REREADING POWE?

MW01275662

Bruce Baum

In his canonical text, *On Liberty*, the English philosopher and social reformer John Stuart Mill (1806–73) looked at the limits imposed by society and the state on individual freedom. Over one hundred years later, Bruce Baum, in *Rereading Power and Freedom in J.S. Mill*, shows how important aspects of Mill's theory of freedom have been misinterpreted. The author recovers lost dimensions of Mill's thought, and in so doing, contributes to a critical sociology of freedom for our time.

Drawing on Mill's thoughts on liberty and power scattered throughout his numerous texts on related subjects, Baum moves beyond what Mill has to say about freedom in *On Liberty*. Baum discovers a consistent purpose behind Mill's advocacy of women's rights, universal suffrage, parliamentary and educational reforms, and workers' co-operatives. Whereas Mill is commonly interpreted as an advocate of negative liberty, Baum argues that Mill possesses a complex theory of freedom that unifies the pursuit of personal autonomy with the quest for collective self-determination through an egalitarian, genuinely participatory democratic politics.

This insightful work traces new connections between Mill's liberalism and the later revisionist liberalisms of theorists such as T.H. Green and John Dewey, as well as between the liberal and socialist traditions. Not only does it break new ground in its demonstration of the complementary relationship between freedom and power, it is the first comprehensive study of Mill's social and political thought that seriously engages his feminism.

BRUCE BAUM is visiting assistant professor in political science at Macalester College.

BRUCE BAUM

Rereading Power and Freedom in J.S. Mill

UNIVERSITY OF TORONTO PRESS
Toronto Buffalo London

© University of Toronto Press Incorporated 2000
Toronto Buffalo London
Printed in Canada

ISBN 0-8020-4761-0 (cloth)
ISBN 0-8020-8315-3 (paper)

Printed on acid-free paper

Canadian Cataloguing in Publication Data

Baum, Bruce, 1960–
Rereading power and freedom in J.S. Mill

Includes bibliographical references and index.
ISBN 0-8020-4761-0 (bound)   ISBN 0-8020-8315-3 (pbk.)

1. Mill, John Stuart, 1806–1873 – Views on liberty.   2. Liberty.
I. Title.

JC585.B385 2000   323.44   C99-932322-9

The University of Toronto Press acknowledges the financial assistance to its
publishing program of the Canada Council for the Arts and the Ontario
Arts Council.

University of Toronto Press acknowledges the financial support for its
publishing activities of the Government of Canada through the Book
Publishing Industry Development Program (BPIDP).

Canadä

Contents

ACKNOWLEDGMENTS ix
ABBREVIATIONS xi

Introduction 3
   I The Politics of Freedom 5
   II The Contribution of John Stuart Mill 10
   III Steps in the Argument 18

1 Mill's Conception of Freedom 21
   I Freedom and Liberty 23
   II Freedom, Autonomy, and Individuality 25
   III Degrees of Autonomy, Degrees of Freedom 31
   IV Freedom and Power 34
   V Freedom, Power, and Culture 36
   VI Conclusions 43

2 Mill's Theory of Modern Freedom 45
   I 'Science,' 'Art,' and 'Theory' in Mill's Political Philosophy 46
   II Freedom and Mill's Moral Theory 52
   III Empirical Theories and Spheres of Freedom 55
        a. The Theory of Social Power 56
        b. The Theory of Individual Development 56
        c. The Theory of Societal Development 57
   IV Secondary Principles 60
        a. The Principle of Liberty 60
        b. Democratic Self-government 61
        c. Social and Distributive Justice 62
        d. Equality 63
   V Conclusions 65

3 The Theory of Social Power   71
   I Mill's Conception of Power   72
  II The Sources of Social Power   77
 III Mill's Theory of Authority   83
          a. Being 'an Authority'   85
          b. Traditional Authority   87
          c. Modern Authority   93
  IV Power and Authority   98
   V Government, Self-government, and the Government
     of Conduct   100

4 Education for Freedom   103
   I Association Psychology and the Development of Autonomy   105
  II The 'Science' of Ethology and the 'Art' of Education   111
 III The Powers of Education   113
          a. Formal Education   113
          b. Education in the 'Larger Sense'   118
          c. Authority, Discipline, and Self-discipline   122
  IV Equality versus Élitism   128
   V Conclusion   131

5 The Principle of Liberty   134
   I Individual Liberty and Modern Democracy   136
  II The Province of Individual Liberty   139
 III Individuality, Utility, and the Diversity of Goods   143
 IV The Domain of Social Morality   150
  V Indirect Utility and the Politics of Rights   159
 VI Individual Liberty and the Powers of Education and Opinion   165
 VII Conclusion   168

6 Freedom, Sex Equality, and the Power of Gender   172
   I Gender and Individual Liberty   174
          a. Autonomy, Freedom, and the Constraints of Gender   174
          b. Life Plans and Career Opportunities   176
          c. Marriage and Divorce   180
          d. Gender, Sexuality, and Sexual Freedom   182
  II Sex Equality and Democratic Self-government   185
          a. Marital Partnership   185
          b. Economic and Political Freedom   191
 III Conclusion   193

7 Economic Freedom   199
   I Mill on Economic Freedom   201
      a. Economic Freedom   201
      b. Maximal Economic Freedom   206
  II The Political Economy of Freedom   207
      a. Individual Liberty   207
      b. Democratic Self-government   221
 III Conclusion   224

8 Political Freedom   228
   I Representative Democracy   233
      a. Equal Representation and Democratic Deliberation   235
      b. Political Equality and Class Division   240
      c. The Principle of Publicity and the Public Sphere   245
      d. Local and National Democracy   252
      e. Popular Participation and the 'Authority of the Instructed'   255
  II Maximal Political Freedom   259
 III Conclusion   262

9 Mill and the Politics of Freedom   267
   I Rethinking Freedom and Power   268
  II Four Principles of Freedom   269
      a. The Principle of Liberty   269
      b. Democratic Self-government   271
      c. Social and Distributive Justice   272
      d. Equality   273
 III Conclusion: The Politics of Freedom   274

NOTES   279
BIBLIOGRAPHY   325
INDEX   351

Acknowledgments

Many people have helped me directly or indirectly with this project. My greatest debts are to Laura Janara, Jim Farr, and my parents, Rosalyn and Charles Baum. I am enormously grateful to Laura for her love and companionship. I thank Laura also for contributing directly to this work through many conversations, her incisive criticism, and her unflagging encouragement.

I want to thank my parents by dedicating this book to them. I am grateful for their love and generosity, and for helping me pursue my goals. I hope in some way that this book reflects the best of what they taught me.

This book is based on my dissertation for the University of Minnesota, where Jim Farr was my dissertation adviser. Without his guidance I might never have completed this project. He helped me transform my rather crude initial ideas about freedom and power into a workable project, and his thoughtful criticism greatly strengthened my arguments. Many thanks to Jim for his role in my scholarly development and for his continuing support.

I also wish to thank a few other mentors. At the University of Minnesota, Ed Fogelman, Doug Lewis, Mary Dietz, and Terence Ball taught me a great deal about political theory and philosophy. Ed and Doug also provided me with crucial support when I needed it most. Two people from my undergraduate years at Vanderbilt University deserve special mention: George Graham, Jr. and John Lachs. They inspired me to follow the path that led to this work.

Thank you to Andy Davison, Byron Miller, Nancy Reist, and Paul Soper for friendship, collegiality, and intellectual exchange that contributed significantly to this project. Thank you to John Mowitt, Naomi

Scheman, Sandy Schram, John Dunn, Diana Saco, Chris Anderson, and Mark Mattern for helpful feedback on various early pieces of this project. Matthew Kudelka, the copy editor for the University of Toronto Press, provided valuable editorial assistance. I also want to thank Virgil Duff and Siobhan McMenemy of University of Toronto Press for supporting this project.

Several other friends and family members have also helped me in less direct ways: Andrea, Jimmy, and Jessica Stewart; Arline, David, Larry, Kevin, and R.J. Widrow; Deb Amster; David Rafferty; Jon and Karen Abels; and Dan Katzeff. Thank you all for your love, friendship, and encouragement. (I owe Dan special thanks for his running promise that if I finished this work he would read it.)

Abbreviations

I. Primary collections of Mill's writings

D&D   *Dissertations and Discussions*, vols 1 & 2.

CW   *The Collected Works of John Stuart Mill.* 1963–91. 33 volumes.

II. Mill's books, articles, and addresses

A   *Autobiography*, CW 1.

'AWEF'   'The Admission of Women to the Electoral Franchise' (1867), CW 28.

'AC'   'Armand Carrel' (1837), D&D, 1.

ACP   *August Comte and Positivism* (1865), CW 10.

'AJ'   'Austin on Jurisprudence' (1863), CW 21.

'ALJ'   'Austin's Lectures on Jurisprudence' (1832), CW 21.

'B'   'Bentham' (1838), CW 10.

'BP'   'Bain's Psychology,' CW 11.

'CFR'   'Carlyle's French Revolution' (1837), CW, 20.

'C'   'Coleridge,' CW 10.

'CC'   'Constraints of Communism' (3 August 1850), CW 25.

'Ce'   'Centralization' (1862), CW 19.

'Civ'   'Civilization' (1836), D&D 1.

'CL'   'The Claims of Labour' (1845), D&D 2.

'COS'   *Chapters on Socialism* (1879), CW 5.

'CPG'   'Comment on Plato's *Gorgias*' (1834/35), in Mill, 1965.

CRG   *Considerations on Representative Government* (1861), CW 19.

'E'   'Endowments,' CW 5.

'EB[1]'   'The Education Bill [1]' (25 March 1870), CW 29.

'EB[2]'   'The Education Bill [2]' (4 April 1870), CW 29.

EHP   *An Examination of Sir William Hamilton's Philosophy*, CW 9.

'FOM'   'A Few Observatons on Mr. Mill' (1833), Appendix D, CW 1.
'FWNI'   'A Few Words on Non-intervention' (1859), CW 21.
'GAYC'   'Grant's Arithmetic for Young Children and Exercises for the
           Improvement of the Senses' (23 October 1835), CW 24.
'GA'   'Grote's Aristotle' (18xx), CW, 11.
'GH[I]'   'Grote's History of Greece [I]' (1846), CW 11.
'GH[II]'   'Grote's History of Greece [II]' (1853), CW 11.
'GP'   'Grote's Plato' (1866), CW 11.
'GELH'   'Guizot's Essays and Lectures on History' (1845), D&D 2.
'IA'   'Inaugural Address Delivered to the University of
           St. Andrews' (1867), CW 21.
'Ire'   'Ireland' (1825), CW 6.
L   *A System of Logic* (1843), CW 7 & 8.
'LTR'   'Land Tenure Reform' (1871), CW 5.
'LLQ'   'Leslie on the Land Question' (1870), CW 5.
'MD[I]'   'Essay on Marriage and Divorce' (circa 1831–32), in Mill and
           Mill, 1970.
'MHF'   'Michelet's History of France' (1844), D&D 2.
'MSPE'   'Miss Martineau's Summary of Political Economy' (1834),
           CW 4.
'MVC'   'Maine on Village Communities' (1871), CW 30.
'N'   'Nature,' CW 10.
'NPE'   'Newman's Political Economy' (1851), CW 5.
'NTA'   'Editorial Notes to *James Mill's Analysis of the Phenomena of the
           Human Mind*' (1869), CW 31.
'NQ'   'The Negro Question' (1850), CW 21.
'OG'   'On Genius' (1832), CW 1.
OL   *On Liberty* (1859), CW 18.
'OLP'   'On the Liberty of the Press,' in Mill, 1959.
'ODPE'   'On the Definition of Political Economy and on the Method
           of Investigation Appropriate to it' (1836), in Mill, 1950.
'ORG'   'On Religion and Guardianship' (1846), in Mill, 1959.
'P'   'Perfectibility' (1828), CW 26.
'PL'   'Periodical Literature: Edinburgh Review' (1824), CW 1.
PPE   *Principles of Political Economy* (1848–1), CW 2 & 3.
'RBP'   'Remark's on Bentham's Philosophy' (1834), CW, 10.
'RP'   'Representation of the People' (five speeches, 12 April
           1866–31 May 1866), CW 28.
'RPL'   'The Right of Property in Land' (1873), CW 25.
'RR'   'Rationale of Representation' (1835), CW 18.

'RRP'	'Reorganization of the Reform Party' (1839), CW 6.
'RWR'	'Recent Writers on Reform' (1859), CW 19.
'SD'	'Sedgwick's Discourse' (1835), CW 10.
SW	*The Subjection of Women*, CW 21.
'SOA'	'Spirit of the Age' (1831), CW 22.
'T'	'Theism' (1874), CW 10.
'TDA[I]'	'De Tocqueville on Democracy in America [I]' (1835),' CW 18.
'TDA[II]'	'De Tocqueville on Democracy in America [II]' (1840), CW18.
'TCL'	'Thornton on the Claims of Labour' (1869), CW 5.
'TI'	'Taine's De L'Intelligence,' CW 11.
'TPR'	'Thoughts on Parliamentary Reform' (1859), CW 19.
'TPV'	'Thoughts on Poetry and its Varieties' (1833), D&D 1.
U	*Utilitarianism*, CW 10.
'UAPT'	'Use and Abuse of Political Terms' (1832), CW 18.
'UR'	'The Utility of Religion,' CW 10.
'VFR'	'Vindication of the French Revolution of February 1848, in Reply to Lord Brougham and Others' (1849), D&D 2.
'WMP'	'Dr. Whewell on Moral Philosophy' (1852), D&D 2.
'WS[I]'	'Women's Suffrage [1],' CW 29.
'WS[II]'	'Women's Suffrage [2]' (26 March 1870), CW 29.
'WS[III]'	'Women's Suffrage [3]' (12 January 1871), CW 29.
'WJR[I]'	'Writings of Junius Redivivus [I]' (1833), CW, 1.
'WJR[II]'	'Writings of Junius Redivivus [II]' (1833), CW 1.

III. Mill, with George Grote

'TS'	'Taylor's Statesman' (1837), CW 19.

IV. Harriet Taylor Mill, with John Stuart Mill

'PWR'	'Papers on Women's Rights' (1847–1850), CW 21.
'RFB'	'Remarks on Mr. Fitroy's Bill for the More Effectual Prevention of Assaults on Women and Children' (1853), CW, 21.

V. Harriet Taylor Mill

'EW'	'Enfranchisement of Women' (1851), in Mill and Mill, 1970.
'MD[II]'	'Essay on Marriage and Divorce' (circa 1831–2), in Mill and Mill, 1970.

REREADING POWER AND FREEDOM IN J.S. MILL

Introduction

After the primary necessities of food and raiment, freedom is the first and strongest want of human nature.

John Stuart Mill, *The Subjection of Women* (1869)

Freedom, power, and hope are the charms of existence.

Harriet Taylor and J.S. Mill, 'Papers on Women's Rights' (circa 1847–50)

In the modern world, the concept of freedom figures prominently in people's self-understandings – including their hopes and ideals – and in their social and political practices. It is intimately connected to ideas about personhood, citizenship, individuality, responsibility, autonomy, and democracy. Moreover, debates about other political goals, such as social justice, equality, the common good, and even a sustainable environment, typically spark further debates about freedom. Yet while many people affirm the centrality of freedom, they continue to disagree sharply about its meaning and requisite conditions.

In this study I draw upon John Stuart Mill's political philosophy to make a modest contribution to what Nicholas Rose calls 'a critical sociology of freedom': My intention is not to be critical *of* freedom, but rather to examine how what we take to be freedom has been historically constituted, along with 'the practices that support it, and the techniques, strategies and relations of power that go to make up what we count as a free society' (Rose, 1995, 213–14). As I write, at the dawning of the twenty-first century, freedom is both a vital ideal and an elusive goal. There has recently been a wave of democratization around the globe, from Africa to Latin America to Eastern Europe and Russia. Many of these emerging democracies are fragile. Moreover, like all modern nation-states, they face the continuing challenge of securing tangible freedom for all of their citizens. This task corresponds with one of Mill's central concerns: to identify the social and political conditions necessary to establish the greatest freedom for each member of a society in a way that is compatible with equal freedom for all. It is hard these days not to wonder whether this modern project is achievable at all, anywhere. At the same time, the struggle for freedom is far too important to abandon, even if it now needs to be tempered with 'postmodern' caution.[1]

I take up these issues primarily through a new interpretation of the theory of freedom developed by John Stuart Mill, the great nineteenth-century English liberal philosopher, focusing on his view of the interplay of freedom and power. This approach to Mill's work offers unique insights into the meaning of freedom and power. My general thesis, apart from my interpretation of Mill, is that freedom and power exist in a complementary relationship that is crucially important if we are to understand the meaning and conditions of freedom. In short, the limits and possibilities that people face in their efforts to direct their own lives must be conceptualized with respect to the various relationships of power in which they are situated. I return to Mill's writings because his analysis of the necessary conditions for freedom in modern societies is informed by a profound understanding of how people's powers of self-determination and self-development are shaped by the power dynamics they encounter in their political, economic, educational, gender, and family relationships.

Mill is best known for his exemplary analysis in his essay *On Liberty* of the limited power that a society can rightfully exercise over its individual members. Based on his famous principle of liberty – which is, that a community can rightfully exercise power to restrict the conduct of its members only to prevent 'harm to others' – Mill is commonly interpreted as a classic defender of 'negative liberty.' According to this view, freedom consists of the absence of constraints and is diminished whenever power is exercised. My claim is that Mill actually *challenges* this understanding of freedom by illuminating positive and negative aspects of freedom as well as the multifaceted and complementary relationship between freedom and power. He develops a far-reaching theory of freedom that builds on his philosophy of the moral sciences and utilitarian moral theory, along with his provocative but little noticed sociology of power.

Regarding the latter, Mill maintains that state power must be understood in relation to the distribution of *social power* – power that is based on such things as wealth and property, strength in numbers, knowledge, and control over the means of communication. Here he has more in common with such classical sociologists as Marx, Weber, and Durkheim than with many twentieth-century liberal political theorists and analytical philosophers who are inspired by his work.[2] I argue, accordingly, that insufficient attention to Mill's ideas about social power has led previous commentators to interpret both his underlying *conception* of freedom and his broader *theory* of freedom too narrowly in terms of his principle of liberty.

My aim, in short, is to offer a new account of Mill's political philosophy in order to challenge the common view that there is an inverse relationship between freedom and power. At the same time, I challenge the prevailing 'negative' view of freedom, which implies that the more society simply leaves people alone – free *from* external interference – the greater is their freedom. In addition, I offer a new perspective on the emancipatory possibilities of the liberal tradition that is relevant to contemporary debates about freedom and equality, individuality and community, struggles for democracy, and the politics of educational, economic, gender, and family relationships. Mill's classic liberal argument for individual liberty – that is, for the freedom of individuals to pursue their own ideas of the good within the limits of their duties to others – is but one part of his larger account of the conditions of freedom. Overall, he provides compelling grounds for adopting the rather radical view that in order for freedom to be realized, individuals must be empowered within their political, educational, economic, gender, and family relationships. Even where Mill's political philosophy is insufficient in itself for achieving his stated goals, it still constitutes an invaluable starting point for freedom struggles.

I The Politics of Freedom

The concept of freedom is now generally understood, at least among English-speaking writers, in terms of two crucial claims. First, freedom is treated essentially as a 'negative' concept so that, as Quentin Skinner explains, its presence is marked 'by the absence of something else; specifically, by the absence of some element of constraint that inhibits the agent concerned from being able to act independently in pursuit of his [or her] chosen ends' (Skinner, 1984, 194). This negative conception has played a prominent role in the development of modern liberalism.[3]

Second, given this prevailing negative view of freedom, freedom is typically seen as inversely related to power, so that freedom is diminished whenever and to the degree that power is exercised. Seen in this light, power is essentially restrictive or repressive in its effects. Thus it is conceived, like freedom, in negative terms.[4] *Political* power, for example, is typically understood in terms of the state's capacity to impose and enforce rules of conduct over and against members of society, thereby limiting their choices and actions.

Both of these claims are problematic because the negative conceptions of freedom and power are flawed. A better understanding of freedom and its requisite conditions must start with the recognition that freedom and power both have positive and negative aspects. In particular, power is not merely an oppressive force that is exercised by some persons over others; it also refers more generally to the capacity of an agent or agents to bring about certain goals or objectives (*OED*, 2nd ed., v. 12, 259). One of the things that powerful agents can *do* with their power is exert control over others; yet power is not always exercised in repressive and thus freedom-diminishing ways (Pitkin, 1972; Hartsock, 1985; Patton, 1989).

This point is central to an alternative tradition that stresses the 'positive' side of freedom.[5] This tradition offers a variety of views of freedom, but it always insists that freedom requires the *presence* of certain enabling conditions – such as rights, resources, and opportunities for choice and self-government – as well as the *absence* of burdensome constraints. As Skinner says, 'someone who wishes at once to be free from an element of interference' seeks at the same time freedom 'to be able (freely, independently) to do or be or become something' (1984, 194n5; cf. MacCallum, 1973). That is, freedom *from* particular constraints is always sought so that a given agent (or agents) can do or be something that he or she wants to do or be, even if this means choosing to be inactive. Freedom from constraint or interference is therefore only one aspect of freedom.

In two respects, this triadic conception of freedom – focusing on agents, obstacles, and fields of possibilities – offers a better basis for considering the complementarity of freedom and power. First, freedom is lacking, and remains an empty promise, if the agent (or agents) in question lacks powers of self-determination. It is misleading to say that someone is *free* to do something when she lacks effective *power* to do it, even if she has legal rights or liberties that permit her (or leave her 'at liberty') to do it (Bauman, 1988, 2). Such a claim rests on a narrow view of the constraints relevant to judgments about freedom. Second, the relationship between freedom and power is integrally related to what Richard Flathman calls the 'situatedness' of freedom. According to Flathman, understanding freedom as a situated concept involves a recognizing that it is 'part of a public, shared, mutually meaningful language of social interaction' (1987b, 2). In other words, freedom cannot be analyzed as an abstract principle as if people are simply free or unfree *per se*. Rather, as Gerald MacCallum points out, whenever freedom is at issue it is *always* the freedom *of* some agent or agents, *from* particular obstacles or constraints, and *to* do, not do, be, or not be certain things (1973, 296). Thus, when we analyze freedom, we need to be clear about the following things: whose freedom is at issue; what things constitute the constraints and enabling conditions of that freedom; and what choices, actions, and possibilities are most important for judging the freedom of the agent or agents. To answer these questions about freedom we need to step down from this high level of abstraction and examine the web of social and political relationships in which people are actually *situated*. Moreover, as Michel Foucault says, the various social and political relationships situating people are relationships of power insofar as they govern their lives by shaping their characters and conduct and by structuring their field of possibilities (1983, 219, 221).

This meaning of 'govern,' Foucault explains, builds upon the broad meaning that the concept of government had in the sixteenth century. At that time, government referred not only to political institutions and the management of states, but also to 'the government of children of communities, of families, of the sick' (1983, 220).[6] Accordingly, political and economic relationships, gender and family relations, educational practices, and practices of 'racial,' ethnic, and religious exclusion and discrimination all constitute *power* relationships in that they govern people's lives by delimiting their field of possible actions. These power relationships govern people's lives in two ways corresponding to distinct but interrelated *internal* (i.e., psychological) and *external* constraints and enabling conditions of freedom (Taylor, 1979). First, power relationships structure the range of external choices and possibilities open or closed to different people – that is, they expand or restrict the range of options open to people or change the character of those options. Second, they shape people's desires, beliefs, identities, and capacities for autonomous action – that is, they socialize people as particular kinds of agents with particular conceptions of their possibilities (Lukes, 1974 & 1986).

This way of understanding power has profound implications for how we think about freedom. Since people are always situated within certain power relationships, they are never completely 'free from' external interference or constraint or power.[7] As Foucault says, 'the important question ... is not whether a culture without restraints is possible or even desirable but whether the system of constraints in which a society functions leaves individuals with the liberty to transform the system' (1988, 294).[8] Thus it is mistaken to construe freedom as simply the absence of power and constraint. Instead, freedom must be conceived in terms of the power of persons to direct the course of their lives, both individually and collectively, with respect to the power relationships that have situated them. This understanding of the interplay between freedom and power has several important implications for how we grasp the relationship between freedom and state power, individuality, equality, distributive justice, and democracy.

First, since state power is not the only form of power that governs people's lives, the relationship between freedom and power must not be construed solely in terms of state power. That being said, state power is particularly important as the means by which other forms of power and other social activities are regulated (Walzer, 1983, 281).

Second, people are socialized in large part by the power relationships situating them. In short, we effectively *internalize* aspects of the social practices and power relationships that are *external* to us as we learn the languages and traditions, rules and norms, and roles and identities through which we make sense of our social world. A commitment to freedom thus requires us to examine whether the particular power relationships or constraints situating people enhance or stunt their autonomy – that is, their capacity reflectively to formulate their goals and objectives. It follows that supporting freedom requires that we organize social relationships – from child rearing and education to economic institutions to the relationship between citizens and the state – in ways that foster autonomy (Nedelsky, 1989).

Third, since power has both positive and negative aspects, it is not strictly a repressive force that stands in an inverse relationship with freedom. Freedom is not automatically diminished whenever and to the degree that power is exercised. Power is sometimes exercised in ways that limit (and occasionally even destroy) freedom, particularly where it is used by some people to dominate or exploit others; but power can also be exercised in empowering ways. In brief, freedom is about the power of persons, individually and collectively, to exercise self-determination.

Fourth, the field of possibilities open or closed to particular people is shaped not only by the power relationships situating them but also by their status within these power relationships. Political, economic, educational, gender, and family relationships distribute the means, resources, and opportunities for free action among individuals depending on their different places within these relationships. That is, people are empowered for self-determination by these relationships to varying degrees, depending on their particular status within them: as citizens or noncitizens, employers or wage earners, men or women, rich or poor consumers, advantaged or disadvantaged children, and so on (Thompson, 1989; Held, 1989). This strongly suggests that freedom and equality are mutually supportive rather than conflicting goals (Lukes, 1991). This is not to deny that some egalitarian policies undermine freedom in certain respects. The point, rather, is that for all members of society to enjoy equal freedom, they must all have relatively equal rights to and resources for self-government in relation to the various power relationships situating them.

Finally, because freedom is always exercised within various power relationships, it needs to be specified in terms of both people's possible actions as independent individuals acting within these relationships, and their opportunities for self-government with respect to these relationships. Freedom, that is, refers to both practices of individual independence – of relatively independent individuals pursuing their own ends – and practices of collective self-government (Friedrich, 1963). Once we accept that collective self-government is an important aspect of freedom, we must also recognize that opportunities for self-government must be conceived in relation to a wide range of power relationships and institutions in modern societies. Self-government is not just a matter for the state, as classical liberal and civic republican theorists contend, since the state is not the only form of power that governs people's lives.

The idea that freedom involves the power of self-determination has been challenged by various commentators, who suggest that it collapses the distinction between freedom and power (cf. Hayek, 1960; Gert, 1972; Wrong, 1988). Yet acknowledging that positive forms of power are an aspect of freedom does not collapse the distinction between the two concepts. While freedom involves the exercise of power for self-determination, such as sharing in practices of self-government, not every exercise of power is an exercise of freedom.[9] Power can be concentrated or dispersed, with various implications for the freedom of those involved. Thus, one of the questions we can ask regarding power relationships is this: To what extent or in what respects are the people embedded within them free?

Once we see how freedom and power are interrelated, we also see that struggles for power and for freedom are deeply intertwined. This is evident in the recent struggles for democratic self-government in South Africa, Latin America, Eastern Europe, and China. These movements to democratize political power are at the same time struggles by citizens to determine more freely the course of their political communities. In the same way, ongoing social movements in democratic capitalist societies to empower women and other disadvantaged groups and to achieve economic or workplace democracy are also struggles for freedom. They are struggles for freedom *because* they centre on the power of persons to shape their lives within the power relationships situating them.

II The Contribution of John Stuart Mill

At first glance, Mill may seem an unlikely source for insights into the complementary relationship between freedom and power. After all, he begins his famous essay *On Liberty* by juxtaposing civil or social liberty with the exercise of societal power and 'social control.' His subject, he says, is 'civil, or social liberty: the nature and limits of the power which can be legitimately exercised by society over the individual' (OL, 217).[10] Nonetheless, Mill's deeper insights lead in a different direction in two respects. First, his conception of freedom includes an emphasis not only on the absence of constraints, but also on the need for autonomy, a 'variety of situations,' and opportunities for self-development and self-government.[11] Second, he builds his view of freedom into a comprehensive theory of modern freedom that places the complementarity of freedom and power in the foreground.

Much of the scholarly attention to Mill's account of freedom focuses on his principle of liberty, whereby the freedom of individuals to pursue their own good in their own way within certain limits is protected. Yet to grasp fully Mill's *conception of freedom* we need to look beyond his liberty principle to clarify his analytically distinct notion of what it means for individuals to be free (Smith, 1984, 183–4). To proceed, we need to consider how Mill complements his analysis of freedom in *On Liberty* with discussions of freedom in his other writings. In particular, we need to carefully attend to how he links his view of freedom to his view of social power. In this regard, his account of 'free will' in terms of the power of individuals over their own characters in *A System of Logic* and his *Examina-*

tion of Sir William Hamilton's Philosophy is especially important (Smith, 1984, 182). At the same time, we must appreciate that Mill develops his theory of freedom in light of the power struggles in various domains of modern societies. These include struggles over working class and women's suffrage, over women's rights more generally, over socialism and industrial 'co-operation,' and over British colonialism, public education, and religious diversity. In short, we need to address how he conceives of the freedom of individuals with respect to the political, economic, educational, gender, and family relationships situating them. For this, we must examine Mill's analysis of freedom and free agency in such works as *Principles of Political Economy, Considerations on Representative Government,* and *The Subjection of Women.*

Mill brings together his inquiries into 'free will' and social and political freedom in relation to his ongoing concern with the development of human capacities for self-determination in a causally determined world. In his view, individuals are not always and inevitably free agents. Rather, they become free agents to the extent that educative social conditions foster their capacities to develop desires and impulses that are really *their own.* What is important therefore in Mill's view is *how,* not just whether, human actions are determined by unalterable causal mechanisms. He considers the necessary conditions for freedom of action in light of both his psychological view of individual character development and his sociological theory of social power. He highlights the link between, on the one hand, the psychological processes through which individuals develop (or fail to develop) capacities for autonomous actions and, on the other hand, the 'educative' effects of social and political relationships in nurturing or stifling these capacities – what Mill calls the 'powers of education' over character. *Only when we appreciate how these issues are interrelated for Mill can we adequately grasp the profound and radical character of his view of freedom.* Among the conditions of freedom he includes not only the absence of coercion or interference (its negative aspect), but also the presence of conditions favourable to self-development, self-determination, and self-governance (its positive aspect), including our capacity to shape our own characters.

Many past interpreters, such as Isaiah Berlin, have contended that Mill says little about material constraints on freedom, such as poverty.[12] This claim, which finds support in Mill's occasional tendency to talk about freedom in 'negative' terms of noninterference, implies that Mill offers a conception of freedom for *already empowered persons* – that is, for persons who, when free from external interference, have the power to pursue their aims and purposes.[13] This reading, however, places undue weight on a few of Mill's select, rhetorically charged comments. It ignores the attention he pays to material constraints to freedom in such works as *The Subjection of Women* and *Principles of Political Economy*.

My claim about what I call Mill's 'theory of freedom' builds on prior 'revisionist' scholarship. Recent scholarship shows that Mill is a more subtle and systematic thinker than previous interpreters have recognized, despite his own claim in his *Autobiography* that he offers 'no system' of political philosophy (A, 169).[14] As Alan Ryan explains, 'one of the many ways in which Mill was unusual among nineteenth century utilitarians, and indeed would still be unusual among their twentieth century successors, too, was in combining ... stress on the role of general principles in morals with an equal emphasis on the historical development of society and personal development in ethics' (1990, x). The systematic character of his philosophy as it pertains to his account of freedom becomes clear when we examine it in light of his framework for social theorizing in his early work, *A System of Logic*. Here Mill discusses the relationship between matters of fact, which he calls the domain of 'science,' and matters of practical reason concerning the ends of human conduct, which he calls the domain of 'art.' The most general 'art' of human conduct he calls the 'Art of Life.' Its purpose is twofold: to clarify the relationship between different ends and modes of conduct, and to identify the portion of the corresponding science – in this case 'sociology,' or the science of society – that addresses the conditions for realizing the ends in question. Mill's theory of freedom thereby encompasses two basic dimensions: an ethical or 'normative' account of how freedom relates to other human ends; and a 'scientific' analysis of the social and political conditions necessary for maximizing the freedom of each person in a manner consistent with the equal freedom of others.

Mill analyses how freedom relates to other ends of life by way of his utilitarian moral theory. As a utilitarian, he contends that social utility, or 'the greatest happiness,' is the ultimate standard for resolving ethical questions. He develops a distinctly qualitative version of utilitarianism, however. He generally rejects any quantitative accounting of pleasure and pain and says that the appeal must be to 'utility in the largest sense, grounded on the permanent interests of man as a progressive being' (OL, 224). His notion of 'permanent interests' builds on his view that people have 'higher faculties' that make them more capable than other animals of 'more elevated' forms of gratification and 'more acute suffering' (U, 211). Mill thus develops a rich conception of happiness by which he counts freedom and individuality among the chief components of human well-being.

Although Mill never expressly articulates a 'theory of freedom,' we can reconstruct a powerful theory of modern freedom from his social, political, and philosophical writings.[15] It encompasses Mill's utilitarian moral theory, three 'empirical theories' about individuals and society, and a set of four 'middle principles' for securing freedom. The latter derive from his moral and empirical theories. I refer to Mill's theory of freedom, then, as a way to illuminate the scope and unity of his efforts to theorize the situatedness of freedom with respect to the social and political conditions necessary to secure maximal freedom for the members of modern societies. Mill's theory confronts many of the problems that arise from the fact that we struggle for freedom in a world we share with others who often have different goals, values, and interests. Notably, he illuminates how our diverse efforts to achieve self-determination are mediated by a variety of power relationships that connect us to others in many-sided and often unequal ways. In this regard, Mill turns our attention to several 'spheres' of freedom and 'unfreedom,' much as Michael Walzer (1983) identifies different 'spheres of justice.'

The three empirical theories on which Mill's theory of freedom is based are as follows: (1) a theory of social power, through which Mill illuminates the social conditions of freedom in relation to the educational, political, economic, gender, and family relationships that govern people's lives in modern, democratizing societies; (2) a theory of individual development, through which he addresses the formation of people's characters and cognitive capacities; and (3) a theory of societal development, through which he distinguishes different 'states of society' to present his ideas about freedom as most immediately suited to modern democratic societies.

Concerning the first of these three empirical theories, I maintain that Mill gives his theory of social power a pivotal place in his theory of freedom. This is so even though, as with his theory of freedom, he offers no sustained account of his theory of social power, and even though previous interpreters have not excavated it.[16] In fact, Mill's theory of social power is central to the more original and radical dimensions of his view of freedom. He provides the outlines of a comprehensive theory of social power that highlights both positive and negative aspects of power in relation to four key features of the complementarity of freedom and power.

First, Mill develops his principle of liberty to address threats to individual freedom posed by the power that society exercises over its individual members through both the force of law and 'the moral coercion of public opinion' (OL, 223). This is the best-known aspect of Mill's treatment of the relationship between freedom and power. Less attention has been given to his insistence that while the state must respect 'the liberty of each individual in what specifically regards himself, [it] is *bound to maintain a vigilant control over his exercise of any power which it allows him to possess over others*' (OL, 301, emphasis added). This point is crucial if we are to appreciate how Mill's distinction between domains of individual liberty and social morality (or duty to others) differs from a straightforward division between 'private' and 'public' domains. Mill construes the province of individual liberty as encompassing some public relationships and activities that involve a 'corresponding liberty in any number of individuals to regulate by mutual agreement such things as regard them jointly, and regard no persons but themselves' (OL, 299, 226). Conversely, he contends that social relationships often counted as 'private,' such as marital, family, and economic relationships, sometimes fall *outside* the province of individual liberty and within the domain of social morality and law.

Second, Mill situates the meaning and conditions of freedom in relation to several kinds of power relationships that govern people's lives.[17] He analyzes freedom in relation to political, economic, educational, gender, and family relationships, clarifying how these power relationships structure what different people are free or unfree to do or be. Moreover, with regard to political, economic, and marital relationships, Mill shows that freedom manifests itself in part in practices of mutual or collective self-government. That is, freedom consists in part in opportunities for people to *share in the exercise of power* with respect to power relationships governing their lives.

Third, Mill shows that the power relationships which situate people affect their freedom not only by structuring their fields of possible actions, but also by shaping their characters, including their capacities for autonomous action. He addresses this point in terms of what he calls the power of 'education and opinion' over people's characters. Accordingly, his call for 'the free development of individuality' does not rest on an atomistic and asocial view of human nature, and is by no means a celebration of individual self-reliance or 'possessive individualism.' Rather, Mill's commitment to freedom and individuality is integrally connected to his understanding of how people's characters develop within social relationships.

Fourth, while Mill highlights the plurality of power relationships and sources of social power in modern societies, he also emphasizes the distinctive role that power plays in governing people's lives. In his view, the control of state power in a given society is always conditioned by the distribution of social power. At the same time, he recognizes the special role of state power in governing all other power relationships and activities in society, including struggles to control state power. Accordingly, he construes political freedom – the freedom of citizens to share in determining the laws by which they are governed – as 'the most important liberty of the nation' (CRG, 432).

The four 'middle principles' that Mill derives from his moral and empirical theories as means for securing maximal freedom for all members of society are as follows: (1) the principle of liberty; (2) a principle of democratic self-government; (3) social and distributive justice; and (4) equality. These principles address both individualistic and collective aspects of freedom and aim at ensuring that the freedom of some does not come at the expense of the rightful freedom of others.

Overall, Mill's theory of modern freedom provides a valuable starting point for my project, which is to contribute to a critical sociology of freedom. By reinterpreting Mill's account of the interplay between freedom and power, I am able to clarify the positive and negative aspects of freedom and also to illuminate how the freedom of individuals is structured by the various power relationships that situate them. Mill's work helps me analyze how freedom has been bound up with the distinctive ways that individuals relate to themselves, with certain ways that some people exercise power over others, and with certain norms and principles through which people organize their activities and experiences (Rose, 1995, 213).

By bringing to the fore Mill's sociology of power, I am able to shed new light on the emancipatory possibilities of liberal political theory. I recover a liberal theory of freedom that powerfully challenges more conventional liberal theories, including those of Isaiah Berlin (1969c), John Rawls (1971, 1996), and Robert Nozick (1974). These theorists focus too narrowly on the negative aspects of freedom, and fail to explore adequately how freedom and power are interrelated. Mill's work also enables me to develop an effective liberal response to contemporary communitarian critiques of liberalism, such as that of Michael Sandel (1982, 1984, 1990). Mill shares with communitarians an appreciation of the social conditions necessary for individual flourishing, and of how individuals derive their characters, beliefs, and ideas of the good life from the traditions and relationships in which they are embedded. Yet Mill also recognizes that modern societies are characterized by a plurality of ideas of the good life, and argues persuasively that individuals should be free within limits to pursue their own good in their own way. His argument thus remains a strong counterpoint to communitarian longings for deeper bonds of 'community' – longings that promote more unitary views of how members of the community ought to live.

More generally, many of Mill's arguments about freedom in relation to political, economic, educational, and gender relationships are as relevant today as they were in his own time. For example, the conformist pressures he found in Victorian England have intensified over time in certain respects, particularly with the advent of television and other electronic mass media, increasingly global communications and popular culture, and new technologies for surveillance and social control. Similarly, his interest in combining aspects of socialism – particularly industrial democracy – with market competition prefigures recent interest in political/economic alternatives to capitalism and state socialism (cf. Nove, 1985; Dahl, 1985; Bowles and Gintis, 1987; Elster and Moene, 1989).

Still, however incisively Mill's work speaks to our contemporary situation, his limitations are notable when he attempts to elaborate the relationship between freedom and power. My disputes with Mill will be clear enough in subsequent chapters, but a few general comments here will set the stage. Compelling critiques of his theories are provided by radical and participatory democratic critics, feminist critics, and critics of Mill's Eurocentrism. Mill's radical democratic critics, while acknowledging the promise of his ideas about education, democratic participation, and self-development, rightly point out that his theory of representative democracy is élitist in certain respects (Pateman, 1970; Macpherson, 1977). I will modify this participatory democratic critique by explaining how Mill qualifies the élitist tendencies of his democratic theory. First, he develops his theory of democratic politics in relation to his own more radically egalitarian proposals for democratizing civil society, particularly industrial and marital relationships. Second, Mill's democratic theory has a crucial *dynamic* or developmental dimension. He insists, for example, that 'the goodness of a government' should be judged not just by how it takes advantage of the 'amount of good qualities' that exist among a people at a given time, but also by 'its tendency to improve or deteriorate the people themselves' (CRG, 390, 392). Mill thus presents some of the more inegalitarian tendencies of his democratic theory – such as his proposal for 'plural votes' for more educated citizens – as transitional measures on the way to a more egalitarian democratic society. The remaining limitations of his democratic theory arise partly from his historical context and partly from his failure to confront adequately the economic, political, and educational inequalities that are produced by capitalism and by the existing sexual division of labour.

Feminist critics also note problems in Mill's understanding of the gender divisions between 'public' and 'private' spheres of social life (Rossi, 1970; Okin, 1979; Coole, 1988; Mendus, 1989a). They show how his analysis of the 'subjection of women' is weakened by his failure to push his questioning of traditional gender roles to its logical conclusions and by his coolness toward issues of sexuality. A few critics have also revealed Mill's failure to account for differences among women (Di Stefano, 1991; Baum, 1997; Shanley, 1998). Nonetheless, I will argue that his deeper theoretical insights can be used against some of his conclusions to develop a feminist theory that moves beyond his immediate practical prescriptions.

Mill's inattention to differences among women is closely connected to the problem of his Eurocentrism (Bhabha, 1985b; Gray, 1991; Said, 1993; Parekh, 1994, 1995). Like other prominent nineteenth-century European political theorists, including Hegel, Marx, and Tocqueville, Mill viewed modern European civilization as the chief agent of change in a universalistic narrative of historical progress. He regarded non-Western societies such as India and China as backward, uncivilized, and 'immature,' and modern Western societies such as England as representing a more advanced stage of societal development. His Eurocentrism led him to build his conception of freedom on a restrictive view of rationality, despite his significant break from the even narrower utilitarian rationalism of Jeremy Bentham and James Mill. However, in contrast to other critics of J.S. Mill's Eurocentrism, I will argue that his view of 'reason' – the capacity for being persuaded and 'improved by free and equal discussion' (OL, 224) – is instructive for grasping the necessary conditions of free agency, though still not unproblematic. Despite his celebrated openness to different 'experiments in living,' he was not sufficiently open to and tolerant of traditional and nonliberal ways of life.[18] This was particularly evident in his support of the 'civilizing' role of British colonial rule in India, in which he participated as an official of the British East India Company.

One further problem concerns Mill's account of social change. His theory of freedom shows that extending freedom more fully and equally demands an enormous *redistribution of power* in economic, political, educational, gender, and family relationships. Yet he underestimates the degree to which achieving such change requires social and political struggle to overcome vested interests.

These shortcomings in Mill's political theory are closely connected to a limitation of his theory of social power. While he develops a profound *sociological* understanding of the forms and sources of social power, he lacks an adequate *interpretive* understanding of the power dynamics at work in clashes between different belief systems, or of the frameworks that compete to validate claims of truth and moral rightness. In short, Mill fails to grasp how the exercise of power is itself culturally shaped. He therefore fails to account for how inequalities of power between England and India contributed to the imposition on India of Eurocentric standards of reason and progress. Similarly, in his account of English politics he fails to address adequately the connections between power and claims of knowledge when he defends a privileged political role for the educated classes in representative democracy.[19]

Even given these problems in Mill's work, his insights into the interplay of freedom and power beg illumination. Moreover, exploration of the problems themselves enables me to deepen the study of how freedom and power interrelate. Mill fails to pursue the more radical implications of his work; even so, he makes a powerful case for some radical reforms so as to extend freedom amid the key power relationships in modern societies: greater equality between the sexes; for practices of democratic self-government in political, economic, and marital relationships; and for education that enables all people to think for themselves. One further implication of my study, then, is that Mill's place in the liberal tradition needs to be reconsidered along with his contributions to democratic theory, feminist theory, and socialist theory. Rather than the classic theorist of 'negative liberty' as he is so often regarded, he is a theorist of both negative and positive aspects of freedom. His sympathetic engagement with socialist thought challenges the usual either/or opposition of liberal and socialist approaches to social reform; he exposes the sexist ways in which modern practices of individual liberty and democratic self-government have been gendered; and he sheds light on how struggles for political democracy are intertwined with broader struggles for a democratic society.

III Steps in the Argument

The bulk of this study consists of my reinterpretation of Mill's political theory in light of how he addresses the interplay between freedom and power. My chief interpretive strategy is to make more explicit the way that Mill addresses – both explicitly and implicitly – this relationship. I do this through a systematic analysis of how Mill examines the freedom–power relationship throughout his writings in light of his broader moral and political theory.[20] Without ignoring the historical and philosophical context of his writings, I am primarily interested in analyzing the cogency of his contribution to an understanding of the conditions of modern freedom. The true strengths and weaknesses of Mill's arguments become clearer as we pay to his writings more explicit attention than he gives to the interconnections between freedom and power and to the positive and negative aspects of both freedom and power. I show that to understand Mill's theory of freedom, we need to place his discussion of individual liberty in *On Liberty* in the broader context of his writings on free agency, ethics, character development, education, politics, economics, and gender and family relationships. In particular, I demonstrate the importance of his analysis of 'the logic of the moral sciences,' in *A System of Logic*, and of his indirect and 'developmental' version of utilitarianism (developed, e.g., in 'Remarks on Bentham's Philosophy,' 'Bentham,' 'Coleridge,' and *Utilitarianism*), for appreciating the unity of his writings on freedom. I pay special attention to how he situates the development of the capacity for autonomy and the exercise of freedom within the web of power relationships that shape people's characters and determine their field of possibilities. This includes his understanding of how changes in the structure and character of political, economic, educational, and gender relations – such as greater democracy in political, industrial, and marital relations and greater equality between the sexes – affect the relative freedom and unfreedom of different people (for example, citizens and noncitizens, property owners and wage earners, and men and women).

My retrieval of Mill's thought proceeds in two parts, as follows. In the first part of the study (Chapters 1–4), I reconstruct the more abstract theoretical underpinnings of Mill's theory of freedom. In Chapter 1, I clarify his underlying *conception* of freedom in light of his discussions of the concept in *On Liberty* (1859) and *A System of Logic* (1843). Chapter 2 outlines his unsystematized and hitherto obscured *theory* of freedom in light of his philosophy of social science. Focusing largely on his *System of Logic*, I explain how his theory encompasses his utilitarian moral theory, three empirical theories concerning individual and social development and social power, and the four 'middle' principles for achieving equal freedom for all members of society.

In Chapter 3 I reconstruct his theory of social power. I focus on such works as 'Bentham' (1838), 'Coleridge' (1840), 'Guizot's Essays and Lectures on History' (1845), and *The Subjection of Women* (1869) to illuminate the depth and breadth of Mill's understanding of the sources of social power as well as the central importance of his view of power to his theory of freedom. In Chapter 4 I examine his theory of the educational conditions of freedom. I sketch the psychological and 'ethological' (roughly, social psychological) underpinnings of the development in individuals of the capacity for autonomous action. Then I turn to his ideas about the social and institutional conditions necessary for people to be educated to achieve autonomous characters. I devote special attention here to such works as *On Liberty, Considerations on Representative Government* (1861), his *Inaugural Address to the University of St. Andrews* (1867), and *The Subjection of Women* (1869), but also refer to lesser known essays in which he develops his notion of 'education in its larger sense.'

In the second half of the study (Chapters 5–9), I investigate Mill's writings on the *situatedness* of people's freedom within the various power relationships that constitute the field of their conduct. This terrain encompasses his famous principle of liberty, with which he seeks to fix the limits of the power that a community can rightfully exercise over the conduct of its individual members; but it also includes the forms that freedom takes or ought to take within political, economic, gender, and family relationships. In Chapter 5 I focus on *On Liberty* to offer a new interpretation of Mill's principle of liberty that brings together both his moral theory and his theory of social power. In Chapter 6 I discuss *The Subjection of Women* to flesh out his analysis of how the freedom of men and women is structured in unequal ways by prevailing gender roles and family relationships. In Chapter 7, through a study of *Principles of Political Economy* (1848) and *Chapters on Socialism* (published posthumously in 1879), I explain his view of economic freedom. In Chapter 8, his political writings – principally *Considerations on Representative Government* – provide me with grounds to explain his view of political freedom. Finally, in Chapter 9 I complete my assessment of Mill's theory of freedom.

1

Mill's Conception of Freedom*

The forms of liberty, are one thing; the substance another. These two things are often confounded, and the consequence is, that the substance is very often sacrificed to the forms.

John Stuart Mill, 'Ireland' (1825)

The *Liberty* is likely to survive longer than anything else that I have written ... [It is] a kind of philosophic text-book of a single truth ...: the importance, to man and society, of a large variety in types of character, and of giving full freedom to human nature to expand itself in innumerable and conflicting directions.

Mill, *Autobiography* (1873)

Mill never systematically articulates his guiding view of freedom, not even in his famous essay *On Liberty*. Nonetheless, he develops a compelling conception of freedom in such writings as *On Liberty*, *The Subjection of Women*, *A System of Logic*, and *Principles of Political Economy*. Despite his reputation for defending a negative conception of freedom, Mill develops a richer view: he highlights both positive and negative aspects of freedom and illuminates the complementary relationship between freedom and power. His conception thus differs strikingly from the negative view of freedom as merely the absence of external constraints on people's efforts to satisfy their desires, whatever these are, which is the view that predominates in the liberal tradition.

Concerning freedom and power, Mill's conception of freedom is best understood in terms of people's capacity for self-determination and self-

*Portions of this chapter originally appeared in 'J.S. Mill on Freedom and Power,' *Polity* 31(2): 186–216.

government. Mill highlights four ways in that the exercise of freedom is integrally related to the exercise of power. First, he maintains that having 'power over our own character[s]' is a necessary precondition of our being fully free (L, 841). This refers to our capacity for individuality or *autonomy* – that is, the capacity to reflectively formulate and pursue our own desires and purposes. Mill sometimes uses morally charged language, but his conception of freedom is significantly different from moralized views in which freedom is equated with virtuous action. Second, Mill maintains that freedom requires the presence of the material resources and of opportunities to realize our aims and purposes. Third, Mill conceives of mental freedom and free agency not in all-or-nothing terms, but rather as capacities that people develop to greater or lesser degrees – that is, basically as *developmental powers*, to use C.B. Macpherson's phrase (1973, 52–3). In short, we are more or less autonomous and, therefore, more or less free overall – all other things being equal – to the *degree* that we have developed our capacity for reflectively pursuing our more important purposes. Mill argues, moreover, that people develop autonomy to the extent that the various power relationships situating them – educational, political, economic, gender, and family relationships – cultivate or stifle their capacities to pursue reflectively their own aims and purposes. Fourth, while Mill emphasizes the 'sovereignty' of the individual in 'self-regarding' matters (OL, 224), he does not conceive of individual freedom solely in terms of the actions of independent individuals. In his view, freedom also involves practices of democratic self-government that enable individuals to share in collective decision-making within the power relationships that govern their lives, particularly at home, at work, and as citizens.

In Mill's view, then, freedom encompasses each of the two distinct kinds of questions that Isaiah Berlin associates with 'negative' and 'positive' senses of freedom, respectively: 'What am I free to do or be?' and 'Who governs me?' (1969c, 130). He regards a free person as someone who has developed her capacity to reflectively formulate and pursue her own distinctive aims and purposes, and who has the power to pursue them in practices of individual and collective self-determination.

There is, however, one aspect of the interplay between freedom and power that Mill fails to address adequately: the relationship between freedom, power, and culture. Mill presents a compelling account of practices of freedom that corresponds to what Michael Sandel (1990) has called 'freedom of choice' – that is, the freedom to choose our own way of life or our own set of beliefs. This view has wide resonance in modern societies – especially modern Western societies – where such practices are basic to the idea of a free person. Yet Mill underestimates the givenness of some religious and cultural identities and incorrectly presents his notion of people as autonomous 'choosers' as universally valid. Consequently, he fails to appreciate that *for some people* freedom of action is more a matter of freedom to pursue deep religious or cultural commitments – what Sandel calls 'freedom of conscience' – than of freedom to *choose* a religious or cultural identity.

I Freedom and Liberty

To adequately grasp Mill's view of freedom, we need to look beyond the well-known 'principle of liberty' that he articulates in *On Liberty*. Only by doing so can we clarify his analytically distinct notion of what it means for persons to be free (Smith, 1984, 183–4). As G.W. Smith points out, we must consider Mill's account of 'free will' in *A System of Logic* and *An Examination of Sir William Hamilton's Philosophy* if we are to comprehend his underlying view of free agency (1984, 182). We must also reckon with Mill's analysis – in such works as *Principles of Political Economy, Considerations on Representative Government*, and *The Subjection of Women* – of the freedom of individuals with respect to the political, economic, educational, gender, and family relationships situating them.

Mill's conception of freedom is often confused with his 'principle of liberty.' The latter prescribes a sphere of 'self-regarding' choices and actions with respect to which the freedom of individuals ought not be restricted. In other words, the liberty principle addresses the issue of when individual freedom should and should not be restricted (Smith, 1984, 182).[1] By contrast, his *conception* of freedom is his view of what freedom means and entails. Mistaking the principle of liberty for Mill's conception of freedom gives rise to three misconceptions about his view of freedom. First, it conveys the false impression that Mill conceives of freedom in essentially negative terms, with the presence of freedom marked by the *absence* of constraints on people's efforts to satisfy their existing desires, whatever these are. Second, it neglects important domains in which freedom, according to Mill, consists of sharing with others in practices of collective self-government rather than simply the choices and actions of independent individuals. Third, it suggests that Mill, like many other liberal theorists, conceives of freedom and power as inversely related rather than complementary but sometimes conflicting.

Mill employs the concepts 'freedom' and 'liberty' distinctly, in ways that correspond to the difference between his principle of liberty and his conception of freedom. Since he does not explicitly distinguish between the two concepts, it would be wrong to overemphasize this distinction.[2] Nonetheless, he generally uses them in ways that capture the different connotations stemming from their different histories and etymologies.[3] Mill typically uses 'liberty' and 'individual liberty' to discuss more bounded practices of freedom. As Hanna Fenichel Pitkin notes, 'Liberty implies an ongoing structure of controls, whether of external laws and regulations or the genteel self-control of the liberal gentleman. That, no doubt is part of its appeal to liberals and ... one reason why John Stuart Mill wrote his essay "On Liberty" rather than on freedom' (1988, 543). Thus, Mill is articulating what he calls 'the principle of individual liberty' when he says in *On Liberty*, 'The only freedom that deserves the name, is that of pursuing our own good in our own way, *so long as we do not attempt to deprive others of theirs, or impede their efforts to obtain it*' (OL, 293, 226, emphasis added). *This* freedom is rightfully bounded by our duties to others, including the respect we owe to the rights of others (OL, 293, 225–6). It refers to the freedom of action to which each mature individual is entitled *by right* (OL, 224). Therefore, we cannot redescribe Mill's 'principle of liberty' as a 'principle of freedom' without distorting his meaning.

Mill typically uses 'freedom' more broadly to encompass a wider range of practices of individual self-determination and collective self-government.[4] He conveys the gist of his conception of freedom in a few remarks in *The Subjection of Women*. He conceives of 'freedom of action of the individual' as 'the liberty of each to govern his own conduct by his own feelings of duty, and by such laws and social constraints as his conscience can subscribe to' (SW, 336).[5] This involves not just the choices and actions of independent individuals, but also practices of democratic self-government that enable individuals to share in the regulating of their affairs within the key power relationships that govern their lives. This emphasis on mutual self-government is a central feature of Mill's view of political freedom. Thus he asks in *The Subjection*, 'What citizen of a free country would listen to any offers of good and skillful administration, in return for the abdication of freedom?' (SW, 337).

Mill further clarifies his understanding of freedom when he identifies the most significant obstacles to freedom. He recognizes, of course, the significance of legal restraints (OL, 223, 276). But as I will explain presently, he also identifies three other significant constraints: psychological constraints upon people's 'mental freedom' and autonomy that limit their capacity to formulate desires and life plans *of their own*; a lack

of material resources and opportunities for people to pursue their chosen occupations and ways of living; and the absence of opportunities for
individuals to share in self-government with respect to the household
and workplace and to the political institutions that govern their lives.

II Freedom, Autonomy, and Individuality

The first aspect of Mill's view of the interplay between freedom and
power concerns what he calls 'the power of self-formation' or 'power
over our own character' (L, 842, 841). This notion is closely linked to the
difference between his notion of the freedom of 'pursuing our own good
in our own way' and the empiricist and negative conception of freedom
that has been dominant within the Anglo-American liberal tradition
(OL, 226).[6] In the latter conception, the presence of freedom is construed merely in terms of the absence of external impediments on an
agent's doing whatever she or he wants to do; the agent's existing desires
are taken as given (Smith, 1991, 240–1; see also Friedman, 1966). One
implication of the negative view is that all laws by definition limit freedom because they either require or prohibit certain actions and thereby
frustrate certain desires. Most proponents of this view – sometimes called
'negative liberty' – acknowledge that some such constraints are desirable, though, since people must not be free to do *anything* they might
want to do.

 For Mill, by contrast, the presence of freedom is not at all the same as
the absence of external impediments to satisfying our unreflective desires, or doing as we please. Mill's conception of freedom includes
notions of self-development and self-mastery according to which, in
Smith's words, 'a free agent is someone who is capable of acknowledging
responsibility for his desire as "his own" because he, rather than others,
has formed the character from which they spring' (Smith, 1984, 211).[7]
Mill maintains that individual freedom is often restricted beyond the
reach of the law by 'the moral coercive of public opinion,' a form of
social power that can lead to a 'social tyranny more formidable than
many kinds of political oppression' (OL, 223, 220; cf. Smith, 1984;
1991). 'Society can and does execute its own mandates,' he says, through
the powers of education and public opinion (OL, 220, 282). This kind of
restraint is particularly insidious 'since ... it leaves fewer means of escape
[than other restraints], penetrating much more deeply into the details
of social life, and enslaving the soul itself' (OL, 220). It restricts people's
freedom of action by stifling their mental freedom. Mill is concerned not

just about the more obvious kinds of coercion or compulsion, such as 'peer pressure' and public reproach, but also about the more thorough-going way that 'society has now fairly got the better of individuality' (OL, 264). As he explains in *On Liberty*,

> the danger which threatens human nature is not the excess, but the deficiency, of personal impulses and preferences ... Not only in what concerns others, but in what concerns themselves, the individual or the family do not ask themselves – what do I prefer? or what would suit my character and disposition? or, what would allow the best and highest in me to have fair play and enable it to grow and thrive? They ask themselves, what is suitable to my position? what is usually done by persons of my station and pecuniary circumstances? ... I do not mean that they choose what is customary in preference to what suits their own inclination. It does not occur to them to have any inclination, except for what is customary. Thus the *mind itself is bowed to the yoke*: even in what people do for pleasure, conformity is the first thing thought of; they like in crowds; they exercise choice only among things commonly done: peculiarity of taste, eccentricity of conduct, are equally shunned with crimes: *until by dint of not following their own nature they have no nature to follow*: their human capacities are withered and starved: they become incapable of ... any opinions or feelings of home growth, or properly their own. (OL, 264–5, emphasis added)

Mill regards the power of education and opinion to shape human character as ever-present and unavoidable features of society (OL, 282; U, 218). Therefore, the mere presence of such power is no cause for concern. Problems arise, however, when the powers of education and popular opinion operate to undermine people's capacities to formulate and pursue aims and purposes 'properly their own.' When this happens, people are unfree with respect to their expressed desires and objectives. Mill made this point emphatically in an 1850 letter to *The Leader*, in which he was responding to a critic who misconstrued his warnings in *Principles of Political Economy* about the threat that 'communistic' reforms pose to freedom. Mill explained that his concern was *not* that a communistic system would make people's lives 'inane and monotonous' by freeing them from want and hunger. *This* freedom, he said, 'is a good in every sense of the word' ('CC,' 1179). His chief concern was the prospect of increased social tyranny – that the 'yoke of conformity' would become more severe in co-operative communities if 'people would be compelled to live as it pleased others, not as it pleased themselves.' He added, moreover, that this kind of 'bondage' was already a problem in existing capitalist societies, even among the rich: 'They do not cultivate and follow opinions, preferences, or tastes of their own, nor live otherwise than in the manner appointed by the world for persons of their class. Their lives are inane and monotonous because (in short) *they are not free*, because though they are able to live as pleases themselves, their minds are bent to an external yoke' ('CC,' 1179, emphasis added). For Mill, then, people who lack the capacity to conceive of desires and life plans that are 'properly their own' are not really self-determining, *even when* they have sufficient resources and opportunities 'to live as pleases themselves.' Such persons have desires and inclinations, but these are not 'of home growth, or properly their own' (OL, 264–5).[8]

Mill's conception of freedom thus differs from the empiricist negative view, in that he insists that the issue of *why* people desire what they desire must be considered in assessing the extent of their freedom (McPherson,1982; Smith, 1991). For Mill, the freedom of 'pursuing our own good in our own way' requires what he calls 'mental freedom,' and what is now commonly called *autonomy*: the capacity of persons reflectively to pursue beliefs, desires, and purposes that are 'properly their own' (OL, 246, 265).

Mill articulates his view of free action most fully in *A System of Logic*, where his chief concern is with the philosophical problem of 'liberty and necessity.' This has led some interpreters, notably J.C. Rees, to insist that particular conclusions about the free-will problem have no bearing on the issue of social and political freedom. 'Questions about human actions being determined by unalterable laws,' Rees says, 'are not questions about legal or social restraints' (1985, 181). Based on Mill's comment that his subject in *On Liberty* is not 'the so-called Liberty of the Will so unfortunately opposed to the misnamed doctrine of Philosophical Necessity; but Civil, or Social Liberty,' Rees even claims that Mills agrees with this proposition (OL, 217). Yet while Mill's focus on societal restraints to freedom in *On Liberty* is distinct from the issue of whether it is possible to speak of human freedom at all in a causally determined world, this point is not decisive. Indeed, the *way* that Mill addresses the question of free will is crucial to his broader conception of freedom (Smith, 1980b; Skorupski, 1989, 250–5).

Mill's view of 'free will' is close to what is now called a compatibilist view: he holds that human actions are causally determined, but that they *can* be free (Smith, 1991, 246; Foot, 1966). People's desires, he says, are not spontaneously chosen but rather flow from their characters, and their *characters* are produced by their circumstances. At the same time, he conceives of the connection between circumstances, on the one hand, and character and desires, on the other, as a *contingent* one that leaves room for freedom. Thus, he criticizes followers of social reformer Robert Owen as fatalists for maintaining that a person's 'character is formed *for* him and not *by* him; therefore his wishing that it had been formed differently is of no use; he has no power to alter it' (L, 840, Mill's emphasis). This is a 'grand error,' according to Mill, since a person has, 'to a certain extent, a power to alter his character' (L, 840). He explains that a person's character is formed 'by his circumstances ..., but his own desire to mould it in a particular way is one of those circumstances, and by no means the least influential.' His character, then, may be 'formed *by* him as one of the intermediate agents' (L, 840, Mill's emphasis). Mill accepts the Owenite claim that we cannot directly 'will to be different from what we are.' Yet he insists that each of us has the potential power to shape our own character that is similar to the indirect power that others have to shape our character by shaping our circumstances: 'We, when our habits are not too inveterate, can, by similarly willing the requisite means, make ourselves different ... We are exactly as capable of making our own character, *if we will*, as others are of making it for us' (L, 840, Mill's emphasis).[9]

This response to the free will problem is fraught with internal tensions. Mill says that our *will* or desire to change our character is a necessary ingredient to our doing so, but that even *this* desire 'comes to us either from external causes, or not at all' (L, 840). He therefore provides an equivocal response to determinism. Nonetheless, the way that he resolves this problem enriches his conception of freedom and illuminates how autonomy is relevant to the issue of free will. By emphasizing our potential power of self-formation, he illuminates the conditions of autonomous agency under which we can claim our desires and purposes as *our own* in the relevant sense that is compatible with determinism (Christman, 1988).

Mill's account of 'our feeling of moral freedom' is particularly instructive in this regard:

A person feels morally free who feels that his habits or his temptations are not his masters, but he theirs: who even in yielding to them knows that he could resist ... It is of course necessary, to render our consciousness of freedom complete, that we should succeed in making our character all we have hitherto attempted to make it; for if we have wished and not attained, we have, to that extent not the power over our own character, we are not free. Or at least, we must feel that our wish, if not our character, is strong enough to conquer our character when the two are brought into conflict ... And hence it is said with truth, that none but a person of confirmed virtue is completely free. (L, 841)

Mill's wording here is deceptive. He appears to conceive of freedom, as Smith says, 'as, essentially, the exercise of virtue' (Smith, 1989, 116). Such a moralized view is deeply problematic and illiberal since it suggests that people achieve true freedom only when they act 'rightly' or in accordance with their 'best self.' According to such a view, people could be compelled to 'choose rightly' in the name of freedom (Smith, 1991, 244; Berlin, 1969c, 134).[10] Mill is better understood, however, as insisting on autonomy rather than the exercise of virtue as a condition of being 'completely free.' His key claim in this regard is that we are fully free agents *only to the extent* that we are able to exercise 'power over our own character[s]' (L, 841). Thus, when he says 'that none but a person of confirmed virtue is completely free,' his point is that only such persons manifestly wield sufficient 'power over [their] own character[s]' to ensure that their desires and purposes are formed *by* them rather than *for* them. Persons 'of confirmed virtue' tend to exhibit the strength of will or character necessary to pursue their more considered aims and purposes even when this requires them to forgo their more transient desires.[11] In his view, then, being 'completely free' is related *directly* to autonomous agency and only *indirectly* to virtuous action. He does not construe freedom *as* the exercise of virtue.

Mill further refines his view of free action in *On Liberty*. He contends that people are fully free only to the extent that their desires and impulses reflect 'their own individual character[s]' – that is, to the extent that they achieve 'individuality' (OL, 262). He says, 'Where, not the person's own character, but the traditions and customs of other people are the rule of conduct, there is wanting one of the principle ingredients of human happiness' (261). Later he equates attaining individuality with 'having character': 'A person whose desires and impulses are his own – are the expression of his own nature, as it has been developed and modified by his own culture – is said to have character. One whose desires and impulses are not his own, has no character, no more than a steam engine has character' (OL, 264). In turn, he regards having character as a necessary condition of the freedom to pursue one's own mode of life.

The gist of Mill's argument is that we can justifiably claim our desires and purposes as 'properly our own' only insofar as we reflectively choose them in light of our own characters and circumstances. In the course of criticizing unreflective obedience to custom, he clarifies his view of the kind of critical reflection required:

> To conform to custom, merely as custom, does not educate or develop in [a person] any of the qualities which are the distinctive endowment of a human being. The human faculties of perception, judgment, discriminative feeling, mental activity, and even moral preference, are exercised only in making a choice. *He who does anything because it is the custom, makes no choice.* He who lets the world, or his own portion of it, choose his plan of life for him, has no need of any other faculty than the ape-like one of imitation. (OL, 262, emphasis added)

This does not mean that we can never freely choose to do what is customary or conventional. It *does* mean that we *freely* follow customs or conventions only when we do so after a process of critical reflection through which we self-consciously affirm the customs or conventions as *our own*.

Although the contemporary terminology of autonomy and heteronomy is foreign to Mill, these concepts refer to precisely the sorts of distinctions that Mill makes (Gray, 1983, 71).[12] According to Mill, we are more fully free, all other things being equal, to the extent that we choose our aims, purposes, and life plans *autonomously* – that is, through critical reflection upon the norms and traditions we confront. Only such autonomous agents are fully self-determining in the sense of pursuing their own good in their own way. In contrast, those who unquestioningly follow custom and those to whom it 'does not occur ... to have any inclination, except for what is customary' are *other*-directed rather than self-determining, heteronomous rather than autonomous. Their conduct is governed or directed by desires and inclinations that, as John Gray says, they have internalized from their 'social and cultural environment without ever subjecting them to critical evaluation' (Gray, 1983, 76).

Thus, what distinguishes Mill's conception of freedom from moralized conceptions is that he construes 'completely free' action in terms of a particular *mode of choosing* rather than in terms of a particular range of 'right' choices.[13] He emphasizes the degree of autonomy or power over their characters that people exercise in the process of determining their own course of conduct. He insists, moreover, that 'different persons ... require different conditions for their spiritual development' and that 'it is important to give the freest scope possible to uncustomary things' (OL, 270, 269). What is important, in his view, is people's capacity to determine the course of their own lives. By contrast, moralized conceptions of freedom focus on the *ends* chosen by agents as the distinguishing mark of whether or not their actions are truly free. People are truly free, in the latter view, when they choose ends that are 'worth choosing' (Berlin, 1969c, 132–4).

These points do not completely clear Mill of the charge that his emphasis on autonomy has moralistic and potentially repressive implications. As we have seen, Mill maintains that only people whose capacities for autonomy have been fully developed can be 'completely free.' His view of freedom thus seems to open the door to paternalistic interference with the conduct of those who are less than fully autonomous – for example, due to 'inveterate' habits or 'infirmities of character' – without this being counted as a restriction of their freedom (L, 840; U, 212). That is, it seems to suggest that certain people can be 'forced to be free' since they are incapable of 'completely free' action without external intervention. He appears to treat these people like children who lack the maturity to take full responsibility for their own lives (OL, 226 & 224; cf. Smith, 1984, 199; 1991). However, as I will explain, Mill's way of addressing this issue is more subtle and less menacing than it first appears to be, although his view of 'completely free' agency is not without limitations (see section V, below).

III Degrees of Autonomy, Degrees of Freedom

Although Mill maintains that only people who have fully developed their capacities for autonomy can be 'completely free' agents, he by no means regards them as the only persons capable of meaningful freedom. Rather than offering a simple dichotomy between the fully autonomous (or 'completely free') and completely heteronomous agents, he recognizes varying *degrees of freedom* corresponding to different degrees of autonomy and heteronomy (Skorupski, 1989, 254). He insists that it is not only 'persons of decided mental superiority who have a just claim to carry out their lives in their own way' (OL, 270). 'If a person possesses any tolerable amount of common sense and experience,' he says, 'his own mode of laying out his existence is the best, not because it is the best in itself, but because it is his own mode' (OL, 270). Mill's understanding of the significance of autonomy for judgments about freedom and unfreedom can be aptly redescribed in terms of the distinction made by some contemporary philosophers of action between *anomic, autarchic,* and *autonomous* agents (Benn, 1975–76; Gray, 1983). These concepts enable us to distinguish a variety of different constraints to *freedom* that are important for Mill.

First, there is the unfreedom of those who are sufficiently autonomous to choose aims and purposes that are 'properly their own,' but who face significant external impediments to their freedom of action (e.g., Andrei Sahkarov and Nelson Mandela during their years in prison). Second, there is the unfreedom of those whose minds are 'bowed to the yoke,' and to whom 'it does not occur ... to have any inclination, except for what is customary' (OL, 264–5). As Gray says, such a person may be free with respect to a particular 'action in so far as his [or her] doing that action is not prevented by the forcible or coercive intervention of an-other' (1983, 74).[14] It would be misleading, however, to describe them as fully or even substantially free. The 'freedom' of such persons is basically the limited freedom of those whom Stanley Benn calls 'anomic' agents and Henry Frankfurt calls 'wantons': they lack capacities of critical reflection and strength of will to such a degree that their desires and inclinations are their own only in a superficial sense.[15] This is not just a hypothetical problem. People sometimes find themselves in such op-pressive and restrictive circumstances that they learn to accept or acqui-esce to their oppression. Mill regards such persons as largely unfree since they cannot pursue their own good in a meaningful sense.

Finally, there is the freedom and unfreedom of those who lack full autonomy but who possess a 'tolerable amount of common sense and experience' (OL, 270). Mill regards this situation as typical of most people. Their freedom corresponds to what Benn and Gray call the freedom of *autarchic* agents. As Gray explains, this notion refers to the freedom of a person who 'while enjoying (over a wide range of actions) the negative freedom which covers the absence of both force and coer-cion, also exercises unimpaired all the normal capacities and powers of a rational chooser by reference to which rational self-direction is defined' (1983, 74). Such persons possess in some measure the capacity to deter-mine their 'own mode' of life insofar as they can articulate reasons for their actions (OL, 270). They are not completely unreflective or impul-sive, like anomic (or heteronomous) persons; but they often fail to exercise the 'second-order' capacity, characteristic of *autonomous* agents, to reflect critically upon their more immediate desires in light of their more considered aims and purposes.[16] Therefore, when people 'exercise choice only among things commonly done' and 'like in crowds' (OL, 265), they are neither completely free nor completely unfree. Moreover, this kind of conformist conduct may be even more common today than in Mill's time. People's characters and desires are now shaped by ever more sophisticated global communications media, while sources of immediate gratification and amusement have multiplied.

These distinctions are often difficult to make with respect to the conduct of actual persons. Nonetheless, they illuminate the subtlety of Mill's conception of freedom and they have a considerable heuristic value. Mill wisely rejects the false dichotomy of either regarding people as free *only* when they are fully autonomous or regarding people as fully free *even when* they are heteronomous. He maintains that people have different degrees of freedom and unfreedom, all other things being equal, in proportion to their relative autonomy or heteronomy. Thus, he is not saying that only persons 'of a better than ordinary mould' ('UR,' 411) are capable of free action and that most others must be 'forced to be free' through external intervention. Rather, and more compellingly, he is insisting that (virtually) all persons tend to develop the capacity for autonomous action to the extent that their educations and life experiences cultivate their capacities for reasoning, judgment, deliberation, and self-control. Clearly, his conception of freedom does not open the door to paternalism in the name of freedom in any simple sense.[17] These considerations have important implications when it comes to assessing Mill's egalitarianism (cf. Smith, 1991, 247–58; Donner, 1991, ch. 8; and chs. 4, 6–8, below).

Mill regards autonomy as a necessary condition of freedom but as insufficient in itself. He clearly recognizes that people may be fully autonomous and yet be largely unfree due to external impediments. His account of free action has one further qualitative dimension that is significant for thinking about the social and political aspects of freedom. While he rejects the view that freedom consists in exercising choice among things 'worth doing,' he highlights an important sense in which the *quality* of the choices and possibilities open to people is important for assessing their overall freedom. He construes freedom in terms of choices and opportunities that enable people to determine their own 'plan of life' or 'mode of existence' rather than as their ability to do whatever they desire. What is crucial is not simply the *number* of choices open to us, but also the *significance* of the choices and possibilities for 'pursuing our own good in our own way.'[18] The extent of a person's freedom, then, depends more on her power to pursue more considered aims and purposes than on her capacity to satisfy 'vague and transient desires' (OL, 261). Therefore, such things as our freedom to express beliefs and opinions, freedom of religion and conscience, and freedom to choose among different ways of life, and our opportunities to choose careers or modes of work, and to share in self-government with respect to the power relationships that govern our lives, are particularly important for assessing the extent of our freedom.

IV Freedom and Power

Mill recognizes that power is often exercised in ways that diminish freedom, both rightfully and wrongfully. Early in *On Liberty*, for instance, he considers how the 'liberty of action' of individuals may be limited by 'physical force in the form of legal penalties,' as well as by 'the moral coercion of public opinion' (OL, 223). But the more innovative part of his argument lies in his attention to four ways in which freedom is directly related to a positive aspect of power that he highlights in 'Bentham': 'the power of making our volitions effectual' ('B,' 96). I have already discussed the most basic aspect of this relationship: 'the power of self-formation,' which is basically the capacity for autonomous action. Mill also emphasizes three other ways that freedom is directly related to the exercise of power: people need material resources and opportunities in order to pursue effectively their aims and purposes; they need to be able to share in practices of self-government with respect to the power relationships that govern their lives; and what Mill calls 'the powers of education' – education in the broadest sense – must cultivate rather than stifle their capacities for freedom of thought and action.

Regarding the significance of material resources, Mill maintains that people require certain material resources – including educational opportunities, occupational choices, and a certain level of disposable income – in order to exercise meaningful freedom. He says, for example, that women to a greater extent than men are unable to enter marriages *freely* because existing laws and customs deny them the 'power of gaining their own livelihood.' Consequently, rather than marriage being 'wholly a matter of choice' for women, it is 'something approaching a matter of necessity; something, at least, which every woman is under strong artificial motives to desire' ('MD[I],' 77). He makes a similar point in the course of comparing the constraints to and prospects for freedom offered by various 'communist' and socialist reform programs to those found in capitalist England. Concerning the existing system he says, 'The generality of labourers in this and most other countries have as little choice of occupation or freedom of locomotion, are practically as dependent on fixed rules and on the will of others, as they could be on any system short of actual slavery' (PPE, 209). Mill's view, in short, is that a sufficient level of material resources 'to make our volitions effectual' is a necessary condition of the freedom of pursuing our own aims, purposes, and life plans.

With respect to practices of self-government, Mill extends the democratic tendencies of the liberal tradition. He addresses questions with respect to the various social and political power relationships in which people's choices and actions are embedded. These include political and economic institutions, gender relations, marital and family relations, educational institutions and practices, and spiritual and recreational activities. Accordingly, he conceives of the extent of people's freedom partly in terms of their opportunities to share in self-government with respect to the key power relationships that govern their lives. Thus, political freedom is not the absence of state power or legal restraints, but rather a matter of each person being 'under no other restraints than ... [the] mandates of society which he has a share in imposing, and which it is open to him, if he thinks wrong, publicly to dissent from, and exert himself actively to get altered' (CRG, 411, 432). Similarly, he conceives economic freedom not just in terms of the economic activities of independent individuals, but also in terms of extending the 'democratic spirit' into economic enterprises. He says that co-operative economic enterprises that give associated workers an equal voice in management would extend 'the freedom and independence of the individual ... [to] the industrial department' in modern societies (PPE, 763). His emphasis on mutual self-government as a component of freedom is also evident in his notion of marital partnerships in which men and women would share in governing 'the affairs of [their] families' (SW, 290–2).

Mill also addresses the interplay between freedom and power with respect to how the various social relationships situating people shape their capacities for self-formation or autonomy. He sees the various social and political relationships situating people not only as the field of their possible choices and actions, but also as 'powers of education' that shape people's characters and cognitive capacities (OL, 282; U, 218; 'IA,' 217; and see ch. 4, below). In Mill's view, the *potential* for autonomous agency is a basic human attribute, but mature powers of free action must be developed. Accordingly, we achieve this potential only to the degree that the social and political relationships situating us call forth and exercise our faculties of reasoning, judgment, deliberation, and imagination, and encourage us to think for ourselves. People, in short, must be educated for freedom, and such education depends not just on quality schooling – education in the narrow sense – but also on mental cultivation within all of their social and political relationships.

V Freedom, Power, and Culture

Mill's understanding of rational autonomy as a condition of 'completely free' agency betrays one significant limitation of his account of the relationship between freedom and power. His view of free action is culturally bounded rather than universally valid. He illuminates to some extent how the religious and cultural commitments of subjugated groups, such as women, often perpetuate their subjection; but his understanding of this problem is limited by his noninterpretive approach to social reality (Skorupski, 1989, 275–82). In particular, he fails adequately to grasp how religious and cultural traditions and identities are sources of meaning and value *as well as* media of power and domination. In sum, he does not address how the exercise of power and practices of freedom are themselves culturally shaped.

Mill displays both the strengths and limitations of his approach when he challenges the ideological power that manifests itself when cultural traditions perpetuate oppression through repressive modes of education or socialization. In *The Subjection of Women* he is eloquent about how English women are educated for subordination. 'All women,' he says, 'are brought up from the very earliest years in the belief that their ideal character is the very opposite to that of men; not self-will, ... but submission, and the yielding to the control of others' (SW, 271). Thus, he rejects the claim that women accept their subordinate status 'voluntarily.' He points out instead that many women 'do not accept it'; and, concerning those who apparently do accept it, he insists that men, preferring 'not a forced slave but a willing one, ... have therefore put everything in practice *to enslave their minds*,' including 'the whole force of education' (SW, 270–1, emphasis added). To the extent that women have learned this 'morality of submission,' their mental freedom has been stifled so that their freedom of action cannot be assessed simply in terms of whether or not they are impeded in their pursuit of their unreflective desires (SW, 294; OL, 290).

Mill rightly emphasizes that traditions are embedded within and expressive of relations of power, which include the patriarchal power of men over women. Even so, his analysis is limited in that he gives short shrift to the symbolic or hermeneutical aspect of religious and cultural traditions and customs. He tends to regard religious and cultural identities and commitments as effects of power, or as signs of intellectual 'immaturity' and 'civilizational' backwardness. Thus, he underemphasizes their importance as sources of meaning and value.[19]

This means, in turn, that Mill also fails to grasp adequately how many 'mature,' rational agents – men as well as women – enact traditional religious or cultural norms and practices *as free agents*. This problem is evident in an important passage from *On Liberty* that I quoted earlier. Mill says, 'To conform to custom, merely as custom, does not educate or develop in [a person] any of the qualities which are the distinctive endowment of a human being ... He who does anything because it is the custom, makes no choice' (OL, 262). In his view, anyone who does something 'because it is the custom' is not fully free because she or he is acting upon premises 'taken from authority, not from reason' (OL, 251). The conduct of such persons is in effect directed by others rather than self-determined. Mill says, 'Not the person's own character, but the traditions or customs of other people are the rule of conduct'; the person is permitting 'the world, or his own portion of it, [to] choose his plan of life for him' (OL, 261–2).

For Mill, then, people can enact a custom or tradition as 'completely free' agents only insofar as they have reflectively chosen their guiding religious and cultural commitments and values. Thus, even when agents self-consciously act in accordance with a valued tradition or belief system, their conduct is not fully free if they have not reflectively chosen their fundamental beliefs and commitments in the first place. Mill is insisting here on a rather radical approach to critical reflection with respect to received moral and religious beliefs. He fleshes out this view in an 1868 letter concerning the role of parents in teaching their children about religion:

> I do not think that there should be any *authoritative* teaching at all on such subjects. I think parents ought to point out to their children when the children begin to question them, or to make observations of their own, the various opinions on such subjects, & what the parents themselves think the most powerful reasons for & against. Then, if the parents show a strong feeling of the importance of truth & also of the difficulty of attaining it, it seems to me that young people's minds will be sufficiently prepared to

regard popular opinion or the opinions of those about them with respectful tolerance, & may be safely left to form definite conclusions in the course
of mature life.[20]

In Mill's view, people can *freely choose* their religion and their religiously informed values only if they are not, as children, instilled with the
belief that any one religion is uniquely true or right. This is a plausible
account of being free with respect to our religious and cultural identities
and commitments. At the same time, it brings to light the idealized and
decontextualized character of Mill's notion of 'completely free' action.
Taken to its logical conclusion, his ideal suggests that we are fully free
only insofar as we are encouraged to choose reflectively our own beliefs
and identities – that is, only insofar as we are not taught authoritatively
any one set of religious and cultural commitments. This implies not only
that all children should have a secular formal education that includes
the comparative study of religious and cultural traditions, but also that
the informal education they receive from their parents or guardians
should be thoroughly nonsectarian (see chapter 4, below). It also implies that people are always more free, in an unequivocal sense, in
proportion to the number of significant possible ways of life, philosophies, and religious and cultural identities that are made available to
them. Thus, even the common practice whereby parents pass on their
religion and culture to their children in some measure constrains the
freedom of the latter.

Mill's standard of 'completely free' agency obscures the givenness –
that is, the unchosen character – of key aspects of *everyone's* social identities, fundamental commitments, and ideas of the good. It follows that
he is posing a false dichotomy when he warns about cases in which 'not
the person's own character, but the traditions or customs of other people
are the rule of conduct' (OL, 261). Our characters, beliefs, and values
are inevitably shaped in some measure by the traditions and customs of
the communities into which we are born. Thus, people always act on the
basis of desires, beliefs, and understandings that they have appropriated
from their social context (Appiah, 1993, 117; Wittgenstein, n.d., 53–
72).[21] Moreover, many (if not most) people choose numerous things –
including important things – because they are their customs. Therefore,
it is misleading to speak of people being 'completely free' with respect to
their aims, beliefs, values, characters, and social identities.

These points are especially salient when we consider people's freedom
with respect to their religious beliefs and identities. Many (if not most)

people are authoritatively taught a particular religious identity as a matter of course. Their earliest encounters with religion commonly consist of being taught 'their' religious identities in their families and/or communities as they learn their language, kinship, nationality, and other basic features of their social identities. People are rarely brought up with the understanding that a wide range of human religious and spiritual practices are available, from which they are free to choose. We typically learn from our families, 'We are Catholic (or Jewish, Muslim, Episcopalian, etc.)' – often through unspoken lessons, such as family or community participation in specific kinds of worship and rituals.[22] Thus, our religious identities are always partly formed by relationships of power and authority. Of course, we learn our religious (or nonreligious) identities in varying ways depending on other aspects of our social identities and social locations (e.g., our nationality, ethnicity, gender identity, 'racial' identity, schooling, and life experiences). Yet this does not undermine the givenness of most people's religious identities.[23] Religious faith typically rests on some received authority and on certain 'rock bottom' beliefs and values that believers do not generally call into question (Wittgenstein, 1984, 45e; Asad, 1993). Many believers question the *meaning* of their religious beliefs, but regard their religion itself as a basic part of their identity rather than as an object of conscious *choice*.[24] Therefore, many people construe freedom with respect to religious beliefs or identities in terms of the capacity to practice religion as they see fit, rather than in terms of choosing fundamental religious commitments.[25]

In this light, Mill misleadingly construes freedom in an essentialist way – that is, transhistorically – in terms of reflective choice, self-realization, and self-government such that any practice of freedom *as freedom* must include these elements. He maintains that 'the peculiar character of the modern world ... is, that human beings are no longer born to their place in life, ... but are free to employ their faculties, and such favourable chances as offer, to achieve the lot which may appear to them most desirable' (SW, 272–3). This modern ethos has led people increasingly to construe freedom in terms of the freedom to choose – and also to share in choosing – how they wish to lead their lives. What Mill fails to see adequately is how the practices of freedom that he rightly regards as the logical expressions of the modern ethos of self-determination are rooted *in a particular historical and cultural constellation of social and political struggles and innovations*. For example, the Protestant Reformation and its aftershocks gave impetus to the development of new ideas and practices of religious freedom and freedom of conscience; the development of modern European nation-states and popular struggles for the extension of basic political rights and liberties produced a distinctively modern form of political freedom linked to representative government; modern capitalist development and class-based struggles against the emergent power of capitalists generated new and conflicting ideas and practices of 'economic freedom'; and concepts and practices of sexual and reproductive freedom are also distinctly modern (cf. Plamenatz, 1960; Hexter, 1983). *Most* of these practices of freedom emphasize individual choice, self-realization, or self-government; yet religious freedom and freedom of conscience require no comparable presumptions of individual choice. The latter freedoms encompass the 'free exercise' of religious creeds, regardless of whether they are inherited or freely chosen, as well as spiritual and philosophical quests through which some people consciously choose their fundamental spiritual and philosophical beliefs and commitments.

This brings us back to my earlier claim that different historical configurations of power and culture have produced different practices of freedom. That is, different contexts generate divergent answers to basic questions concerning freedom – questions such as, 'Freedom from what? For whom? To do what?'[26] For example, Dorothy Lee explains that in traditional Navaho society in Arizona and New Mexico, learning to be free 'involves learning to observe a large number of taboos and procedures, which are aspects of every act ... All this could be seen as inhibiting, or negative, or as interfering with the individual; but to the Navaho it is guidance in the acquisition of an essential skill – the freedom to act and to be' (1959, 11). This Navaho practice of freedom has striking affinities to other historical practices of freedom that involve similar modes of self-discipline, such as the ancient Greek view of freedom as 'self-mastery,' early Christian practices of 'spiritual freedom,' and the later Puritans' view of freedom as requiring 'subjection ... [to] the authority of Christ' and his worldly representatives.[27]

One way to regard such practices of self-discipline is to start from the perspective of modern pluralistic societies, as Mill and Isaiah Berlin do, and then find them wanting as general conceptions of freedom (OL, 68–70; Berlin, 1969c, 135ff).[28] Alternatively, we can acknowledge that such practices are forms of freedom while recognizing that, as Lee says, they are not general models of freedom for modern pluralistic societies, 'but rather food for thought, the basis of new insights' (1959, 14). This approach offers a fresh perspective on modern practices of freedom that involve analogous unchosen commitments, and makes possible a respectful consideration of nonmodern practices of freedom. Still, the close connection between freedom and subordination in some nonmodern practices makes these practices suspect from a modern perspective – particularly to people with liberal, democratic, feminist, and secular commitments. In the same breath, it is worth recalling that Western practices of freedom have often combined freedom for some persons with the subordination of others. For instance, the political freedom of ancient Athenian male citizens and of propertied white men in the ante-bellum United States went hand-in-hand with slavery and the subordination of women. Furthermore, Mill himself insists that *existing* practices of economic freedom in modern capitalist societies conjoin considerable freedom and power for capitalists with unfreedom and subordination for the labouring classes.[29] Accordingly, one of the great merits of Mill's account of freedom and power is his insistence that democratic and critically reflective ways of organizing relations of power and authority uniquely foster the equal freedom of all persons.[30]

To comprehend the interplay of freedom, power, and culture, we need a more pluralistic approach than Mill offers. Besides recognizing how modern practices of freedom emphasize autonomy, choice, and self-realization – at least in principle – we need to recognize that people in various contexts also exercise freedom when they carry out religious and cultural commitments that they have not reflectively chosen. At the same time, we must not jump to the false conclusion that any enactment of cultural or religious norms and rules is an expression of freedom regardless of the power dynamics under which it occurs.

Distinguishing free from unfree agency is not simply a matter of distinguishing conduct that emanates from conscience from that imposed by external authority. This distinction is untenable, since people's fundamental religious and cultural beliefs and commitments are always partly constituted by *some* external authorities – by parents, teachers, ministers, or rabbis, or, in more pernicious cases, by missionaries and colonial educators. Yet this crucial point can be elaborated in ways that leave us without any adequate conception of free agency. For instance, Stanley Fish argues that just as it makes no sense to speak of actions *free from all constraints*, since people always act within background conditions that make some actions possible while making others unavailable, 'it follows, too, that there can be no continuum which differentiates institutions or structures as being more or less constrained, or more or less free' (1989, 459).[31] As Mill points out, however, such situational 'constraints' are not equally constraining (or freedom-generating) for all people. The asymmetries of power, including relationships of oppression, leave differently situated people with different degrees of freedom. This is one of Mill's key insights in *The Subjection of Women*: while many women and men may do things *because* they are traditional or customary, this tendency is particularly burdensome to women. Pervasive patriarchal traditions and relationships sharply constrain women's available choices and possibilities relative to those of men (SW, 272–82; cf. Hirshmann, 1996, 57–63). Women, to a far greater extent than men, find themselves in situations where they face extremely severe penalties for noncompliance with the rules of conduct prescribed by their inherited religious and cultural traditions. This was true, for example, of the practice of self-immolation by widowed (usually upper-caste) Hindu women in India, and it is true of practices of 'female circumcision' in Sahelian Africa (particularly Sudan, Somalia, and Mali), some Arab countries, and parts of Asia.[32] In such circumstances, women often *yield* to prevailing norms and practices without freely *consenting* to them (Mathieu, 1990; Spivak, 1994).

Freedom, therefore, requires that women and men be *agents* rather than passive objects of their social and political practices. But it also requires that their conduct represents, in a meaningful sense, their own way of affirming a valued way of life. Mill rightly insists that to affirm freely an inherited religious or cultural identity, a person must be in a position to freely reject this identity without being unduly penalized (see OL, 290). Moreover, he rightly insists that people are unfree with respect to a received custom insofar as they reduce it to a 'hereditary creed, ... received passively, not actively' (OL, 248). Nonetheless, we need a more interpretive and pluralistic account than Mill offers of how the interplay of power and culture shapes possibilities for free agency. Such an account must not prejudge *just* when agency should be regarded as free, but it can offer some guideposts. First, like Mill, we should be wary of regarding actions taken under notably constrained conditions as an exercise of freedom. Second, since people always start with some pre-given concepts and understandings, we ought to take seriously their own self-understandings – their own reasons for doing what they do and their own conceptions of freedom. Third, insofar as people are never fully aware of all the social forces and power dynamics that shape them, their self-understandings will not tell the whole story of their freedom or unfreedom.

This last point has important implications. We need to acknowledge practices of freedom that do not conform to Mill's secular modernist notion of reflective choice; but at the same time, we also need to be aware of agents' unarticulated or barely articulated forms of resistance (Jones, 1994, 36; Walzer, 1994, 175, 173; Spivak, 1994). The latter will indicate situations where people yield to religiously or culturally pre-scribed rules of conduct without freely enacting them. Furthermore, prevailing ideas and self-understandings about freedom in *all* societies may be open to criticism. In this vein, Mill astutely criticizes many prevailing ideas about freedom in modern democratizing societies like his own (see chs. 5–8, below).[33]

VI Conclusions

Mill's developmental view of individuality and autonomy leads him to articulate an indispensable account of the relationship between freedom and power. Freedom, he maintains, consists of the absence of burden-some constraints on people's possible actions as well as the capacity of persons for self-determination and self-government. While recognizing that the exercise of power often diminishes the freedom of individuals, he shows that there is no opposition between freedom and power *as such*. In his view, people are always embedded in power relationships that shape their capacities for free action and delimit their field of possibili-ties. Therefore, the real opposition is between forms of power that stifle people's autonomy and freedom of action and forms of power that support freedom. In this regard, Mill maintains that freedom must not be conceived solely in terms of what we are free to do or be (or not do or not be) *within* the power relationships that govern our lives, but must also be assessed in terms of our opportunities to effectively share in self-government with respect to the various power relationships situating us. This requires more than merely formal opportunities for self-government, since freedom entails individuals having 'influence in the regulation of their affairs.' In the same breath, Mill's argument implies that individuals can be free in reflectively choosing *not to participate* in processes of collective self-government. Such choices are free, however, only given certain conditions. The agents must have developed capaci-ties for self-government, and institutions and practices must be available that would enable them, if they so chose, to share meaningfully in self-government. He construes freedom, then, as an 'exercise-concept' rather than merely as an 'opportunity-concept,' to use Charles Taylor's terms. The presence of freedom requires that we actually exercise a directing influence over the course of our lives (Taylor, 1979).

Mill recognizes the potential tensions between individual liberty and democratic self-government; yet he regards both as indispensable and neither one as more essential than the other. Accordingly, he develops his principle of liberty – that a community can rightfully exercise power over the conduct of its individual members only to prevent 'harm to others' (OL, 223) – as a means to reconcile democratization of the state, industrial relations, education, and marital relations with protection for individuals against tyrannical majorities (see chs. 5 and 7, below).

Regarding the interplay of freedom, power, and culture, my account of Mill's views shows that we need a conception of freedom that is more pluralistic than his if we are to grasp how different contexts of power and culture constitute different modes of free agency. In particular, we need a view which accommodates practices of freedom whereby individuals pursue fundamental commitments and beliefs that they have not reflectively chosen, along with as practices of freedom that emphasize reflective choice, self-realization, and self-government. In this way we can grasp how supporting freedom of choice in Mill's sense (i.e., the freedom of individuals to choose their fundamental commitments and ways of life) may sometimes conflict with freedom of conscience (i.e., the freedom of individuals to practise their beliefs). In this regard, Mill's view of free action can hardly as congenial to, say, people for whom a powerful god is a living presence, as it is to people who lack such a belief. Fundamental religious commitments may lead the former to pursue 'correct' moral and religious practices as prescribed by their religion (as they understand it) rather than to seek personal independence, self-creation, and self-government.

Yet adopting this pluralistic view of freedom should not lead us to overlook Mill's insight into the special significance of freedom of choice in modern societies. Even members of modern (and 'modernizing') societies who are especially concerned with freely pursuing their fundamental religious or cultural commitments typically seek freedom of choice in other areas of their lives. Moreover, it is crucial to appreciate how Mill's notion of freedom of choice differs from the 'freedom of choice' that is so widely celebrated in modern capitalist societies such as the United States. According to Mill, the freedom of choice that matters is *not* the limited freedom of choosing our favourite products in the marketplace (e.g., the 'freedom' to choose between Coke and Pepsi). Rather, it is the freedom of 'pursuing our own good in our own way' – the freedom of choosing our own 'mode of existence' or 'plan of life.' This sort of freedom encompasses not only our field of possibilities as independent individuals, but also our opportunities for self-government.

2

Mill's Theory of Modern Freedom

No one who attempts to lay down propositions for the guidance of mankind, however perfect his scientific acquirements, can dispense with a practical knowledge of the actual modes in which the affairs of the world are carried on, and an extensive personal experience of the actual ideals, feelings, and intellectual and moral tendencies of his own country and his own age. The true practical statesman is he who combines this experience with a profound knowledge of abstract political philosophy.

J.S. Mill, 'On the Definition of Political Economy' (1836)

Starting with Mill's conception of freedom, his ongoing and varied inquiries into the conditions of freedom can be brought together as a coherent theory of modern freedom in light of his philosophy of social scientific inquiry. With his philosophy of the social sciences, which he explains in *A System of Logic*, he connects questions of fact to questions of value and outlines the underpinnings of his 'social philosophy.' Through his social philosophy he seeks to explain societal tendencies toward stability or change in relation to the various forms of social power. This sociology of power leads Mill to examine 'agencies lying deeper than forms of government, which, working through forms of government,' produce certain effects in states and societies ('AC,' 234; cf. Ashcraft, 1989). This is also the basis upon which Mill situates his analysis of the meaning and conditions of freedom in the context of the web of social and political relationships that shape people's characters and capacities and structure the extent and character of their freedom (i.e., that delimit what they can and cannot do or be).

Along with Mill's theory of social power, there are a few other theoretical cornerstones of his theory of freedom. In particular, he elaborates his view of freedom as a chief element of human well-being in light of his utilitarian moral theory; and he advances theories of individual and societal 'development' to assess the utility of freedom and its proper scope and character in relation to other political goals in different social and historical contexts. He is especially concerned, however, with the flourishing of freedom in modern democratizing societies.[1] Finally, drawing upon his theoretical inquiries regarding freedom, he employs four secondary or 'middle principles' (*axiomata media*) with which he aims at *achieving* an optimal balance of freedom among the various members of modern democratic societies: individual liberty, democratic self-government, justice, and equality.

I 'Science,' 'Art,' and 'Theory' in Mill's Political Philosophy

To grasp the sense in which Mill can be fruitfully read as offering a comprehensive theory of modern freedom, we first need to be clear about how he views of the role of general 'theories' in the social sciences. He devotes considerable attention to this topic, especially in Book VI of *A System of Logic*, entitled 'On the Logic of the Moral Sciences.' In turn, we can deduce his theory of freedom by bringing together his methodological prescriptions for studying social phenomena with his own efforts to illuminate the meaning and conditions of freedom in relation to people's 'position[s] in the world' ('B,' 89). At the most general level, Mill defines 'theory' in a way that applies to propositions of *science*, which concern matters of fact – what *is*, or what will be – as well as to propositions of *art*, which concern 'whatever speaks in rules or precepts' in the domain of what *ought* to be (L, 943, 949). Properly understood, he says, theory 'means the completed result of philosophical induction from experience. In that sense, there are erroneous as well as true theories, for induction may be incorrectly performed, but theory of some sort is the necessary result of knowing anything of a subject, and having put one's knowledge into the form of general propositions for practice. In this, the proper sense of the word, Theory is the explanation of practice' (L, 812). Both 'art' and 'science,' then, are theoretical endeavors in the broadest sense of the term. Moreover, *theory* in this broad sense is central to Mill's effort to establish a rational basis for both aspects of the moral sciences: the *science* of systematically explaining the causes of social phenomena, and the *art* of systematically relating the ends of human conduct to the rules of their realization in light of general principles (Ryan, 1990, 193).

Since the two aspects of social scientific inquiry correspond to different kinds of propositions, Mill relates them to two different kinds of theories and theorizing. He explains this distinction as follows. Propositions of science are 'indicative' propositions that 'assert a matter of fact: an existence, a co-existence, a succession, or a resemblance' (L, 949). Science, therefore, is essential for explaining how certain phenomena come into being, how they can be (or are) maintained, and how and why they change. In contrast, propositions of art 'do not assert that anything is, but enjoin or recommend that something should be' (L, 949). Mill says that defining the end in a particular field of human conduct 'belongs exclusively to Art, and forms its peculiar province,' even though ends can only be attained in light of theoretical knowledge derived from science (L, 949). Thus, art has an intimate connection to science, which provides knowledge of what *causes* the state of affairs we desire, but it is a distinct endeavor.

In short, once we move from choosing the ends or goals of conduct to evaluating whether or not, how, to what extent, and at what cost they can be achieved given existing resources and circumstances, we have shifted away from the domain of art to the domain of science. In a passage that is directly relevant to how he theorizes the conditions of freedom, Mill says,

> the grounds ... of every rule of art are to be found in theorems of science. An art, or a body of art, consists of the rules, together with as much of the speculative propositions as compromise the justification of those rules. *The complete art of any matter includes a selection of such a portion from the science as is necessary to show on what conditions the effects which the art aims at producing depend* ... [Art] brings together from parts of the field of science most remote from one another the truths relating to the production of the different and heterogeneous conditions necessary to each effect which the exigencies of practical life require to be produced. (L, 947, emphasis added)

The art of a matter, then, involves both assessing the desirable ends of human conduct and identifying the scientific knowledge that is necessary for achieving these ends. In the same vein, scientific inquiry concerns the task of identifying the factors or conditions that are necessary for bringing about our chosen ends. In addition, we need science in order to determine whether particular ends are attainable in light of existing conditions and possibilities, or, alternatively, the conditions under which they might become attainable.

Mill goes on to explain that the art applicable to the human sciences is a branch of what he calls the 'Art of Life.' This comprehensive art has three departments – morality, prudence or policy, and aesthetics – which correspond to the three main provinces of human conduct: 'the Right, the Expedient, and the Beautiful or Noble' (L, 949). Mill construes the Art of Life as the art to which 'all other arts are subordinate; since its principles are those which must determine whether the special aim of any particular art is worthy and desirable, and what is its place in the scale of desirable things' (L, 949). It includes a notion of 'Teleology, or the Doctrine of Ends,' which consists of practical reasoning about appropriate rules or precepts for different types of human conduct, and about the status of different ends of human conduct 'in the scale of desirable things' (L, 949–50). With respect to the ends of morals and politics, this task falls specifically to moral philosophy. Mill explains that the only premise that the art contributes to social scientific inquiry and practical policymaking 'is the original major premise, which asserts that the attainment of the given end is desirable'; then we need to turn to the corresponding science (L, 944). The science enables us to take the proposed end 'as a phenomenon or effect to be studied,' illuminate its causes or conditions, and, finally, derive a theorem for the art that identifies the conditions 'by which it can be produced' (L, 944). Ideally, he says, the science 'lends to Art the proposition (obtained by a series of inductions or deductions) that the performance of certain actions will attain the end. From these premises Art concludes that the performance of these actions is desirable and, finding it also practicable [i.e., when it *is* practicable], converts the theorem into a rule or precept' (L, 944–5).

Mill models his approach to the social sciences on the logic of the natural sciences. Accordingly, he maintains that a field of inquiry becomes scientific when it becomes deductive and theoretical – where being 'theoretical' means that the phenomena in question can be explained in relation to general laws or generalizations. 'What is known of a subject, only becomes a science,' he says, 'when it is made a connected body of truth; in which the relation between the general principles and the details is definitely made out, and each particular truth can be recognized as a case of the operation of wider laws' (ACP, 285; L, 462). He insists, moreover, that this logic holds true for the social or 'moral' sciences as well as for the natural sciences. Insofar as they aspire to scientific status, the 'methods of investigation applicable to moral and social science ... [must be] those of science in general' (L, 835). Therefore, what Mill says in 'Bentham' concerning philosophy succinctly characterizes his view of the basic commonality between the science of matter and the human sciences: 'to build either a philosophy or anything else, there must be materials. For the philosophy of matter, the materials are the properties of matter; for moral and political philosophy, the properties of man, and of man's position in the world' ('B,' 89). The social sciences, like the natural sciences, must begin by comprehending the basic properties of their subject matter and go on to analyze the factors that affect the character and conduct of the subject matter. In the social sciences this entails comprehending the basic properties of human beings and the effects upon them of their 'position[s] in the world.' In addition, human conduct is amenable to being treated as a subject of science because the 'law of causality,' according to which the succession of the phenomena are the effects of causes, holds true for human actions just as it does for natural phenomena.[2]

These considerations are closely related to Mill's 'compatibilist' view of 'liberty and necessity' (see ch. 1). Mill maintains that accepting that the law of causality applies to human conduct – that is, that we can usually predict a person's conduct *if* we have sufficient knowledge of her 'character and disposition,' circumstances, and motivations – does not 'conflict in the smallest degree with what is called our feeling of freedom' (L, 837). Human freedom does not entail unpredictability or an absence of causes of human actions, but rather the power of persons to modify their own character if they wish.[3] The key difference between the social and natural sciences, according to Mill, is that the former are more complex; there is no essential difference in kind. Understanding the forces or 'agencies' that affect the subjects of social science requires consideration of the multiplicity of intertwined circumstances that shape human character and conduct. These include the various social practices, relationships, material artifacts, forms of government, and patterns of social development that are the products of human conduct.

In this light, Mill sees the various social sciences as related to one another in a particular way, with psychology being the most basic and history being the most comprehensive. He proceeds, as Henry Magid notes, from psychology (the science of the 'general laws of mind'), to what he calls ethology (the science of the formation of character), to sociology (the science of society, which includes the science of government), and, finally, to history (1965, xxii). Psychology and ethology are both 'sciences of individual man,' whereas sociology and history are sciences 'of the actions of collective masses of mankind' (L, 875). Only the latter, therefore, are full-blown *social* sciences. Still, Mill regards psychology and ethology as essential building blocks for all social scientific inquiry because all social phenomena are ultimately based on laws of 'individual human nature' – that is, basic mental processes common to all persons. He explains: 'The laws of the phenomena of society are, and can be, nothing but the laws and actions and passions of human beings united together in the social state. Men, however, in a state of society, are still men; their actions and passions are obedient to the laws of individual human nature ... Human beings in society have no properties but those which are derived from, and may be resolved into, the laws of the nature of individual man' (L, 879). In other words, our ability to explain social phenomena is predicated on our understanding of 'general laws of the mind,' because these presocial properties determine *how* the character and capacities of individuals unfold in relation to social practices, relationships, and institutions. Thus, individual human beings are the basic unit of social scientific explanations.

Basically, Mill is committed to a *social* version of 'methodological individualism': the doctrine that changes within all social institutions and collectives must ultimately be explained in terms of the dispositions, beliefs, and actions of individual human beings (Lukes, 1974, 110–22). He insists that social phenomena are ultimately explainable in terms of the laws of mind. Yet he does not subscribe to what Karl Popper calls *psychologism*: the more questionable view that sociological laws are reducible to psychological laws (Popper, 1950, 283, cited in Capaldi, 1973, 409). Rather, Mill maintains that the characters, beliefs, and motivations of individuals are shaped *by their circumstances*, but he does not lose sight of the role that people play in shaping those circumstances. In this way, his methodological individualism is integrally related to his social and developmental conception of individuality. Thus, Mill says that human beings in society 'have no properties but those which are derived from ... the laws of the nature of individual man,' but he regards this as true only in a minimal sense. The 'laws' of the nature of individual human beings to which Mill refers are 'laws of association' that explain the succession of psychological states in the minds of individuals (L, 853–56; see ch. 4, below). He emphatically insists, however, that attending to these presocial aspects of human nature is merely a first step in social scientific analysis since human beings are always found *in society*. 'It is certain,' he says, 'that our mental states, and our mental capacities and susceptibilities, are modified, either for a time or permanently, by everything which happens to us in life' (L, 863–4).[4] In sum, psychology is an essential but limited tool for explaining social phenomena such as people's conduct within their social and political relationships.

Mill gives the name 'Ethology, or the Science of Character,' to the science that has as its subject the 'derivative' or intermediate laws that determine 'the kind of character produced in conformity to those general laws [of the mind], by any set of circumstances, physical and moral' (L, 869). He presents ethology as a complement to psychology insofar as it provides a means of relating the 'inner,' psychological workings of the self to the 'outward' social relationships that shape its development. Ethology occupies a pivotal place in Mill's philosophy of social science and, in turn, in his theory of freedom. Since the capacity for free action, or autonomy, entails the development of a particular kind of character, including a significant measure of reflectiveness and self-control (or strength of character), ethology promises to yield knowledge that is essential to the *end* of cultivating the capacity for free agency among people.

Mill explains further that the science of ethology corresponds 'to the art of education, in the widest sense of the term, including the formation of national or collective character as well as individual' (L, 869). Whereas ethology seeks to explain how people's characters are formed, the *art* of education – in its 'widest sense' – encompasses all those social practices and relationships that actually shape people's characters and cognitive capacities. For this reason, Mill regards the perfection of ethology as of vital importance for the perfection of education, including education for freedom. He never fulfills his aim of developing the science of ethology; yet he does pursue ethology informally throughout his writings to develop a few middle-range propositions regarding how people's characters and cognitive capacities are shaped by their social and political relationships and institutions (see Feuer, 1976; Gibbons, 1990; and ch. 4, below). Moreover, as I will explain shortly, both ethology and education are integrally connected to his view of the sources of social power.

Mill's theory of freedom, however, involves a wider body of knowledge than can be provided by psychology and ethology alone. It also requires knowledge of sociology – which in Mill's view encompasses government and economics – and history. Sociology and history build upon psychology and ethology, but they seek to formulate general 'empirical laws' – that is, contextually bounded, law-like generalizations – that explain the 'actions of collective masses of mankind' (L, 875). Mill expects these 'laws' to explain such things as tendencies for stability and change in social practices and institutions. The sciences of collective human action are necessarily more tentative and inexact than psychology and ethology,

Mill says, 'because the number of concurrent causes, all exercising more or less influence on the total effect, is greater, in proportion in which a nation, or the species at large, exposes a larger surface [that is, more persons and circumstances] to the operation of agents, psychological and physical, than any single individual' (L, 875). He says, moreover, that 'the multitude of the causes is so great as to defy our limited powers of calculation' (L, 846). This multitude of causes includes the actions of persons, individually and collectively, to change their circumstances and shape their characters.

Given these complexities, Mill maintains that although social phenomena are *in principle* amenable to scientific explanation, the more comprehensive social sciences can identify only tendencies of social phenomena. He emphasizes, though, that even if the science of society can never be a predictive science due to the complexity of the causes of social phenomena, 'an amount of knowledge quite insufficient for prediction may be valuable for guidance' (L, 878). He explains, 'It is enough to know that certain means have a *tendency* to produce a given effect ... When the circumstances of an individual or of a nation are in any considerable degree under our control, we may, by our knowledge of tendencies, be enabled to shape those circumstances in a manner much more favorable to the ends we desire than the shape which they would of themselves assume. This is the limit of our power, but within this limit the power is a most important one' (L, 869–70, Mill's emphasis). In short, even though we cannot predict the effects of actions and policies with any certainty, our knowledge of general tendencies and likely results enables us to act purposefully to pursue desired ends. For instance, we may lack the ability to predict the precise consequences of stiffer legal penalties on certain activities, or of new programs aimed at improving education or health care, but we often have sufficient knowledge of the likely consequences of such policies to enable us to make sound policy judgments.

II Freedom and Mill's Moral Theory

Regarding the end of human freedom, then, social science can provide us with 'empirical laws' – generalizations about the *tendencies* of a particular class of phenomena – that will help us choose appropriate institutions and policies for given social contexts, or states of society.[5] Yet theorizing freedom also requires the appropriate art to enable us to determine the status of freedom in relation to other desirable ends, and to select the portion of the corresponding science that 'is necessary to show on what conditions the effects which the art aims at depend' (L, 949). Mill explains that the department of teleology appropriate for determining the status of ends such as freedom in relation to other ends and 'to how great a length ... [they] ought to be pursued' is moral philosophy, which concerns principles of conduct and moral rules (L, 950–1).

A necessary first step for this endeavour, of course, is specifying the subject of the inquiry; and here, Mill's conception of freedom provides us with important clues for identifying the social scientific knowledge that we need to foster freedom. He uses his utilitarian moral philosophy to clarify the relative importance of freedom in the scale of human ends. As a utilitarian, Mill maintains that utility, or the 'greatest happiness' principle, is the 'ultimate appeal on all ethical questions' (OL, 224). He defines utility as 'the conduciveness to the happiness of mankind, or rather, of all sentient beings: in other words, ... the promotion of happiness is the ultimate principle of Teleology [that is, the Doctrine of Ends]' (L, 951). In *Utilitarianism*, he says that utility is 'the ultimate end of life ... with reference to and for the sake of which all other things are desirable – whether we are considering our own good or that of other people' (U, 214). He explains that he does not mean that 'the promotion of happiness should be itself the end of all actions, or even all rules of action'; rather, he says, promoting happiness 'is the justification, and ought to be the controller of all ends, but it is not itself the sole end' (L, 952).[6] Moreover, he says that 'the happiness of mankind, or ... of all sentient beings' – or 'the greatest happiness principle' – is not an end that can be achieved *directly* ('B,' 110–11). He explains in 'Bentham' that 'utility, or happiness, [is] much too complex and indefinite an end to be sought except through the medium of various secondary ends, concerning which there may be, and often is, agreement among persons who differ on their ultimate standard' ('B,' 110). Such 'secondary principles' include freedom, individuality, and justice.[7]

With respect to Mill's commitment to freedom, his utilitarianism has a crucial but often misunderstood role. Some commentators, notably Maurice Cowling and C.L. Ten, contend that Mill's defence of the primacy of freedom is inconsistent with his utilitarianism. They claim that his commitment to utility entails that freedom can legitimately be sacrificed to promote the greater good of society (Ten, 1969, 1991; Cowling, 1975). Mill is not completely consistent in this regard, and as I will explain later, this criticism has some merit. Nonetheless, his qualitative and indirect form of utilitarianism is not so obviously incompatible with his defence of freedom. While Mill appeals to utility, he insists that it must be 'utility in the largest sense, grounded on the permanent interests of man as a progressive being' (OL 224). In turn, he offers a utilitarian defence of freedom as being, along with individuality, among the 'permanent interests' of human beings (Gray, 1983, ch. 3). He builds upon his understanding of the 'higher faculties' that distinguish human beings from other animals and that make them suited for 'more elevated' and more complex forms of gratification and happiness, along with 'more acute suffering,' than other animals (U, 210–12).[8] He explains in *The Subjection of Women*, 'After the primary necessities of food and raiment, freedom is the first and strongest want of human nature' (SW, 336).[9] In sum, Mill regards freedom as desirable both as means to happiness and as part of that end. Freedom is instrumental to fostering 'the greatest happiness,' since it enables people to pursue their own good – that is, what makes *them* happy. In addition, it is so integrally linked to the special 'sense of dignity' distinctive to human beings that it is itself a key component of human flourishing or happiness once people's basic needs have been met (U, 212; OL, ch. 3). Therefore, it is ultimately desirable as a *part of* the end of utility rather than merely as one of those things that is 'a means to a collective something termed happiness, and to be desired on that account' (U, 235). Enhancing freedom, then, contributes to general utility – that is, the greatest happiness – at least insofar as the freedom gained by some people does not come at the cost of the rightful freedom of others.[10]

We can gain a fuller appreciation of how Mill links his utilitarian moral theory to the empirical, or 'scientific,' aspects of his theory of freedom by comparing his view to Rousseau's famous pronouncement that 'Man was born free, and he is everywhere in chains' (1979 [1762], 49). Rousseau bases this claim on a notion of 'natural rights.' From Mill's perspective, by contrast, there can be no appeal to 'abstract right, as a thing independent of utility' (OL, 224). People are not 'born free,' but rather are born with a *potential* for freedom. This potential, which is evident in the development of people's mental states and faculties in accordance with the general laws of the mind, is either cultivated or stifled among different people depending on the educative character of their social circumstances. Moreover, people have no unlimited rights to freedom according to Mill. On the contrary, he argues that while people *should have* certain moral and legal rights to freedom of thought and action (the latter within appropriate limits), these rights are rooted in utilitarian

considerations concerning their permanent interests as progressive beings (U, ch. 5; OL, chs. 3–4). He maintains that freedom, like equality
and democracy, remains a conditional and qualified good in important
respects. Thus, he does not support the same freedom for all persons in
all societies; rather, he insists that the proper scope and character of
freedom must be qualified by utilitarian considerations, especially in
relation to claims of justice, expedience, and existing states of individual
and societal development. At the same time, based on his utilitarianism,
he defends roughly equal freedom for all members of modern societies
as a condition of social and distributive justice. I will return to this point
later.

III Empirical Theories and Spheres of Freedom

When Mill turns to the social and political domains that constitute the
field of people's freedom, he develops three interrelated empirical theories to discern the conditions of freedom. These three theories, with
which he relates questions about the realization of freedom to people's
'position[s] in the world,' concern social power, individual development, and societal development. As I noted earlier, with respect to Mill's
aim of securing freedom for each member of society, his Art of Life
highlights two basic tasks: placing freedom 'in the scale of desirable
things' – a task for moral theory; and selecting aspects of the appropriate
science that are necessary to identify the conditions necessary to achieve
the desired end (L, 949).

In the case of freedom, however, there is not just one relevant science.
Systematic knowledge from psychology, ethology, history, and sociology
is necessary, as well as knowledge of political economy and the science of
government, which Mill regards as parts of the 'general Science of
Society' (L, 906).[11] Psychology and ethology provide knowledge of the
social and political conditions necessary to foster autonomy, or free
agency. History is needed to comprehend the developmental tendencies
of different states of society and, thereby, to assess the extent to which
freedom contributes to well-being in societies at different stages of development. Finally, sociology is necessary to understand the agencies of
social power that shape human character, govern people's conduct,
shape government policies, and constitute the field of people's actual
and potential self-determination and self-government. Drawing upon
these sciences, Mill develops his three guiding empirical theories of
social power, individual development, and societal development.

Since Mill's theories of social power and individual development are central to his view of the interplay between freedom and power, I discuss them at length in the two chapters that follow. Therefore, I will discuss them only briefly here to clarify their status within his theory of freedom. Since Mill's theory of societal development is less central, I discuss it only in passing in subsequent chapters. I will discuss it at some length here, however, to clarify the sense in which his theory of freedom is basically a theory of freedom for modern democratizing societies.

a. The Theory of Social Power

Considerations of power lie at the heart of Mill's theory of freedom. He emphasizes the fundamental role of various power relationships in situating people and determining their prospects for self-development and self-determination. In this regard, his goal of achieving maximal freedom for all members of a given society *requires* a theory of social power – that is, a comprehensive view of the power relationships that govern people's lives. Mill illuminates how people's conduct is governed by the political, economic, educative, gender, and family relationships in which their lives are embedded. Moreover, he shows that we can adequately understand state power only by examining how it is shaped by forms of social power that lie outside the state but that work through it to produce certain effects ('AC,' 234; CRG, 380).[12] His theory of social power also includes a theory of authority with which he considers the distinctive implications of authority relationships for freedom.

b. The Theory of Individual Development

Mill summarizes his view of individual development in *On Liberty* when he says, 'Human nature is not a machine to be built after a model, and set to do exactly the work prescribed for it, but a tree, which requires to grow and develop itself on all sides, according to the tendency of the inward forces which make it a living thing' (OL, 263). He views the faculties of reasoning, judgment, deliberation, discrimination, and self-control, which are constitutive of mental freedom and autonomy, as common human potentialities. He maintains, however, that individuals develop these faculties only insofar as they are called forth and exercised by the various power relationships situating them. Thus, people must be educated for freedom, and this process depends largely on the educative character of the power relationships in which they are embedded. Moreover, as I explain in Chapter 4, Mill focuses on two aspects of individual development: the 'inward forces' that are the basis of autonomy (the psychological aspect); and the 'educational' conditions that foster or stifle autonomy (the ethological aspect).

c. The Theory of Societal Development

Mill's theories of individual and societal development highlight the 'dynamic' character of his theory of freedom. He says that to attain valid 'empirical laws' about societies we need to 'combine the statical view of social phenomena with the dynamical' (L, 925). In other words, empirical laws of society must explain both the causes of stability within 'the social union' – what Mill (following Auguste Comte) calls *social statics* – and the succession of different states of society, or 'sequences of social conditions' – what Mill (again following Comte) calls *social dynamics* (L, 917–8, 924). His attention to both static and dynamic aspects of social and political life is particularly evident in his views concerning freedom, colonialism, democratic citizenship, and socialism.

Mill's interest in 'social dynamics' is integrally related to the historical approach to social science that he adopts from his study of continental thinkers such as Comte and the St. Simonian school, and of English conservative thinkers Samuel Taylor Coleridge and Thomas Carlyle (A, 169–73). He develops the view 'that any general theory or philosophy of politics supposes a previous theory of human progress, and that this is the same thing with a philosophy of history' (A, 169). Accordingly, he affirms the historicist position 'that all questions of political institutions are relative, not absolute, and that different stages of human progress not only *will* have, but *ought* to have, different institutions' (A, 169, Mill's emphasis; cf. ACP, 323). He explains in the *Logic* that the science of society does not provide 'laws of society in general,' but only contextual propositions that 'declare how some given cause would operate in [a set of] circumstances, supposing that no others were combined with them' (L, 900). Thus, he says that the 'laws' of social and political inquiry are always applicable only to specific circumstances or states of society (L, 898–900).

Yet while Mill emphasizes the historical relativity of social and political truths, he also contends that understanding the laws of social development – that is, 'the laws according to which any state of society produces the state which succeeds it' – is the 'fundamental problem' of social science (L, 912). He says that finding a law that explains both the static and the dynamic aspects of social phenomena in different societies 'would become the real scientific derivative law of the development of humanity and human affairs' (L, 925). For his part, Mill boldly asserts, without claiming to have found such a law, that 'the evidence of history and that of human nature combine' to show that there is one central causal agent of social progress. 'This,' he says, 'is the state of the speculative faculties of mankind, including the nature of the beliefs which by any means they have arrived at concerning themselves and the world by which they are surrounded' (L, 926). Basically, he sees a reciprocal relationship of agents and circumstances, as mediated by the state of the speculative faculties in a given society, as the primary motivating force of social change. 'The circumstances in which mankind are placed,' he says, 'operating according to their own laws and to the laws of human nature, form the characters of the human beings; but human beings, in their turn, mould and shape the circumstances for themselves and those who come after them' (L, 913). These circumstances include prevailing beliefs.

Mill's rationalist-historicist view that the development of human speculative faculties is the chief factor in social development informs the scope and character of his theory of freedom. Following Comte, he identifies three successive stages of speculative thought and social development: theological, metaphysical, and positive. He maintains that earlier modes of thought – first theological and later metaphysical – have been superseded in modern Europe by the 'positive stage,' in which people increasingly seek rational and scientific explanations of natural and social phenomena (ACP, 267–79, 317; A, 173; L, 928). Mill's view of social progress is also informed by the St. Simonians' idea that history alternates between 'organic' periods – periods in which 'some positive creed' is widely accepted – and 'critical' periods – transitional eras in which received doctrines are widely challenged and in which social division and unrest are prevalent (A, 171; cf. Williams, 1976a, 23; Gibbons, 1990).

In light of these ideas, Mill develops his own linear theory of human progress according to which people advance from savage to barbarian to civilized states of societies. He places modern European societies at the pinnacle of historical development as 'civilized' societies in opposition to societies such as India and China, which he regards as 'barbarian' or 'backward' and thus in need of 'civilizing' ('Civ'; OL, ch. 1; CRG, ch. 18; and 'FWNI'). Moreover, he regards this modern trend toward 'civilized' societies as unequivocally liberating insofar as it marks the arrival of a state of society 'when mankind have become capable of being improved by free and equal discussion' (OL, 224). In his view, this development enables people to become emancipated from uncritical and, therefore, unfree acceptance of the authority of received myths, legends, and religions (cf. OL, 224; L, 928–9n; 'GH[I],' 278–90; 'GH[II],' 321; 'UR,' 411). Mill's view of historical development betrays considerable ethnocentrism, however. It also has some troubling political implications, particularly with regard to Mill's support for the 'civilizing' efforts of the British East India Company in India, and to his one-dimensional view of non-Western ways of life more generally (Parekh, 1994, 1995; Gray, 1996).

With respect to Mill's theory of freedom, his theory of societal development is notable because he aims his generalizations and prescriptions concerning the conditions and utility of freedom are aimed primarily at modern, 'civilized' societies (Williams, 1976a, 35–6). For instance, he explicitly restricts his principles of liberty and democratic self-government – two key components of the theory – to those societies which have attained a level of intellectual development such that their members are swayed more by 'free and equal discussion' than by 'mere authority' (OL, 224). He says in *On Liberty*, 'Liberty, as a principle, has no application to any state of things anterior to the time when mankind have become capable of being improved by free and equal discussion'; and he adds, 'Despotism is a legitimate mode of government in dealing with barbarians, provided the end be their improvement, and the means justified by actually affecting that end' (OL, 224). Similarly, he maintains that the political freedom offered by representative government – which he views as 'ideally the best form of government' – is suited only to societies that have achieved 'a sufficiently advanced state' of social development (CRG, 567; Thompson, 1976, ch. 4).

Despite the limitations of Mill's theory of stages of historical development, his historicism has the virtue of leading him to recognize that the conditions of freedom that he identifies for modern Western societies like Victorian England may not be readily applicable to different societies with divergent social and cultural conditions. At the same time, though, he expects all societies to go through the same stages of social development so that his theory of freedom will eventually become universally applicable. In this regard, as I explain in Chapter 3, his progressivist view of history gives rise to some limitations in his view of freedom and authority.

IV Secondary Principles

Finally, based on the theoretical components of his theory of freedom, Mill derives a set of four guiding principles as means for achieving roughly equal freedom for different members of society. These four principles are the principle of liberty; democratic self-government; social and distributive justice; and equality. Within his theory of freedom, they operate as what he calls 'secondary' or 'intermediate' principles that mediate between his aim of securing equal freedom for all and the realm of social and political relationships that is the domain of human freedom ('B,' 110–11).[13] In other words, the four principles provide practical rules or axioms by means of which Mill believes we can achieve the end of securing for 'all persons complete independence and freedom of action, subject to no restriction but that of not doing injury to others' (PPE, 208–9), within the social and political relationships and institutions in which they exercise freedom. I will briefly summarize these four principles as a prelude to my later examination of his view of the situatedness of freedom.

a. The Principle of Liberty

Mill articulates and defends his 'principle of liberty' more fully and explicitly than the other principles. He makes it the subject of his famous essay *On Liberty*.[14] The *principle of liberty*, in short, is 'that the sole end for which mankind are warranted, individually or collectively, in interfering with the liberty of action of any of their number is ... to prevent harm to others' (OL, 223). It is meant to govern not just the conduct of independent individuals, but also 'the liberty, within the same limits, of combination among individuals; freedom to unite, for any purpose not involving harm to others' (OL, 226). It can be fully understood, however, only in light of his moral theory – particularly his understanding of rights and justice – and other aspects of his political theory.

Mill offers the principle of liberty to distinguish a discreet 'province' of conduct – the 'self-regarding' domain – within which individuals should be completely free to pursue their own good in their own way. He differentiates this domain of conduct, within which 'the individual is not accountable to society for his [or her] actions,' from the domain of 'social morality,' or 'duty to others,' which concerns conduct that is 'prejudicial to the interests of others' in the sense of violating distinct and assignable moral obligations to them (OL, 282, 292). In the latter domain, the individual is accountable to society for his or her conduct and, thus, may be legitimately 'subjected either to social or to legal punishment, if society is of the opinion that the one or the other is requisite for its protection' (OL, 292). The domain of social morality, moreover, encompasses *any social relationship* in which the conduct of some person (or persons) poses harm to others. In addition, it includes 'vigilant control' by the state with respect to any relationship in which some person or persons exercise power over others (OL, 301).

b. Democratic Self-government

Although Mill never expressly articulates a principle of democratic self-government, this notion conveys a central aspect of how he construes individual freedom with respect to key power relationships that govern people's lives.[15] He emphasizes the interdependence of persons within marital, economic, and political relationships. Accordingly, he conceives of freedom with respect to these relationships less in terms of making people independent of others than in terms of enabling them to share with others in practices of self-government. He articulates this broad notion of democratic self-government at the end of *The Subjection of Women* when he speaks of individual 'freedom of action' as 'the liberty of each to govern his [or her] conduct by his own feelings of duty, and by such laws and social restraints as his [or her] own conscience can subscribe to' (SW, 336).

Democratic self-government fosters freedom by extending to each person a voice in matters that concern him or her (Berger, 1984, 187). Moreover, in light of Mill's view of the multiple sources of power that govern people's lives, he seeks to extend opportunities for individuals to share in self-government beyond the domain of state power. In short, where Mill's principle of liberty concerns the self-regarding conduct of independent individuals (or combinations of independent individuals), his principle of democratic self-government extends freedom of individuals into three key sets of social relationships within the domain of 'social morality': the state, marital relationships, and economic enterprises.

Mill elaborates the democratic principle somewhat differently with respect to marital, economic, and political relationships in light of considerations of justice, equality, educational attainments, and differences between these relationships. Mill in principle supports equal freedom and the 'equal claim of everybody to happiness' (U, 258), but he stops short of prescribing strictly equal rights to democratic self-government for all adult members of modern democratizing societies. His reticence on this score arises from his views concerning the peculiarities of the different social relationships and the unequal readiness of different members of society for self-government in any given state of social development.

c. Social and Distributive Justice

Considerations of 'social and distributive justice' are central to Mill's goal of securing to each individual the maximum freedom compatible with the same freedom for others.[16] His aim is not the greatest *sum* of freedom, which could mean great freedom for some and little for others, but rather maximal freedom for all. Given Mill's fundamental commitment to the aggregative principle of 'utility as the ultimate appeal on all ethical questions' (OL, 224), it is important to be clear about just how he applies distributive rules of justice in his theory of freedom. There are some tensions in his utilitarian approach to justice, to which I will return, but his formal account of justice and rights has considerable merit. As I noted earlier, Mill develops an indirect form of utilitarianism; he says that utility is 'the ultimate appeal on all ethical questions; but it must be utility in the largest sense, grounded on the permanent interests of man as a progressive being' (OL 224). In turn, based on his view of freedom as a vital human interest, he regards promoting freedom as intimately connected to promoting human happiness or well-being (SW, 336; OL, ch. 3).

In light of his view that freedom requires resources and opportunities for education, self-determination, and self-government, Mill regards the goal of extending freedom to all members of society as integrally linked to achieving 'social and distributive justice' (U, 257). He derives from his enlarged conception of utility the right to 'equality of treatment' for all members of society as a matter of justice. He says,

> The equal claim of everybody to happiness in the estimation of the moralist and the legislator, involves an equal claim to all the means of happiness except in so far as the inevitable conditions of human life, and the general interest, in which every individual is included sets limits to the maxim ... All persons are deemed to have a *right* to equality of treatment, except when some recognized social expediency requires the reverse. And hence all social inequalities which have ceased to be considered expedient, assume the character not of simple inexpediency, but of injustice. (U, 258)[17]

Justice, then, entails a commitment to respect the equal claim of each individual to happiness. In principle, considerations of justice protect against the possibility that the dignity of some individuals might be sacrificed in the name of achieving the 'greatest happiness.'[18] His theory of justice thus has significant egalitarian implications with respect to his theory of freedom insofar as freedom is one of the key ingredients of happiness or well-being.

In light of these considerations, Mill asserts, 'The perfection of both social arrangements and practical morality would be, to secure to all persons complete independence and freedom of action, subject to no restriction but that of not doing injury to others' (PPE, 208–9). In short, he offers a utilitarian case for what I will call *maximal freedom*: the most extensive freedom for each member of society consistent with the same freedom for others. This entails that no one can have 'complete' freedom of action, except within certain limits. Moreover, maximal freedom requires that resources and opportunities for education or self-development, self-determination, and self-government be justly distributed with respect to the various social relationships that govern people's lives. This goal requires both the principle of liberty and the principle of democratic self-government.

It is beyond the scope of this study to give a comprehensive account of Mill's theory of justice, but a few additional points are crucial to his theory of freedom. First, Mill maintains that the state, as the enforcer of *rights*, has a special responsibility to secure claims of justice. Justice, he says, 'implies something which it is not only right to do, and wrong not to do, but which some individual person can claim from us as his [or her] moral right' (U, 247). Second, he appeals to considerations of justice to mark off the rightful domain of individual liberty in two respects: he defends unlimited freedom of action for individuals in 'self-regarding' matters as a basic right; conversely, he justifies *legal restricitons* of individual freedom of action – as opposed to restraints of public opinion – only to prevent individuals from violating what he calls their obligations of justice to others (OL, 224, 276). Third, Mill insists that the while the state must respect 'the liberty of each individual in what specifically regards himself, [it] is bound to maintain a vigilant control over his exercise of any power which it allows him to possess over others' (OL, 301).

d. Equality

Equality, as we have seen, plays a key role in Mill's theory of justice. His commitment to the 'equal claim [of everyone] to all the means of happiness' entails a commitment to securing to all persons equal means and conditions of freedom. He accepts certain inequalities, however, notably some inequality of incomes, but only insofar as these inequalities are justified by differences of merit and are compatible with the equal moral status of all persons as free agents. Thus, one of the grounds on which Mill condemns as *unjust* the existing capitalist economic system, restrictions of voting rights, and the unequal and subordinate status of women concerns how these inequalities systematically undermine the free and equal status of many members of society.

Yet Mill views the relationship between freedom and equality as a complementary but contingent one. On the one hand, he emphasizes several ways in which freedom and equality are mutually supporting goals: his theory of justice implies the equal right of all adult persons to freedom; his principle of democratic self-government points toward steadily more equal rights and powers among virtually all adult members of society to determine the rules that govern their lives; and he challenges systematic social and political inequalities that impose unequal restraints on the freedom of some members of society – particularly women and members of the working class. On the other hand, Mill follows Alexis de Tocqueville in arguing that tendencies toward social equality and the government of public opinion in modern democratic societies threaten to stifle individual freedom of thought and action with political and social tyranny. Thus, in his second review of de Tocqueville, he remarks, 'Equality may be either equal freedom, or equal servitude' ('TDA[II],' 159). And he warns elsewhere that state-sponsored efforts to ameliorate social inequalities, such as public education and redistributive policies, tend to increase the scope of state power and decrease the scope of individual initiative and spontaneity ('Ce'; OL, ch. 5; PPE, 950).

On balance, Mill defends a complex and qualified egalitarianism. In 'Thoughts on Parliamentary Reform,' for example, he expressly rejects the idea that all persons possess an unqualified claim 'to be equal in every description of right recognized in society' ('TPR,' 323). In particular, he rejects the claim that all adults are entitled absolutely to an 'equal voice' in their government. He favours political equality as an ultimate goal, but adds that it needs to be qualified in the near term until everyone is more equally prepared to exercise this power ('TPR,' 323).[19] In his article on 'Centralization,' however, he argues more forcefully for equal freedom in opposition to the prospect of some persons having 'power over others.' The only 'solid security' for the freedom of each person, he says, is 'the equal freedom of the rest' ('Ce,' 610).

Overall, he maintains a consistent commitment to what Fred Berger calls a 'baseline' conception of equality. He regards inequalities as justified only insofar as they respect the moral status of persons as free and equal, including the equal claim of each person to the means of happiness (Berger, 1984, 199).[20] In other words, Mill maintains that some inequalities are justified only insofar as (1) there are good practical reasons for them in existing circumstances – for example, if they correspond to unequal abilities of different persons to exercise power in a responsible way – *and* (2) they are consistent with respect for the equal moral standing of all persons as free agents.[21] Thus, Mill justifies some inequalities concerning political rights, economic power, and the sexual division of labour without abandoning his basic commitment to equal freedom. Where he argues against simple equality of rights, resources, and opportunities, he either holds out the promise of progressively greater equality (e.g., more equal political rights and economic power with more equal educational attainments) or upholds some other egalitarian principle (e.g., he opposes strictly equal incomes because this policy conflicts with the principle of reward proportionate to exertions). Moreover, in each case where he rejects simple equality he upholds the equal moral standing of all persons. Finally, Mill's egalitarian commitment is especially evident in his insistence that (with a few qualifications) all persons are *basically* equal with respect to their potential capacities for self-determination and self-government. He contends that differences among people in their intellectual powers are, for the most part, produced by differences in their educations and life experiences; conversely, he says that virtually everyone is fully capable of freedom if she or he is given a suitable education (see ch. 4).

V Conclusions

Mill never presents us with a systematic 'theory of freedom,' and it is not his style to offer such a general theory.[22] Nonetheless, his analysis of freedom is quite systematic, especially when we consider it in light of the framework for social theorizing that he develops in *A System of Logic*. His theory of modern freedom consists of an interrelated set of ethical propositions based on the Art of Life – concerning the ends of human conduct – and empirical propositions from social science – consisting of generalizations about the nature and conduct of individuals and of 'the collective masses of mankind.' With these propositions he clarifies the status of freedom in relation to other ends of human conduct and provides a framework for grasping the situatedness of freedom.

Mill's theory of social power is particularly important to his under-standing of the situatedness of freedom. He highlights the role of several different power relationships in governing people's conduct in modern democratic societies. In turn, he contends that the relevant domain of democratic self-government extends beyond the state to encompass eco-nomic and marital relationships. Moreover, in light of his theory of individual development, his emphasis on 'the powers of education' – the power exercised over people's characters and cognitive capacities by their various social and political relationships – leads him to deem education, in both its narrower and broader senses, a crucial condition of freedom.

Mill's theory of freedom highlights two overlapping divisions of the broad domain of human conduct – divisions which correspond to rela-tively distinct spheres of freedom. First, he offers us his well-known division between the province of individual liberty (the domain of self-regarding conduct) and the domain of social morality (the domain regarding which society can rightfully interfere with individual conduct) (OL, 223). This division cuts across some social relationships that are often considered 'private,' particularly gender and family relationships, property ownership, and economic enterprises. Therefore, it does not correspond to a straightforward distinction between 'public' and 'pri-vate' spheres of conduct. Some conduct within economic relationships, marital and family relations, gender relations, and educational practices falls into the protected province of individual liberty. At the same time, certain kinds of conduct within these relationships fall within the do-main of social morality. This applies especially to conduct that involves the exercise of power by some persons over others. Such power includes the power of parents over children, men over women, employers over employees, and some citizens over other citizens. When such power is present in these relationships, according to Mill, there is a legitimate role for authoritative state regulation and, in some cases, for claims of mutual self-government.

This last point is closely connected to the second division that Mill makes among spheres of freedom. Within what he calls the domain of 'social morality, of duties to others' (OL, 283), he distinguishes three sets of power relationships as relatively distinct sites of democratic self-government: marital relationships, economic enterprises, and political institutions.[23] As I explain in subsequent chapters, Mill examines both individual and collective practices of freedom with respect to each of these sets of relationships in relation to his principles of individual liberty, democratic self-government, justice, and equality, and utilitarian considerations of expedience.[24] He also addresses the distinctive ways in which each of these power relationships structures the barriers to and opportunities for freedom that different people face.

In Mill's theory of freedom, political and gender relationships in particular have a distinctive status. Regarding gender, he illuminates how gender cuts across and shapes the character of all other social relationships and institutions, including families, schools, economic enterprises, and political institutions. He recognizes that although gender relations do not constitute a distinct site of self-government, they have a considerable impact in determining the relative freedom of women and men in every domain of human conduct. For instance, he illuminates how prevailing gender roles and expectations produce unequal barriers and opportunities for women and men with respect to political power, education, careers, child rearing, marriages, and household labour. Concerning politics, Mill shows how state power has special importance because it regulates all other activities and forms of social power, even though control of political power is largely dependent on the distribution of social power. Therefore, he regards political freedom – the freedom of citizens to shape state policies – as having special importance among the various forms of freedom in modern democratic societies (see ch. 8, below).

Finally, Mill's commitment to the aggregative principle of utility ultimately poses certain problems for his attempt to secure roughly equal freedom for all members of society on grounds of justice. As H.L.A. Hart points out, there is a fundamental tension between the 'general form of the analysis' that Mill uses to account for valid claims of moral rights, and his appeal to 'general utility' as the basis of moral obligations (1982, 91). Mill makes a strong case for recognizing certain interests, such as individual liberty, as so vital to individual well-being that they ought to be considered as rights (see ch. 5, below). Yet his appeal to general utility in the sense of the 'equal claim of everyone for happiness' provides an uncertain foundation for his goal of promoting freedom equally for every person as a moral right (U, 257–8). This appeal to utility ultimately leaves him open to the criticism made by John Rawls and Hart, among others, that his utilitarianism is no better than Bentham's hedonistic utilitarianism in adequately recognizing the separate dignity of different persons (Rawls, 1971; Hart, 1982). In short, Mill's utilitarianism, like Bentham's, ultimately offers no protection to individuals against gains in the general welfare of their community that could be achieved at the expense their individual rights (Hart, 1982, 96–7; Gray, 1989a, 136).

The problem is evident in Mill's argument that the utilitarian commitment to the 'equal claim of everyone to happiness' implies that 'all persons are deemed to have a *right* to equality of treatment, except when some recognized social expediency requires the reverse' (U, 257–8, Mill's emphasis). This concern for equality stems from 'the very meaning of utility, or the greatest happiness principle,' according to which 'one person's happiness, supposed in degree (with proper allowance made for kind), is counted for exactly as much as another's.' In this regard, he quotes Jeremy Bentham's maxim that 'everybody to count for one, nobody for more than one,' as a short-hand statement of his own view (U, 257). Then he elaborates on this point, in a footnote, in response to Herbert Spencer's claim that the principle of utility provides an insufficient 'guide to right; since ... the principle of utility presupposes the anterior principle that everybody has an equal right to happiness' (U, 258n). Mill comments, 'It may be more correctly described as supposing that equal amounts of happiness are equally desirable, whether felt by the same or by different persons. This, however, is not a presupposition; not a premise needful to support the principle of utility, but the very principle itself ... If there is any anterior principle implied, it can be no other than this, that the truths of arithmetic are applicable to the valuation of happiness, as of all other measurable quantities' (U, 258n). On this point, Mill takes the standard Benthamite position – a position that, as Hart says, conflicts with his prior formal analysis of what it means to have a *moral right*. By insisting that utilitarianism presupposes no ethical standard anterior to the principle of utility itself, understood in a way that permits 'measurable quantities' of happiness, he undermines his aim of establishing a utilitarian basis for protecting fundamental rights and the equal dignity of all persons.

In effect, Mill's appeal to measurable quantities of happiness reduces the right of all persons to 'equality of treatment,' which he officially endorses, to a weighting principle with which to calculate the happiness of different people *as part of* the happiness of all. That is, insofar as Mill construes utility as a measurable quantity that can be aggregated to determine the overall happiness of all members of society, the moral rights of individuals become merely instrumental to the fundamental goal of general utility. The happiness of everyone would count equally in tallying the 'greatest happiness' regardless of whether a given person is rich or poor, a woman or a man, young or old, and so on; yet the equal 'right' posited here is not the kind of 'moral right' that figures so prominently in Mill's formal analysis of rights (see ch. 5, below). In Hart's words, 'The right of equal treatment which Mill speaks of here exists as a right, in his view, independently of any question of enforcement: it exists solely on the distributive and egalitarian aspects of the principle of utility as Mill and Bentham both interpret it' (1982, 100).[25] Within this mode of utilitarian calculus, then, individuals lack the separate moral status that they seem to have in Mill's formal analysis of rights (Hart, 1982, 97; Lyons, 1982b, 134–5). It follows that Mill's utilitarianism does not foreclose the possibility of suppressing the rights or freedom of some persons for the sake of promoting the greatest happiness, despite his aim of protecting the equal claim of each person to the means of happiness as an obligation of justice (U, ch. 5).

At the same time, Mill's formal analysis of moral rights remains a valuable basis for a democratic politics of rights, even though it is not distinctively utilitarian (see ch. 5, below). As Hart explains, it provides guidelines for identifying 'what individuals need and can reasonably demand from each other (by way either of restraint or of active provision) in order to pursue their own ends through the development of distinctive human powers' (1982, 104). Mill offers this guidance by illuminating what is implied in the notions of 'moral obligations' and 'moral rights' (Lyons, 1982b, 134). With this conceptual analysis he calls upon people, as citizens, to reserve the notion of *moral rights* for those obligations of justice that 'concern the essentials of human well-being more nearly ... than any other rules for human conduct' (U, 255).

Moreover, Mill generally construes the greatest happiness principle as a more pragmatic and less reductive approach to ethical reasoning than his remark about measurable quantities of utility suggests. In this vein, he presents his notion of the Art of Life as a framework for practical reasoning that draws upon commonly recognized distinctions between conduct that primarily raises questions of prudential or aesthetic judgment, and conduct that falls within the domain of *morality* because it involves 'distinct and assignable' duties to others (OL, 281). Similarly, in 'Sedgwick's Discourse' he presents utilitarianism as a mode of practical reasoning that seeks to provide grounds for moral judgments – judgments of 'right' and 'wrong' – independently of particular religious or theological doctrines or of any other notions of 'eternal and immutable morality' ('SD,' 51). He explains that utilitarianism insists upon 'human happiness as the foundation of morality,' which gives it a thoroughly consequentialist character; but he also insists that there is always a degree of 'indefiniteness' in utilitarian prescriptions ('SD,' 64–5, 74). Moreover, he points out that this indefiniteness has a great advantage over doctrines that claim to provide 'immutable' moral truths, because it recognizes that 'moral judgments and feelings ... [are] susceptible of ... improvement' ('SD,' 74; cf. ch. 5, below). Furthermore, Mill contends in 'Bentham' – in stark contrast to his more rigid formulation at the end of *Utilitarianism* – that 'utility, or happiness, [is] much too complex and indefinite an end to be sought except through the medium of various secondary ends, concerning which there may be, and often is, agreement among persons who differ in their ultimate standard' ('B,' 110). He adds, moreover, that whether or not happiness is accepted as the proper end on questions of morality, 'that it be referred to an *end* of some sort, and not left in the dominion of vague feeling or explicable internal conviction, that it be made a matter of reason and calculation, and not merely one of sentiment, is essential to the very idea of moral philosophy; is in fact what renders argument or discussion on moral questions possible' ('B,' 111, Mill's emphasis). Elsewhere he says, 'According to the theory of utility ... the question, what is our duty, is as open to discussion as any other question' ('SD,' 74). Accordingly, he generally uses utilitarianism as a means of identifying certain basic moral rules, such as the principle of liberty, that will indirectly promote the greatest happiness. In this regard, then, Mill's indirect utilitarianism provides an exemplary model for political ethics in which the fundamental importance of certain rights or goods as 'essentials of human well-being' can be given its due weight (cf. Caillé, 1992).

3

The Theory of Social Power

There are in society a number of distinct forces – of separate and independent sources of power. There is the general power of knowledge and cultivated intelligence. There is the power of religion; by which, speaking politically, is to be understood that of religious teachers. There is the power of military skill and discipline. There is the power of wealth; the power of numbers and physical forces ... Each of these, by the influence it exercises over society, is fruitful of certain beneficial effects; none of them is favourable to all kinds.

John Stuart Mill, 'Guizot's Essays and Lectures on History' (1845)

Mill's previous interpreters have offered little systematic analysis of his understanding of power.[1] This inattentiveness is unfortunate because, although he never systematically analyses power, he continually addresses the topic in a way that is pivotal to his theory of freedom. Moreover, he offers considerable insight into the positive and negative aspects of power and the diverse sources of social power in modern societies. In addition, his attention to the 'power over human character' that is wielded by 'education and opinion' (U, 218) foreshadows the investigations by more recent radical social theorists, such as Steven Lukes and Michel Foucault, into the more subtle effects of power relationships in shaping people's opinions, desires, and self-understandings (see Lukes, 1974; Foucault, 1983). Mill's understanding of social power goes hand in hand with his view that political science, or the 'Science of Government,' must be viewed as a branch of sociology, or 'the general Science of Society' (L, 906). He contends that state power must always be understood in relation to how social power is distributed and exercised in society. And while he highlights the distinctive status of state power, he also shows how various other forms of social power involve different modes of governing people's conduct.

Mill is well aware of the ways in which freedom is limited by various oppressive forms of power – including but not limited to state power. In fact, he sometimes writes as if he believes that the exercise of power always diminishes the exercise of freedom. In 'Centralization,' for instance, he says that while 'all alike may be free, ... the appetite for power is essentially selfish; for all cannot have power; the power of one is power over others' ('Ce,' 610). Nonetheless, he moves beyond a one-dimensional view to develop a rich account of both nonrepressive and repressive forms of power, and of how freedom requires nonrepressive forms of power. Furthermore, his theory of social power includes a theory of authority as one of its central components. He regards authority as both a distinctive *mode* of power – a way of bringing about certain ends – and as a distinct *source* of social power – a resource with which individuals or institutions exercise power.

I Mill's Conception of Power

Mill conceives of power in its most basic sense as a capacity to affect change or to achieve desired goals. Mill explains this aspect of power most explicitly in his notes to the 1869 edition of his father's *Analysis of the Phenomena of the Human Mind*:

> Power ... seems to me to express, not causingness and causedness taken together, but causingness only. Some of the older philosophers certainly talked of passive power, but neither in the precise language of modern philosophy nor in common speech is an effect said to have the power of being produced, but only the capacity or capability. The power is always conceived as belonging to the cause only. When any co-operation power is said to reside in the thing said to be acted upon, it is because some active property in the thing is counted as a con-cause – as a part of the total cause. ('NTA,' 198)

Power, then, belongs to agents or agencies that bring about certain effects – that is, that cause things to happen – and not in the things being acted upon. Power may also reside in the things acted upon *if and when* they also have an 'active' role in shaping some final effect. Mill articulates this point in a more politically salient way in 'Bentham,' in the course of criticizing Bentham's narrow understanding of human nature.

Bentham, he says, fails to recognize in human nature such expansive qualities as 'the love of *power*, not in the limited form of power over other human beings, but abstract power, the power of making our volitions effective' ('B,' 96).[2] Mill links this aspect of power closely to freedom (see ch. 1).

In an important passage in *Considerations on Representative Government*, Mill builds upon this basic conception of power and outlines his broader understanding of social and political power. He begins by stating his view that control of state power is rooted in social agencies lying outside – and, as he says elsewhere, 'deeper than' – the machinery of government (CRG, 380; 'AC,' 234). Then he considers the meaning of power with reference to the theory that the 'government of a country ... is, in all substantial respects, fixed and determined by the state of the country in regard to the distribution of the elements of social power' (CRG, 380):

> When it is said that the strongest power in society will make itself the strongest power in the government, what is meant by power? Not the thews and sinews; otherwise pure democracy would be the only form of polity that could exist. To mere muscular strength add two other elements, property and intelligence, and we are nearer the truth, but far from having reached it. Not only is the greater number often kept down by a less, but the greater number may have a preponderance in property, and individually in intelligence, and may yet be held in subjection forcibly or otherwise. To make these various elements politically influential, they must be organized; and the advantage in organization is necessarily with those who are in possession of the government. (CRG, 381)

He further explains the relationship between social power and political power in light of a distinction between 'active power' and 'merely passive' power: 'The power in society which has any tendency to convert itself into political power, is not power quiescent, power merely passive, but active power; in other words, power actually exerted; that is to say, a very small portion of all the power in existence. Politically speaking, a great part of all power consists in will. How is it possible, then, to compute the elements of political power, when we omit from the computation anything that acts on the will' (CRG, 381). In other words, control of political power consists of the capacity to control the state. Political power is dependent, however, on the distribution and exercise of social power, the 'real power' that underlies the 'distribution of constitutional power' ('Civ,' 173). *Social* power includes both active power ('power actually exerted') to bring about certain ends, and passive or potential power (dormant power that may become active in certain circumstances). Moreover, Mill identifies property and knowledge as among the key sources of social power, along with strength in numbers; and he emphasizes the significance of forms of social power that 'act on the will' of people and thereby move them to action or inaction.

Three aspects of Mill's discussion of power in *Representative Government* are central to his broader understanding of power. *First*, he contends that an empirically adequate account of social and political power must not limit itself to the more readily observable ways in which people bring about certain ends or exercise control over others; it must also account for more covert ways that some agents or agencies shape people's conduct by *acting on their wills*. Mill addresses these more subtle forms of power as they affect control of state power as follows:

> To think that, because those who wield the power in society wield in the end that of government, therefore it is of no use to attempt to influence the constitution of government by acting on opinion, is to forget that opinion is itself one of the greatest active social forces. One person with a belief, is a social power equal to ninety-nine who have only interests. *They who can succeed in creating a general persuasion that a certain form of government, or social fact of any kind, deserves to be preferred, have made nearly the most important step which can possibly be taken towards ranging the powers of society on its side.* (CRG, 381, emphasis added)

He goes on to state, 'It is what men think that determines how they act; and ... no little power is exercised over them by the persuasions and convictions of those whose personal position is different, and by the united authority of the instructed' (CRG, 382).

Elsewhere Mill articulates two corollaries to this power to shape other people's thoughts – corollaries which foreshadow recent ideas about 'second' and 'third' faces of power.[3] (1) Concerning the 'second face' of power, Mill maintains that virtually all persons have at least some potential power to realize their interests if they act accordingly, especially under democratic forms of government. Such potential power may include knowledge, wealth, or votes. He adds, however, that this power remains merely *passive* rather than *active* power unless it is combined with the capacity to form and express opinions, along with the will to make these opinions a basis for collective action. Thus, when he says that 'one person with a belief, is a social power equal to ninety-nine who have merely interests,' his point is as follows: Merely having interests is by itself a passive phenomenon that corresponds to merely passive or potential power. Having interests gives rise to *active* power, or 'power actually exerted,' only among people who develop *the will to act upon* their interests. In contrast, a 'person with a belief' is someone who has an active conviction about what 'deserves to be preferred' and, thus, possesses a will to act to achieve this end.[4] For instance, Mill says in *On Liberty* that the 'yoke of opinion' is greater and the weight of legal prohibitions is lighter in England than in most other European countries; but he adds that the law is likely to become more intrusive in England as the majority learns 'to feel the power of government their government, or its opinions their opinions' (OL, 223).

(2) With respect to the 'third face' of power, Mill contends that some people exercise power over others indirectly *by shaping what they think*, thereby acting on their wills. As I will explain shortly, he generally discusses this power in terms of 'all the powers of education' over human character (OL, 282; U, 218). A full account of social and political power, therefore, must include an account of those individuals, groups, and institutions that influence how people act by shaping what they think – for instance, by persuading them to support a particular policy or agenda (CRG, 382). In this regard, Mill's view of power has what Steven Lukes calls a 'radical' dimension, in that it locates the exercise of social power in part in the effects of social relationships and institutions in shaping people's opinions, desires, cognitive capacities, and self-understandings.[5]

Second, Mill illuminates both repressive and nonrepressive aspects of power. That is, he highlights both *positive* modes of power, or 'power to,' in both individual and collective manifestations, and *negative* or repressive modes of power, or 'power over,' such as the 'power of coercion and compulsion' ('Ce,' 610). Moreover, he implicitly considers what Hanna Pitkin calls *relational* and *nonrelational* forms of power (1972, 277). While power always signifies a relationship between an agent or agents and certain ends, consequences, or potentialities, it does *not* always refer to a direct relationship between people (e.g., with one person or more persons exercising power over others).[6] Mill does not explicitly develop the distinctions between 'power to' and 'power over' or between nonrelational and relational forms of power, but he includes each of these aspects within his conception of social power. Like several current writers, he conceives of the power that some people have *over* others – including powers of coercion – as a subcategory of 'power to' (Pitkin, 1972; Patton, 1989). That is, he understands that one of the things that powerful agents can typically *do* with their power is get others to do something or do something to others. Regarding the broader notion of 'power to,' Mill considers both the power of individuals *as individuals* to shape their own characters and achieve their goals as well as collective and institutional forms of power. His general tendency is to focus on collective and institutional forms of power, such as the power of individuals acting collectively to pursue common goals (particularly through politics), the power of men over women and of employers over employees, and the power of government to promote the public welfare (SW, 288; 'C,' 158, 156; CRG, 435).

Mill summarizes his view of the relationships between 'power to' and 'power over,' and between consensual and coercive forms of power, in 'Thoughts on Parliamentary Reform.' He defends the right of (virtually) every adult in England – women as well as men – to share in the exercise of political power. Yet he rejects the claim made by more radical democratic reformers that every person has a right to an '*equal* voice' and an 'equal claim to control over his own government' ('TPR,' 323, Mill's emphasis). Mill supports equal political rights as an ultimate goal; but adds that in light of existing social conditions (between 1859 and 61), strictly equal rights would be warranted only if they consisted merely of 'control [by each person] over his own government' (see ch. 8, below). Suffrage must be treated differently since it gives people power to govern others – or at least what he calls *potential* power – as well as over their own self-government. 'The power which the suffrage gives,' he explains, 'is not over himself alone; it is power over others also; whatever control the voter is enabled to exercise over his own concerns, he exercises the same degree over those of everyone else' ('TPR,' 323). In his two reviews of Alexis de Tocqueville's *Democracy in America* in 1835 and 1840, he also discusses collective forms of power. He maintains that 'the capacity of cooperation for a common purpose, heretofore a monopolized instrument of power in the hands of the higher classes, is now a most formidable one in those of the lowest' ('TDA[I],' 51). He also speaks of the 'power of combined action' or 'power of combination,' particularly as it is increasingly exercised by organized labourers, as a defining feature of modern democratizing societies ('TDA[II],' 165; 'RRP,' 484). Mill repeatedly refers to this power of persons to act collectively to achieve common purposes. In addition, he continually considers how the 'power of combined action' exercised by particular groups or classes can be repressive 'power over others.'

Third, Mill considers the connection between social and political power in *Representative Government*, largely with regard to the control of political power. Elsewhere, however, he complements this focus by analyzing how various forms of social power, such as the power of men over women, and of employers over employees, and 'the powers of education,' govern people's conduct in ways that are at least partially independent of their influence on state power. As I will explain later, his overall understanding of different forms of social power is the linchpin of his views about both political freedom and freedom in other domains of social action.

II The Sources of Social Power

Regarding the sociology of power, Mill locates the sources or bases of social power in a web of enduring but not unchanging social relationships that extend well beyond 'mere physical and economic power' (CRG, 382). His approach to power thus has important affinities with 'situated' conceptions of power that draw upon 'realist' views of underlying causal mechanisms that constitute social reality (see Isaac, 1987, 16–19; Wartenberg, 1988).[7] Mill traces the relative social power of different agents – both passive or active – to their different positions within the social and political relationships situating them. He conceives of the power of agents (or agencies) to bring about certain ends in terms of their status within enduring social relationships that empower or disempower them relative to other agents – for example, men versus women with respect to economic, political, and marital relations; and wage labourers versus capitalists with regard to economic and political institutions.

In 'Coleridge,' for instance, Mill notes the power conferred to some persons over others by property ownership. He says that 'when the state allows any one to exercise ownership over more land than suffices to raise by his own labour his subsistence and that of his family, it confers on him power over other human beings – power affecting them in their most vital interests' ('C,' 157–8). Similarly, in *The Subjection of Women* he discusses patriarchal power in light of the oppressive effects of 'the almost unlimited power which present institutions [including existing laws and customs] give to the man over at least one human – the one with whom he resides, and who he has always present [that is, his wife]' (SW, 289). In each case, Mill situates the power of the dominant party in relation to a broader structure of social relationships that establishes the specific power dynamics in question – a structure that encompasses prevailing property rights; laws concerning economic enterprises; the tendency of capitalist economies to generate accumulations of capital that give capitalists power over wage labourers; and prevailing traditions, customs, and laws the give men power over women (COS, 749–53; PPE, Bk. IV, ch. 7; SW, ch. 1). Meanwhile, he considers not just the power of the powerful but also the potential or actual power of those relatively powerless agents who are primarily *acted upon* by others – that is, those persons or classes of persons who are subordinate within power relationships. For example, he maintains that employees have *some* power in relation to their employers in wage-labour relations, and that wives have *some* power in relation to their husbands within patriarchal marital and family relationships, even though these structured relationships make employers and husbands the more powerful parties.

Mill expands these insights into a comprehensive account of three different aspects of social power. First, he illuminates the sources of social power in relation to various social relationships that produce and distribute the resources that differentially empower different social agents. Second, he highlights the role of a wide array of social relationships as media of 'the powers of education' with regard to their educative role in shaping people's desires, beliefs, self-understandings, and capacities. Third, he regards *authority* as a distinctive form of social and political power.

Mill presents his most wide-ranging account of the sources of social power in a review article on the essays and lectures of the French historian and foreign minister François Guizot. In discussing Guizot's view of how different societies are characterized by different dominant agencies of social power (that is, groups and institutions), Mill outlines his own view as follows:

> There are in society a number of distinct forces – of separate and independent sources of power. There is the general power of knowledge and cultivated intelligence. There is the power of religion; by which, speaking politically, is to be understood that of religious teachers. There is the power of military skill and discipline. There is the power of wealth; the power of numbers and physical forces; and several others might be added. Each of these, by the influence it exercises over society, is fruitful of certain beneficial effects; none of them is favourable to all kinds. ('GELH,' 236)

In other words, social power derives from a wide variety of social relationships and institutions that tend to unequally empower different groups of people with the resources to make their volitions effective. The power acquired by social agents is rooted in such things as social institutions and relationships, which transmit knowledge and 'cultivate' people's intelligence; religious institutions, which define and interpret the guiding principles that govern people's moral and spiritual pursuits; trade unions and political associations, through which people organize to pursue common interests; economic enterprises, which generate income and wealth and determine the conditions in which people work; and gender and family relationships, which determine (in part) the relative power of men and women to pursue their objectives in such areas as education, careers, politics, and leisure pursuits, as well as their relative power and possibilities with respect to marriages and families.

In other writings, Mill develops a more sustained account of the primary sources of social power in modern societies. He maintains in his essay on 'Civilization' that in 'advancing civilization' social power 'passes more and more from individuals, and small knots of individuals, to masses' ('Civ,' 163). He explains that property and the 'powers and acquirements of the mind' become 'widely diffused' in such societies, and that this tends to enhance the 'powers of combination' of the masses ('Civ,' 163, 165). He presents a related but more sophisticated picture of the 'powers which are even now at work in society' in his second essay on de Tocqueville ('TDA[II],' 163). He repeats his observation that the power of individuals is decreasing 'in comparison with the mass'; but rather than seeing a clear 'tendency toward equality of condition' in this diffusion of power, he highlights conflicting tendencies and class differences ('TDA[II],' 163, 194). In England 'inequalities of property are apparently greater than in any former period of history' ('TDA[II],' 163); yet at the same time, 'the power of the higher classes, both in government and in society, is diminishing; while that of the middle and even the lower classes is increasing' ('TDA[II],' 163). In light of the prospect of manhood suffrage, Mill foresees the development of a new constellation of class-based power in democratizing capitalist societies: one in which the *active* power of the 'middle' or capitalist class, which is based on its 'accumulation of capitals,' is opposed to the *potential* power of the working class, which is based on its electoral strength as 'the numerical majority' ('TDA[II],' 165–6, 191–200; CRG, 467; COS, 707).

Mill explains that the working classes have considerable *potential* power. Manhood suffrage, such as would arise with the abolition of property requirements for voting, would soon give them potentially 'absolute power, if they chose to exercise it' (CRG, 467). That is, *if* they were organized effectively to exercise 'the power of combined action,' the working classes could use their potentially superior numerical strength to promote 'their collective objects' in political elections ('TDA[II],' 165; COS, 707). Mill claims, moreover, that the diffusion of knowledge and intelligence 'to the lower, and down even to the lowest rank' that is characteristic of modern democratizing societies tends to foster increasing 'power of combined action' among the working classes ('TDA[II],' 164–5; cf. PPE, Bk. IV, ch. 7). While the working classes may not possess the most advanced 'intelligence,' this is not so important with respect to their active power. 'The knowledge which is power,' he explains, 'is not the highest description of knowledge only; any knowledge which gives the habit of forming an opinion, and the capacity of expressing that opinion, constitutes a political power, and, if combined with the capacity and habit of acting in concert, a formidable one.' Mill adds that what 'the power of combined action' can accomplish is evident in the work of 'Political Unions, Anti-Slavery Societies, and the like; to say nothing of the less advanced, but already powerful organization of the working classes' ('TDA[II],' 165).

Despite these advances of the working classes, Mill notes several 'tendencies of modern commercial society' that favour the middle class ('TDA[II],' 191). As we have seen, he conceives of politically effective as opposed to merely potential power as 'active power ... [or] power actually exerted.' It depends upon the will to act to pursue particular goals. An adequate account of 'the elements of political power' must therefore include 'anything that acts on the will' (CRG, 381). In this regard, he suggests that the middle class possesses unmatched power to shape what other people think and, thus, to 'create a general persuasion in society' favouring their interests ('TDA[II],' 191; CRG, 381–2). Thus, after saying that power is gradually passing to 'the mass,' Mill adds, 'Hardly anything now depends upon individuals, but all on classes, and among classes mainly upon the middle class. That class is now the arbiter of fortune and success' ('TDA[II],' 194). Furthermore, he says that the development of political democracy heralds the political supremacy of public opinion, but he also emphasizes the unmatched power of the middle class to *shape* public opinion ('TDA[II],' 162, 189, and 194–200). For instance, due to the dominant economic power of the middle class, the 'daily actions' of aristocratic members of the British House of Lords 'are falling more and more under the yoke of *bourgeois* opinion,' and middle class tastes are increasingly shaping the production of even literature and art ('TDA[II],' 194–5). 'The ascendancy of the commercial class in modern society and politics is inevitable,' he adds, so that 'it is chimerical to hope to overbear or outnumber the middle class' ('TDA[II],' 200).[8]

Extending this line of analysis, Mill intimates an additional source of middle class power. Immediately after discussing the 'power of combined action' manifest by various political associations, he says,

> The real Political Unions of England are the Newspapers. It is these which tell every person what all other persons are feeling, and in what manner they are ready to act: it is by these that the people learn, it may be truly said, their own wishes, and through these that they declare them. The newspapers and the railroads are solving the problem of bringing the democracy of England to vote, like that of Athens, simultaneously in one *agora*; and the same agencies are rapidly effacing those local distinctions which rendered one part of our population strangers to another; and are making us more than ever (what is the first condition of a powerful public opinion) a homogeneous people. ('TDA[II],' 165)

In Mill's time newspapers were the most important means of mass communication. They not only linked people together as a 'public,' with some common knowledge and ideas about public affairs, but also taught people 'their own wishes' and (ideally) provided them with a forum in which to 'declare' their wishes. Consequently, they were a crucial medium for 'the habit of forming an opinion, and the capacity of expressing that opinion, [that] constitutes a political power' ('TDA[II],' 165). It follows that the prospect that any one group or class in society might control or dominate newspapers (and mass communications more generally) has enormous significance with regard to their power to shape what other people think and, thus, to act on their wills (CRG, 381–2). In addition, the fact that in 'modern commercial societies' newspapers (along with other major communications media) are largely *commercial enterprises* further advantages the middle or capitalist class in a way that Mill only vaguely foresaw: the ownership and control of newspapers (along with other mass media) by large capitalist corporations in democratic polities has increasingly become a major source 'middle class' social and political power.[9]

Mill's never did develop this last point despite his appreciation of the social power that the 'accumulation of capitals' confers on the capitalist class. It is perhaps unfair to criticize him on this score, since in his time the capitalist class did not yet exert oligopolistic control over the communications media. In addition, his expectations about how a post-capitalist economic order would evolve gave him special reasons to gloss over the danger of capitalist domination of the mass media: as I explain in Chapter 7, he rather optimistically expected that capital itself would become increasingly diffused and ultimately *democratically controlled* within co-operative enterprises. Accordingly, Mill only 'partially' agreed with the view that the middle class, aided by the aristocracy, would be able to gain unchecked ascendance by using its 'property, intelligence, and power of combination, against any possible growth of those elements of importance in the inferior classes' ('TDA[II],' 166). Nonetheless, his account of social and political power supports a stronger conclusion: concentration of ownership and control of the means of communication leads to considerable concentration of power to shape what other people think. This, in turn, profoundly conflicts with democratic ideals (see ch. 8).

In light of these considerations, it is important to appreciate that Mill regards such 'power over human character' as one of the most significant and far-reaching forms of power in society, and not just as a means of class domination. In 'Utility of Religion,' he goes so far as to say, 'The power of education is almost boundless: there is not one natural inclination which it is not strong enough to coerce, and, if needful, to destroy by disuse' ('UR,' 409). In *Utilitarianism* he refers to the 'vast ... power over human character' wielded by 'education and opinion' (U, 218; cf. OL, 282). Three aspects of Mill's view of the 'powers of education' – or what I will call *educative power* – are especially central to his overall view of freedom and power. *First*, he maintains that the powers of 'education and opinion' *always* play a role in shaping the characters and capacities of individuals. The key question, therefore, is not *whether or not* such power should be exercised, but *what kind* of educative power should be exercised and for what purposes (see ch. 4, below).

Second, Mill maintains that educative power is a feature of virtually all social and political relationships, practices, and institutions that play a significant role in shaping people's characters and capacities. A complete account of the powers of education, therefore, must include not only that 'which has any tendency to convert itself into political power' (CRG, 381), but any power that shapes how people act by shaping what they think. Mill shows that educative power is sometimes used in repressive ways, as when men, preferring 'not a forced slave but a willing one[,] ... put everything in practice to enslave [women's] minds,' including 'the whole force of education' (SW, 271). When employed in this way the power of education has an obvious 'negative' aspect, since it consists of the capacity of some person or persons to repress others. Yet in Mill's view educative power is not always repressive; it also has a 'positive' or freedom-supporting aspect. He regards an invigorating education – in the broadest sense – as necessary for developing people's powers of free action (see ch. 4).

Third, Mill gives authority relationships, particularly 'the authority of the instructed' and the authority of received ideas, a distinctive place in his understanding of 'the powers of education.' He says in *Representative Government* that 'speculative thought is one of the chief elements of social power' (CRG, 382; cf. 'TDA[II],' 197–8). Thus, considerable power is exercised over average people 'by the persuasion and convictions of those whose personal position is different, and by the united authority of the instructed' (CRG, 382). Similarly, he refers in *On Liberty* to 'the ascendancy which the authority of a received opinion always exercises over the minds who are least fitted to judge for themselves' (OL, 282; cf. 'UR,' 410–11). As I will explain presently, Mill maintains that such authority, like educative power more generally, sometimes supports and sometimes stifles freedom.

III Mill's Theory of Authority

Mill conceives of authority as a particular mode of securing compliance that depends on the acceptance of those subject to it. He considers authority as a characteristic of prevailing traditions, norms, and beliefs as well as of persons and institutions; and he emphasizes the power over human character of certain forms of authority.[10] His guiding notion of authority basically coincides with Steven Lukes's recent definition of authority as 'a distinctive mode of securing compliance which combines in a peculiar way power over others and the exercise of reason' (1987, 62). For Mill, compliance with or obedience to authority is rooted not in coercion, but rather in acceptance of the authoritativeness of certain traditions, norms, and values or of the right of certain persons to issue commands to others. He contends that authority is not always rooted in an appeal to reason *per se*, since people sometimes accept the authority of certain norms or leaders simply because they have been taught to do so. He maintains, however, that reasoned acceptance, narrowly construed, is the distinguishing feature of legitimate modern authority, which he therefore regards as the kind of authority that is most compatible with the freedom of those who are *subject to* authority.

Mill gives questions of authority an especially central place within his

theory of democratic politics. He introduces his view of political authority in 'Bentham' in relation to the 'three great questions in government,'
as follows:

> First, to what authority is it for the good of the people that they should be
> subject? Secondly, how are they to be induced to obey that authority? The
> answers to these two questions vary indefinitely, according to the degree
> and kind of civilization and cultivation already attained by a people, and
> their peculiar aptitudes for receiving more. Comes next a third question,
> not liable to so much variation, namely, by what means are the abuses of
> this authority to be checked. ('B,' 106)

Following both Bentham and Samuel Taylor Coleridge, Mill maintains
that political authority is indispensable in all political communities. He
recognizes that political authority has an equivocal character: it is necessary for order and security and to protect weaker members of the community, but it also gives rulers potentially repressive power over others
(OL, 217–8). Moreover, he seeks increasing and inclusive democratization in virtually all areas of modern societies, including political authority, but he is not a radical or egalitarian democrat – at least not in any
simple sense. He argues that inequalities of knowledge and understanding an inevitable in modern societies – even in democracies – and
require some division between those who command and those who obey.
Thus, as Bruce Kinzer notes, Mill's 'politics of inclusion partly hinged
upon its enlistment of a valid principle *and* process of authority' (1988,
lxi, Kinzer's emphasis; cf. Hamburger, 1982). Specifically, Mill reserves a
place for 'the authority of the instructed' in a rational and deliberative
democracy, based on his view that some people are *authorities* in public
affairs (CRG, 382; 'TDA[II],' 188–9; and ch. 8, below). Such authority
plays a related though less developed role in how Mill extends the
principle of democratic self-government into economic and marital relations (see chs. 6 and 7, below).

Despite his well-known allusion in *On Liberty* to a grand 'struggle between Liberty and Authority' (OL, 217), overall, Mill construes authority, like power, as having a complex and complementary relationship
with freedom. Since authority refers a distinctive mode of exercising
power, the relationship between freedom and authority differs somewhat
from the relationship between freedom and other forms of power.
According to Mill, the relationship between authority and freedom

depends largely on whether the authority in question is legitimized on traditional or 'modern' grounds, and on whether it is exercised within its 'proper bounds.'

a. Being 'an Authority'

The sense of authority conveyed in the notion of a person being 'an authority' on certain matters is fundamental to Mill's broader view. He was influenced by John Austin's argument in *The Theory of Jurisprudence Determined* that with regard to specialized scientific and ethical subjects, only persons who have studied these matters in depth can have real knowledge as opposed to mere opinions (Friedman, 1968, 386). According to Austin, ordinary persons must depend on the judgment of specialists to gain authoritative opinions on such matters. Austin contends, moreover, that the deference of nonspecialists to the authority of such 'experts' is perfectly rational: 'I freely believe ... that the earth moves round the sun; though I know not a tittle of evidence from which the conclusion is inferred. And my belief is perfectly rational, though it rests upon mere authority. For there is nothing in the alleged fact, contrary to my experience of nature; whilst all who have scrutinized the evidence concur in confirming the fact' (Austin, quoted in T. Pateman, 1982, 18). In other words, most people are ill-equipped to understand the *grounds* upon which many scientific 'truths' are based. Yet it is nonetheless perfectly reasonable for the many nonspecialists to defer to the opinions of those who have 'scrutinized the evidence,' since the former *can* appreciate the expertise of the latter. In addition, such deference to authority is, in principle, perfectly consistent with our freedom insofar as we defer *upon reflection* and, therefore, *freely*.

Austin's influence is most evident in Mill's 1831 articles on 'The Spirit of the Age.' Mill's argument is a bit more subtle than Austin's but is basically consistent with it. He says the division of labour in modern societies enables some people to 'dedicate themselves to the investigation and study of physical, moral, and social truths, as their peculiar calling' so that they

> can alone be expected to make themselves thorough masters of the philosophical grounds of those opinions which it is desirable that all should be firmly *persuaded*, but which they alone can entirely and philosophically *know*. The remainder of mankind must, and, except in periods of transition

like the present [when accepted knowledge is most in flux], always do, take the far greater part of their opinions on all extensive subjects upon the authority of those who have studied them. ('SOA,' 242)[11]

Like Austin, then, Mill generally maintains that there are inequalities of knowledge and insight that distinguish certain persons as *authorities*. He qualifies this point in four respects, however. First, he challenges the view that there is a *natural division* between those who are and those who are not able to attain authoritative knowledge. He maintains that the existing inequality is largely due to unequal social circumstances that favour intellectual achievement by some people more than by others ('SOA,' 242; U, 213–16; COS, 746–8). Second, he says that 'the proofs of the moral and social truths of greatest importance to mankind, are few, brief, and easily intelligible to persons of the most limited faculties, with moderate study and attention' ('SOA,' 242). In the same breath, though, Mill argues that while there are no clear limits to the intellectual '*powers* of the mass of mankind,' most people's circumstances – especially their occupational burdens – substantially limit 'their possible *acquirements*' ('SOA,' 242, Mill's emphasis). Not many people, he says, have sufficient opportunities for study and reflection 'to be able to appreciate the force of reasons [regarding great moral and social truths] when laid before [them]' ('SOA,' 242). Therefore, 'when all is done, there still remains something which [most people] must always and inevitably take upon trust ... [on] the authority of the best-informed' ('SOA,' 243–4). Third, he distinguishes three kinds of 'authorities' who have commanded people's submission through history: 'the authority of superior minds, ... the interpreters of divine will, ... [and] superiors in rank and station' ('SOA,' 290). He maintains, however, that only the authority of 'superior minds' or of the 'best informed' is appropriate for modern, civilized societies. Fourth, Mill is ultimately somewhat sceptical about the prospect of attaining truly 'authoritative' knowledge in social and political matters.

He explains this last point and its political implications in a later work, *Auguste Comte and Positivism* (1865). He challenges Comte's defence of the rule of a philosophical-scientific élite of 'positive' sociologists who would base their policy prescriptions on authoritative sociological knowledge. As we have seen, Mill argues that the facts of social or moral sciences are more complicated than those of the natural sciences because they depend upon 'a greater concurrence of forces' and circumstances (ch. 2, above). Consequently, the difficulty of arriving at firm conclusions regarding the causes of particular phenomena is much greater for subjects that concern the social sciences (ACP, 326). He explains,

> It is therefore, out of all proportion, more uncertain than in any other science, whether two inquirers equally competent and equally disinterested will take the same view of the evidence, or arrive at the same conclusion. When to this intrinsic difficulty is added the infinitely greater extent to which personal or class interests and predilections interfere with impartial judgment, the hope of such accordance of opinion among sociological inquirers as would obtain, in mere deference to their authority, the universal assent which M. Comte's scheme of society requires, must be adjourned to an indefinite distance. (ACP, 326)

In short, the prospect of obtaining *authoritative* knowledge of social and political matters as a guide for political practice is undermined by two factors: the complexity of social phenomena; and inevitable personal and class biases of social scientists.[12]

Still, Mill's doubts about the possibility of gaining complete and impartial knowledge in social and political matters does not stop him from giving expert authority a pivotal role in his democratic theory. He maintains that knowledge of tendencies in social and political life is both attainable and valuable for good government (see ch. 2). He then argues that a 'rational democracy' must reserve a special role for the authority of persons with 'superiority of intellect and knowledge' in matters relevant to politics ('TDA[I],' 73; PPE, 765; 'TPR,' 323ff; CRG, chs. 5–8). In this regard, Mill never fully abandons his early view that on many issues most people 'must, in the last resort, fall back upon the authority of still more cultivated minds' ('SOA,' 244).

b. Traditional Authority

Mill does not use the term 'traditional authority,' but it corresponds to the kind of authority relationships that he sees as characteristic of pre-modern or 'uncivilized' societies. Max Weber explains that traditional authority rests 'on an established belief in the sanctity of immemorial traditions and the legitimacy of the status of those exercising authority under them' (1973 [1922], 105). Mill examines this kind of authority most fully in his 'Spirit of the Age' articles. He focuses on 'the authority of ancestors' in what he calls the 'best constituted' ancient commonwealths – those of the Athenians, Spartans, and Romans. He says that for them 'the great authority for political doctrines ... was the wisdom of ancestors: their old laws, their old maxims, the opinions of their ancient statesmen' ('SOA,' 291). He goes on to say that the 'authority of ancestors' that was so revered in Athens and Rome was at the same time 'the authority of the wisest and best men' ('SOA,' 293). Accordingly, he rejects the view that this authority had 'more than its just weight' in relation to the claims of reason: 'it did not supersede reason, but it guided it' ('SOA,' 293).

Mill offers two observations concerning the distinctiveness of this kind of traditional authority. First, it is rooted in what he calls a '*natural* state of society' – that is, a stable condition where there is a unifying body of settled doctrines – which is quite different from the 'transitional' and unsettled state of opinions and feelings of modern societies ('SOA,' 304, Mill's emphasis).[13] Second, the ancient commonwealths represent one of two kinds of societies in which 'there is found a united body of moral authority, sufficient to extort acquiescence from the uninquiring, or uninformed majority' ('SOA,' 304–5). The others are those societies in which one cohesive religion is the dominant force. Mill refers to Hindu and Turkish societies and 'Christendom in the middle ages' as examples; he also regards the Catholic church, though no longer quite so dominant, as exemplifying this kind of authority. Catholics, he says, 'received the priest from God, and their religion from the priest' ('SOA,' 312). Thus, they regard priests as authoritative 'interpreters of the divine will' ('SOA,' 290).

In subsequent writings Mill focuses on the second form of traditional authority. He summarizes his view of its limitations in *On Liberty* when he contrasts conclusions based on premises 'taken from authority' with conclusions based on premises taken 'from reason' (OL, 251). He explains that students who were involved in the 'school disputations of the Middle Ages' – where they learned to understand the grounds of both their own opinions and opposing opinions so that they 'could enforce the grounds of the one and confute those of the other' – advanced beyond an unquestioning acceptance of received opinions. In his view, though, these 'contests had indeed the incurable defect, that the premises appealed to were taken from authority, not from reason' (OL, 251). Likewise, he criticizes traditional Christian morality for being reactionary since it is 'essentially a doctrine of passive obedience; it inculcates submission to all authorities found established; who indeed are not to be actively obeyed when they command what religion forbids, but who are not to be resisted, far less rebelled against, for any amount of wrong to ourselves' (OL, 255; see also 'SOA,' 312). According to Mill, then, traditional authority holds sway where the rules governing human conduct among a particular people 'appear to them self-evident and self-justifying' (OL, 220).

Mill's criticism of traditional authority is integrally related to his concern with what he calls the 'despotism of custom' and, thus, to his conception of free thought and action (OL, 272). As I explained in Chapter 1, he insists that a person is unfree when he or she does 'anything because it is the custom' (OL, 262). By extension, we are unfree when we act in accordance with traditional authority, or the 'authority of a received opinion,' because this entails letting 'the world, or [our] portion of it, choose [our] plan of life for [us]' (OL, 282, 262). I also noted in Chapter 1, however, that Mill relies on overly narrow – basically, modern rationalist – standards of reason and 'rationality' when he juxtaposes premises taken 'from authority' with those taken 'from reason.' He implicitly appeals to an ideal of 'pure reason' that presumably is independent of any traditional moorings. Therefore, he fails to grasp that what constitutes a 'good reason' for conclusions or actions is always rooted in some prior prerational commitment to a particular belief system or mode of reasoning (MacIntyre, 1987, 405; Tully, 1989; Appiah, 1993). Furthermore, Mill fails to adequately appreciate that people who rely on premises taken from the authority of religious and cultural traditions often exercise considerable reasoning in light of these premises. Conversely, he also fails to account adequately for how even the most confirmed rationalists typically rely on their own taken-for-granted premises and, thus, on the 'authority of a received opinion' (Appiah, 1993, 117; Fish, 1996).

Mill tests the limits of his rationalist approach to traditional authority in an essay on ancient Greek history and mythology. Here he seems to acknowledge that people in traditional cultures use reason in following their immemorial customs for traditional reasons. He says that a modern scientific 'interpretation of nature,' in which explanation is grounded on 'natural causes' rather than on 'the personal agency of a hidden supernatural power, ... is not only offensive to the reverential feelings of the hearer [who regards a religious interpretation as paramount], *but actually repugnant to his reason*, so contrary is it to the habitual mode of interpretation' ('GH[I],' 290, emphasis added). In the end, though, he regards this as an archaic mode of reasoning, calling it a 'state of mind perfectly intelligible by our knowledge of the Hindoos ... who reproduce in so many respects the infancy of the human race' ('GH[I],' 290).[14]

Mill's understanding of acting on premises 'taken from authority, not from reason,' is rooted in his theory of societal development, and has some troubling political implications. With regard to the development of modern societies, he maintains in *Principles of Political Economy* that 'the progress of the mass of the people in mental cultivation, and in the virtues which are dependent on it,' generally makes people less willing to be governed 'by the mere authority and *prestige* of superiors' (PPE, 764, Mill's emphasis; cf. PPE, 200). People in such progressing or improving societies increasingly insist upon consensual forms of authority that respect their status as free agents. In contrast, he sees societies in which a tradition-bound frame of mind prevails as caught under the 'despotism of custom.' This despotism, he says, 'is everywhere the standing hindrance to human advancement, being in unceasing antagonism to that disposition to aim at something better than customary, what is called, according to circumstances, the spirit of liberty, or that of progress or improvement' (OL, 272).[15] He notes that the 'spirit of liberty' and the 'spirit of improvement' are sometimes in conflict – for instance, where the latter seems to require 'forcing improvements on an unwilling people.' Yet he maintains that the 'progressive principle ... in either shape, whether as the love of liberty or of improvement, is antagonistic to the sway of Custom, involving at least emancipation from that yoke' (OL, 272). Mill thus contends that it is 'the privilege and proper condition of a human being ... to use and interpret [inherited human] experience in his [or her] own way' (OL, 262), and that the hold of traditional forms of authority undermines the fullest flourishing of human life.

Therefore, in spite of his concern about 'forcing improvements' on people, he justifies British colonial rule over India as a civilizing force. 'Despotism,' he says in *On Liberty*, 'is a legitimate mode of government in dealing with barbarians, provided the end be their improvement, and the means justified by actually effecting that end' (OL, 224). His hope was that British colonialism would guide the Indian people to that state of society where they would be prepared for self-government (OL, 224; CRG, ch. 18; 'FWNI'). Since Mill regards *unreasoned* acceptance of the authority of immemorial traditions as itself a form of 'despotism,' he maintains that people may need to be liberated from its 'yoke' *even when* they perceive their freedom and well-being as deeply entwined with their customs and traditions. In some of his writings on India (see 'MVC') he ventures beyond a narrow and unreflective form of Eurocentrism, but his arguments about non-European societies typically betray the civilizing ethos that was common among nineteenth-century European intellectuals.[16]

But there is another, more liberating aspect of Mill's view of traditional authority. He emphasizes that received traditions and customs sometimes perpetuate oppression. In such cases, some people perpetuate their own oppression by deferring to the authority of received traditions. Mill expresses this point most forcefully in *The Subjection of Women*. In response to the argument that the 'authority of men over women' is justified because it is 'natural,' he asks, 'was there ever any domination which did not appear natural to those who possessed it?' (SW, 269). He points out how such things as slavery, absolute monarchy, 'the law of force,' and the rule of the feudal nobility in the Middle Ages were all justified as 'natural' by those who benefited. Then he adds, 'The subjection of women to men being a universal custom, any departure from it quite naturally appears unnatural. But how entirely, even in this case, the feeling is dependent on custom appears by ample experience' (SW, 270). In short, the laws, customs, and traditional beliefs that support the authority of men over women can be traced to 'a mere physical fact' of male dominance gained by force, to which they give 'the sanction of society ... Those who had already been compelled to obedience became in this manner legally bound to it' (SW, 264). Thus, as was the case with slavery, the existence of patriarchal authority does not *justify* such authority. 'No presumption in its favour,' Mill says, 'can be drawn from the fact of its existence' (SW, 264). Moreover, as I noted earlier, Mill maintains that the fact that many women *accept* the authority of men over them is partly due to how men have 'put everything in practice to enslave [women's] minds,' including 'the whole force of education' (SW, 271). A key implication of his argument is that *acceptance of traditional authority by dominated groups may itself be a product of the same asymmetries of power between groups that this authority sanctions* (SW, 263). In this regard, his notion of reasoned engagement with received traditions offers a means by which oppressed parties can liberate themselves by becoming aware of the power dynamics that have shaped their customs and traditions (see ch. 1, sec. V, above).

Finally, it is important to note that Mill is rarely interested in understanding traditional authority in its own right. Although he refers to 'the whole East,' and China in particular, as his models of societies under the 'sway of Custom,' he is *primarily* concerned with developing a theory and practice of authority for 'advanced' societies like England. He is only secondarily concerned with traditional authority in 'backward' societies that have not yet 'attained the capacity' for self-government (OL, 224; Parekh, 1994, 89–90).[17] In Mill's time, due to the progress of commerce and industry, modern democratizing societies such as England and France were in the midst of revolutionary changes in their self-understandings, beliefs, social and political relationships and institutions, and views of authority. Thus, regarding 'the ancient structure of English society,' he says, 'it may now be said that in all relations of life, except those to which law and religion have given permanence, change has become the general rule, and constancy the exception' ('TDA[II],' 194; cf. 'SOA'). In the face of such change, traditional forms of authority are being undermined as social norms and practices come to be seen as less fixed and more subject to human volition. One of the prominent features of such transitional societies is 'the decay of authority, and diminution of respect for traditional opinions,' where the authority in question is traditional authority, rooted in the passive acceptance of 'traditional opinions' ('TDA[II],' 195).

Here, Mill articulates his great fear for modern democratizing societies: that traditional authority will be replaced by a similarly despotic kind of modern authority – that of popular opinion ('B,' 107). In his second article on Tocqueville's *Democracy in America*, he contrasts traditional authority with the increasing authority of public opinion in the 'democratic' United States. He begins by citing Tocqueville's view that Americans both profess and

> carry into practice, on all subjects except the fundamental doctrines of Christianity ... the habit of mind which has been so often inculcated as the one sufficient security against mental slavery – the rejection of authority, and the assertion of the right of private judgment. They regard the traditions of the past merely in the light of materials ... They are not accustomed to look for guidance either to the wisdom of ancestors, or to eminent contemporary wisdom but require that the grounds on which they act shall be made of their own comprehension. ('TDA[II],' 178–9)

Mill comments that this democratic mode of thought might be expected to encourage excessive 'individual independence of thought,' but 'the fact is the reverse' ('TDA[II],' 179). He maintains (following Tocqueville) that even when people ostensibly reject all forms of authority as the basis for their opinions, such a basis 'always exists in fact. That law above them, which older societies have found in the traditions of antiquity, or in the dogmas of priests or philosophers, the Americans find in the opinions of one another' ('TDA[II],' 179). In other words, as traditional authority is being gradually eclipsed in the United States, popular opinion is increasingly gaining the unquestioned and thereby despotic character of traditional authority. Yet whereas the power of the latter is rooted in people's belief in or acceptance of the sanctity of 'immemorial traditions' or the wisdom of ancestors, the despotic authority of public opinion is an ironic accompaniment to the modern 'democratic' aspiration of people to govern themselves.

Mill's concern, in short, is that despite the evident 'improvement' of social relationships and social consciousness in democratizing societies, many members of these societies are still bound by the sway of custom or prevailing opinion (OL, ch. 3). He presents the example of Eastern societies, in which 'the despotism of Custom is complete,' as a warning for England and the other nations of Europe:

> A people, it appears, may be progressive for a certain length of time, and then stop: when does it stop? When it ceases to possess individuality. If a similar change should befall the nations of Europe, it will not be in exactly the same shape: the despotism of custom with which these nations are threatened is not precisely stationariness. It proscribes singularity, but it does not preclude change, provided all change together. We have discarded the fixed costumes of our forefathers; every one must still dress like other people, but the fashion may change once or twice a year. (OL, 273)

As I will explain in the following section, Mill regards neither such stagnation nor the 'despotism' of public opinion as inevitable. Still, he sees the modern 'spirit of liberty' being threatened in democratizing societies by a tendency toward conformity that resembles submission to traditional authority.

c. Modern Authority

Mill's notion of legitimate authority in modern societies is similar to but somewhat different from Max Weber's notion of legal or legal-rational authority. Legal authority, for Weber, rests 'on a belief in the "legality" of patterns of normative rules and the right of those elevated to authority under such rules to issue commands' (1973 [1922], 105). Mill, by contrast, emphasizes that laws may be judged through critical scrutiny to be *unjust* and thus illegitimate. He notes that it is sometimes thought to be 'just to respect, unjust to violate the *legal rights* of any one.' He asserts, however, that 'the legal rights of which [a person] is deprived may be rights which *ought* not to have belonged to him; in other words, the law which confers on him these rights may be a bad law' (U, 241–2, Mill's emphasis). In Mill's view, then, legitimate modern authority rests on something more than mere legality or acceptance of relations of command and obedience between rulers and ruled. It requires expressly consensual and reasoned acceptance by both parties of the prevailing normative rules and of the prerogative of rulers to command others based on these rules.

Mill elaborates his view of legitimate modern authority in light of his early account of the inevitable inequalities of knowledge and understanding among people concerning public affairs. In his view, this situation requires some division between those who command and those who obey, but it does not preclude democratic government. Modern societies, he says, increasingly adopt modes of critical thought in which 'the yoke of authority has been broken, and innumerable opinions, formerly received on tradition as incontestable, are put upon their deference, and required to give an account of themselves' ('B,' 78; cf. 'TDA[II],' 194). Changes wrought by modern science and commerce have increasingly led people to reject the 'old theory' that the course of people's lives should be laid down for them by 'superior wisdom,' for the 'modern conviction' that things go best when individuals are left free to choose their own course of life, without 'any regulation of them by authority, except to protect the rights of others' (SW, 272). For Mill, this modern development is integrally connected to the progress of the 'democratic spirit' whereby people increasingly regard any authority over them as legitimate only insofar as it rests upon their consent (PPE, 793; 'TDA[II]'). Moreover, while he strongly supports this development as an advance in political freedom (CRG, ch. 3), he rejects the kind of democratic radicalism according to which the unchecked will of the numerical majority is the only legitimate basis for political authority.[18]

Mill develops this point in the course of discussing Bentham's view that the will of the 'numerical majority' is the proper basis for political authority. Bentham, he explains, holds that the will of the numerical majority is the proper basis for establishing political authority, because this creates an 'identity of interest' between the rulers and the ruled. Mill himself is more sceptical of this presumed 'identity of interest.' He agrees with Bentham's view that political authority should be responsible to persons whose interest corresponds 'with the end in view – good government,' but he offers the following qualification: 'since power given to all, by a representative government, is in fact given to a majority; we are obliged to fall back upon the [question of] ... under what authority is it for the good of the people that they be placed?' ('B,' 106). Accordingly, he questions Bentham's unqualified faith in the authority of the numerical majority:

> Is it, at all times and places, good for mankind to be under the absolute authority of the majority of themselves? We say the authority, not the political authority merely, because it is chimerical to suppose that whatever has absolute power over men's bodies will not arrogate it over their minds – will not seek to control (not perhaps by legal penalties, but by the persecutions of society) opinions and feelings which depart from its standard; will not attempt to shape the education of the young by its model, and to extinguish all books, all schools, all combinations of individuals for joint action upon society, which may be attempted for the purpose of keeping alive a spirit at variance with its own. Is it ... the proper condition of man, in all ages and nations, to be under the despotism of Public Opinion? ('B,' 106)

Mill's argument here foreshadows his later emphasis in *On Liberty* on the form that the 'struggle between Liberty and Authority' takes in modern democratic societies (OL, 217). He regards the movement toward popular government as a progressive achievement that is essential for political freedom; but he does not see it as a simple solution to the tensions between liberty and authority (CRG, chs. 3, 5, 7; OL, 217–20). Popular government offers a partial answer to the danger of tyranny by unaccountable rulers, but it also opens the door to new political and social forms of 'tyranny of the majority' – or of 'those who succeed in making themselves accepted as the majority' – including the tyranny of public opinion over what people think and feel (OL, 219–23; 'TDA[II]').

Mill insists, therefore, that legitimate political authority in modern societies must be based on the consent of all the governed; but he also maintains that majority rule must be balanced by the 'authority of the instructed.' He holds that authority is consistent with the freedom of those who are subject to it when it is established in a way that affirms their desire to be 'essentially self-governed' ('B,' 125, 124). Consequently, he regards democracy as the only basis for legitimate political authority in modern societies, since only democracy gives ultimate control over all officials and agencies of government to 'a common Superior – the People' ('TDA[I],' 65). The legitimacy of modern political authority, then, ultimately depends on the consent and *authorization* of the people. At the same time, he contends that the complexities of modern society require a special guiding role for the 'authority of the instructed' to ensure 'rational' democracy and good government.

Mill maintains that the guidance of persons with special knowledge and insight concerning public affairs is a necessary check against the new dangers of political and social 'majority tyranny' that are characteristic of modern democratizing societies. The majority tyranny he most fears is 'a tyranny not over the body, but over the mind' as members of such societies increasingly rely on 'the opinions of one another' ('TDA[II],' 178; OL, 219–20). Concerning this threat, he highlights two tendencies of modern commercial societies that encourage such 'democratic' despotism. First, there are practical limitations that preclude the mass of people from attaining the knowledge and capability to carry out the day-to-day business of government. We need to guard against not only the 'ascendancy which the authority of a received opinion always exercises over the minds who are least fitted to judge for themselves' (OL, 282), which can be partially offset through improved education, but also the 'dogmatism of common sense.' Mill describes the latter as a kind of intellectual mediocrity whereby the general public demands, as a corollary to claims of self-government, 'that all things shall be made clear to each man's understanding – an indifference to the subtler proofs which address themselves to more cultivated and systematically exercised intellects' ('TDA[II],' 196, 179).[19] Second, he warns of potentially degrading effects upon democracy by 'the ascendancy of the commercial class in modern society,' including the ascendancy of 'the commercial spirit' ('TDA[II],' 200, 198). Democratic politics, he says, is degraded not by 'the preponderance of a democratic class, but by the preponderance of any class' ('TDA[II],' 196, 202). Moreover, as I noted earlier, he offers some reasons to expect that the 'public opinion' that is likely to become dominant in modern commercial societies will be '*bourgeois* opinion' rather than the considered views of the majority ('TDA[II],' 194).

For these reasons, Mill concludes that attention to the 'subtler proofs' and truly public interests that are crucial for good public policy requires a special role for persons with 'more cultivated ... intellects.' What is necessary 'in politics ... is not that public should not be, what it is and must be, the ruling power; but that, in order to [foster] the formation of the best opinion, there should exist somewhere a great social support for opinions and sentiments different from those of the mass' ('TDA[II],' 198). In short, he contends that a 'rational' or 'true' democracy requires a combination of popular sovereignty and a legislative process that reserves a special role in law making for a class of political experts. Ideally, this 'governing class' would not only analyze subtle arguments that are beyond the comprehension of ordinary citizens, but would also be somewhat insulated from 'the unbalanced influence of the commercial spirit' ('TDA[II],' 198, 196, 200–4; CRG, chs. 5–6). 'The people' would exercise 'ultimate control' of their government, but they would not govern themselves directly. 'The interest of the people is,' Mill explains, 'to choose for their rulers the most instructed and ablest persons who can be found, and having done so, to allow them to exercise freely, or with the least possible control – as long as it *is* in the good of the people, and not some private end, that they are aiming at' ('TDA[I],' 72, Mill's emphasis). Popular control over the government should include the power of the people 'to dismiss their rulers as soon as the devotion of those rulers to the interests of the people becomes questionable,' but the people should cede to the governing class the authority to make laws and policies ('TDA[I],' 71–2). Mill describes the power of the people to choose governing *authorities* as 'that intervention of popular suffrage which is essential to freedom' (CRG, 527). At the same time, he warns that political 'freedom cannot produce its best effects' unless it is combined 'with trained and skilled administration' (CRG, 440).

He tempers the élitist tendency of his argument somewhat with the developmental aspect of his political theory. He envisions increasing democratization of social and political relationships as a fitting consequence of ongoing 'progress in the mass of the people in mental cultivation, and in the virtues dependent on it' (PPE, 764). Therefore, although he refrains from offering unqualified support for equal rights of all persons to share in practices of self-government, his *ideal* of progressive reform points in a more thoroughly egalitarian direction (see chs. 6–8, below). In the end he offers a complex ideal of democratic equality: increasingly equal rights for people to share in self-government in political, economic, and marital relationships, but without everyone having a strictly equal role in practices of self-government. In this regard, Mill construes his emphasis on the deference of most citizens to the authority of experts on particular subjects as consistent with self-government and the unwillingness to be governed by 'mere authority.' Deference to political authorities with respect to day-to-day governance would be reasoned and freely given.[20] Ideally, the trust that people place in the authority of public officials would be part of a broader democratic political order. Furthermore, given the difficulties of gaining authoritative knowledge in matters of social science and policy – including serious obstacles to impartial judgment – such deference would never be unconditional or uncritical.[21]

IV Power and Authority

To return to the broader topic of power, Mill insightfully distinguishes between power and authority. In *The Subjection of Women* he contrasts the limited form of power that women possess with the power and authority that men have over them. Men have traditional *authority* over women because their power over women's lives is (or *was* in Mill's time) the widely accepted 'established custom' (SW, 263). Yet women are not completely powerless despite their subordinate position. They exercise some marginalized and *unauthorized* power by acting in relation to men (particularly their husbands) to get what they want or achieve some of their desires. Mill says that in the face of the 'despotic power which the law gives to the husband' over his wife, 'the wife, if she cannot effectively resist, can at least retaliate; she, too, can make the man's life extremely uncomfortable, and by that power is able to carry many points which she ought, and many which she ought not, to prevail in' (SW, 292, 289). One striking feature of this women's power is that it goes hand in hand with their relative powerlessness, their lack of freedom, and their exclusion from significant *authority*.[22] They must resort to the 'power of the scold' to achieve their aims through their husbands because they have so little authorized power aside from their power over their children (SW, 289). Even the power that wives exercise with respect to their children may be limited, however, if their husbands demand to exercise their full 'legal authority' as the rulers of 'their' families. Where laws and customs acknowledge exclusive authority of men over women, then, whatever power women exercise is typically power without authority.

Similarly, Mill considers how a central government can have 'much authority' but only limited 'actual power' in the affairs of local governments. Ideally, he says, a central government would disseminate resources and information and establish general governing principles, but without monopolizing *power* in local matters. 'This central organ,' he says, 'should have a right to know all that is done, and its special duty should be that of making the knowledge acquired in one place available for others' (OL, 309). He adds that due to its distance from 'the petty prejudices and narrow views of a locality [the central government's] advice would naturally carry much authority; but its actual power, as a permanent institution, should ... be limited to compelling the local officers to obey the laws laid down for their guidance' (OL, 309).

In sum, Mill shows that authority is a distinct form of power, and that not all power is authority. For example, in 'Thoughts on Parliamentary Reform,' when he speaks of the 'power which suffrage gives' some persons 'over others,' this power is distinct from authority ('TPR,' 323). The vote gives voters potential political power over others as well as over themselves. This power *may* also constitute a form of authority, but it carries authority *only* within societies in which the right of voters to exercise this power is widely accepted and affirmed. In other words, belief in the principle of popular sovereignty is necessary for it to exist *as authority*. Even then, it is generally limited authority insofar as it typically entails direct control over the state's legislative, executive, and judicial powers. Voters are the ultimate *source* of authority in democratic polities, but they usually lack the authority to make, execute, or interpret the law, except when they are elected or appointed to positions in government, or serve on juries. Conversely, Mill recognizes that being *an authority* or even *having authority* is sometimes only indirectly related to exercising power. For example, when someone is an authority in certain matters, others may be especially inclined to seriously consider her opinions; but this will not always translate into effective power to achieve her goals, particularly if other authorities express contrary opinions.

Finally, the distinction between power and authority has important implications for Mill's view of the proper bounds of political authority. As I noted earlier, Mill says that the 'modern conviction' is that things go best for individuals when they are free to choose their own course of life, without 'any regulation of them by authority, except to protect the rights of others' (SW, 272). Thus, while he says that the common sense of the numerical majority should not be regarded as completely authoritative in democratic politics, he insists that the 'common sense and experience' of each mature individual ought to be regarded as authoritative with regard to laying out his or her own mode of life, at least in 'self-regarding' matters (OL, 270, 280–4, 232; see ch. 5, below). Similarly, he holds that no person or persons can *authoritatively* decide what constitutes 'the good' of other mature and competent adults. Consequently, the legitimate reach of political authority in regulating people's conduct is limited to matters of 'social morality, of duties to others' (OL, 283). Mill warns, however, that members of modern democratic societies may *claim* the authority to regulate the self-regarding conduct of others, and that the majority has potential *power* to dictate what others can and cannot do. Even so, in his view the majority has no such rightful authority in modern societies. This means that there is a continuing tension between liberty and authority in modern democratic societies, since at any time the majority may claim such authority with respect to others. Moreover, this tension will persist in a more covert way as long as the 'authority of a received opinion' wields undue influence.

V Government, Self-government, and the Government of Conduct

We can now put together a general picture of how Mill's theory of social power relates to his theory of freedom. His theory of social power illuminates the situatedness of freedom, including both its conditions and the forms that it takes. It brings to the fore key forms of social power that govern people's lives by delimiting what they can do or be in different spheres of action and by shaping their capacities for autonomy. As I explained in Chapter 2, Mill conceives of the freedom of individuals in terms of both their powers of self-determination *within* the various power relations situating them, and their opportunities for self-government with respect to the social relationships that govern their lives. Therefore, his theory of social power clarifies the forms that freedom takes in modern societies.

It is important to note that Mill sometimes uses the concept of 'government' in a broad sense that refers to various modes of governing human conduct as well as in the narrower sense that refers to 'the government' or the state. He uses the broad sense of government, for example, in *The Subjection of Women* in response to the claim that no society can exist without government – a claim posed as an objection to his arguments for equality between the sexes. Mill writes, 'But how, it will be asked, can any society exist without government? In a family, as in a state, some one person must be the ultimate ruler. Who shall decide when married people differ in opinion? Both cannot have their way, yet a decision one way or the other must be come to' (SW, 290). Mill accepts the claim that families, like states, must be governed. Yet he emphatically rejects the notion 'that in all voluntary association between two people, one of them must be absolute master: still less that the law must determine which of them it shall be' (SW, 290). He contends that nothing from experience proves that there must be an inequality of decision-making power between a husband and wife (SW, 291–8; see ch. 6, below). Mill also employs the broader sense of government in other contexts. In *Chapters on Socialism*, for instance, he refers to the 'nearly despotic power' that the head of the family had in early states of society 'in governing the family'; and in 'Michelet's History of France' he discusses the power of the clergy in Europe during the Middle Ages to

'admonish and govern' their followers (COS, 750; 'MHF,' 155). He argues in *Principles of Political Economy* that co-operative government within
economic enterprises would extend 'the best aspirations of the democratic spirit' to 'the industrial department' in modern societies (PPE,
793). Finally, in 'Bentham' and in other writings he considers the
motivations by which human conduct is *governed* ('B,' 94).[23]

In light of these observations, Mill examines the prospects for self-
government by the different members of society as an aspect of their
freedom within marital and economic relationships as well as with respect to the state (see chs. 6–8, below).[24] At the same time, he emphasizes the special status of state power in modern societies in relation to
other forms of social power. He explains this point in 'Recent Writers on
Reform' in the course of rejecting the notion that the voting rights of
citizens can be compared to the voting rights of shareholders in joint
stock companies. The 'business of government,' he says, is not concerned solely with property; instead, 'the stake which an individual has
in good government [by the state] is ... nothing less than his entire
earthly welfare, in soul, body, and mind. The government to which he is
subject has power over all his sources of happiness, and can inflict on
him a thousand forms of intolerable misery' ('RWR,' 354–5). In Mill's
view, political power has a sovereign status in relation to all other pursuits, including other forms of power. That is, in modern societies the
state has potential power to regulate, alter, or protect any or all social
relationships and activities. This is true, according to Mill, *even though* the
exercise of state power itself depends on the balance of *social power* in a
society. His analysis of the prospects for political freedom in a democratic state thus has a special status in relation to other forms of modern
freedom. At the same time, the interdependence of social and political
power implies that the capacity of the state to carry out its responsibilities may be undermined if certain sources of social power, such as
transnational corporations, become too powerful in relation to modern
states.

Overall, Mill offers a persuasive account of social power in modern
societies. Still, his view has several limitations, as I will show in later
chapters. First, his theory of authority is weakened somewhat by his
Eurocentrism. His distinction between traditional and modern forms of
authority presumes an overly sharp dichotomy between supposedly
'unreasoned' deference to traditional authority and the 'reasoned'
deference that characterizes modern authority. Consequently, his claim
that modern authority is uniquely grounded in *rational* deference is

misleading. In this regard, Mill does not adequately address the interplay between power and culture, and between power and knowledge. He fails to address adequately how forms of power and authority are always culturally shaped. For example, he fails to grasp how the production of knowledge about stages of societal development, including his own, has been shaped by and implicated in asymmetrical power relationships between different cultures and societies, such as colonial struggles between European and non-European societies.

Similarly, Mill lacks an account of how oppressive power relationships involving people's racial, gender, and sexual identities have been partly constituted by the production of bodies of knowledge regarding these identities. He *does* consider how some prevailing ideas and discourses about gender and race are used to justify the oppression of women, the Irish, and people of African descent (SW, ch. 1; 'NQ'; 'MHF,' 145–7; PPE, 319). In Mill's view, though, such oppressive discourses are typically lingering remnants of outmoded traditions and customs that will be eclipsed by the advance of reason. Consequently, he was unable to foresee how the production of new scientific 'knowledge' – for example, in 'race science' and eugenics – could produce new modes of domination, and how struggles over knowledge about cultural, racial, class, and sexual identities would figure in struggles for power and freedom.

4

Education for Freedom

Who speaks of liberty while the human mind is in chains?

Francis Wright, 'On Existing Evils and Their Remedy' (1837)

Education, in its largest sense, is one of the most inexhaustible of all topics. Not only does it include whatever we do for ourselves, and whatever is done for us by others, for the express purpose of bringing us somewhat nearer to the perfection of our nature; it does more: in its largest acceptation, it comprehends even the indirect effects produced on the character and on the human faculties, by things of which the direct purposes are quite different; by laws, by the forms of government, by the industrial arts, by modes of social life; nay even by physical facts not dependent on human will; by climate, social, and local position. Whatever helps to shape the human being – to make the individual what he is, or hinder him from being what he is not – is part of his education.

John Stuart Mill, 'Inaugural Address Delivered to the University of St Andrews' (1867)

As we have seen, Mill's conception of freedom contains both psychological and sociological aspects. It encompasses both the cognitive capacity for autonomous thought and action, and the field of social and political relationships in which people develop autonomy and exercise self-determination. Mill views the capacity for free action as a *potentiality* of all human beings, and as enhanced or stifled in proportion to the development of their faculties of reasoning, deliberation, imagination, judgment, and self-control. For this reason he takes an abiding interest in education 'in its largest acceptation' as a means of empowering people for freedom.

Mill addressed the issue of education for individual liberty and democratic self-government in the context of the challenges posed by political democratization in nineteenth-century England, particularly the struggles to extend suffrage reflected in the Reform Bills of 1832 and 1867. In Mill's time, as Geraint Parry notes, 'the newly enfranchised classes had not only no practical adult education in popular politics, but also little in the way of schooling' (1994, 54).[1] Against this backdrop, Mill maintains that the freedom of individuals depends in large part on what he calls 'mental freedom' – that is, the capacity of people to think for themselves and reflectively pursue their own aims and purposes. The extent of their mental freedom depends, in turn, on the character of their educations. He expresses the guiding thread of his view of education for freedom in an 1852 letter to Rev. Henry William Carr on the question of (in Mill's words) 'how to teach social science to the uneducated, when those who are called the educated have not learnt it; and nearly all the teaching given from authority is opposed to genuine morality.' Mill responds: 'What the poor as well as the rich require is not to be indoctrinated, is not to be taught other people's opinions, but to be induced and enabled to think for themselves' (CW 14, 80).

For Mill, the 'education' relevant to achieving this end includes all those social relationships, institutions, and life experiences that 'make the individual what he is, or hinder him from being what he is not' ('IA,' 217). In this view, the domain of education overlaps with the domain of social power. All relationships of social power – political, economic, gender, and family relationships as much as schools – have an educative dimension insofar as they all play a formative role in shaping people's characters and cognitive capacities. Regarding this aspect of the interplay of freedom and power, Mill joins his analysis of 'the powers of education' (OL, 282) with two key issues within his theory of freedom: cultivating the 'mental freedom' or autonomy that is a necessary condition of free agency; and instilling the kind of moral restraint among free agents – in exercising both individual liberty and democratic self-government – that is necessary to sustain equal freedom for all.

Mill's account of education for freedom is comprehensive and discerning. At the same time, it also highlights the tensions between egalitarian and élitist tendencies in his thought and in his account of freedom and determinism. He maintains that while there are some differences among people in 'the vigour of their intellectual powers,' virtually everyone can be educated for freedom ('TPV,' 67; COS, 744). He expresses ambivalence, however, regarding the 'authority of received opinion' in moral education, and about whether or not there will always be some persons with 'too little understanding, or too little virtue, to be capable' of being fully included in a life of self-determination (OL, 282; PPE, 793).

I Association Psychology and the Development of Autonomy

Mill builds his theory of education for freedom upon his account of the psychological processes through which people develop autonomy. Regarding the moral and political significance of psychology, Mill explains in *An Examination of Sir William Hamilton's Philosophy* that 'a true Psychology is the indispensable scientific basis of Morals, of Politics, and of the science and art of Education' (EHP, 2). He adds in his preface to the 1869 edition of James Mill's *Analysis of the Phenomena of the Human Mind* that psychology is concerned with the elemental 'laws of the mind' that are instrumental in 'moulding our thoughts' and 'forming our thinking powers' ('NTA,' 97–8). John Stuart Mill works within the tradition of association psychology, which was developed by Thomas Hobbes, John Locke, David Hartley, David Hume, and his father, James Mill. Associationists contend that complex mental phenomena develop out of rudimentary mental phenomena – notably sensations of pleasure and pain – through the universal laws of association. The latter explain what John Mill calls 'the uniformities of succession' of mental phenomena – that is, 'various feelings or states of consciousness of sentient beings' (L, 848). Thus, associationists give a naturalistic account of such things as ideas, emotions, desires, and volitions as products of experience, in opposition to the view that these things are innate or original to the human mind.[2]

For John Mill, as for his father, these psychological premises are closely related to his reformist political philosophy. He emphasizes these connections in his *Autobiography*, where he says that his father's associationist doctrine of the formation of human character by circumstances demonstrates the 'unlimited possibility of improving the moral and intellectual condition of mankind by education' (A, 109, 111). Elsewhere he summarizes his own view of the importance of psychology for the cultivation of 'the nobler phenomena of the mind' as follows: 'If these nobler parts of our nature are not self-sown and original, but are built or build themselves up, out of no matter what materials, it must be highly important to the work of education and improvement of character, to understand as much as possible of the process by which those materials are put together' ('BP,' 349).

Mill regards the human capacities for mental freedom and autonomy as 'nobler parts of our nature.' People are not born free, in his view; rather, we are born with the *potential* for mental freedom and free action. This potential comes to fruition, however, only insofar as the educative relationships situating us nurture our faculties of reasoning, imagination, judgment, deliberation, and strength of character in relation to universal laws of association. Mill conceives of the development of autonomy in terms of three stages of increasingly complex associations. First, as infants we develop 'the initiary stage of volition' in response to our rudimentary inclinations to increase sensations of pleasure and diminish those of pain ('NTA,' 251, 215; 'BP,' 356). Later, we refine our volitional powers so that 'the will has power over the attention,' where 'attention' refers to our capacity to *reflect upon* our feelings and desires ('NTA,' 247, 213). As we gain the power to wilfully direct our attention toward desires, our volitions become the basis for voluntary action. We learn to fix our attention on thoughts that 'are not themselves so painful or pleasurable ... by a voluntary act' ('NTA,' 247). In this way we become less dependent on sensations of pleasure and pain as we learn to fix our attention on ends that are not 'sufficiently pleasurable to fix it spontaneously' ('NTA,' 247; L, 842). This process is characteristic of the capacity to delay gratification: we forgo immediate pleasures in order to achieve a more distant aim.

The third and most complex stage involves developing the strength of character to will a particular course of action, or life plan, independently of our more transient desires. This is the mark of deliberate and purposeful action. As Mill explains in *A System of Logic*, although the will is always determined by *motives*, 'we gradually ... come to desire the means without thinking of the end: the action itself becomes an object of desire' (L, 842). In other words, we learn to develop more deliberate 'habits of willing' that constitute *purposes* rather than mere desires.[3] The laws of association no longer operate directly in relation to sensations of pleasure and pain, since such purposes as the desires for self-formation and self-determination are basically second-order desires. That is, they are deliberate preferences for a certain order or priority among our various desires that require us to exercise our faculties of discrimination and judgment (see ch. 1, above).

This last developmental stage is essential for achieving the 'confirmed character' that is essential for autonomy. Mill explains, 'It is only when our purposes have become independent of the feelings of pain or pleasure from which they originally took their rise, that we are said to have a *confirmed character*' (L, 843, emphasis added; U, 238). Having a confirmed character is a necessary condition of mental freedom because, as Mill says in *On Liberty*, it is only the person of character 'whose desires and impulses are his own – are the expression of his own nature' (OL, 264). In short, only insofar as we develop 'confirmed characters' do we have desires, impulses, and purposes that are determined *by* us rather than *for* us. Only then are we fully capable of the freedom of 'pursuing our own good in our own way' (OL, 226).

Mill further argues that the cognitive capacities that comprise our powers as free agents are not limited to analytical reasoning. They also include our moral and aesthetic capacities, or what he calls the 'internal culture of the individual' (A, 147). Therefore, education for freedom must also cultivate these capacities. He addresses this point in his critical essay on Bentham with respect to the power of imagination. Imagination supports freedom of thought and action by enabling us to envision new possibilities of thought and to know ourselves. 'Without it,' Mill says, 'nobody knows even his own nature, further than circumstances have actually tried it and called it out' ('B,' 92; cf. 'SD,' 109–38). He describes imagination as 'the power by which one human being enters into the mind and circumstances of another,' and he adds that it 'constitutes the poet, in so far as he does anything but melodiously utter his own feelings' ('B,' 92; 'TPV,' 79–82). Insofar as imagination is essential to know our 'own nature,' it is also, by implication, a necessary condition of the freedom to pursue our own good in our own way.

Mill's effort to explain the development of all these cognitive capacities within the contours of association psychology highlights the lingering tensions in his view of freedom and determinism (see ch. 1). Since association psychology posits that differences in people's characters and cognitive capacities are due to differences in their experiences, it seems to conflict with his contention in *On Liberty* that 'different persons require different conditions for their spiritual development; and can no more exist healthily in the same moral, than all the variety of plants can in the same physical, atmosphere and climate' (OL, 270). There are three interrelated aspects of this problem concerning human individuality, diversity, and freedom: whether or not human beings have any core characteristics of individuality or difference; what the moral and philosophical grounds are for fostering individuality; and whether or not there are any active powers of the mind that are irreducible to laws of association. If people *acquire* distinctive characters, identities, and cognitive abilities only through different experiences and associations, then their *need* of different conditions for their development is merely an artifact of their having been individuated by their life experiences. Consequently, the grounds for Mill's insistence on 'the full freedom of human nature to expand itself in innumerable and conflicting directions' (A, 259) would be obscure. For instance, if one type of character could be shown to be the *best* for people, then there would be a utilitarian rationale for arranging social institutions and practices to cultivate this ideal type of character in all persons.[4] Likewise, if the *self* is nothing more than a cipher filled with received thoughts and desires, then its status as the subject of *self-determination* is unclear.

Mill ponders this challenge to association psychology in 'Bain's Psychology.' He says that 'the great problem' of associationism is determining 'how much of the apparent variety of the mental phenomena it is capable of explaining; what ultimate elements of the mind remain, when all are subtracted, the formation of which can in this way be accounted for' ('BP,' 347–8). He never provides a sustained defence of his associationist view of the mind and self against such criticisms, but he does provide some intimations of a defensible view. One source of difficulty is that he oscillates between 'phenomenalist' and 'realist' accounts of the nature of mind and the self (Anschutz, 1953; Britton, 1989; Quinton, 1989; Ruben, 1989). At times he defends the phenomenalist view that all we can know of things, including our own minds, is based on our perceptions of them. In this vein he construes the mind as merely the 'Permanent Possibility' of our various states of thinking and feeling (EHP, 189; cf. 'TI,' 444). Yet Mill also conceives of 'the Mind, or Ego,' as the locus of personal identity, or the self; and he conceives the latter in terms of our awareness of ourselves as distinct beings. The self is 'the thread of consciousness which composes the mind's phaenomenal life, [and which] consists not only of present sensations, but likewise ... of memories and expectations ... [It is] a series of feelings which is aware of itself as past and future' (EHP, 194; cf. 'NTA,' 211–13). As Mill acknowledges, however, these considerations pose a problem for a phenomenalist account of the mind and the self. Conceiving of the mind as having this capacity for self-awareness leaves us with 'the alternative of believing that the Mind, or Ego, is something different from a series of feelings, or possibilities of them, or of accepting the paradox, that something which *ex hypothesis* is but a series of feelings can be aware of itself as a series' (EHP, 194).

Therefore, Mill moves toward a realist view of the mind as an active entity and a core component of the self that *organizes* sensations through associations, inferences, deductions, and theories (Ryan, 1974, 226; 1990; Loesberg, 1986; Carlisle, 1991). According to this view, mental phenomena such as imagination and deliberation are manifestations of underlying causal powers or properties of the mind (Anschutz, 1953, 120). Mill comes close to adopting a realist view in 'Nature.' After declaring that human virtues are acquired rather than innate, he adds 'that there is hardly anything valuable in the natural [that is, unsocialized] man except capacities – a whole world of possibilities, all of them dependent upon eminently artificial discipline for being realized' ('N,' 393). He goes a step further in 'Bain's Psychology' in response to the charge that association psychologists lack 'recognition of any active element ... in the mind itself' ('BP,' 354). He acknowledges that insofar as associationism focuses on 'sensation, and the memory of sensations,' it highlights 'passive phenomena' through which the mind 'does not act, but is acted upon.' He contends, though, that the mind 'is active as well as passive'; and he adds, 'Activity cannot possibly be generated from passive elements; a primitive element must be found somewhere' ('BP,' 354). Mill seems to regard this active capacity as an 'ultimate' element of the mind that cannot itself be accounted for by laws of association ('BP,' 348–51). He never develops this point, but he does say that this active element is fundamental to our powers of voluntary action ('BP,' 354–6; 'NTA,' 215).

In adopting this quasi-realist perspective, Mill suggests a way to reconcile 'universal laws of human nature' with his celebration of human 'diversities' and free agency ('TPV,' 81). The pre-socialized mind, in his view, lacks desires, purposes, beliefs, 'moral feelings,' and a social identity – including a distinct gender identity – since these aspects of personal identity are learned. At the same time, the mind constitutes an active locus of selfhood and of each person's potentialities for reasoning, imagination, deliberation, judgment, choice, and self-control – the 'mental powers' constitutive of autonomy (OL, 262–3; Robson, 1976, 150). Here, Mill is offering some intimations of an interactive view of the self according to which our mature selves are formed through our interactions with others.

In addition, Mill refines his account of individual differences by augmenting association psychology with physiology. This enables him to highlight both differences in experiences and divergent effects of similar experiences among different people. He explains in the *Logic* that among human beings 'differences in education and in outward circumstances are capable of affording an adequate explanation of by far the greatest portion of [differences in] character; and ... the remainder may be in great part accounted for by physical differences in the sensations produced in different individuals by the same external or internal cause' (L, 859; cf. 'TVP,' 81). He also notes the role of instincts in explaining character, while emphasizing that instincts can be modified significantly 'by other mental influences, and by education' (L, 859).

Mill draws out the implications of these refinements to his view of human diversity in the course of examining our capacities for genius and imagination. Genius, he contends, is less the capacity to discover 'new truths' than the originality of insight to arrive at 'truths' through one's own reason ('OG,' 334). More to the point, he declares that genius is 'no peculiar mental power, but only mental power possessed in peculiar degree ... By aid of suitable culture all might possess it, although in unequal degrees' ('OG,' 331, 334). Similarly, Mill says that the capacity for imagination is in some measure common to us all. We develop imagination as well as reasoning abilities when our educations exercise these powers: 'As the memory is trained by remembering, so is the reasoning power by reasoning; the imaginative by imagining; the analytic by analyzing; the inventive by finding out' ('OG,' 338). At the same time, he associates the power of imagination with a 'poetic nature,' and says that there are 'natural differences' in people's mental predispositions and susceptibilities, such as 'the vigour of their intellectual powers' and whether or not they possess poetic natures ('TPV,' 67, 79–82).[5] In brief, virtually all people have some potential for genius and imagination, but not equal potential.

Taken together, Mill's arguments support his claim that there is a natural tendency for 'human nature to expand itself in innumerable and conflicting directions' (A, 259). The existence of 'universal laws' of association entails that as long as people have different experiences they will inevitably have at least somewhat different characters and desires. Individual differences may well be largely the product of different experiences; nonetheless they are real differences. Yet Mill also notes the subtle contribution that physiological differences make among people.[6] In this light, he provides sufficient grounds for concluding that if each person has opportunities to develop his or her mental freedom and individuality, he or she will do so in distinctive ways according to his or her 'own notions of the individual good' ('N,' 395).

There is, however, a related difficulty in Mill's view of the development of free agents. He ultimately *does* posit an ideal type of character as a condition of being a fully free agent. He contends that an autonomous, reflective character is uniquely conducive not only to appreciating such 'higher pleasures' as freedom, but also for exercising the freedom 'to use and interpret [human] experience' in our own way (OL, 262). Therefore, he maintains that fostering this kind of character should be the aim of education for freedom. As I explained in Chapter 1, Mill's view of the relationship between free agency and rational conduct smuggles a particular conception of the good life into the criteria of what it means to be free. Moreover, this 'perfectionist' aspect of his thought introduces a certain degree of narrowness into his view of education for freedom that fits uneasily with his liberalism (Gray, 1996, 142–5; cf. Cowling, 1975; Parekh, 1994). That being said, *any* such theory of education for freedom will inevitably privilege some account of civic virtues, so we should not discount Mill's view outright (Parry, 1994). In addition, as I will explain later, Mill addresses this problem with respect to the danger of sectarian formal education with considerable subtlety.

II The 'Science' of Ethology and the 'Art' of Education

Mill proposes 'Ethology,' or the 'Science of the Formation of Character,' as a tool to provide systematic knowledge about how desired kinds of characters and capacities are produced by particular forms of education, in relation to the 'laws of the mind' (L, 869). He regards it as the science that corresponds to the 'art' of education. He explains hopefully that 'when Ethology shall be thus prepared, practical education will be the mere transformation of those principles into a parallel system of precepts' (L, 874). He insists that even though it is unavoidably an 'imperfect' science, it promises significant practical insight into the general *tendencies* concerning how different circumstances produce different kinds of character (L, 869–70; see ch. 2, above).

Unfortunately, Mill gives no examples of substantial ethological laws when he explains ethology. He offers a few examples of the kind of hypothetical propositions that he expects ethological laws to be, but they hardly establish ethology as a full-fledged science: 'It is a scientific proposition, that bodily strength tends to make men courageous; not that it always makes them so: that an interest on one side of a question tends to bias the judgment; not that it invariably does so: that experience tends to give wisdom; not that such is always the effect' (L, 870). He does offers some propositions, however, that can be restated as ethological laws, and two of these are directly related to his goal of educating people for freedom. First, there is Mill's response to Rev. Henry William Carr's question about 'how to teach social science to the uneducated,' which I quoted earlier: 'What the poor as well as the rich require is not to be indoctrinated ..., but to be induced and enabled to think for themselves' (CW 14, 80). Second, he says in *Representative Government*, 'Whatever invigorates the faculties in however small a measure, creates an increased desire for their more unimpeded exercise: and a popular education is a failure, if it educates the people for any state but that which it will certainly induce them to desire, and most probably demand' (CRG, 243). These two remarks can be restated as 'ethological laws' concerning the education of people as free agents, as follows:

1 For people to develop mental freedom they must be encouraged to arrive at conclusions through their own reasoning, rather than merely be inculcated with received truths.
2 To the degree that the social relationships situating people exercise their cognitive faculties, they will tend to foster in them a continuing desire to exercise and develop their faculties; conversely, social relationships that fail to exercise people's faculties will tend to stifle their subsequent intellectual exertion.

As hypothetical propositions, these 'laws' do not entail that the desired results – autonomy, and a desire for intellectual growth – will *always* be achieved, but rather that these outcomes will generally result from the specified causes unless they are counteracted by other causal factors (L, 898). Although Mill does not explicitly offer these two propositions as ethological laws, he gives them the status in his theory of education that he envisions for such laws: they serve as guiding precepts for organizing educative practices to foster people's capacities as free agents.

Drawing upon these precepts, Mill conceives of the educational conditions of freedom as encompassing both formal education, or schooling, and what he refers to in his 1867 inaugural address at St. Andrews as education 'in its largest acceptation.' The latter includes 'even the indirect effects produced on the character and on the human faculties, by things of which the direct purposes are quite different; by laws, by the forms of government, by the industrial arts, by modes of social life'; it consists of 'whatever helps to shape the human being – to make the individual what he is, or hinder him from being what he is not' ('IA,' 217). Mill uses the phrase 'educate ... for freedom' in passing in an illuminating passage in *On Liberty*. While discussing a proposal to restrict the sale of 'stimulants,' he supports a policy of licensing sellers. He says, however, that limiting the number of beer and spirit houses to limit occasions for temptation among the labouring classes 'is suited only to a state of society in which the labouring classes are avowedly treated as children or savages, and placed under an education of restraint, to fit them for future admission to the privileges of freedom' (OL, 298–9). Then he adds, 'This is not the principle on which the labouring classes are professedly governed in any free country; and no person who sets due value on freedom will give his adhesion to their being so governed, unless after all efforts have been exhausted to educate them for freedom and govern them as free men, and it has been definitely proved that they can only be governed as children' (OL, 299).

For Mill, these remarks are a logical extension of his premise that virtually every human being has the potential for mental freedom and individuality. At the same time, his call to educate the labouring classes for freedom highlights his developmental view that people realize their capacities as free agents only through education that calls forth such capacity. As he explains in *Utilitarianism*, capacity for such 'nobler feelings' as the love of freedom and independence 'is in most natures a very tender plant, easily killed, not only by hostile influences, but mere want of sustenance' (U, 213). He goes on to say that the only thing standing in the way of 'almost all' people attaining the 'mental cultivation' to be fully free and self-governing is 'the present wretched education, and wretched social arrangements' (U, 215).

III The Powers of Education

a. Formal Education

Taken together, formal education, or schooling, and the educative effects of all the social relationships and practices situating people comprise what Mill calls 'all the powers of education' (OL, 282). Concerning formal education, he explains the vital role of 'elementary education' in *Principles of Political Economy*. 'There are certain primary elements and means of knowledge,' he says, 'which it is in the highest degree desirable that all human beings born into the community should be able to acquire during childhood' (PPE, 948). Then he adds: 'Instruction, when it really is such, does not enervate, but strengthens as well as enlarges the active faculties: in whatever manner acquired, its effect on the mind is favourable to the spirit of independence' (PPE, 949). In 'The Claims of Labour' Mill links a basic education directly to people's capacities for self-government and for knowing their own interests. He says that due to their lack of education, English working people are so deficient 'in the power of reasoning and calculation' that they are 'insensible to their own direct personal interests' ('CL,' 202). He goes on to contrast the English worker with the Scottish peasant who, due to strong parish schools, 'has been a reflecting, an observing, and therefore naturally a self-governing, a moral, and a successful human being – because he has been a reading and a discussing one' ('CL,' 203). Mill concludes that schooling is crucial for 'converting' English workers 'into rational beings – beings capable of foresight, accessible to reasons and motives addressed to their understanding; and therefore not governed by utterly senseless modes of feeling and action' ('CL,' 204). The gist of his argument is that primary education is crucial for cultivating mental freedom among all members of a community insofar as it calls forth and exercises their cognitive faculties.

Mill outlines his view of empowering instruction in two early articles in which he distinguishes instruction that merely fills students up with facts from instruction that teaches them to think for themselves. He explains in a review of Horace Grant's educational theories, 'One of these is the system of *cram*; the other is the system of cultivating mental *power*. One proposes to stuff a child's memory with the results which have been got at by other people; the other aims at qualifying its mind to get at results by its own observation, experience, and reflection' ('GA,' 786, Mill's emphasis).[7] Grant, he says, shows the value of an approach that seeks to bring 'reason into exercise from the very earliest' by giving children not only sounds to memorize, but also ideas that challenge them to use 'all [their] perceptive faculties, and [their] first nascent powers of judgment and reasoning' ('GA,' 787). Mill reiterates this argument in 'On Genius.' The chief limitation to most people achieving their potential for 'genius,' he contends, is their narrow educations. Modern schooling typically fails because it discourages young people from thinking of anything other than what they are told, or what is 'professed by other people'; it is 'all *cram*' as if the world already knows everything ('OG,' 337). As an alternative, he recommends the educational approach of the ancient Greeks and Romans, which

> consisted not in giving what is called knowledge, that is grinding down other men's ideas to a convenient size ... it was a series of exercises to form the thinking faculty itself, that the mind, being active and vigorous, might go forth and know ... With powers [of reasoning] thus formed, and no

possibility of parroting where there was scarcely anything to parrot, what a man knew was his own, got at by his own senses or his own reason; and every new acquisition strengthened the powers, by the exercise of which it had been gained. ('OG,' 335–6)

That is, schooling is an important means of cultivating people's capacities to think for themselves when it engages them as active participants in the learning process and exercises their capacities for reasoning and understanding.

With respect to educational policy, Mill's guiding principle is the same one as frames his broader theory of freedom. Social and political institutions should be arranged 'to secure to all persons complete independence and freedom of action, subject to no restriction but that of not doing injury to others' (PPE, 208–9). Education, he says, must not teach people 'to exchange the control of their own actions for any amount of comfort or affluence, or to renounce liberty for the sake of equality, [since this] would deprive them of one of the most elevated characteristics of human nature' (PPE, 209). As we have seen, Mill sees no simple trade-off between freedom and equality. Rather, he seeks to reconcile the two, and he regards education for mental freedom and moral responsibility as crucial means to achieve this end. The broad system of education should be organized to support the maximum freedom for each member of society within the limits marked by considerations of justice, equality, and general utility. The equal right to freedom implies an equal right of every person to an education – in both senses of the term – that fosters her or his capacities for autonomous action. Although Mill is not explicit on this point, he implicitly regards such an education as a right – that is, a matter of justice – since it is so integrally connected to the equal right to freedom and to the means of happiness more generally (U, 257–8). This requires not only that all members of society have roughly equal access to stimulating schooling, but also that they have the prospect of living and working within social and political relationships that exercise their mental powers. Moreover, it entails an obligation on the part of the state to promote the education of all members of society for freedom – in schooling and in broader educative practices – within the limits constituted by its other obligations. I will return to Mill's view of the narrower, economic aspects of educational policy when I consider his conception of economic freedom (see ch. 7).

With regard to the kind of formal education required, Mill emphasizes the value of a wide 'diversity of education.' He explains in *On Liberty*,

'All that has been said of the importance of individuality of character, and diversity of opinions and modes of conduct, involves, as of the same unspeakable importance, diversity of [formal] education' (OL, 302). It follows that the duty of the state to ensure that everyone has access to a good education must not lead to a state monopoly over the provision of education. A state monopoly would give government officials almost complete power to 'mould the opinions and sentiments of the people from youth upwards' and, in turn, the power – at least potentially – to 'do with them whatever it pleases' (PPE, 950). Mill himself, as I will explain later, is not completely consistent on the question of diversity, since his notion of mental freedom calls for a particular mode of secular and 'liberal' education (sec. III:C, below).

It is important to emphasize that Mill's concern for diversity does not preclude a dominant state role in providing education. As Amy Gutmann (1995) points out, it is not clear that a system of predominantly state-sponsored education is incompatible will diversity. The danger that state-supported schooling poses to diversity can be substantially mitigated with institutions that establish local, democratic accountability. More-over, a largely state-supported system is probably necessary to secure quality schooling for everyone. Conversely, any alternative to a largely state-sponsored system must be judged, at least in part, in light of Mill's goal of equality of educational opportunity (see ch. 7, sec. II:A). Still, a state monopoly over formal education would likely entail at least some notable limits to diversity.

Concerning the role of formal primary and secondary education in fostering freedom, then, Mill favours diversity in settings, approaches, and institutions. Moreover, given his emphasis on the educative value of self-government, one further implication of his theory is that schools will foster people's active powers most fully when they also encourage citizens to participate in their management and direction. Thus, Mill's theory lends support to efforts to involve students, parents, and teachers as active participants in schools – for example, through student councils and parent-teacher associations (Garforth, 1980, 185).

Finally, Mill addresses the contribution of higher education in cultivating freedom and civic responsibility. With respect to curriculum and teaching methods, he favours a classic model of 'liberal education,' including an emphasis on logic, mathematics, classics, languages, history, analytical psychology, and political economy ('IA,' 220). In his view, the purpose of a university education is not to teach people vocational skills, but rather to make them 'capable and cultivated human beings'

('IA,' 218). Higher education should cultivate people's faculties of reasoning, judgment, observation, and imagination, rather than training them to adopt particular conclusions ('IA'; 'WMP,' 452; 'Civ,' 196). These capacities are essential for people 'to judge between conflicting opinions which are offered to us as vital truths' and 'to form a rational conviction on great questions' of legislation and policy ('IA,' 234).

Mill's view of higher education still has considerable value, but it also has some notable limitations for contemporary democratic societies. The limitations stem largely from how he takes the élite English universities of the mid-nineteenth-century as his models. He looks to higher education to form the 'great minds' that can authoritatively instruct the broader democratic public on matters of legislation and policy ('Civ,' 195, 201). In principle, he favours opening higher education to all men and women who demonstrate an aptitude for it ('E,' 628), but he upholds a sharp dichotomy between liberal and vocational modes of education. As a result, his view would largely restrict traditional liberal education to economically advantaged members of society, while relegating most students to vocational training that prepares them to work under the control of others. The problem here is that in industrialized and 'postindustrial' societies, some form of higher education has become a prerequisite for desirable employment. Accordingly, colleges and universities are increasingly being pressed to promote vocational objectives at the expense of liberal education, and few postsecondary students now have the luxury of pursuing mental cultivation without any vocational orientation. At the same time, a vocational emphasis need not preclude attention to the aims and values of liberal education, and a classical curriculum of the sort Mill favours is not indispensable to his broader goal of engaging people's active faculties (Garforth, 1980, 174–5, 188–9).

Mill's more lasting contribution here lies in his abiding emphasis on cultivating people's capacities for reasoning, judgment, and imagination. He maintains that the mental cultivation necessary for people to pursue reflectively their own life plans and to be responsible democratic citizens can be made 'the inheritance of every person in the nation' (COS, 746). This broader ideal of education for freedom implicitly challenges the kind of educational 'tracking' systems that relegate many members of modern societies to vocational 'tracks' that lack meaningful engagement with 'great questions' of legislation and ways of life. At the same time, affirming the desirability of extending *this aspect* of liberal education to all citizens does not require that all citizens obtain a traditional postsecondary liberal education. What it does require is that, as much as possible, all citizens be engaged sufficiently during their formal education with teaching and curriculum that call forth their faculties of reasoning, judgment, deliberation, and imagination. This means that economic, political, and cultural pressures that promote vocational relevance in schooling must not be permitted to displace entirely the liberal education objective, which is to teach students to think critically and imaginatively.

b. Education in the 'Larger Sense'

Regarding education in the 'larger sense,' throughout his writings Mill highlights the educative effects of social and political relationships and institutions on the formation of character. 'Whatever can be learnt in schools is important,' he says, 'but not all important. The main branch of the education of human beings is their habitual employment, which must be either their individual vocation, or some matter of general concern, in which they are called to take part' ('TDA[II],' 169). Based on this premise, he contends that both types of education are indispensable to human development. Education in the narrower sense does little for the development of people's capacities when it is not complemented by education in the larger sense. As he explains in 'The Claims of Labour,'

> when education, in ... its narrow sense, has done its best, and even to enable it to do its best, an education of another sort is required, such as schools cannot give. What is taught to a child at school will be of little effect, if the circumstances which surround the grown man or woman contradict the lesson. We may cultivate his understanding, but what if he cannot employ it without becoming discontented with his position, and disaffected to the whole order of things in which he is cast? Society educates the poor, for good or for ill, by its conduct to them, even more than by direct teaching. ('CL,' 204)

In other words, while formal instruction is a necessary condition of mental freedom, it is not a sufficient one. An education that empowers individuals to act as 'rational beings' (PPE, 763; OL, 282), capable of effective self-determination, must encompass both formal and informal forms of education.

In this regard, Mill finds parallels to the 'cram' mode of education in virtually all modern social relationships and institutions. Just as the 'system of cram' in schooling stifles people's mental freedom and autonomy, these powers are likewise dulled when they are treated as passive or dependent beings within other educative social relationships. He describes this process in 'On Genius' as follows: 'When he leaves school, does not everything which a young person sees or hears conspire to tell him, that it is not expected he shall think, but only that he shall profess no opinion on any subject different from that professed by other people?' (OG, 337). This pressure to 'go along' is found in such relationships of command and obedience as the subjection of women by men, of labourers by employers, and of all persons who live under despotic governments. It is also present, he says, whenever individuals let others choose their life plans for them, since such persons have need of no 'other faculty than the ape-like one of imitation' (OL, 262).

Mill develops his view of freedom-nourishing modes of informal education in opposition to such constricting modes. In the latter, the conduct of some persons is dictated by the will of others, and the subordinates are forced into routines that stifle their tendencies toward spontaneity and originality. Typically, such paternalism is rationalized by the claim that some adults, like young children, are unable to govern themselves, so their conduct must be regulated for them. Yet this directly limits the freedom of self-government of those so regulated; it also restricts their opportunities to develop their capacities for free agency by assuming the responsibility for their choices and actions. As Mill says in *Representative Government*, 'Between subjection to the will of others, and the virtues of self-help and self-government, there is a natural incompatibility' (CRG, 410).

Mill sets out the negative side of his argument through a critical analysis of the existing paternalistic organization of economic enterprises. He contends that the hierarchical structure of capitalist firms stifles the development of working people's capacities for self-dependence and self-government:

It is by discussion that the manual labourer, whose employment is a routine, and whose way of life brings him into contact with no variety of impressions, circumstances, or ideas, is taught that remote causes, and events which take place far off, have a most sensible effect on their personal interests; and it is from political discussions, and collective political action, that one whose daily occupations concentrate all his interests in a small circle around himself, learns to feel and with his fellow citizens. (CRG, 469)

He extends this analysis in *Principles of Political Economy* to challenge the prevailing theory that the work lives of labourers 'should be regulated *for* them, not *by* them' (PPE, 759, Mill's emphasis). According to this theory, working people 'should not be required or encouraged to think for themselves, or give to their own reflection or forecast an influential voice in the determination of their destiny' (PPE, 759). He explains, 'The rich should be in loco parentis to the poor, guiding and restraining them like children. Of spontaneous action on their part there should be no need. They should be called on for nothing but their day's work, and to be moral and religious' (PPE, 759). In Mill's view, this kind of routinized paternalism characterizes the largest part of the practical education of most labouring women and men. Employers exercise their faculties by managing their enterprises; the general run of labourers find little in their jobs that invigorates their faculties or broadens their understandings.

Mill further develops this line of argument through his analysis of the subjection of women. Labouring *men*, in his view, are at least able to exercise their faculties to some degree when they make decisions and wield authority within their families – authority that is generally denied to women (see ch. 6). Yet even men suffer under existing gender and family arrangements. Men who wield nearly exclusive power over their families learn the habits and sensibilities of despots rather than the 'virtues of freedom' (SW, 295). On the whole, the lessons taught within patriarchal families conflict with education for freedom in three respects. Women are taught 'the exaggerated self-abnegation which is the present artificial ideal of feminine character'; men are 'taught to worship their own will as such a grand thing that it is actually law for another rational being'; and children are 'school[ed] in despotism' rather than in freedom and equality (SW, 293–5). Under such unequal gender relations, neither women nor men learn the qualities of free agents who support the equal freedom of others. Mill argues that this patriarchal educational regime is particularly detrimental to the development of autonomy among women. 'The masters of women wanted more than simple obedience,' he says, 'and they turned the whole force of education to effect their purpose. All women are brought up from the very earliest years in the belief that their ideal of character is the very opposite to that of men; not self-will, and government by self-control, but submission, and yielding to the control of others' (SW, 271). That is, the prevailing education of women undermines their capacities for self-determination. They are *taught* that the desire for equal freedom and authority is unfeminine, and are inculcated with the 'feminine' virtue of living for others rather than for themselves.

Critical reflection upon these repressive aspects of existing social relationships enables Mill to envision freedom-supporting alternatives. Social and political institutions will tend to educate people for freedom, in his view, to the degree that they are organized to recognize all the people situated within them as potentially autonomous and to cultivate their capacities for autonomy. He summarizes this point in the *Principles*:

> It is ... of supreme importance that all classes of the community, down to the lowest, should have much to do for themselves; that great a demand should be made upon their intelligence and virtue as it is in any respect equal to; that the government should not only leave as far as possible to their own faculties the conduct of whatever concerns them alone, but should suffer them, or rather encourage them, to manage as many as possible of their joint concerns by voluntary co-operation; since this discussion and management of collective interests is the great school of that public spirit, and the great source of intelligence of public affairs, which are always regarded as the distinctive character of the public of free countries. (PPE, 944)

For instance, trade union and political organizing by labouring men and women around matters of collective interest tends 'to awaken [their] public spirit ... and to excite [their] thought and reflection' (PPE, 763–4). Likewise, while he regards prevailing gender relations within the family as 'a school of despotism,' he contends that the family can become a 'real school of the virtues of freedom' if it is 'justly constituted' on the basis of gender equality (SW, 294–5). He sees analogous benefits to be gained from a policy that leaves adult members of society completely free to do as they please in 'self-regarding' matters:

> The human faculties of perception, judgment, discriminative feeling, mental activity, and even moral preference are exercised only in making a choice ... The mental and moral, like the muscular powers, are improved only by being used ... He who chooses his plan for himself, employs all his faculties. He must use observation to see, reasoning and judgment to foresee, activity to gather material for decision, discrimination to decide, and ... firmness and self-control to hold to his deliberate decision. And these qualities he requires and exercises exactly in proportion as the part of

his conduct which he determines according to his own judgment and feeling is a large one. (OL, 262–3)

In short, people's capacities for autonomy are cultivated to the extent that they are empowered to direct the course of their own lives. He insists, moreover, in *Representative Government, Principles of Political Economy*, and *The Subjection of Women* that this educative effect is not limited to choices made by individuals acting alone; it also depends upon their opportunities to share in collective decisions.

For Mill, then, the prospect of educating all persons for freedom and self-dependence is intertwined with his goal of extending democratic self-government to politics, industry, and marital relations. Thus, rather than supporting a strict *laissez-faire* policy by the state with respect to the institutions of civil society (for example, schools, families, businesses), he encourages selective government regulation to enable people to share in 'manag[ing] as many as possible of their joint concerns' (PPE, 944). Specifically, the state should support the principle of democratic self-government, along with the principle of individual liberty.

c. Authority, Discipline, and Self-discipline

Mill is optimistic regarding the *possibilities* for liberating social change; but there is also a more measured and conservative side to his view of education for freedom. Mill says in 'Coleridge' that the character of the national education is 'at once the principle cause of [a society's] permanence as a society, and the chief source of its progressiveness: the former by the extent to which that education operated as a system of restraining discipline; the latter by the degree in which it called forth and invigorated the active faculties' ('C,' 140; cf. 'Civ,' 198). He defends unrestricted freedom for individuals to pursue their own good in their own way within the limits imposed by their duties to others, including 'the freest scope possible to uncustomary things' (OL, 226, 269). But at the same time, he emphasizes that people require self-discipline if they are to exercise freedom in a way that is compatible the rights and interests of others. As he says in an early article, 'By properly regulating his actions, a man becomes a blessing to his species' ('PL,' 323). He contends that establishing a free society requires a broad system of education that instils a 'restraining discipline' among its members. Thus, moral restraint must be cultivated in order to secure voluntary submission to legal and moral obligations while sustaining the 'vigour and manliness of character' essential for free action. Mill explains,

> There has existed, for all who are accounted as citizens, – for all who were not slaves, kept down by brute force, – a system of *education*, beginning with infancy and continued through life, of which, whatever else it might include, one main ingredient was *restraining discipline*. To train the human being in the habit, and thence the power, of subordinating his personal impulses and aims, to what were considered the ends of society; of adhering, against all temptation, to the course of conduct which those ends prescribed ... this was the purpose, to which every outward motive that the authority directing the system could command. ('C,' 133, Mill's emphasis)[8]

Such a restraining discipline is important not only to instil in people a 'confirmed will to do right,' but also to enable them to subordinate their fleeting impulses and temptations to their more considered aims and purposes ('N,' 395; OL, 261).

Mill's view of 'restraining discipline' is rooted in his conviction that a 'will to do right' is a learned trait rather than a 'natural' or intuitive one (U, 238–9). In short, we have to be taught to be moral. We develop distinctly *moral* feelings only insofar as we are disciplined from childhood to differentiate between 'right' and 'wrong,' and 'moral' and 'immoral.' He maintains that we learn to distinguish between what is a duty or moral obligation and 'what we merely regard as useful,' along with what gives the former feeling its distinctive strength and urgency, by associating certain kinds of conduct with the idea of punishment ('NTA,' 241):

> From our earliest childhood, the idea of doing wrong (that is, of doing what is forbidden, or what is injurious to others) and the idea of punishment are presented to our mind together, and the intense character of the impressions causes the association between them to attain the highest degree of closeness ... In most cases the reason [for the judgment] has never, in our early education, been presented to the mind. The only ideas presented have been those of wrong and punishment, and inseparable association has been created between these directly, without the help of an intervening idea. (EHP, 463; cf. 'NTA,' 241–2; U, 218, 238–9)

In other words, learning what kinds of conduct merit punishment is crucial to developing moral feelings. Mill contends, moreover, that punishment plays a special role in teaching people to fulfil their moral obligations *even when* this conflicts with their more immediate desires: 'Punishment can alone produce the associations which make the conduct that incurs it, ultimately hateful in itself, and which by rendering that which is injurious to society, sincerely distasteful to its members, produces the fellowship of feeling which gives them a sense of common interest' (EHP, 458–9n).

In this light, he insists that the virtue of self-control must also be cultivated. He says in 'Nature' that even 'the commonest self-control for one's own benefit – that of sacrificing a present desire to a distant object or a general purpose which is indispensable for making the actions of the individual accord with his own notions of the individual good' – is an acquired virtue ('N,' 395). The extent to which this virtue is 'unnatural to the undisciplined human being ... may be seen by the long apprenticeship which children serve to it' ('N,' 395). In Mill's view, self-control differs from other virtues in the degree to which it is learned through personal experiences and, thus, 'self-taught'; but he insists that such 'self-culture' is largely a cultural artifact: 'Even those gifted organizations [that is, gifted individuals] which have attained the like excellence by self-culture, owe it essentially to the same cause; for what self-culture would be possible without aid from the general sentiment of mankind delivered through books, and from the contemplation of exalted characters real or ideal?' ('N,' 396).

These remarks highlight a significant tension in Mill's account of the relationship between educational discipline, freedom, and moral responsibility. He is ambivalent about the educative value of received moral standards. He observes in *On Liberty*, for instance, that society has considerable 'powers of education' to bring its 'weaker members up to its ordinary standard of rational conduct': it 'has ... absolute power over them during all the early portion of their existence: it has ... the whole period of childhood and nonage in which to try whether it could make them capable of rational conduct in life' (OL, 282). This power also includes 'the ascendancy which the authority of received opinion always exercises over the minds who are least fitted to judge for themselves' (OL, 282; 'UR,' 411). Yet insofar as we learn our society's 'standard of rational conduct' – including our understandings of what is right and wrong, acceptable and unacceptable – from the authority of received opinions, we are vulnerable to the 'social tyranny' that Mill criticizes in *On Liberty* (OL, 219–20). In this regard, his 'restraining discipline' bears a discomforting resemblance to the 'disciplinary society' that concerned Michel Foucault: individuals may be left free to act upon their existing desires, but their desires and inclinations already reflect the cramped, 'normalizing' effects of internalized cultural norms, imposed through educative institutions.[9]

Mill broaches this problem in 'Utility of Religion.' After explaining that people are generally unaware of the degree to which their motivations are shaped by prevailing opinions and beliefs, he adds, 'Of course the public opinion for the most part enjoins the same things which are enjoined by the received social morality; that morality being, in truth, the summary of the conduct which each one of the multitude ... desires others should observe towards him' ('UR,' 410). From Mill's perspective, the danger is that the 'rules of conduct' that constitute the basis for a 'restraining discipline' may be rooted in nothing more than 'the likings and dislikings' of the majority, or of the most powerful portion of society (OL, 221–2).[10] He warns that given the current state of education, such unreflective acceptance of the authority of received opinions is the general tendency of 'ordinary minds.' Only persons 'of a better than ordinary mould' tend to develop the capacity to accept or reject received ideas based upon their own reasoning and judgment and, thus, *freely* ('UR,' 411; OL, 262–9). Most people tend to believe that they are justified in imposing their preferred rules of conduct on others, yet feel no obligation to justify their own actions with reasons (OL, 220–3; 'WMP,' 498–9). Consequently, prevailing 'rules of conduct' are likely to reflect the interests of the dominant group, culture, or class, or prevailing prejudices, rather than a 'fitting adjustment between individual independence and social control' (OL, 220–1).

Ultimately, Mill's view of these matters is more consistent and defensible than it first appears to be, though it is not without difficulties. His view of the proper role of education in teaching people to be morally responsible free agents parallels his useful distinction in *On Liberty* between legitimate and illegitimate rules of conduct: 'To be held to rigid rules of justice for the sake of others, develops the feelings and capacities which have the good of others for their object. But to be restrained in things not affecting their good, by their mere displeasure, develops nothing valuable' (OL, 266). Part of our education *necessarily* consists of being schooled in certain moral rules – for example, learning that some things are right and some things are wrong. Furthermore, any society that seeks to establish freedom for all must foster a 'restraining discipline' that leads its members to exercise their freedom in ways that are compatible with the rightful freedom of others (OL, 226).[11] Mill's goal, therefore, is to educate people to become free agents *with respect to* received moral doctrines. 'Moral doctrines,' he says, 'are no more to be received without evidence, nor to be sifted less carefully, than any other doctrines' ('SD,' 158; cf. 'WMP,' 452). Accordingly, teaching children some guiding moral rules and concepts – such as the meaning of 'right' and 'wrong,' 'just' and 'unjust' – is essential to enable them to discuss and debate moral issues and to make their own moral judgments as free agents.[12]

Still, Mill's approach to educating everyone to be morally responsible free agents has a deeper limitation – one that is rooted in his narrow conception of rationality. Although he maintains that virtually everyone can become a free and 'cultivated' agent if provided with suitable education, his standard of 'rational conduct,' as I noted earlier, is Eurocentric and unduly rationalistic.[13] The Eurocentric aspect of his view is evident in how he distinguishes between 'backward' and 'civilized' societies. Mill draws this distinction in a way that corresponds to his distinction between conclusions based on premises 'taken from authority' and those derived from 'reason' (OL, 251; see ch. 1, above). He holds that non-Western societies such as India are civilizationally 'immature' because they have not yet 'attained the capacity for being guided to their own improvement by conviction and persuasion' – a capacity that he regards a precondition for rational inquiry (OL, 224). Consequently, he offers an insufficient account of the diverse ways that people exercise rationality. For instance, he fails to grasp how some people with fundamental religious commitments employ their powers of critical reflection to work out the meaning and implications of their doctrines without questioning their fundamental beliefs (cf. Tully, 1989; Appiah, 1993, ch. 6).

Mill outlines the educational implications of his conception of rational conduct in the 1868 letter to Charles Friend that I cited in Chapter 1. Concerning the proper role of parents in teaching their children about religion, he writes,

> I do not think that there should be any *authoritative* teaching at all on such subjects. I think parents ought to point out to their children when the children begin to question them, or to make observations of their own, the various opinions on such subjects, and what the parents themselves think the most powerful reasons for and against. Then, if the parents show a strong feeling of the importance of truth and also of the difficulty of attaining it, it seems to me that young people's minds will be sufficiently prepared to regard popular opinion or the opinions of those about them

with respectful tolerance, and may be safely left to form definite conclusions in the course of mature life.[14]

Authoritative teaching in such matters encourages children to accept received doctrines uncritically. Consequently, it tends to limit people's freedom to 'use and interpret [human] experience' in their own way (OL, 262; see ch. 1, above).[15] Ideally, then, parents would teach their children to appreciate the variety of religious and moral perspectives so that they will be able to freely make their own informed judgments as adults. Thus, despite Mill's emphasis on diversity in formal education, his conceptions of reason and autonomy lead him strongly to favour a particular mode of secular education as uniquely suited to the fostering of freedom.[16]

As a matter of public policy, however, Mill took a more pluralistic stance. Most importantly, he supported the right of parents to determine the religious education of their children. For instance, in an 1846 article he defended the right of a Catholic mother, in a case of paternal intestacy, to determine the religious education of her children ('ORG,' 222–4). He took up the issue again in response to the government's 1870 Education Bill. He criticized the bill for proposing to teach 'the religion of a part [of the community] with funds raised by taxation from the whole'; it would have enabled clergy of the Church of England to educate children in England and Wales 'in their religion' at public expense ('EB[I],' 382). He went on to emphasize that those like himself who opposed state-supported religious teaching on grounds of freedom of conscience were not seeking 'to prohibit all schools except secular ones ...; all we demand is, that those who make use of the religious teaching shall pay for it themselves instead of taxing others.' As long as the latter used their own resources, he added, 'they are free to found schools of their own' ('EB[I],' 384–5). Such a position permits some parents and private schools to teach religion and morality *authoritatively* to children within the broader system of national education. Mill proposed to regulate this disunited approach to national education through a system of public examinations 'to make the universal acquisition ... of a certain minimum of general knowledge, virtually compulsory'; but he added that these examinations would not hinder the rising generation 'from being taught religion, if their parents chose, at the same schools where they were taught other things' (OL, 303).[17] In short, while he favoured a system of national education fostering thoroughgoing critical reflection as a basis for mental freedom and autonomy, he objected to *imposing* such an education on all children – at least in modern 'civilized' societies such as England.[18] Moreover, leaving the door open to authoritative forms of schooling supported another aspect of Mill's vision of education for freedom: diversity among educational institutions (OL, 302; 'E,' 617).

Finally, there is another, more ironic limitation of Mill's view of rationality. He seeks to overcome the rationalism of previous utilitarians, particularly Bentham and James Mill, with a more nuanced account of the human mind (see 'B,' 92ff). But he is not completely successful. As he says in his *Autobiography*, from the earlier utilitarians' neglect of 'the cultivation of feeling, naturally resulted, among other things, an undervaluing of poetry, and of Imagination generally, as an element of human nature' (A, 115). He attempts to improve upon the earlier doctrine by addressing 'all the more subtle workings both of the mind upon itself, and of the external things upon the mind,' in a way that encompasses the cultivation of feeling and imagination ('B,' 93). Nonetheless, the rationalist legacy of utilitarianism and association psychology is evident in his restrictive view of what autonomous and rational agents will tend to do or be. This position is closely related to his distinction between 'higher' and 'lower' pleasures. Mill starts with plausible though still debatable premises. He assumes, for instance, that autonomous agents will generally recognize that there are good reasons to abstain from certain types of conduct, such as unprovoked violence toward others; and he emphasizes that the capacity to forgo immediate gratification is crucial for people to pursue successfully their 'own notions of the individual good' ('N,' 395). At the same time, Mill wrongly insists that people with 'cultivated minds' will not only tend to favour 'higher pleasures' of the intellect over 'lower' pleasures of the body, but will also tend to forgo the 'bodily pleasures' of sensualists, as if these are mutually exclusive alternatives (see ch. 6, below). Thus, while he rightly aims to foster both free agency and moral responsibility, his disembodied notion of rational conduct leads him to leave too little latitude for nonrational and opaque aspects of the self. As a result, his view of education for freedom goes too far in seeking to suppress rather than accommodate the self's passions, emotions, and fantasies; and his view of imagination remains too rigidly analytical.

IV Equality versus Élitism

Mill's rationalist tendencies are closely related to a broader tension between the egalitarian and élitist aspects of his theory of education for freedom. He believes that virtually everyone has the potential for autonomy and self-government, but he is sceptical about the short-range prospects for most people *achieving* their potential given their day-to-day preoccupations. Moreover, while he offers a basically egalitarian view of human capabilities – he consistently warns against overemphasizing innateness and underestimating the role of circumstances – he also posits some inborn differences in people's cognitive potentials (Garforth, 1980, 218n32). For example, in 'Civilization,' he says that higher education should aim at 'forming great minds' with the 'greatest possible quantity of intellectual *power*, and ... the interests *love of truth*' ('Civ,' 195, 201, Mill's emphasis). He reiterates this theme in his address at St Andrews:

> It is not given to us all to discover great general truths that are a light to all men and to future generations; though with a better general education the number of those who could do so would be far greater than it is. But we all require the ability to judge between conflicting opinions which are offered to us as vital truths ... We all observe, and we all reason, and therefore, more or less successfully, we all ascertain truths: but most of us do it very ill, and could not get on at all were we not able to fall back on others who do it better. If we could not do it in any degree, we should be mere instruments in the hands of those who could. ('IA,' 234)

He further elaborates this emphasis on 'great minds' in *On Liberty* with regard to the value of originality and genius in democratizing societies:

> There is always need of persons not only to discover new truths, and to point out when what were once truths are no longer, but also to commence new practices, and set the example of more enlightened conduct, and better taste and sense in human life ... It is true that this benefit is not capable of being rendered by everyone alike ... Persons of genius, it is true, are, and are always likely to be, a small minority. (OL, 267; cf. L, 937)

He maintains that only a few people can develop the genius to discover new 'truths' and better practices. A class of such people is important both for arriving at rational convictions on 'extensive subjects' and for 'maintaining a victorious struggle with the debilitating influences of the age' ('Civ,' 200, 181–5).

At the same time, Mill says that genius flourishes only under suitable social conditions (OL, 267); and he insists that we all have sufficient capacity to 'ascertain truth' to share in self-government, though not necessarily on completely equal terms. Moreover, his argument in *On Liberty* about the prospects for individuality and intellectual vitality relies more on his assessment of 'debilitating influences' of democratizing societies than on any belief in innate differences. Thus, while Mill supports democratization, he warns that the eclipse of the sharp class distinctions of the past by more equal conditions of life threatens individuality and intelligent government. He elaborates this point in the course of affirming Wilhelm von Humboldt's view that 'freedom, and variety of situations' are the two necessary conditions of individual development:

> The second of these two conditions is in [England] every day diminishing. The circumstances which surround different classes and individuals, and shape their characters, are daily becoming more assimilated. Formerly, different ranks, different neighborhoods, different trades and professions, lived in what might be called different worlds; at present to a great degree in the same ... And the assimilation is still proceeding. All the political changes of the age promote it ... Every extension of education promotes it, because education brings people under the common influences, and gives them access to the general stock of facts and sentiments. Improvements in the means of communication promote it ... The increase of commerce and manufactures promotes it. (OL, 274–5)

In other words, the democratic levelling of social and political conditions tends to undermine the sociological basis for diversity of conduct and ideas. By empowering the masses, this trend threatens any diversity and eccentricity that the majority shuns.

Mill is not completely consistent, however, with respect to the negative conclusions that he draws from the tendencies 'towards a democratic constitution of society' (OL, 286). He says that nothing better than 'collective mediocrity ... [is] compatible ... with *the present low state of the human mind*' (OL, 286, 268–9, emphasis added). The last part of this remark qualifies his pessimism. It brings together the 'static' aspect of his political theory – that is, his assessment of the existing state of society – with the 'dynamic' aspect of his theory – his attention to the succession of social states and, thus, prospects for societal improvement (L, 917, 920, 924–5). Regarding these two tendencies, Mill seeks the kind of balance that he describes in *Representative Government* between 'the preservation of all kinds and amounts of good which already exist, and ... the increase of them' (CRG, 219). Overall, then, he wavers between pessimism and optimism concerning the prospects of educating all members of society for freedom. On the one hand, he says that with suitable education virtually everyone can develop more fully his or her capacities for reasoning and judgment (U, 215). On the other hand, he sees the widening reach of formal education as part of the 'assimilation' of social conditions that threatens individuality.

The internal tension in Mill's argument becomes clearer when we recall that he himself regards one kind of 'assimilation' of social conditions as a necessary condition for fostering mental freedom: an education that encourages people to think for themselves. In this light, he seems to be overstating if not misstating his case. As one early critic points out concerning the 'assimilation of social conditions' that worries Mill, rather than being 'a process fatal to the due development of individualities of character, ... [it] enlarged, the sphere of individual freedom' by making such freedom more widely available (Hutton, 1975 [1859], 124–5). Indeed, since Mill's time wider access to formal education in democratic societies has enabled proportionally more members of these societies to develop individuality of character and life plans. In this regard, it is important to remember that Mill is prescribing a policy *both* of 'giv[ing] the freest scope possible to uncustomary things' (OL, 269) – in order to foster diversity, individuality, and innovation – *and* of improving education, in both senses of the term, for everyone. Therefore, his warning in *On Liberty* and elsewhere regarding the 'mediocrity' of the masses is best read as a cautionary tale.

V Conclusion

Mill's understanding of education for freedom is pivotal to his theory of freedom: it is basic to the dynamic, developmental aspect of his theory of freedom and to his view of the interplay between freedom and power. His understanding of 'all the powers of education' is a key aspect of his broader view that power has both freedom-limiting and freedom-generating effects. Powers of education are *always* exercised over people, in a wide variety of ways. These powers tend to diminish mental freedom when they are exercised in ways that treat people as passive receivers of knowledge and commands rather than as active agents of understanding. Educative power tends to foster freedom when it is exercised in ways that engage people's capacities for reasoning, judgment, deliberation, imagination, and self-discipline. Accordingly, Mill conceives of education for freedom as intertwined with, and partly dependent on, the achievement of two of his primary political goals: achieving maximal

individual liberty; and democratizing key social and political relationships. The latter goal concerns not just the relationship between citizens
and the state, but also economic, gender, and marital relations. Mill's
aim is not to overthrow all forms of authority, but to prepare people for
more democratic authority relationships that are more compatible with
the equal freedom of all.

For societies that aim at such equal freedom, Mill's goal of educating
everyone for freedom is compelling. Nonetheless, his theory of education for freedom has two significant limitations. First, his faith in the
'unlimited possibility of improving the moral and intellectual condition
of mankind by education' (A, 111) is naïve. Even so, this does not detract
from his more measured educational aims. Second, his associationist
psychology is too one-dimensional to grasp all the complex factors at
play in the development of individual autonomy and heteronomy.[19]
From his perspective, it is relatively easy to comprehend – though not
necessarily *to establish* – the educative conditions that would enable virtually everyone to think for themselves. Yet despite his attention to the
'internal culture of the individual' (A, 147), his association psychology
cannot account adequately for such subtleties as how adult dispositions
are instilled by infantile dependency, and the impact of early education
in 'authoritative' religious beliefs and cultural traditions. Mill himself
astutely raises the latter issue in 'The Utility of Religion,' when he notes
that in almost all countries children are 'taught from their earliest years
some kind of religious belief' by their parents. He says that 'the impressions of this early education ... possess what is so much more difficult for
later convictions to obtain – command over the feelings' ('UR,' 408).
These 'first impressions' often exert a powerful hold even over people
'who have given up the opinions which they were first taught' ('UR,'
408). Still, Mill's association psychology cannot adequately explain the
role, in forming such deep impressions, of such things as childhood
dependency, bonds of affection and intimacy, and early struggles for
recognition and independence.[20]

This point has important implications when we come to evaluate Mill's
theory of education for freedom. His notions of psychology and ethology provide a useful account of *some* of the psychological and sociological dynamics at work in the development of mental freedom. He rightly
emphasizes how the faculties that comprise our capacities for mental
freedom and moral agency tend to be cultivated insofar as they are
called out and exercised. In this regard, he provides an instructive vision
of education that teaches people to think for themselves and to be
morally responsible. Nonetheless, a comprehensive account of educa-

tion for freedom must contend with a more intricate and opaque web of formative influences than Mill addresses.[21] It must grasp not only the role played by schools and other social and political institutions, including new mass media, but also the complex interplay between these institutions and the early education provided to children by parents, guardians, and other significant others – education that varies widely, sometimes with devastating effects.[22] To his credit, Mill is certainly aware that various 'powers of education' often have conflicting effects; but he only begins to confront the challenge of crafting national policies of education for freedom in light of how his liberalism wisely places many educative relationships beyond direct public control.

This difficulty is evident in Mill's effort to balance his commitment to individual autonomy with that of respecting religious and cultural pluralism. In light of his view that mental freedom is a necessary condition of full freedom, he proposes a few basic precepts to establish education for freedom: schools and other social institutions should be organized to foster autonomy; parents should teach their children nothing 'authoritative' in matters of religion and morality; and the state should 'require for every child a good education' (OL, 302). Yet he also supports considerable freedom for parents to determine the character of their children's education, including the power to determine the religious education of their children. There is considerable tension between these commitments, but it is not exclusive to Mill's liberalism. The same tension is present in two educational goals that are still widely embraced by liberal thinkers: teaching liberal values of intellectual freedom, critical thinking, and tolerance for diverse ways of life; and leaving individual families and diverse religious and cultural communities, including *nonliberal* families and communities, free to practise and pass on their own distinct beliefs and values (cf. Stolzenberg, 1993; Gutmann, 1995; Macedo, 1995).

In the end, one of the merits of Mill's approach to political theory is that it can accommodate some of these difficulties. He holds that as a general rule, educative institutions and practices can be organized to foster mental freedom; but he also recognizes that they cannot produce mental freedom in everyone equally and without exception. He says that even though we cannot expect complete predictability and control in the human sciences, a mature science of ethology would provide guiding precepts for practical education. These precepts cannot surmount all the contingencies of human existence, but they can clarify the general tendencies concerning how different circumstances produce different kinds of character (L, 869–70). On this score, Mill's theory of education for freedom largely succeeds.

5

The Principle of Liberty

If I go to church on Sunday,
and Cabaret all day Monday,
It ain't nobody's business if I do ...
Ain't nothing I can do, or nothing I can say,
that folks won't criticize me,
but I'm gonna do just what I want to anyway.

Porter Granger and Everett Robbins, 'Ain't Nobody's Business (If I Do)'

Can ... the judgment of society sanction every invasion of a man's privacy, however extreme? Theoretically that must be so ... Society must be the judge of what is necessary to its own integrity if only because there is no other tribunal to which the question can be submitted.

Lord Patrick Devlin, *The Enforcement of Morals* (1965)

There is a limit to the legitimate interference of collective opinion with individual independence: and to find that limit; and maintain it against encroachment, is as indispensable to the good condition of human affairs, as protection against political despotism.

John Stuart Mill, *On Liberty* (1859)

Mill's principle of liberty is the best-known component of his theory of freedom. Building upon his conception of freedom and his theories of individual development, social power, and societal development, he presents it as 'one very simple principle' for determining 'the nature and limits of power which can be legitimately exercised by society over the individual' (OL, 223, 217). The principle, in short, is that members of a society can rightfully interfere 'with the liberty of action of any of their number,' individually or collectively, whether through the force of law 'or the moral coercion of public opinion,' only to prevent 'harm to others' (OL, 223–4). The liberty principle is not quite so 'simple,' however. Actually, it is a sophisticated response to the threat to individual freedom posed by two forms of power in modern, democratizing societies: legal interference, and 'the moral coercion of public opinion' (OL, 223). The subtlety with which Mill employs the principle is evident in two ways. First, Mill provides different criteria to justify legal penalties and the coercion power of public opinion, respectively. Second, Mill gives the principle of liberty a relatively straightforward role in limiting coercive uses of political power and the power of public opinion; but he does not cast it as in direct opposition to either political power or the power of public opinion *per se*.

With respect to the power of public opinion, it is important to recall Mill's view that the powers of education and opinion are always present in societies but are not always repressive. Thus, the principle of liberty seeks not to limit the powers of education and opinion in general, but rather to limit only *coercive aspects* of the powers of education and opinion. Similarly, Mill seeks to limit the reach of political power and legal penalties regarding the freedom of individuals, but he does not see a simple opposition between political power and individual liberty. Instead, he ultimately reserves to politics, and thus to the political freedom of citizens, a key role in defining the proper bounds of individual liberty and political authority. In his view, it is a political task to determine those interests of individuals that are so vital that they 'ought to be considered as rights' (OL, 276).

Overall, Mill offers the principle of liberty as a precept for citizens in democratic societies to secure for one other the widest individual liberty that is compatible with the same freedom for all. It does not provide us with definitive and noncontroversial guidelines, but it does offer a persuasive framework for determining the rightful limits to individual liberty. It helps us identify the kinds of considerations that justify restrictions of the freedom of individuals to pursue their own good in their own way in modern democratic societies that are characterized by a plurality of often conflicting moral doctrines and conceptions of the good. To fully appreciate the merits and limitations of the principle of liberty, however, we need to understand how Mill develops it in light of his support for representative democracy as a means of securing popular political freedom; his utilitarian moral theory, with which he articulates his notions of moral obligations, justice, and rights; his pluralistic view of the good – particularly as it relates to his emphasis on happiness, autonomy, and individuality; and his view of the powers of education and opinion.

I Individual Liberty and Modern Democracy

Mill's defence of individual liberty goes hand in hand with his commitment to his principle of democratic self-government, particularly as it applies to democratic politics. Thus, when he turns in *On Liberty* to the task of protecting individual liberty against burdensome social and political interference in modern democratic societies, he is far from diminishing the importance of political freedom. In fact, he says in *Representative Government*, his chief work on democratic politics, that the political freedom 'of being governed only by laws assented to by ... elected representatives' is 'the most important liberty of the nation' (CRG, 432). He says in *On Liberty* that the authority of rulers originally derived 'from inheritance or conquest' rather than from 'the pleasure of the governed.' He maintains, though, that this authority was vital to secure order and to prevent 'the weaker members of the community from being preyed upon by innumerable vultures' (OL, 217). Eventually, he adds, 'patriots' saw the need to 'set limits to the power which the ruler should be suffered to exercise over the community; and this limitation was what they meant by liberty' (OL, 217–18). Political authority, then, has a fundamentally equivocal character: it is necessary for order and security and to protect weaker members of the community, but it gives rulers potentially repressive power.

Mill notes that some European liberals presumed that the development of political democracy would resolve this dilemma. With democracy the people no longer had to look upon 'their governors ... [as] an independent power, opposed in interests to themselves ... What was now wanted was, that the ... interest and will [of the rulers] should be the interest and will of the people. The nation did not need to be protected against its own will' (OL, 218). The hope was that government by the people themselves would reconcile liberty and authority. Mill strongly supports the establishment of representative democracy to extend political freedom to all citizens in modern 'civilized' societies (CRG, ch. 3). Yet he also points out that democratic government by no means eliminates the tension between 'liberty and authority.' One problem, he says, is that such phrases as 'self-government,' and 'the power of the people over themselves,' do not express the true state of the case. The 'people' who exercise the power are not always the same people with those over whom it is exercised; and the 'self-government' spoken of is not the government of each by himself, but that of each by the rest. The will of the people, moreover, practically means the will of the most numerous or the most active part of the people; the majority, or those who succeed in making themselves accepted as the majority; the people, consequently, may desire to oppress a part of their number; and precautions are as such much needed against this as any other abuse of power. (OL, 218)

That is, under democratic government the people who succeed in transforming their will into collectively binding laws and policies are rarely identical with the whole community. It follows that some portion of the community is inevitably subject to laws and policies that reflect the will of others.

Democratic government, however, is not the problem, according to Mill. Political communities must be governed by some rules of conduct, and he regards democratic governments as preferable to undemocratic governments, at least in 'civilized' societies. In the same breath, he maintains that democratic government and a democratic basis for prevailing opinion are not panaceas. The relevant questions are not just *who* should make the law and establish authoritative opinion, but also 'where to place the limit – how to make the fitting adjustment between individual independence and social control' (OL, 220). In this regard, democratic government, like any form of government, undermines individual liberty when it resorts to the force of law to regulate the conduct of individuals *in matters that do not rightfully concern the broader community*. The danger in a democracy is that general rules of conduct and laws will be based on nothing more principled than 'the feeling in each person's mind that everyone should be required to act as he, or those with whom he sympathizes, would like them to act' (OL, 221).

In addition, Mill explains that political tyranny – 'tyrannizing' that operates through 'the hands of political functionaries' (OL, 219–20) – is not the only threat to individual liberty in modern democratic societies. The increasingly pervasive role of the power of 'public opinion' poses a new danger: the prospect of a 'social tyranny' that operates outside of political and legal channels.[1] Mill explains, 'Society can and does issue its own mandates: and if it issues wrong mandates instead of right, or any mandates at all in things with which it ought not to meddle, it practices a social tyranny more formidable than many kinds of political oppression, since, though not usually upheld by such extreme penalties, it leaves fewer means of escape, penetrating much more deeply into the details of life, and enslaving the soul itself' (OL, 220). In other words, society imposes rules of conduct on individuals independently of the force of law through 'the moral coercion' of public opinion. Mill explains that public opinion can limit individual freedom in two ways: by establishing a 'hostile ... censorship' – for example, through widespread attitudes of scorn, castigation, or condemnation – that leads people to renounce or relinquish their own desires and life plans; and by exercising a deeper, more covert power over what people think so that 'they exercise choice only among things commonly done' (OL, 265). He maintains, therefore, that individual liberty needs to be guarded not only against the potential tyranny of public authorities, but also 'against the tyranny of prevailing opinion and feeling; against the tendency of society to impose, by other means than civil penalties, its own ideas and practices as rules of conduct on those who dissent from them; to fetter the development, and, if possible, prevent the formation, of any individuality not in harmony of its ways' (OL, 220).

The principle of liberty is one of Mill's answers to these dangers, along with education for freedom and a properly constituted democratic state. It addresses what Mill sees as the absence of any principled basis on which to 'place the limit' between individual freedom and the impera- tives of social control. He says of the prevailing situation, 'The likings and dislikings of society, or of some powerful portion of it, are ... the main thing which has practically determined the rules laid down for general observation' (OL, 222). That is, many people feel unrestrained in imposing their ideas of the good life – that is, their notions of propriety, taste, and morality – on others. Accordingly, Mill offers the principle of liberty as 'one very simple principle, as entitled to govern absolutely the dealings of society with the individual in the way of com- pulsion and control, whether the means used be physical force in the form of legal penalties, or the moral coercion of public opinion' (OL, 223). He recommends the liberty principle in part as a precept for balancing individual liberty with political freedom in modern demo- cratic societies. Basically, he intends it to serve as what in *Representative Government* he calls a maxim of 'positive political morality': an 'unwrit- ten' normative rule that ordinary citizens and public officials should use to guide their relations with other members of democratic societies (CRG, 422).[2]

Concerning the broader relationship between individual liberty and democratic politics, two further aspects of Mill's view need to be stressed from the start. First, not only does Mill support both individual liberty and political freedom, but he also ultimately reserves for democratic politics the task of determining the proper domains of individual liberty and 'of social morality, of duty to others' (OL, 283). I will return to this point later. Second, it is crucial to remember that Mill's principle of liberty relies on a logically distinct conception of freedom (see ch. 1). In contrast to his conception of freedom, his liberty principle is essentially a 'negative' principle of noninterference that prescribes, in G.W. Smith's words, 'an area within which individuals ought to be free' (Smith, 1984, 182). Therefore, although it is a necessary condition of individual liberty – the freedom 'of pursuing our own good in our own way, so long as we do not attempt to deprive others of theirs' (OL, 226) – it is not a sufficient condition for achieving it. As we have seen, Mill maintains that people are not made free by simply leaving them to do as they please regardless of their circumstances or of the genesis of their desires and purposes (see ch. 1). Thus, the principle of liberty is not – and is not intended by Mill to be – his complete response to the problem of securing individual liberty in the face of the 'moral coercion of public opinion.' Mill also emphasizes the need to educate people for freedom so that they can respond to prevailing opinion as autonomous or free agents.

II The Province of Individual Liberty

Mill outlines his principle of liberty as follows:

> The sole end for which mankind are warranted, individually or collectively, in interfering with the liberty of action of any of their number, is self-protection. That the only purpose for which power can be rightfully exercised over any member of a civilized community, against his will, is to prevent harm to others. His own good, either physical or moral, is not sufficient warrant. He cannot rightfully be compelled to do or forbear because it will be better for him to do so, because it will make him happier, because, in the opinions of others, to do so would be wise, or even right. (OL, 223–4)

The notion of 'harm to others' is pivotal to Mill's distinction between the domain of 'self-regarding' conduct – that is, the province of individual liberty – and that of 'social morality, of duty to others' (OL, 282–3).

Concerning conduct that falls within the self-regarding category, Mill maintains that the freedom of action of individuals is 'of right, absolute' (OL, 224). In contrast, individuals are responsible to society for conduct that poses harm to others. Accordingly, society can rightfully restrain the freedom of action of individuals with regard to such conduct. Understanding his view of just what constitutes 'harm to others' is therefore crucial to understanding how he distinguishes the two domains of conduct.

Mill's notion of 'harm to others' is rooted in his view of the Art of Life and, in turn, his view of moral obligations (see ch. 2). He explains in *A System of Logic* that the task of conceiving of the ends of human conduct in general involves 'the Art of Life, in its three departments, Morality, Prudence or Policy, and Aesthetics; the Right, the Expedient, and the Beautiful or Noble, in human conduct and works' (L, 949). He regards the domain of morality, or duty to others, then, as just one department of a much broader category of human conduct. *Some* conduct raises distinctly moral considerations; much conduct, however, raises considerations of prudence or aesthetics, but does not involve moral obligations (Ryan, 1965, 1990). In this light, he contends that the rightful authority of society with respect to the conduct of individuals extends only to the domain of moral obligations properly construed.

Mill explains his view of moral obligations that underlies his notion of 'harm to others' in *Utilitarianism*. He says that the idea of 'penal sanction, which is the essence of law,' is basic not only to our conception of injustice, but also to our broader notion of moral wrong. We call something *wrong*, that is, only when 'we mean to imply that a person ought to be punished in some way or other for doing it – if not by law, by the opinion of his fellow creatures, by the reproaches of his conscience' (U, 240). Mill adds that our understanding of this distinction and our judgments regarding the appropriateness of punishment are the basis for the distinction between 'morality and simple expediency' – that is, between what ought to be done *as a matter of moral obligation* and what we would find merely useful, convenient, or desirable.[3] Duty or moral obligation, therefore, refers to something

> that a person may rightfully be compelled to fulfill ... Unless we think that it may be exacted from him, we do not call it his duty. Reasons of prudence, of the interests of other people, may militate against actually exacting it, but the person himself ... would not be entitled to complain. There are other things, on the contrary, which we wish that people should do, which

we like or admire them for doing, perhaps dislike or despise them for not doing, but yet admit that they are not bound to do; it is not a case of moral obligation. (U, 246)

Mill construes 'harm to others,' then, in terms of violations of our moral obligations or duties to others. Only conduct that poses 'a definite damage, or a definite risk of damage, either to an individual or to the public' *in this sense* properly falls within the domain of morality – or what he calls the domain of 'social morality' in *On Liberty* (OL, 283, 282). He says, therefore, that this is the only conduct of individuals regarding which society has a *direct* interest.[4] Conversely, he maintains that conduct that does not involve 'distinct and assignable' duties to others may be an appropriate subject for judgments about *prudence* or *aesthetics*, including praise or honour, but not for *moral* reproach (OL, 281). Such conduct constitutes the 'self-regarding' domain of individual liberty, which is the 'sphere of action in which society, as distinguished from the individual, has, if any, only an indirect interest' (OL, 225, 281).

For example, how I choose to dress is usually a matter of aesthetics. Whether or not I wear sufficiently warm clothes on a cold winter day raises considerations of prudence, but still not of moral obligations. Yet if I took a small child with me on a winter walk without properly dressing her for the cold, or if I wore shorts and a soiled T-shirt to a funeral, I would be crossing a line and violating a moral obligation – an obligation to care for the child in the first case, and one to show due respect for a grieving family in the second.

Mill also says that in certain circumstances conduct that is generally self-regarding can *become* a matter of moral obligation or duty. For instance, he says that drunkenness is not *by itself* a matter of social morality; individuals have no general duty to others not to be drunk. He adds, though, that 'a soldier or a policeman should be punished for being drunk on duty' (OL, 282). *This* conduct violates distinct duties to others so that it 'is taken out of the province of liberty, and placed in that of morality or law' (OL, 282). Today this point is commonly extended to people who drive cars while drunk. At the same time, Mill insists that conduct which merely offends or is a nuisance to others but which does not violate any distinct or assignable obligation to some other person or persons falls within the 'province of liberty.' In such cases, individuals should have 'perfect freedom, legal and social, to do the action and stand the consequences' (OL, 276).

According to Mill, then, the rightful domain of individual liberty consists of the broad domain of 'self-regarding' conduct that is of *direct* concern only to the individual agent herself because it is does not impinge upon any moral obligations or duties to others. This domain also encompasses some conduct by individuals that directly affects others – including conduct that is done jointly with others – but only when this involves 'their free, voluntary and undeceived consent' so that it respects their integrity as free agents (OL, 225). Mill delineates this 'appropriate region of human liberty' as follows:

> It comprises, first, the inward domain of consciousness; demanding liberty of conscience in the most comprehensive sense; liberty of thought and feeling; absolute freedom of opinion and sentiment on all subjects, practical or speculative, scientific, moral, or theological. The liberty of expressing and publishing opinions ... [since this is] almost of as much importance as the liberty of thought itself ... Secondly, the principle of liberty requires liberty of tastes and pursuits; of framing the plan of our life to suit our own character; of doing as we like, subject to such consequences as may follow: without impediment from our fellow-creatures, so long as what we do does not harm them, even though they should think our conduct foolish, perverse, or wrong. Thirdly, from this liberty of each individual, follows the liberty, within the same limits, of combination among individuals; freedom to unite, for any purpose not involving harm to others: the persons combining being supposed to be of full age, and not forced or deceived. (OL, 225–6)

These basic liberties are the substance of Mill's notion of individual liberty. Accordingly, the province of individual liberty encompasses a range of religious, spiritual, economic, artistic, recreational, personal, and economic activities, but not all such activities.

Concerning this last distinction, two further points are crucial for a complete picture of the domain of individual liberty. *First*, it does not correspond directly to common notions of 'personal' or 'private' spheres of life, such as family relationships and 'private property.' Some critics have argued that this is a shortcoming insofar as Mill does not adequately acknowledge the special character of *personal* relationships between people, such as marital relations and the relations between parents and children (cf. Chopra, 1994, 418). Yet this is actually one of the *strengths* of Mill's argument. He recognizes that while such personal relations often fall firmly within the province of individual liberty, they do not always do so. He points out that within such relationships one person (or persons) often exercises significant power over another (or others), and that such relations are often sites of domestic violence and abuse, and other less egregious violations of basic moral obligations – for example, by men against women, and by parents against children (OL, 301; SW, 287–9). Mill insists, therefore, that while the state must respect 'the liberty of each in what especially regards himself [or herself, it] is bound to maintain a vigilant control over his [or her] exercise of any power it allows him [or her] over others' (OL, 301).[5]

Second, as I explain in Chapter 7, Mill insists that the principle of liberty is distinct from the economic principle of *laissez-faire*, or government noninterference. In turn, he maintains that property rights are rightfully subject to collective regulation and alteration where this 'would be beneficial to the public' (COS, 753). Many economic activities of individuals and of combinations of individuals fall within the province of individual liberty, but not *all* economic activities. For instance, matters of trade and property ownership, being intrinsically social relationships, do not fall strictly within the protected domain of individual liberty (OL, 293; and see ch. 7).

III Individuality, Utility, and the Diversity of Goods

Given Mill's utilitarianism, it is important to understand his view of how the principle of liberty contributes to utility, or the greatest happiness, by fostering individual liberty and individuality. He recognizes that the freedom of 'pursuing our own good in our own way,' independent of any superior wisdom, expresses a distinctly modern view of the good life. He says in 'Guizot's Essays and Lectures on History,' for instance, that the 'modern spirit of liberty' consists of 'the love of individual independence; the claim for freedom of action, with as little interference as is compatible with necessities of society, from any authority other than the conscience of the individual' ('GEL,' 244–5). 'The whole mode of thought of the modern world,' he declares in *Representative Government*, 'is ... pronouncing against the claim of society to decide for individuals what they are and are not fit for, and what they shall and shall not attempt (CRG, 479).

Accordingly, Mill takes the 'modern conviction ... that things in which the individual is the person interested, never go right but as they are left to his [or her] discretion' as a basic premise of his argument that individual freedom is a basic element of well-being (SW, 273; CRG, 479; OL, ch. 3). In older European societies – and in many non-European societies still – authoritative knowledge concerning what is good for each member of the community was found in 'received doctrines' – generally religious in nature – and in the 'superior wisdom' of the authoritative interpreters of these doctrines ('SOA,' 290–5, 304–7; SW, 273). In modern Western societies, no one creed or doctrine enjoys such hegemony; yet religion remains a key source from which people draw their ideas of right and wrong and of the good. The proliferation of religions, religious denominations, and nontheistic philosophies has given rise to a plurality often conflicting moral doctrines and ideas of the good (OL, chs. 1 and 4; and 'SOA'). Mill points out that the struggle for religious liberty and freedom of conscience became the first great 'battle field' on which 'the rights of the individual against society have been asserted on broad grounds of principle' (OL, 222; cf. 'EB[I],' 385). The perils of religious conflict and persecution gradually produced increasing (if often grudging) support for religious toleration and freedom of conscience as general principles (OL, 222). These principles entail that individuals are not responsible to others in matters of religious conviction and conscience.

For Mill, these principles are vitally important, but they constitute only the starting point for a more complete defence of individual liberty. He maintains that the broader freedom 'of pursuing our own good in our own way,' within the limits necessary to protect the vital interests of others, is one of 'the principle ingredients of human happiness, and quite the chief ingredient of individual and social progress' (OL, 261). His utilitarianism appears to entail yet another comprehensive view of the human good, since he maintains that 'the greatest happiness principle' is 'the ultimate end of life ... with reference to and for the sake of which all other things are desirable – whether we are considering our own good or that of other people' (U, 214).[6] His appeal to utility, though, does not entail a comparable comprehensive doctrine of the good. Instead, he appeals to happiness as a general standard, since it is one thing that virtually all persons pursue, *despite* their differing religious and philosophical creeds and the different ways they seek happiness (U, 217; OL, ch. 3).[7] Moreover, he construes happiness as a complex or inclusive end that is achieved in different ways by different persons (Hoag, 1987). In short, a wide range of disparate activities and experiences contribute in different ways to the happiness of different persons.

Mill regards happiness itself as a complex good, and he considers some components, such as freedom, as so fundamental to happiness that they are themselves desired as *part of* that end. 'The ingredients of happiness are very various,' he says, 'and each of them is desirable in itself, and not merely when considered as swelling an aggregate ... They are desired and desirable in and for themselves; besides being means, they are part of the end' (U, 235; 'B'; cf. Hoag, 1987, 422–3). This is particularly evident, according to Mill, with respect to freedom and individuality, both of which he regards as means to happiness and as part of that end. They are instrumental to the capacity of persons to achieve happiness by 'framing the plan of our life to suit our own character' (OL, 226). Therefore, they are integrally related to that special 'sense of dignity' of human beings which corresponds to what he calls 'utility in the largest sense, grounded on the permanent interests of man as a progressive being' (U, 212; OL, 224).

Mill's view of happiness as a complex and inclusive end has two important implications for his principle of liberty. First, since people differ in their characters, abilities, needs, and tastes, they *require* 'a corresponding diversity in their modes of life' in order to 'grow up to the mental, moral, and aesthetic stature of which they are capable' and obtain their 'fair share of happiness' (OL 270; cf. OL, 261). He explains,

> If it were only that people have diversities of taste, that is reason enough for not attempting to shape them all after one model. But different persons all require different conditions for their spiritual development ... The same things which are helps to one person toward the cultivation of higher nature are hindrances to another. The same mode of life is a healthy excitement to one, keeping all his faculties of action and enjoyment in their best order, while to another it is a distracting burden, which suspends or crushes all internal life. (OL, 270)

Mill is somewhat vague about the extent to which differences in people's characters and impulses are ultimately due to nature or nurture (see ch. 4). Nonetheless, he insists that a person's character and impulses can be 'the expression of his [or her] own nature as it has been developed and modified by his [or her] own culture' (OL, 264). Accordingly, he contends, 'If a person possesses any tolerable amount of common sense and experience, his own mode of laying out his existence is the best, not because it is the best in itself, but because it is his own mode' (OL, 270). The mode of existence chosen by any competent adult may not be 'best' in any transcendent sense, but it will be the way of living most likely to bring that person happiness. This will be so, moreover, partly *because* the choice is an expression of the individual's freedom.

Mill is not claiming that competent individual agents never make mistakes regarding their 'own good.' Rather, each individual 'is the person most interested in his well-being: the interest which any other person, except in cases of strong personal attachment, can have in it, is trifling, compared with that he himself has; ... while, with respect to his own feelings and circumstances, the most ordinary man or woman has means of knowledge immeasurably surpassing those that can be possessed by any one else' (OL, 277). So once we reject the idea that any one mode of existence is best for everyone, we should recognize that each mature and competent individual is far better suited than anyone else to know what will promote her own well-being.

In light of these considerations, Mill emphasizes the costs of permitting the general public 'to make every one conform to the approved standard' (OL, 271). When the public or the 'over-ruling majority' imposes its view of acceptable and unacceptable conduct on others in *self-regarding matters*, it is 'quite as likely to be wrong as right; for in these cases public opinion means, at the best, some people's opinion of what is good or bad for other people' (OL, 283). In this regard, he considers the objection that we are not 'restricting individuality, or impeding ... original experiments in living' when we prevent people, even in matters that concern their own good, from doing things that experience has shown to be disagreeable 'to any person's individuality' (OL, 281). He mentions gambling, drunkenness, incontinence, idleness, and uncleanliness as examples (OL, 280). Mill acknowledges that we can learn much from accumulated human experience, but he also contends that it is wrong to insist that individuals should be bound to 'the traditions and customs of other people.' Customs and traditions, he says, are evidence of what other people's 'experience has taught *them*'; therefore, they constitute 'presumptive evidence ... that one mode of existence, or mode of conduct, is preferable to another' (OL, 262, Mill's emphasis). Mill maintains, however, that 'customs are made for customary circumstances, and customary characters.' Consequently, to insist that everyone should simply do what is customary or commonly done ignores the fact that the characters and circumstances of some people 'may be uncustomary' (OL, 262). In turn, to enable everyone to flourish 'it is important to give the freest scope possible to uncustomary things,' and to permit each person to 'use and interpret [inherited] experience' in his or her own way (OL, 269, 262).

The second key component of Mill's utilitarian case for the principle of liberty concerns the link between individual freedom, self-development, and paternalism. The principle of liberty precludes paternalistic interference with the freedom of mature individuals in self-regarding matters – that is, matters which concern strictly their own good. Mill maintains not only that the liberty principle directly promotes individual liberty, but also that it indirectly supports freedom by fostering individual self-development. He says that when individuals take responsibility for 'carry[ing] out their lives in their own way' (OL, 270), they also exercise and expand their capacities for autonomous action:

> He who chooses his plan [of life] for himself, employs all his faculties. He must use observation to see, reasoning and judgment to foresee, activity to gather materials for decision, discrimination to decide, and when he has decided, firmness and self-control to hold to his deliberate decision. And these qualities he requires and exercises exactly in proportion as the part of his conduct which he determines according to his own judgment and feelings is a large one. (OL, 262–3)

By making decisions concerning our own lives, we exercise and expand the reasoning faculties that are constitutive of our capacity to pursue our own good in our own way. In contrast, individuals who do not choose their own mode of living – because others choose for them or because they let 'the world, or [their] own portion of it, choose for [them]' – do not exercise their faculties. Such persons have 'no need of any other faculty than the ape-like one of imitation' (OL, 262). Mill insists on the benefits of individuals choosing their own mode of living, moreover, even when people are short-sighted or mistaken in their choices. He says that it is proper for people to give others advice and exhortations to aid their judgment in their self-regarding choices, but adds that all the errors an individual 'is likely to commit against advice and warning are far outweighed by the evil of allowing others to constrain him to what they deem his own good' (OL, 277).

Mill elaborates on these points by asking us to consider the hypothetical 'extreme case' of a person who would 'sell himself, or allow himself to be sold, as a slave' (OL, 299). 'The reason for not interfering, unless for the sake of others, with a person's voluntary acts,' he says, 'is consideration for his liberty. His voluntary choice is evidence that what he so chooses is desirable, or at least endurable, to him, and his own good on the whole best provided for him by allowing him to take his own means in pursuing it' (OL, 299). In this light, he presents the prospect of someone selling himself or herself into slavery as a limiting case with respect to the relationship between a person's 'voluntary' choices and his or her liberty. He contends that a person's 'power of voluntarily disposing his own lot in life' may rightfully be limited in such a case because the person's act would defeat 'the purpose which is justification for allowing him to dispose of himself' – that is, it would subvert his freedom (OL, 299).

This example has generated considerable commentary and controversy (see La Selva, 1987). For present purposes, what is important is how Mill offers this example to qualify the general rule that the freedom of independent individuals in self-regarding matters 'implies a corresponding liberty in any number of individuals to regulate by mutual agreement such things as regard them jointly' (OL, 299). He says that this conclusion 'presents no difficulty, *so long as the will of all persons implicated remains unaltered*' (OL, 299, emphasis added). The slavery example shows how the general rule concerning mutual agreements is complicated by the fact that a person's will may change with respect to such agreements. Mill explains, 'The principle ... which demands uncontrolled freedom of action in all that concerns only the agents themselves, requires that those who have become bound to one another ... should be able to release one another from the engagement' (OL, 300). He applies this point, moreover, to marriage contracts as well as to the slavery example (PPE, 953–4).

At the same time, Mill's conception of free action (see ch. 1) implies that if we were to come across 'extreme cases' such as a person 'voluntarily' choosing slavery, we would have good reason to question whether the choice was really freely made. That is, while it is possible to imagine a hypothetical situation in which a person *voluntarily* sells herself or himself into slavery, if we found someone who actually did this we would have good reason to wonder what circumstances *forced* her or him to make this choice. The general rule to respect the free choices of individuals is called into question, then, in cases where an individual lacks information that is vital to making a free choice, lacks an adequate 'reflecting faculty' – either temporarily or permanently – to pursue objectives that are properly his or her own, or acts under duress (see OL, 294, 226).

At first glance, Mill's emphasis on competent choosers and autonomous choices appears to license paternalism for persons who do what is customary or 'commonly done' simply *because* it is customary or commonly done (OL, 262, 264). He says that 'the faculties are called into no exercise by doing a thing merely because others do it, no more than by believing a thing only because others believe it' (OL, 262). Moreover, he regards people who act in this way as unfree in an important sense even when they are able to do as they please, since they do not actively choose their own mode of conduct (OL, 262, 265). Thus, paternalistic interference with the voluntary conduct of these persons would appear to involve no clear infringement of their freedom. As I noted in Chapter 1, however, Mill regards this scenario as the most extreme case of how 'society has now fairly gotten the better of individuality' such that some individuals have no desires or inclinations that are really their own (OL, 264–5). Moreover, as we have seen, he maintains that any adult with 'the ordinary amount of understanding' – or with 'any tolerable amount of common sense and experience' – is 'immeasurably' better equipped than anyone else to decide what will serve his or her well-being than anyone else (OL, 276–7, and 270). In most cases, then, Mill insists that such interference clearly restricts freedom.[8] Still, his argument implies that *in those rare cases* where people's minds are so 'bowed to the yoke' by prevailing opinion or oppressive circumstances that their expressed preferences are not their own in a meaningful sense – that is, where they are heteronomous or anomic agents (see ch. 1) – paternalistic interference would impose no real infringement of their freedom.

Finally, Mill further refines his argument by explaining that the principle of liberty and its prohibition of paternalism applies 'only to human beings in the maturity of their faculties' and not to 'young persons' who still need to be 'taken care of by others' (OL, 224). More problematically, he adds that the principle does not apply to 'backward states of society in which the race itself may be considered in its nonage' (OL, 224). Regarding children, his point is simply that paternalistic guidance is justified for those persons who have not yet developed their capacity to take care of themselves. He also regards such paternalism as justified with respect to persons with severe mental illnesses or cognitive disabilities. As a general rule, though, Mill regards such paternalism as only justified insofar as it aims to empower agents to govern themselves.[9]

Mill's notion of 'immaturity' is inappropriate, however, with respect to non-European traditional cultures and societies. What is at stake in such cases is not 'immaturity,' but rather different understandings of selfhood, identity, community, freedom, and authority. From Mill's perspective, despotism and colonialism are justified in 'backward states of society' where people have not 'attained the capacity of being guided to their own improvement by conviction or persuasion' (OL, 224). Moreover, 'backward' societies and cultures seem in his view to include *any* culture or subculture in which the authority of received traditions is regarded with greater reverence and deference than he regards as fitting for free persons and free societies (Mendus, 1986/87; Parekh, 1994b). Mill is right to ponder the universality of the principle of liberty, but his conclusions are dubious. Insofar as different cultures and societies are characterized by distinctive conceptions of self and society or community, they are also often characterized by different kinds of moral obligations. Thus, although Mill's principle of liberty is relevant to many cultures and societies, it is questionable whether it is applicable to all kinds of communities in the same way.

IV The Domain of Social Morality

As we have seen, Mill construes individual liberty as the freedom to pursue our own good in our own way 'within the limits imposed by the rights and interests of others' (OL, 226, 266). Thus, he recognizes that individual freedom must be limited by some general rules of conduct. Yet he offers the prospect of arriving at general rules of 'social morality' for modern pluralistic societies that different individuals or groups can endorse, at least in principle, despite divergent moral outlooks. Basically, Mill defends a version of what has been called the priority of the right over the good (Rawls, 1988; Larmore, 1990; cf. Sumner, 1979; Weinstein, 1991). He maintains that since members of such societies fundamentally disagree about comprehensive religious, philosophical, and moral doctrines of the good life – for example, the Catholic view that there is no salvation outside of the Church, and the existentialist view that life has only the meaning we give it – no one such view can properly serve as the basis for general rules of social morality.[10] Therefore, we need to base general rules of conduct on generally acknowledged moral obligations, particularly considerations of justice, that the various members of society can endorse despite their different moral outlooks and views of the good life.

Regarding the importance of moral rules, Mill says in *Utilitarianism* that 'the moral rules which forbid mankind to hurt one another (in which we must never forget to include wrongful interference with each other's freedom) are ... vital to human well-being' (U, 255). He elaborates on this point in an 1862 letter in which he maintains that the 'greatest happiness' principle is fully consistent with the conviction that 'general rules must be laid down for people's conduct to one another.'[11] The good of all, he says, can only be achieved by each person taking primary responsibility for his or her own good 'with due precautions to prevent these different persons ... from hindering one another.'[12] In turn, he contends that human happiness is most successfully achieved when people act in accordance with general rules that regulate their conduct toward

> one another, or in other words, rights and obligations must ... be recognized; and people must, on the one hand, not be required to sacrifice even their own less good to another's greater, where no general rule has given the other a right to the sacrifice; while, when a right *has* been recognized, they must, in most cases, yield to that right even at the sacrifice, in the particular case, of their own greater good to another's less. These rights and obligations are (it is of course implied) reciprocal.[13]

This reciprocal quality, he says, has two important implications. First, each person has fairly definite duties toward others, just as others have toward her, that she must respect and which are delineated by the distinct domain of moral wrongs. Second, as long as individuals act within the limits imposed by their duties toward others, other people are obliged to refrain from interfering punitively with their conduct.

With regard to how a society actually regulates individual freedom, Mill distinguishes two *kinds* of moral wrongs (or harm to others) that justify two different modes of coercive interference with the conduct of individuals (Berger, 1984, 242, 257). Thus, whenever individuals by their conduct violate or pose a definite risk to 'a distinct and assignable obligation' to some other person or persons, their conduct is 'taken out of the province of liberty, and placed in that of *morality or law*' (OL, 281–2, emphasis added; see Ryan, 1986; 1990, 236–7). All such conduct falls within the broad domain of 'social morality, of duty to others,' and so is rightfully subject to 'moral disapprobation' or punishment (OL, 281). Mill maintains, though, that while punishment through the moral coercion of public opinion is justified for any violation of moral obligations, punishment by legal penalties (or the force of law) is justified only for a smaller subcategory of moral wrongs. He explains in *On Liberty* that every person who receives protection from his or her society 'owes a return for the benefit,' which obligates them to observe certain basic rules of conduct toward the rest of their society:

> This conduct consists first, in not injuring the interests of one another; or rather certain interests, which, either by express legal provision, or by tacit understanding, ought to be considered as rights; and secondly, in each

person's bearing his share (to be fixed on some equitable principle) of the labours and sacrifices incurred for defending the society or its members from injury and molestation. These conditions society is justified in enforcing, at all costs to those who endeavor to withhold fulfillment. Nor is this all that society may do. The acts of an individual may be hurtful to others, or wanting in due consideration for their welfare, without going to the length of violating any of their constituted rights. The offender may then be justly punished by opinion, though not by law. (OL, 276)

In other words, when and only when an individual's conduct violates or poses a definite danger to certain interests of others that are so vital that 'they ought to be considered as rights,' can the agent rightfully be punished by legal penalties. At the same time, Mill says there are other acts that are 'hurtful to others' in the sense of violating distinct moral obligations to them, but that do not violate their rights. Such acts may be justly punished by the moral censure of opinion, but not by law (OL, 276).

Mill's understanding of the distinction between these two kinds of moral wrongs is basic to his view of the kinds of punishment that are justified in different cases of harm to others. He elaborates this key distinction in *Utilitarianism* when he distinguishes between the 'perfect' obligations of justice and the 'imperfect' obligations of benevolence or generosity. While cautioning that these expressions are somewhat 'ill-chosen,' he says that duties of imperfect obligation concern matters, such as acts of charity or beneficence, where the act is morally obligatory but 'the particular occasions of performing it are left to free choice' (U, 247). That is, we have a moral obligation to be charitable or benevolent to others, but it is an indefinite obligation that we are not bound to practice 'toward any definite person, nor at any prescribed time' (U, 247).[14] Still, insofar as obligations of benevolence are moral obligations, our failure to carry them out is a rightful subject of moral reproach.

Mill says that 'duties of perfect obligation' are obligations of *justice*. Justice, he says, 'implies something which is not only right to do, and wrong not to do, but which some individual can claim as his moral right' (U, 247). He explains that obligations of justice correspond to 'those duties in virtue of which a correlative *right* resides in some person or persons; duties of imperfect obligation are those moral obligations which do not give birth to any right' (U, 247, Mill's emphasis). 'Wherever there is a right,' he adds, 'the case is one of justice, and not of the virtue of beneficence' (U, 247–8). Regarding the special character of obligations of justice, Mill adds, 'Justice is a name for certain classes of moral rules which concern the essentials of human well-being more nearly, and are therefore of more absolute obligation, than any other rules for the guidance of life; and the notion which we have found to be the essence of the idea of justice – that of a right residing in an individual – implies and testifies to this more binding obligation' (U, 255; and U, 259). Obligations of justice, in short, are the special class of moral obligations that correspond to those interests of a particular person or persons which are so important to human well-being that they ought to be considered as rights.

Regarding the correlative notion of rights, Mill maintains that when we call something a person's right 'we mean that he has a valid claim on society to protect him in possession of it, either by force of law or by that of education and opinion. If he has what we consider a sufficient claim, on whatever account, to have something guaranteed to him by society, we can say that he has a right to it' (U, 250). Conversely, he says that when we want to demonstrate that someone is not entitled to something *by right*, 'we think this is done as soon as it is admitted that society ought not to take measures for securing it to him, but should leave it to chance, or to his own exertions' (U, 250). Moreover, Mill ultimately links obligations of justice directly to *moral* rights rather than to *legal* rights – that is, to those rights recognized by the law. He says that the legally constituted rights that a person has 'may be rights which ought not to have belonged to him.' The law cannot be taken as 'the ultimate criterion of justice,' since existing laws may 'give to one person a benefit, or impose on another an evil, which justice condemns' (U, 242). In contrast, having a *moral right* means having an interest that *ought to be constituted as a legal right* and protected as such, regardless of whether it currently has this status.[15]

For Mill, then, when we claim that a person has a moral right to something we are saying that it is due to them as an obligation of justice. This means, in turn, that society is bound to guarantee it to her insofar as it is practicable with the 'utmost exertions' (U, 247). Mill maintains, moreover, that morally speaking there are two different senses of *having a right* to do a thing ('UAPT,' 8–10; Donner, 1991, 161–5). We might think of the thing in question as the right to worship or not worship as we please, or to express unpopular ideas, or the right to basic medical care. First, in a negative sense, having a right to do something means simply that we are entitled to do it without facing legal prohibitions. This includes having a moral and legal right to do some things that violate obligations of benevolence, such as being uncharitable. Therefore, we can rightfully be punished by moral censure, but not by law, for some things that we have a right to do.[16] In addition, Mill maintains, as I will explain shortly, that while other people have no right to punish others for conduct that neither violates nor poses a definite risk to any moral obligation, they are entitled to think the worse of us if they disapprove of our conduct, and even to express their disapproval. Second, in a more positive vein, having a right to something sometimes means not just that other people are morally obligated not to hinder us from obtaining it, but also that positive action must be taken by society to secure it for us (U, 250). This may involve such things as legal protection for our right to worship as we please, legal protection for private property, government provision for a subsistence income, and government guarantees that adequate educational opportunities are available to everyone.

Mill applies this line of reasoning to the principle of liberty as follows. He says that individual conduct that violates definite duties to others but without infringing upon their moral rights – that is, conduct that violates obligations of benevolence but not of justice – may 'be justly punished by opinion but not by law' (OL, 276). Society can rightfully resort to legal penalties only to prevent people from violating the constituted *rights* of others, or those vital interests of others that 'ought to be considered as rights' (OL, 276). Regarding obligations of benevolence, he says that there are also 'certain acts of individual beneficence, such as saving a fellow-creature's life, or interposing to protect the defenseless against ill-usage, things which whenever it is obviously a man's duty to do, he may rightfully be responsible to society for not doing' (OL, 225). This last comment is rather vague since it begs the question of *just when* it is obviously a person's duty to, say, save a fellow creature's life. But Mill's basic point is clear: Insofar as something is an obligation of individual beneficence rather than an obligation of justice, people can be rightfully punished by moral censure, though not by law, for failing to do their duty.

Furthermore, Mill insists that moral wrongs are distinct from the offence, distress, or inconvenience we bring to others through our conduct. For instance, we may offend or disturb other people, by doing things that conflict with their tastes, their prejudices, their judgments about what is prudent, or their beliefs about what is religiously right or wrong, without committing a moral wrong in Mill's sense.[17] He explains this point in *On Liberty* with respect to religious differences and differences of taste, as follows:

There are many who consider it as an injury to themselves any conduct which they have a distaste for, and resent it as an outrage to their feelings, by persisting in their abominable worship or creed. But there is no parity between the feeling of a person for his own opinion, and the feeling of another who is offended at his holding it; no more than between the desire of a thief to take a purse and the right of the owner to keep it. And a person's taste is as much his own peculiar concern as his opinion or his purse. (OL, 283)

For Mill, the distinction between moral obligations and matters of prudence or taste does not depend on any direct utilitarian tallying of the amount of offence or distress entailed by different kinds of conduct. Instead, these distinctions require practical judgments concerning whether or not certain conduct is rightly punishable, and whether or not certain interests ought to be considered as rights that do not rely upon any particular moral outlook. Moreover, he insists that we can all understand the difference between what we would merely like others to do or not do and those things that we regard them as morally obligated to do.[18] In short, violations of duties to others are not reducible to such things as offence, distress, or discomfort.

In this regard, Mill's distinction between the domains of individual liberty and social morality requires some qualitative judgments concerning the vital or 'permanent' interests of human beings. He contends that while we may never all agree on what constitutes 'the good life,' we can reach more modest agreement about moral norms. For instance, we can agree that the desire of a thief for someone else's purse has a qualitatively lesser moral standing than the right of the owner to keep it, and that an individual's freedom to pursue her own religious, spiritual, or existential calling in her own way has a qualitatively greater moral standing than the fact that others might be distressed by her spiritual strivings. In this way, Mill's argument offers a strikingly different response to modern pluralism than that which is implied in views of morality that appeal to more sectarian beliefs about what is right and wrong, praiseworthy and impious, as the basis for general rules of conduct. From Mill's perspective, we all have a right to believe what we believe and, within certain limits, to act on our beliefs insofar as our society affirms the principles of religious freedom and freedom of conscience. These principles entail, however, that we do not have a right to impose our beliefs upon others or to hold others liable for our religious observances and abstinences (OL, 284). To do so would be to resort to what Mill calls the 'logic of persecutors, and to say that we may persecute others because we are right, and that they must not persecute us because they are wrong' (OL, 285). This would make general rules of conduct dependent upon nothing other than sheer force, whether through majority tyranny or the tyranny of a powerful minority. Moreover, as Mill says, it would mean 'admitting a principle of which we should resent as a gross injustice the application to ourselves' (OL, 285).

A few further distinctions are central to Mill's view of the domain of morality. *First*, this domain consists not only of the 'negative' obligation to avoid harming the essential interests of others, but also 'many positive acts for the benefit of others, ... such as [giving] evidence in a court of justice' and bearing our 'fair share in the common defense, or in any other joint work necessary to the interest of the society' in which we enjoy protection (OL, 224–5). Each person, he says, must bear his or her 'share (to be fixed on some equitable principle) of the labours and sacrifices incurred for defending the society and its members from injury or molestation' (OL, 276). This includes paying his or her fair share of taxes (PPE, 806–8). The *rightful* liberty of individuals, therefore, does not include the freedom to evade such obligations.

Second, Mill explains that there are many things that are desirable for people to do, and highly commendable, that are not matters of moral obligation. An example is for a person to volunteer one day per week to help others. Mill says in *August Comte and Positivism*, 'It is not good that persons should be bound, by other people's opinion, to do everything that they deserve praise for doing' (ACP, 337). There is, in short, a 'region of positive worthiness' in human conduct that denotes virtuous but not obligatory conduct (ACP, 337). Such morally praiseworthy conduct falls within the domain of individual liberty, within which individuals are equally free to be self-centred or indifferent toward others. Mill explains elsewhere that utilitarianism fully acknowledges 'the distinction between the province of duty and that of virtue' even as it maintains that 'the standard and rule of both is the general interest' ('TCL,' 650). 'From the utilitarian point of view,' he says,

> there are many acts, and a still greater number of forbearances, the perpetual practice of which by all is so necessary to the well-being, that the people must be held to it compulsorily, either by law, or by social pressure. These acts and forbearances constitute duty. Outside these bounds there is the innumerable variety of modes in which the acts of human beings are

either a cause, or a hindrance, of good to their fellow-creatures, but in regard to which it is, on the whole, for the general interest that they be left free; being merely encouraged, by praise and honour, to the performance of such beneficial actions as are not sufficiently stimulated by benefits flowing from them to the agent himself. This larger sphere is that of Merit or Virtue. ('TCL,' 650–51)

Overall, then, Mill identifies a wide range of conduct in modern pluralistic societies regarding which both moral reproach and legal restraint have no place. It includes conduct that raises considerations of prudence or aesthetics but not of duties to others, and conduct that is morally virtuous but not obligatory. He recognizes that virtually all individual conduct *affects* others, but insists that strictly speaking, the domain of morality encompasses only conduct through which some person (or persons) poses a definite risk to 'a distinct and assignable obligation to any other person or persons' (OL, 280, and 281).

Finally, Mill also considers how people can rightfully respond to conduct by others that does 'no wrong to any one' in the strict sense, but that arouses their distaste or contempt, or that offends or distresses them. This may include, for example, conduct that reveals an extreme degree of 'lowness or depravation of taste' or a 'defect of prudence or personal dignity' (OL, 278–9). Insofar as the conduct in question does 'no wrong' – that is, neither violates nor poses any definite risk to any distinct and assignable obligation – it falls within the protected province of individual liberty. Therefore, we cannot rightfully *punish* a person who does it, either by law or opinion. Whatever 'inconvenience' is caused by such conduct, he says, 'is one that society can afford to bear, for the greater good of human freedom' (OL, 282). Mill contends, however, that just as each of us is entitled to pursue our own good in our own way *as long as we do no wrong*, we have a correlative right, 'in various ways, to act upon our unfavourable opinion of any one, not to oppression of his individuality, but in the exercise of ours' (OL, 278). He adds, 'We are not bound, for example, to seek his society; we have a right to avoid it (though not to parade the avoidance), for we have a right to choose the society most acceptable to us. We have a right, and it may be duty, to caution others against him' (OL, 278). Regarding people's relations to another person whose conduct they find objectionable, Mill explains further, 'It makes a vast difference both in our feelings and in our conduct ... whether he displeases us in things in which we think we have a right to control him, or things in which we know that we have not' (OL, 279). In short, whereas we can rightfully punish a person who poses definite harm to others, our proper recourse is quite different with respect to a person who exhibits merely 'self-regarding faults, ... which are not properly immoralities' (OL, 279). In such cases, Mill says, 'it is not our part to inflict any suffering on him, except what may incidentally follow from our using the same liberty in the regulation of our own affairs, which we allow him in his' (OL, 280).

To summarize, no coercive or punitive interference, whether by law or by moral condemnation, is justified in matters of the self-regarding conduct of others. We may, however, rightfully express our disapproval of self-regarding conduct by others; and we may rightfully seek to influence such conduct through 'advice, instruction, persuasion, and avoidance' as an expression of our freedom as long as we do not resort to coercion (OL, 292, 269). Moreover, Mill says that 'a person may suffer very severe penalties at the hands of others' for such conduct, *but only insofar as* these 'penalties' are an incidental consequence of the 'same liberty' in self-regarding conduct of their fellow citizens and 'not ... purposely inflicted on him for the sake of punishment' (OL, 278).

These considerations pose thorny dilemmas that Mill does not squarely address. Consider, for instance, his claims that 'we have a right to avoid' the company of a person whose self-regarding conduct we find distressing so long as we do not 'parade the avoidance,' and that 'we have a right, and it may be a duty, to caution others against him.' In relation to contemporary conflicts over such things as the rights of homosexuals, bisexuals, and transgender persons, and the rights of religious minorities, Mill's advice here is characteristically sound, but also rather vague. His argument seems to sanction, for example, the freedom of people to publicly declare their views of the 'immorality' of homosexuality and of unconventional religious practices, but not punitive or hateful crusades against such ways of life.[19] In addition, Mill's argument expressly licenses people to inflict certain incidental 'suffering' on others for their disfavoured self-regarding conduct as long as this merely follows from the former 'using the same liberty in the regulation of [their] own affairs' as they allow to the latter. In this regard, Mill would likely support such things as laws that prohibit discrimination based on 'race,' sex, religion, or sexual orientation in housing and employment, but might also support *some* principled exemptions to antidiscrimination laws to accommodate religious convictions that require certain kinds of discrimination. For instance, he might support the right of people whose religious beliefs condemn the 'sins' of homosexuality and extramarital sex to refuse to rent an apartment on their property to gay and lesbian couples and unmarried heterosexual couples.[20] Similarly, while he would probably support public education curricula that teach tolerance and respect for diverse ways of life, he would also support the right of parents to seek alternative private education for their children that teaches children that some ways of life, such as homosexuality, are 'immoral.'

The power of public opinion raises further complications in such matters. Insofar as public opinion shapes people's conduct by shaping what they feel and think, even putatively noncoercive expressions of distaste or disapproval for self-regarding conduct pose a potential problem for Mill's attempt to protect individual liberty. He says that the 'mandates' society imposes on individuals through prevailing opinion can produce a 'social tyranny' that strikes more vehemently than political tyranny because it 'penetrat[es] much more deeply into the details of life, enslaving the soul itself' (OL, 220). Thus, widespread disapproval or castigation of certain kinds of self-regarding conduct, even when it is purportedly noncoercive, is likely to foster a repressive environment. This is often the case today, for example, with respect to homosexuality. In this regard, the increase in legal protections for gay men and lesbians in many countries, while welcome, only partly redresses the bigotry and disrespect they commonly face.[21] Even when individuals have the right (or are *at liberty*) to pursue their own distinctive modes of existence, they may nonetheless find their freedom constrained by 'the eye of a hostile and dreaded censorship' (OL, 264).[22] As Mill notes, moreover, this kind of restraint tends to especially burden those whose economic circumstances make them dependent on 'the good will of other people' (OL, 241). As I will explain later, Mill wisely regards the principle of liberty as a partial response to these difficulties rather than as a cure-all.

V Indirect Utility and the Politics of Rights

Leaving aside for now the difficulties posed by the power of public opinion, it is crucial to understand how Mill's appeal to rights, in light of his rejection of any appeal to 'abstract right' (OL, 224), reserves for democratic politics the task of establishing legal limits to individual liberty.[23] His utilitarianism requires general rules that delineate obligations of justice and correlative rights to secure 'certain social utilities which are vastly more important, and therefore more absolute and imperative, than any others' (U, 259). Yet he provides no simple formula to tell us precisely what interests are so important that they 'ought to be considered as rights' (OL, 276; and see ch. 2, above). On the contrary, Mill maintains that determining the scope and character of rights is ultimately a *political* matter and as such a task for democratic politics.

Mill states the basic point in *On Liberty*. He says, 'On questions of social morality, of duty to others, the opinion of the public, that is, of an overruling majority, though often wrong, is likely to be still oftener right; because on such questions they are only required to judge their own interests; of the manner in which some mode of conduct, if allowed to be practiced, would affect themselves' (OL, 283). Likewise, he says in *Representative Government* that one of the two general principles on which the 'superiority' of popular government rests 'is, that the rights and interests of every person are only secure from being disregarded, when the person is himself able, and habitually disposed, to stand up for them' (CRG, 404). Accordingly, the task of determining those essential interests of persons which ought to be considered as rights must involve the general public, or the 'overruling majority,' since it concerns fundamental rights and interests of every person. He insists, however, that authoritative decisions must be based not on the mere 'likings and dislikings' of the majority – or those who get themselves accepted as such. Rather, they must be based on a deliberative form of democratic politics that expresses the considered judgments of the majority, through elected representatives, concerning those interests which are so fundamental to human well-being that they ought to be considered as obligations of justice.

Mill does not explicitly address the role of democratic politics in this regard. Implicitly, though, his case for a democratic politics of rights is basically a corollary to his defence of the 'perfect freedom' of individuals in the self-regarding domain of individual liberty. He maintains that the well-being of individuals is best achieved in the latter domain when they are free to pursue their own good in their own individual ways; that being said, issues of social morality, or duty to others, ought to be decided democratically, by the overruling majority, since this similarly empowers people to judge what is in their own interests.

In this regard, Mill's vision of democratic deliberation and law-making in representative assemblies in *Representative Government* is in some ways a rather attenuated conception of democratic politics. He proposes that the actual *drafting* of laws be left to a special Commission of Legislation selected by and accountable to the representative assembly, so that ordinary citizens would have no direct law-making role (see ch. 8). Nonetheless, the representative assembly would ideally express the will of the general public in determining what laws are established and for what purposes (CRG, 430). It would ensure that the nation is 'governed only by laws assented to by its elected representatives,' and it would decide what interests are constituted as legal rights (CRG, 432). Mill's ideal, as I explain in Chapter 8, is a legislative process in which 'those whose opinion is overruled, feel satisfied that it is heard, and set aside not by a mere act of will, but for what are thought superior reasons, and commend themselves as such to the representatives of the majority of the nation' (CRG, 432).

His view of the politics of rights becomes clearer when we consider one of the standard criticisms of his appeal to 'harm to others' as marking the rightful limit of individual liberty. As John Gray articulates this view, 'for Mill's principle to be the "one very simple principle" that he sought to enunciate, he needs a conception of interest that is fairly determinate in its applications, and which can be deployed non-controversially by persons with divergent moral outlooks' (Gray, 1991, xviii; cf. Gray, 1989c, 1996). According to Gray, Mill fails to offer any such notion. Gray concludes, therefore, 'If, ... as seems highly plausible, conceptions of harm, and in particular of the relative severity of harms, vary with different moral outlooks, then Mill's principle will be virtually useless as a guide to policy' (Gray, 1991, xviii). In contrast, Jonathan Riley offers a different reading of Mill's harm principle, which he believes saves Mill from this difficulty. According to Riley, Mill construes harm 'in a way that transcends the laws and customs of any particular civil society' by equating it 'with "perceptible hurt" or "perceptible damage" experienced by a competent agent against his wishes.' In this way, he says, Mill excludes mere distress or dislike experienced by others 'without any other evidence of injury' from being counted as harm (Riley, 1991b, 22).

Both of these interpretations underestimate the subtlety of Mill's approach. Gray is right that Mill does *not* conceive of 'harm to others' in a way that transcends the traditions and customs of particular societies or removes from politics disputes about what counts as harm (Gray, 1991, xx). Moreover, Mill never articulates a notion of 'perceptible damage' that would remove questions of moral obligation from contextual practical judgments.[24] His 'simple principle' is not quite so simple. Rather, in rejecting any appeal to 'abstract right' he simultaneously rejects the idea that the rightful limits of individual liberty and social morality can be fixed once and for all, independently of traditions, customs, and politics. As he says in *August Comte and Positivism*, moral expectations and obligations change as societies change; therefore, 'the domain of moral obligations, in an improving society, is always widening. When what was once uncommon virtue becomes common virtue, it comes to be numbered among obligations, while a degree exceeding what has grown common, remains simply meritorious' (ACP, 338). Although Mill presents an overly optimistic picture of social progress, his insight about moral obligations remains valid. As social relationships, institutions, practices, and technologies change, societies face not only new possibilities and amenities, but also new dangers and new understandings of old practices. Consequently, judgments about the kinds of conduct that are punishable and the interests that should be protected with the utmost exertion (i.e., *by right*) inevitably change in relation to people's changing needs, expectations, and circumstances.

More generally, Mill's approach to rights and duties is contextual in several ways. First, he says that the liberty principle applies only to 'civilized' societies that are capable of being 'improved' and governed by 'free and equal discussion' (OL, 224). This restriction betrays his Eurocentrism, but it also contains a valid observation about the conditions necessary for the kind of politics of rights he envisions. Second, Mill relies on the kind of practical reasoning that people routinely engage in when they distinguish between those things they would merely like others to do or not do, and those things they are morally obligated to do or not do ('UAPT,' 9; cf. Lyons, 1982b). This point, of course, does not resolve the problem of arriving at general notions of duties and rights that are acceptable to persons with divergent moral outlooks. Yet Mill joins it effectively with his focus on pluralistic modern societies in which people are generally willing to be persuaded by 'free and equal discussion.' In his view, for democratic politics to be effective in determining legal rights in a pluralistic society, the members of that society must generally recognize the need to provide one another with general, secular grounds for constituting certain interests as rights.

Current conflicts about homosexuality and individual rights are an important test case for Mill's approach. Homosexuality is regarded as 'immoral' within several traditional religious and moral perspectives.[25] In addition, Western societies like England and the United States have a long history of prohibiting homosexual relations by law, and of persecuting homosexual men and women. Furthermore, this legal and extra-legal persecution and discrimination typically has been justified in terms of prevailing beliefs about what is regarded as (in Mill's phrase) 'religiously wrong' (OL, 289). As Mill warns, 'No stronger case can be shown for prohibiting anything which is regarded as a personal immorality, than is made out for suppressing these practices in the eyes of those who regard them as impieties' (OL, 285). Western societies have been dominated by 'Judeo-Christian moral standards, so this tradition has been the *de facto* basis for many basic laws and constituted rights in Western societies (OL, 284–91; Mitchell, 1970). Mill insists, however, that legislation must not be based on any one group's beliefs about what is religiously wrong or impious, even if they are in the majority. 'The notion that it is one man's duty,' he says, 'that another should be religious, was the foundation of all the religious persecutions ever perpetuated, and if admitted, would justify them ... It is a determination not to tolerate others in doing what is permitted by their religion because it is not permitted by the persecutor's religion' (OL, 289).

Mill's framework for resolving such moral conflicts is valuable independently of his own ambivalent views about sexuality.[26] As Alan Ryan notes, we misconstrue Mill's view of the 'enforcement of morals' – that is, the right of the majority to impose its moral views on others – if we interpret him as supplying an answer to the question of whether the state has a right to suppress 'private immorality' (1965; and 1990, 245–7). This concept has no place in Mill's moral theory since he construes the domain of morality more narrowly in terms of violating 'a distinct and assignable obligation' to some other person or persons – that is, an obligation that is *generally acknowledged*.[27] Accordingly, activities that many people regard as 'private' or 'personal' immoralities, such as homosexual sex and heterosexual sex outside of marriage, are *not moral wrongs* in Mill's sense. Such conduct has usually been designated 'immoral' based on religious doctrines that are infused by notions of 'sin' and 'impiety.' In turn, it is regarded by some people as *intrinsically* immoral regardless of whether or not it involves any tangible harm to others.[28]

From Mill's perspective, individuals who hold beliefs about what is 'religiously wrong' are entitled to act on their beliefs in pursuing their *own good* in their own way, but only within the limits of their *duties to others*. Thus, they are entitled to avoid the company of people whose conduct they regard as 'immoral,' and to express their disapproval of such conduct, and to advise against it; but at the same time they have no right to punish people for such conduct or 'to inflict any suffering on [them], except what may incidentally follow' from the exercise of their own rightful liberty (OL, 280). Mill's position, then, is that the rightful freedom of individuals to act upon religiously grounded beliefs that homosexuality is wrong (that is, sinful) is limited by *their obligation* to respect those interests of gay men, lesbians, and bisexuals which 'ought to be considered as rights.' Moreover, this restriction concerns not the current legal rights of these persons – since these may well reflect dominant religious beliefs – but rather their *moral* rights as equal members of society, unless there is some sound secular basis for giving them lesser rights. Thus, Mill's principle of liberty permits Orthodox Jews and Christian fundamentalists to avoid the company of homosexuals and bisexuals in their personal lives; but it precludes efforts by such groups to deny gay men and lesbians equal rights and equal recognition with respect to such things as education, privacy, employment, public services, and the use of public spaces.

Mill's principle of liberty offers no unambiguous guide to balancing all the competing interests at stake here, such as the claims of nondiscrimination, on the one hand, and free expression of religion, on the other. Yet it does help us clarify the various considerations that ought to count in making such judgments. According to Mill, the distress or offence that a given type of conduct causes to some members of society is never sufficient justification to prohibit or punish such conduct. The fact that many people are deeply distressed by homosexuality – even to the extent of finding it abhorrent – is no more a justified reason for imposing moral or legal penalties against homosexuals than is the fact that orthodox Moslems and Jews regarding eating pork as an impiety a sufficient reason for prohibiting pork eating as a matter of public or social morality (see OL, 284). Mill says, 'There are many who consider it as an injury to themselves any conduct which they have a distaste for, and resent it as an outrage to their feelings, by persisting in their abominable worship or creed. But there is no parity between the feeling of a person for his own opinion, and the feeling of another who is offended at his holding it' (OL, 283). Thus, the principle of liberty precludes any reductive utilitarian calculus of the happiness that is (or would be) produced by prohibiting homosexual affectional and sexual relations in comparison to the 'unhappiness' or displeasure that is (or would be) caused by permitting it.

Mill's line of argument provides further support for claims of equal rights and equal recognition for gay men, lesbians, and bisexuals. To paraphrase Mill, there is no parity between the interest that people have in their own sexual orientations and relationships and the interests that others have in their sexual orientations and relationships.[29] Once a society acknowledges the vital importance of people's intimate sexual and affectional relationships to their well-being, it is difficult to imagine a plausible secular argument that would justify more extensive sexual freedom for heterosexual persons than for persons who are homosexual or bisexual.[30]

This does not mean, however, that *any* sexual – or sexually oriented – conduct ought to be permitted. Indeed, Mill's argument implies that mature and mentally competent individuals should have 'perfect freedom' to express their sexual orientation and inclinations only as long as they do so within the bounds of their 'distinct and assignable' duties to others. This, in turn, entails that we should regard any sexual choices made, or sexual acts performed, by consenting adults, as within the protected domain of individual liberty, *as long as* those choices or acts do not involve coercion or deception, or one party physically or psychologically injuring another. Therefore, *with whom* a person chooses to have sex should not be regarded as a moral issue, as long as it is another consenting adult or adults. At the same time, *how* people act toward others in their sexual and affectional relationships may well raise legitimate moral concerns. Sexual abuse and sexual harassment are moral wrongs, according to this view, regardless of who abuses whom.[31] Similarly, if someone knows that he or she has a sexually transmitted disease but chooses not to share this knowledge with his or her sexual partner or partners, *this conduct* would violate a distinct moral obligation, although not necessarily an obligation of justice. If, however, he or she shares this information with a partner, who then willingly agrees to a sexual relationship, then their mutual choices arguably fall within the domain of individual liberty rather than that of social morality.[32]

Mill's narrow conception of the domain of morality obviously conflicts with how many people think about 'morality.' Moreover, his view implicitly privileges a conception of the good life that emphasizes individuality, freedom, and autonomy. Nonetheless, it offers distinct advantages for determining generally binding rules of conduct in pluralistic modern societies – particularly where religious freedom and freedom of conscience are accepted fundamental rights. It calls upon citizens to exhibit the same consideration for the moral outlooks of others that they expect from others for their own moral outlooks.

VI Individual Liberty and the Powers of Education and Opinion

For Mill, the power of public opinion to shape what people think and feel poses special dangers to individual liberty. Without imposing any visible restraints, public opinion can create a repressive atmosphere that stifles the freedom of individuals to pursue their own good in their own way (Hamburger, 1991). It leads some individuals to abstain from doing what they really want to do; and it bows the minds of others 'to the yoke,' stifling their capacity to develop their own characters, preferences, and life plans (OL, 264–70). For these reasons, the principle of liberty is only one part of Mill's response to the potentially repressive power of public opinion.

He regards public opinion as a mode of education, since it shapes people's characters, feelings, and opinions ('IA,' 217). He says that 'the power of public opinion' consists 'of the praise and blame, the favour and disfavour, of their fellow creatures; and is a source of strength inherent in any system of moral belief which is generally adopted' ('UR,' 410). Like all the powers of education, Mill regards this one as a basic and unavoidable feature of society. Thus, freedom is achieved not by eradicating this form of power, but rather by securing people against its repressive tendencies. He says, for instance, that because 'education and opinion have so vast a power over human character,' their power should be used 'to establish in the mind of every individual an indissoluble association between his [or her] own happiness and the good of the whole; especially between his [or her] own happiness and the practice of such modes of conduct ... as regard for the universal happiness pre-scribes' (U, 218). The powers of education and opinion can be misused to impose on all individuals the 'likings and dislikings' of the majority or of a dominant minority.[33] Still, these powers cannot be wished away, and they *can also be used* to help establish a principled balance 'between individual independence and social control' (OL, 220–1).

Mill's response to this challenge has three key components. First, he insists that the power that education and opinion exert over human character is an additional reason to avoid using coercion with respect to the self-regarding conduct of individuals. Society, he says, already pos-sesses considerable means of

bringing its weaker members up to its ordinary standard of rational con-duct, [aside from] waiting till they do something irrational, and then punishing them, legally or morally, for it. Society has had absolute power over them during all the early portion of their existence: it has had the whole period of childhood and nonage in which to try whether it could make them capable of rational conduct in life ... [It is a]rmed not only with all the power of education, but with the ascendancy which the authority of a received opinion always exercises over the minds who are least fitted to judge for themselves; and aided by the *natural* penalties which cannot be prevented from falling on those who incur the distaste or the contempt of those who know them. (OL, 282, Mill's emphasis)

He goes on to say that society 'should not pretend that it needs, besides all this, the power to issue commands and enforce obedience in the personal concerns of individuals' (OL, 282). In brief, society already possesses vast educative powers to teach its individual members to take care of themselves and to act in ways that are compatible with the well-being of others; commands and mandates are not its only recourse. If a society is dissatisfied with how some of its members act in self-regarding matters, it has noncoercive means of redressing this. Specifically, before interfering in the personal concerns of its adult members, it should examine whether its various educative institutions and practices are adequately teaching people to be free and responsible agents. 'If society lets any considerable number of its members grow up mere children, incapable of distant motives,' Mill says, 'society has itself to blame for the consequences' (OL, 282). This point, of course, leads back to questions about what kinds of education are appropriate in pluralistic modern societies (see ch. 4, above).

None of this, however, addresses the more hidden dangers posed by public opinion. In particular, it does not prevent public opinion from establishing an atmosphere that stifles mental freedom and autonomy, or unconventional or eccentric conduct that does 'no wrong.' Mill addresses these threats to freedom more directly through his second notion, which involves educating people to be free and morally responsible agents. People need to learn to obey certain rules of conduct as limits to their freedom, but they can and should be taught these rules in a manner that supports their mental freedom and autonomy. 'Moral doctrines,' he says, 'are no more to be received without evidence, nor to be sifted less carefully, than any other doctrines' ('SD,' 158). In other words, insofar as people are encouraged to exercise their reasoning powers and to think for themselves, they can learn to freely endorse some general rules of conduct without uncritically embracing whatever rules prevail at a given time. In addition, they will also be empowered to critically appropriate received traditions and prevailing opinions *as free agents* – that is, in terms of what suits their characters and purposes (OL, 262–4).

Finally, Mill suggests that to the extent that people adopt the spirit of toleration implied in the principle of liberty, they will be more likely to avoid employing public opinion coercively. Thus, along with emphasizing the need to instil certain general rules of conduct, he insists 'that it is important to give the freest scope possible to uncustomary things' (OL, 269). Society can and should use the powers of education and opinion to encourage moral and rational conduct, but it should be careful not to assume that one mode of existence is suitable for everyone. Society must leave sufficient room for individuality and eccentricity, not only in imposing general rules of conduct but also in employing the powers of education and opinion.

VII Conclusion

Mill's principle of liberty provides a persuasive means for protecting individual freedom against both excessive political legal restraint and 'the moral coercion of public opinion' (OL, 223). The principle is relatively straightforward in its broad contours. Yet rather than being 'one very simple principle,' Mill gives it a measure of subtlety that matches the complex interplay of individual liberty and social and political power. In this regard, we will fail to grasp its richness if we abstract it from Mill's broader view of freedom and power and see it *merely* as a principled limit to the power that 'can be legitimately exercised by society over the individual' (OL, 217). The principle is meant to help guard individual freedom against repressive power, but it is also part of Mill's broader account of both repressive and freedom-supporting aspects of social and political power.

Because of its influence as a precept for balancing individual freedom and social control, Mill's principle has generated considerable critical commentary. To further clarify his position, I will briefly consider a few of the most significant criticisms. First, Mill – along with other liberal theorists – has been criticized for basing his defence of individual liberty on a defective, atomistic understanding of individualism that misleadingly opposes individuals to society (cf. Bosanquet, 1899; Dewey, 1954 [1927]; Wolff, 1968; Norman, 1987; Di Stefano, 1991). For example, Henry David Aiken claims that Mill fails to adequately appreciate that people are thoroughly social beings, and that he presents a false separation 'between spheres of private activity within which the individual person is alone concerned and a sphere of public interest which is the exclusive interest of something called "society"' (1962, 296).[34] Yet Mill himself emphasizes that people's desires, characters, and conceptions of the good life are socially formed. Even their capacities for individuality and autonomy, in his view, are dependent upon supportive educations and social arrangements (see ch. 4). Moreover, he is well aware that almost everything a person does affects others in some ways. 'No person,' he says, 'is an entirely isolated being; it is impossible for a person to do anything seriously or permanently hurtful to himself, without mischief reaching at least to his near connexions, and often far beyond' (OL, 280). In this regard, his aim is not to distinguish conduct through which individuals affect only themselves, from conduct through which individuals affect others. Rather, he distinguishes conduct through which individuals violate or pose a definite danger to 'a distinct and assignable' moral obligation to another person or persons, from conduct that neither violates nor threatens any such duties to others. The issue is not *whether* our conduct affects others, but rather *how* it affects them.

Critics such as John Gray and Bhikhu Parekh challenge the way Mill privileges individuality and autonomy as vital to human well-being. In Gray's words, Mill fails to adequately 'acknowledge the dependence of personal individuality and human flourishing on a cultural tradition' (1989c, 226). There is considerable merit in this criticism. As we have seen, Mill acknowledges that people can learn from received customs and traditions. Still, in claiming that people can be neither free nor fulfilled unless they critically distance themselves from received customs and traditions, he fails to adequately grasp what people with fundamental commitments to nonliberal ways of life would have to give up to adopt his conception of the good life. Mill strongly defends the value of social pluralism, but he offers a distinctly liberal model of pluralism and toleration (Baum, 1997). That is, he consistently favours the freedom of individuals *as individuals* to pursue their own life plans over diversity among distinct *ways of life*. Thus, despite his tendency to celebrate diversity of individual modes of existence, his emphasis on autonomy and individuality leads him, as Parekh says, to 'display considerable intolerance ... [toward] non-liberal ways of life,' so that the diversity he celebrates is 'confined within the narrow limits of the individualist model of human excellence' (1994, 12). Consequently, Mill's view of 'harm to others' insufficiently attends to the significant injury that an individual may well experience when the community or group that is the source of his identity and way of life – which may be a nonliberal or communitarian way of life – is undermined (see Galeotti, 1993; Galston, 1995; Kukathas, 1995).

In this regard, however, the indefiniteness of the liberty principle in light of Mill's emphasis on the relativity of moral obligations and the role of democratic politics is a *strength* rather than a weakness. Although

Mill expresses considerable intolerance toward nonliberal and non-European cultures, his account of the logic of religious toleration and the politics of rights offers a promising approach to the challenges posed by religious and cultural pluralism. Mill provides a classic liberal rationale for the important distinction that Martha Minow makes between 'a subcommunity's desire to export to the rest of society its values that contradict the broader society's own commitments [and] ... its desire to secure space free from intrusion to develop and perform its own practices' (1990b, 90). From Mill's perspective, which he summarizes in his critique of the logic of persecutors, it is one thing for members of a community or subcommunity to seek toleration and respect for their way of life, but it is quite another thing for them to attempt to impose their view of what is 'religiously wrong' on others (OL, 285–91). As Minow points out, the distinction between a subcommunity's desire to preserve its way of life and its desire to impose its values on others breaks down when groups seek to discriminate against or oppress some of their own members in ways that violate antidiscrimination principles of the larger society (1990b, 90). In this regard, the merit of Mill's liberal pluralism resides in how he attends to just this problem while tentatively supporting toleration for groups, such as the Mormons *as a group*, to practise their distinctive ways of life (OL, 290–1).

In sum, Mill's principle of liberty does not provide all the resources necessary for balancing conflicting claims of individual and group autonomy, or of individual rights and group rights (cf. Green, 1995; Baum, 1997). Nonetheless, it provides a valuable framework for balancing claims of individual freedom with moral obligations. He recognizes that what people regard as morally obligatory necessarily varies with changes in social conditions. Therefore, he maintains that the task of determining fundamental rights and duties is irreducibly political and open to debate. The best we can do, according to Mill, is determine, through a process of free and democratic deliberation and decision-making, those interests which ought to be considered as rights. The alternative of appealing to some notion of 'abstract right' would involve a couple of insuperable problems: it would establish one particular and controversial comprehensive moral outlook – say, the natural law philosophy of St. Thomas Aquinas or John Locke – as the basis for general rules of conduct; and it would close off the possibility of establishing new rights and new obligations as required by new circumstances. There is no guarantee, of course, that the kind of democratic politics that Mill proposes will adequately respect individual liberty, but this is also true of appeals to 'abstract' or 'natural' rights. Moreover, Mill highlights not only the kinds of considerations that are crucial for making such judgments in pluralistic modern societies, but also the extent to which the justness of decisions depends on the democratic character and integrity of the processes of public deliberation and decision-making (see ch. 8).

Finally, Mill's utilitarianism broaches but does not resolve a further issue regarding the rightful limits of individual freedom of action. Following Bentham, Mill construes the greatest happiness, 'so far as the nature of things admits,' in relation to 'the whole sentient creation' (U, 214). This raises important questions regarding the obligations that human beings may have with respect to nonhuman nature. Mill offers little guidance for weighing the harm to other species caused by human activities against the benefits that may accrue to human beings – as beings capable of more 'elevated' kinds of gratification than other animals (U, 210–12) – except in terms of the value that humans place on nonhuman nature. Mill addresses this issue in a limited way in the *Principles*, where he argues that preserving spaces of 'solitude in the presence of natural beauty and grandeur' is important to human well-being (PPE, 756). In his view, however, human ends remain the measure of all such valuations.

6

Freedom, Sex Equality, and the Power of Gender

Everyone, for himself, values his position just in proportion to the freedom of it: yet the same people think that freedom is the very thing which you may subtract from in the case of others, without doing them any wrong.

Harriet Taylor and J.S. Mill, 'Papers on Women's Rights' (circa 1847–50)

So long as Man is equal to human but Woman is non-Man (and therefore nonhuman) how could we possibly invent anything so comparatively simple as mere freedom?

Robin Morgan, *The Anatomy of Freedom*

Mill regards gender relations as among the most significant power relationships that govern people's lives. His book *The Subjection of Women*, published in 1869, can be read as a feminist analysis of how gender relations – relations through which sex differences are given social and political meaning – structure unequally the constraints to and opportunities for freedom that men and women face. He sees prevailing gender relations as relationships of unequal power and unequal freedom that favour men at the expense of women. Moreover, he illuminates how gender relations structure people's freedom in a distinctive way compared to other power relationships – for example, educative, familial, economic, and political relationships – due to how gender cuts across, shapes, and is shaped by all other social relationships and institutions. The power of gender, then, does not refer to any one distinct site for governing conduct or of potential self-government.

Mill's account of the subjection of women also extends his insights into how the psychological and sociological aspects of freedom and unfreedom are intertwined. He highlights two distinct but interrelated forms of patriarchal power that impose special constraints upon women's freedom.[1] First, men control the powers of education and opinion and use them in ways that stifle women's capacities for mental freedom and autonomy. Second, men largely control the law, customs, 'the moral coercion of public opinion,' and the distribution of resources, and thereby restrict the options open to women relative to those of men. In more current terminology, he sees women's freedom as limited by both *repressive* power – 'internalized notions of their own incapacities' – and *oppressive* power – 'systematically imposed rules and customs that guaranteed sex inequality' (Elshtain, 1991, 153).[2]

Besides elucidating the distinctive constraints to freedom that women face relative to men, Mill shows that achieving equal freedom for women and men is more than just a matter of removing repressive and oppressive forms of power. It also requires equal power and equal opportunities for women to share in practices of self-formation and self-government with respect to education, paid employment and careers, marriage and divorce, self-government in economic enterprises, political freedom, and self-government in families. He employs his principles of liberty, equality, justice, and democratic self-government to outline the necessary conditions for maximizing the freedom of both women and men. At the same time, he shows how the ways in which individuals are gendered has important implications for both forms of modern freedom: individual liberty and democratic self-government – the freedom to pursue our own life plans as independent individuals and the freedom to share in governing ourselves (see ch. 1, above).

Along with its considerable merits, Mill's feminism has three significant limitations for addressing the relationship between freedom and the power of gender. First, despite his challenge to existing gender conventions, he uncritically accepts prevailing ideas about the 'most suitable' sexual division of labour between women and men. Second, he takes for granted the Victorian view of heterosexual marital relations as the basic and 'normal' unit structuring sexual, affectionate, and familial relations. Third, due to his noninterpretive approach to social criticism – that is, his failure to grasp how social reality is partly constituted by agents' self-understandings – he fails to address adequately differences among women and among men of culture, nationality, class, 'race,' and religion.

I Gender and Individual Liberty

Mill explores several ways in which the power of gender unequally structures the individual liberty of women and men. Regarding the 'inward,' psychological dimension of freedom, gender shapes their relative autonomy – that is, their capacity to reflectively determine their own desires and purposes. This calls for what Mill calls 'ethological' analysis (see chs. 2 and 4). Within the 'outward' field of social and political power relationships, gender structures the effective freedom of women and men with respect to life plans, marriage, divorce, and sexuality.

a. Autonomy, Freedom, and the Constraints of Gender

In light of his concern for character formation and education for freedom, Mill shows that the force of law is only one aspect of the subjection of women to men. Prevailing traditions and customs, which are sustained by education and popular opinion, also perpetuate unequal freedom and power between the sexes (Mendus, 1994). The existing education of women for traditionally 'feminine' characters and customary 'women's' roles (that is, their gender socialization) is a powerful constraint on women's freedom.[3] Such education limits their autonomy by instilling in them a truncated sense of their own capacities and possibilities (see chs. 1 and 4 above). Consequently, it conflicts with the modern spirit of freedom that Mill characterizes in an address on women's suffrage as 'the desire to take off restrictions – to break down barriers – to leave people free to make their own circumstances, instead of chaining them down by law and custom to circumstances made for them' ('WS[I],' 375).

He explains in *The Subjection of Women* that men want 'not a forced slave but a willing one.' Accordingly, they have 'put everything in practice to enslave their minds,' including 'the whole force of education' (SW, 271).[4] 'All women,' he says, 'are brought up from the very earliest years in the belief that their ideal character is the very opposite to that of men; not self-will, and the government by self-control, but submission, and the yielding to the control of others. All moralities tell them that it is the duty of women, and all current sentimentalities that it is their nature, to live for others' (SW, 271–2, 293). He adds that this restrictive education extends beyond the early upbringing of young girls into the daily lives of adult women. The existing gender roles and responsibilities of women, including the 'superintendence of a household, ... [are] extremely onerous to the thoughts' and impose limitations 'from which the person responsible for them can hardly ever shake herself free' (SW, 318). These tasks constrain their 'freedom of mind' by expending their 'time and mental power' (SW, 318–19). 'If it were possible that all this number of little practical interests (which are made great to them) should leave them either much leisure, or much energy and freedom of mind, to be devoted to art or speculation, they must have a much greater original supply of active faculty than the vast majority of men' (319). Compared to men, then, the education of women is repressive. Women are taught to minister to the needs and desires of others rather than to think about and pursue their own aims and purposes; and thus, they face special barriers to developing their speculative faculties and freedom of mind.[5]

Mill is open to criticism insofar as he implies that most women are essentially passive and powerless in the face of social conditioning, except for the 'few individuals superior to their age' ('PWR,' 387; cf. SW, 270–1). He regards most men, however, in a similar light, and his basic insight is sound regarding the constraints faced by many (if not most) women of his time. Many women had internalized restrictive notions of their possibilities and of their rightful claims in relation to men.[6] Moreover, women whose ambitions might have led them to consider nontraditional roles and life plans often curtailed their stated aims and desires in response to sexist laws and customs. These women may well have achieved 'mental freedom' in Mill's sense, but their expressed preferences and actual choices within such constraining circumstances can hardly be taken as a sign that they were fully free to pursue their own life plans.[7] Furthermore, women in many countries continue to face similar constraints (Hirschmann, 1996).

Mill's remedy for this limitation of women's mental freedom is to reform social and political institutions to foster equally the 'free development' of both men and women. He calls for 'giving to women the free use of their faculties, by leaving them the free choice of their employments, and opening them to the same field of occupation and the same prizes and encouragements as to other human beings' (SW, 326). This must include an equal education for freedom to foster the qualities of character essential for self-government (see ch. 4, above). 'Strong feeling,' he says, 'is the instrument and element of strong self-control: but it requires to be cultivated in that direction' (SW, 309). Later he adds, 'Women in general would be equally capable of understanding business, public affairs, and the higher matters of speculation with men in the same class of society ... [through] better and more complete intellectual education

... raising their education to the level of men' (SW, 326). Women's desires and sentiments will remain 'artificial products,' he explains, 'as long as the social institutions do not admit the same free development of originality in women which is possible in men' (SW, 280). Conversely, simply by opening opportunities for women to freely use their faculties and choose their employments,

> the mere consciousness a women would then have of being a human being like any other, entitled to choose her pursuits, urged or invited by the same inducements as any one else to interest herself in whatever is interesting to others, entitled to exert the share of influence on all human concerns which belongs to an individual, whether she attempted actual participation in them or not – this alone would affect an immense expansion of the faculties of women, as well as enlargement of the range of their moral sentiments. (SW, 327)

That is, opening opportunities for women to choose their own pursuits and to have a voice in matters that concern them would foster their autonomy and self-determination. Rather than merely living *for* others, women would learn to regard themselves, like men, as having the capacity and the moral right to control their own lives.

b. Life Plans and Career Opportunities

Important tensions in Mill's feminism are evident when he examines the relative freedom and unfreedom of women and men with regard to pursuing their own life plans and career choices. His deepest insights support the egalitarian view that women and men are equally suited for, and entitled to, the freedom to influence 'the regulation of their affairs' in all areas of modern life (SW, 337). In this vein, he provides grounds for thoroughgoing domestic, social, and political equality between women and men as a necessary condition of equal freedom for all.[8] At the same time, he fails to carry the radical dimension of his argument to its logical conclusions, and as a result accepts some unequal constraints on the freedom of women. This shortcoming needs to be understood, however, in its historical context: although Mill's overall view of women's liberation seems moderate by contemporary feminist standards, it was fairly radical for its time (Nicholson, 1998).[9]

On the egalitarian side of his argument, Mill maintains that equal opportunities for men and women in all areas of modern life are necessary for equal freedom. He declares in a speech on women's suffrage that justice requires 'equal chances, equal opportunities, equal means of self-protection for both halves of mankind' ('WS[I],' 374; cf. SW, 300). A crucial component of his argument is his critique of prevailing assumptions about the 'nature' of women. He says in *The Subjection of Women* that such assumptions are misleading because they take the effects upon women of social customs and traditions as evidence of what is 'natural' for women to do or be. 'What is now called the nature of women is an eminently artificial thing – the result of forced repression in some directions, unnatural stimulation in others. It may be asserted that no other class of dependents have had their character so entirely distorted from its natural proportions by their relation with their masters' (SW, 276). That is, given the limitations that women have historically faced, their achievements to date offer us no valid grounds for deducing what they can and cannot do or be. Their true capabilities are something 'nobody knows, not even [women] themselves, because they have never been called out' (SW, 278). Until women have the same freedom as men to develop their potentialities, he says, it is presumptuous to conclude

> what women are or are not, can or cannot be, by natural constitution. They have hitherto been kept, as far as regards spontaneous development, in so unnatural a state, that their nature cannot but have been greatly distorted and disguised; and no one can safely pronounce that if women's nature were left to choose its direction as freely as men's, and if no artificial bent were attempted to be given to it except by the conditions of human society, and given to both sexes alike, there would be any material difference at all in character and capacities which would unfold themselves. (SW, 305; cf. SW, 280)[10]

His underlying philosophical position is a variant of the empiricist view that only experience can teach us about such untried things as what women are really like 'by nature' and, thus, the limits of their capabilities (SW, 275–8, 310–19).[11] Consequently, current appeals to what is 'natural' for women, to justify laws and customs that relegate women to certain predetermined roles and responsibilities, are either fallacious or disingenuous.

Mill maintains, therefore, that his arguments for individual liberty apply equally to women and men. 'Freedom of individual choice,' he explains,

> is now known to be the only thing which procures the adoption of the best processes, and throws each operation into the hands of those who are best

qualified for it ... In consonance with this doctrine, it is felt to be an overstepping of the proper bounds of authority to fix beforehand, on some general presumption, that certain persons are not fit for certain things ... At present, in the more improved countries, the disabilities of women are the only case, save one, in which laws and institutions take persons at their birth, and ordain that they shall never be allowed to compete for certain things. (SW, 273–4)

In other words, despite the increasingly acknowledged benefits of leaving individuals free to succeed or fail in various pursuits according to their desires and abilities, prevailing laws and customs prevent most women from freely choosing their own life plans (SW, 305). Such restrictions not only conflict with the principle of careers open to merit, but also constitute a basic injustice since they exclude women 'from the greater number of lucrative occupations, and from almost all high social functions,' even though many women have proven 'themselves capable of everything ... done by men' (SW, 299–300). Even if society can do without women in lucrative positions, he asks, 'would it be consistent with justice to refuse them their fair share of honour and distinction, or to deny them the equal right of all human beings to choose their occupation (short of injury to others) according to their own preferences, at their own risk?' (SW, 300). He insists that even if we accept the questionable premise that being a wife and mother is 'the natural vocation of a woman,' there is no need to *prohibit* them from choosing other vocations. With equal opportunities, women and men will tend to end up doing what they are best suited to do as a result of the 'free play of competition' (SW, 280–1, 304).[12]

In illuminating how prevailing gender norms restrict the individual liberty of women relative to that of men, Mill begins to outline a far-reaching case for equal individual liberty for women and men. Yet he undermines his egalitarianism by uncritically accepting as the norm the then-prevailing sexual division of labour in middle-class families (cf. Hall, 1992, 151–71). He asserts that 'the most suitable' division of labour between a husband and wife is one in which 'the man earns the income and the wife superintends the domestic expenditure' and takes care 'of the children and of the household' (SW, 297–8).[13] He says that once a woman chooses marriage, she 'chooses a profession' that includes the 'choice of the management of the household, and the bringing up of a family as the first call upon her duties' (SW, 298). He insists that women can *freely choose* this vocation only if alternative vocations are fully open to them (see below), but he assumes that this is the 'natural' choice for most women and the choice that most women will freely make.[14] In addition, he maintains that once a woman makes *this choice* she effectively renounces 'all other objects and occupations' that conflict with taking care of her children and managing her household (SW, 298). This position relegates most women to the very constraints of domesticity that Mill criticizes elsewhere. To the degree that women are largely responsible for domestic labour, their freedom to develop their talents and to pursue their own life plans in other directions is sharply restricted relative to that of men: 'The actual exercise, in a habitual or systematic manner, of outdoor occupations, or such as cannot be carried on at home, would by this principle be practically interdicted to the greater number of married women' (SW, 298). In contrast, men face no such trade-off between a career and a family, since the prevailing middle-class roles of husband and father are compatible with careers, *provided* that their wives fulfill their prescribed supporting roles. Clearly, equal freedom for married men and women requires a more radical rethinking of gender roles than Mill provides. He does not consider an equal division of domestic labour, including child rearing, housework, and other caregiving activities.[15]

Mill's uncritical acceptance of the patriarchal middle-class sexual division of labour is an uncharacteristically weak link in his broader argument for sex equality. It flies in the face of his own critique of prevailing assumptions about the 'nature' of women, and he gives no grounds for his conclusion apart from the claim that if the woman is 'disabled' from caring for children and the household, 'nobody else' will do this work (SW, 298). In fact, while perpetuating the human species requires that some women must bear children – at least for now – it by no means entails that women must take primary responsibility for children's 'care and education in early years' (297). He fails to consider that just as women are capable of vocations other than that of wife and mother, men are quite capable of sharing in the 'mothering' and 'housewife's' work of child care and housework. Children clearly need care and nurturance in order to flourish, but accumulated human experience shows that no one kind of family arrangement is uniquely and cross-culturally suited to this task. Moreover, just what constitutes 'effective,' 'successful,' or 'good' child rearing is itself an intrinsically contestable issue.[16] Furthermore, the privileging of the middle-class heterosexual nuclear family as the 'normal' family unit in modern democratic societies is arguably an ideological supposition rather than a measured assessment of the necessary conditions for effective child rearing. It is one thing to acknowledge the profound meaning and value that this family structure holds for many people; it is quite another thing to construe it narrowly as an elemental and unchanging feature of human society.

The logic of Mill's argument supports a more egalitarian policy than he officially endorses. It is possible that one sex is better suited to be the primary care giver for children, but Mill makes a persuasive case for being wary of claims about the supposedly 'natural' roles of women and men.[17] It remains possible, of course, to argue that women *should be* primarily responsible for child care and other domestic labour – for example, based on religiously informed views of women's and men's 'proper' roles – and that this obligation should take precedence over their freedom to pursue other goals. The persuasiveness of such arguments, however, depends upon prior acceptance of the particular moral outlooks on which they rest. Finally, Mill's acceptance of the prevailing sexual division of labour also poses a problem for his aim of equally educating both women and men for freedom. As I noted earlier, he contends that this gender dichotomy tends to undermine the development of mental freedom and individuality of women relative to that of men. Accordingly, his view of educative conditions for freedom lends further support to the conclusion that equal freedom requires a more thoroughly equalized sexual division of labour.

c. Marriage and Divorce

Mill also considers the relative freedom of men and women with respect to choosing marriage and divorce. He insists in his early essay on this topic that without the 'power of gaining their own livelihood,' women are less free than men in this domain because they are less able to choose marriage freely. In this situation, marriage is 'something approaching a matter of necessity; something, at least, which every woman is under strong artificial motives to desire,' rather than 'wholly a matter of choice' ('MD[I],' 77).[18] He suggests that those women who wish to choose other vocations will only be fully free to do so when existing laws and customs, which dictate that women 'have no vocation or useful office to fulfill in the world, [by] remaining single,' are transformed to support the pursuits of 'single women' ('MD[I],' 72; SW, 298). Once again, his argument is limited somewhat by how he presents women with the choice of *either* being single career women *or* being wives and mothers.

Mill also supports liberalized divorce laws, but a bit more hesitantly.

He notes certain dangers inherent in liberalized divorce laws, particularly when children are involved ('MD[I],' 80–1; OL, 300). In addition, he suggests that unrestricted freedom to marry and divorce would be appropriate for ideal circumstances of equal respect between partners, but not for existing marriages. In his view, existing marriages undermine equality and mutual respect because they are based primarily on sensual bonds that subordinate women to men. 'The law of marriage, as it now exists, has been made *by* sensualists, and *for* sensualists and to *bind* sensualists' ('MD[I],' 70, Mill's emphasis). As a consequence, women 'have a habitual belief that their power over men is chiefly derived from men's sensuality' ('MD[I],' 71).

Still, he regards equal freedom for women and men to get divorces as necessary to establish marital relations on the basis of mutual freedom and equality:

> If all, or even most persons, in the choice of a companion of the other sex, were led by any real aspiration towards, or sense of, the happiness which such companionship in its best shape is capable of giving to the best natures, there would never have been any reason why law or opinion should have set any limits to the most unbounded freedom of uniting or separating: nor is it probable that popular morality would ever, in a civilized or refined people, have imposed any restraint upon that freedom. ('MD[I],' 70)

Mill says that even in current circumstances there are 'numerous cases in which the happiness of both parties would be greatly promoted by dissolution,' and adds that divorces will be even more likely to satisfy both partners 'when the social position of the two sexes shall be perfectly equal' ('MD[I],' 79, 78). On balance, then, 'the arguments in favour of the indissolubility of marriage, are as nothing in comparison with the far more potent arguments for leaving this like other relations voluntarily contracted' ('MD[I],' 83; PPE, 953–4).[19] While an indissoluble tie may have been beneficial to women when the best they could hope for was 'to find a protector,' it is inappropriate now that they are 'ripe for equality.' Women, he says, are 'no longer a mere property' of their husbands or fathers; they are independent agents in their own right. 'But it is absurd to talk of equality when marriage is an indissoluble bond' ('MD[I],' 83).

At the same time, based on his view of equal political freedom (see below), Mill refrains from taking a definite position on the reform of marriage and divorce laws while women lack an equal voice in law making. He says in an 1870 letter, 'It is impossible, in my opinion, that a right marriage law can be made by men alone, or until women have an equal voice in making it.'[20]

d. Gender, Sexuality, and Sexual Freedom

Regarding sexuality and sexual freedom, Mill offers some valuable insights into how gendered power undermines mutual freedom and fulfilment within sexual relations, even though he takes a dim view of sexuality.[21] Generally speaking, he maintains that what he calls 'a merely animal connexion' between men and women gets in the way of a deeper relationship ('MD[I],' 78). In this spirit, he says in the early draft of his *Autobiography* that in his marriage to Harriet Taylor he and Harriet 'disdained, as every person not a slave of the animal appetites must do, the abject notion that the strongest and tenderest friendship cannot exist between a man and a woman without a sensual relation.'[22] In addition, he reinforces Victorian gender stereotypes concerning male and female sexuality by reiterating the prevailing view that women are less strongly motivated than men are by sexual passions ('MD[I],' 70–1).[23] More interestingly for present purposes, he traces the worst features of human sexual relationships to the patriarchal character of existing marriages. He even provides a critique of what is now recognized as marital rape (cf. Pateman, 1983).

In Mill's view, women at the time were so thoroughly denied independence by prevailing laws and customs that they were effectively denied freedom with respect to sexual relations with their husbands. In contrast to an English wife, even

> a female slave has (in Christian countries) an admitted right, and is considered under moral obligation, to refuse to her master the last familiarity. Not so the wife: however brutal a tyrant she may unfortunately be chained to – though she may know that he hates her, though it may be his daily pleasure to torture her, and though she may feel it impossible not to loathe him – he can claim from her and enforce the lowest degradation of a human being, that of being made the instrument of an animal function contrary to her inclinations. (SW, 285)

In short, in the absence of laws that offer women legal protection against abusive husbands, domestic abuse by husbands, including rape, is in effect legally sanctioned. Existing laws perpetuate the idea that married women are the 'property' of their husbands and must cater to their husbands' sexual desires; *women's* desires and inclinations in such matters are given no legal standing.

On the whole, then, patriarchal power tends to degrade sexual relations into something like an 'animal function' – or in the case of rape to something worse, an act of violence. Where women are treated merely as the objects of men's sexual desires, the distinctly human aspects of sexuality – love, caring, intimacy – are absent. In this light, Mill's ideal of 'true marriage' as a partnership provides a vision of the kind of reciprocal relationships in which sexuality can express mutual freedom rather than being an 'animal function' (Shanley, 1998). The equal power and equal respect that his marital ideal implies is indispensable if sexual relations are to be an expression of freedom between consenting adults.

Mill also broaches important connections between population control, reproductive freedom, and economic inequalities between men and women. As I noted in Chapter 5, his account of the distinction between the domain of individual liberty and that of moral obligations entails that the sexual conduct of consenting adults falls within the self-regarding domain of individual liberty. Here the freedom of action of individuals is 'of right, absolute' (OL, 224). Thus, his principle of liberty calls upon society to abstain from punitively interfering with the sexual conduct of consenting adults – at least as long as such conduct involves no force or deception and no harm to third parties. He qualifies this policy only with regard to sexual relations that produce children; here, he supports efforts to develop safe and effective methods of birth control.[24] In his view, reproduction raises issues of social morality or duty to others in two respects.[25] First, parents take on responsibilities to their children, and to society to nurture and educate their children. Second, people's individual reproductive decisions indirectly raise broader moral obligations to society with respect to population control.

The latter point is especially relevant for present purposes. Drawing upon Thomas Malthus's arguments about population growth, Mill maintains that some limits to population growth and, thus, to human reproduction are necessary in order to secure sufficient means of subsistence for all persons who are born, and in order for people to maintain a healthy balance with nonhuman nature (i.e., by leaving unspoiled habitats for other creatures) ('VFR,' 385–7; PPE, 756, 762; and Coole, 1988, 136–8).[26] In his view, these considerations are indirectly related to the goal of sex equality insofar as increasing social and economic equality between women and men tends to promote population control. Mill says that an increase in intelligence, education, and 'the love of independence among the working classes' will foster 'provident habits of conduct' that restrain population growth. This will ease the pressure on employment opportunities and wages (PPE, 765). Furthermore, he says that 'the opening of industrial occupations freely to both sexes' will significantly contribute to this trend by leading some women to choose vocations other than motherhood (PPE, 765). He shies away from pursuing the more radical implications of this thought with respect to marriage and motherhood. Nonetheless, he alludes to a more fundamental line of questioning by criticizing how existing gender roles make the reproductive function 'fill the entire life of one sex, and interweave itself with all the objects of the other' (PPE, 766).

Once we acknowledge that child bearing constitutes only one of many things that women can do, and that bearing children has no necessary connection to being the primary care giver for children, then we must also recognize a broader range of options for women than the ones Mill affirms. He does not consider the range of new possibilities (and challenges) that open up for women and men, consistent with limiting population growth, once we open paid employment equally to women. For instance, it is clearly easier for couples *jointly* to combine parenting with 'outside' vocations when they have only one or two children in their care.[27]

Finally, Mill's account of the interplay between freedom and power with regard to gender and sexuality is also limited by his acceptance of prevailing norms concerning heterosexuality. He naturalizes key gender and sexual norms by framing his analysis in terms of 'the relations of Man and Woman' ('MD[I],' 68). Men, in his view, are always 'Men,' defined primarily in terms of public vocations and sexual attraction to women and secondarily in terms of the responsibilities of fathers and husbands. Women are always 'Women,' defined primarily though not exclusively in terms of domesticity, motherhood, wifehood, and sexual attraction to men. Manhood and womanhood, so conceived, are always *natural* counterparts of each other in relation to the norm of heterosexuality. In taking this view, Mill is very much a product of his time. For that reason he is unable to see the subtle way in which the powers of prevailing opinion and received 'knowledge' operate to constitute as 'deviant' those modes of gender, sexuality, and family that transgress these norms – a case in point being same-sex relationships (Foucault, 1980a). Consequently, he fails to question deeply enough the role received gender roles and expectations, and the norms governing sexual, affectionate, and family relations.

Contrary to Mill's Victorian assumptions, there are no necessary conditions of human existence that require manhood and womanhood to be enacted according to the prevailing English middle-class norms of gender and sexuality. Indeed, changes in politics, economics, and technology, and differences of religion, culture, sexual orientation, and 'experiments in living,' offer other possibilities.[28] At the same time, his defence of 'experiments in living' (OL, 281) lends support to sexual, affectionate, and family relationships that present more far-reaching challenges to prevailing gender norms. (see ch. 5, above).

II Sex Equality and Democratic Self-government

As I noted at the start of this chapter, Mill illuminates how the power of gender structures both practices of democratic self-government and practices of individual liberty. He examines the gendered character of practices of democratic self-government with respect to marital relations, politics, and economic enterprises.

a. Marital Partnership

Perhaps the most striking aspect of Mill's analysis of the interplay between freedom and gender concerns his ideal of marital partnership. For Mill, men's and women's freedom with regard to marriage involves not only the freedom to choose whether to marry (and divorce), but also an equal share in governing their marriages and families. Accordingly, besides highlighting the special constraints that prevent women from making marriage a matter of 'free and voluntary choice' ('MD[I],' 69ff), he brings to light the severe constraints to women's freedom imposed by patriarchal rule within marriages. His solution is not to somehow banish power from marital relations, but rather to democratize power and authority between spouses. Although he by no means seeks to require such marriages by law, he calls for the state to facilitate greater marital equality by guarding against domestic tyranny and abuse by men, and by protecting women's property.

Mill maintains that for women, the existing institution of marriage is basically a form of enslavement. Thus, he rejects the prevailing view 'that civilization and Christianity have restored to the woman her just rights' after a past in which all power was given to husbands (SW, 284). 'The wife,' he says, 'is the actual bond-servant of her husband: no less so, as far as legal obligation goes, than slaves commonly so called' (284). She takes a marital vow of 'obedience' whereby 'she can do no act whatever but by [her husband's] permission, at least tacit. She can acquire no property but for him; the instant it becomes hers, even if by inheritance, it becomes *ipso facto* his' (284). One indication of the extent to which a married woman loses her own independent existence, property, and freedom is the way that she and her husband are 'called "one person in law,"' for the purpose of inferring that whatever is hers is his, but the parallel inference is never drawn that whatever is his is hers' (284). Moreover, on top of this condition 'of slavery as to her own person,' a woman's husband is given exclusive legal standing as the guardian of their children: 'They are by law *his* children. He alone has any legal rights over them' (285, Mill's emphasis). Therefore, if a woman wishes to leave her husband she must be prepared to leave everything that she had within her marriage, including her children. Her only legal recourse to this situation, he says, is a 'legal separation by a decree of a court of justice, which entitles her to live apart, without being forced back into the custody of an exasperated jailer – or which empowers her to apply any earnings to her own use' (SW, 285).

Mill believes that it is possible for some couples to establish more egalitarian marriages within the limits set out by the existing social and political power relationships. Indeed, he and Harriet Taylor attempted to create an equal partnership when they married in 1851. He emphasizes, though, that existing laws and customs make fully equal freedom and power unattainable by most married women, regardless of the best efforts of individual couples. Individual men can disavow their given rights, powers, and privileges; but they cannot wish away the broader social, legal, and cultural context of gender inequality.[29]

The 'present social institutions,' in Mill's view, give men 'almost unlimited power' over their wives and families and sharply restrict the freedom of married women (SW, 289). Married women are not completely powerless with respect to their husbands and children, but their power with respect to their husbands is largely that of subordinates who can influence their superiors. He explains, 'the wife, if she cannot effectually resist, can at least retaliate; she, too, can make the man's life extremely uncomfortable, and by that power is able to carry many points which she ought, and many which she ought not, to prevail in. But this instrument of self-protection – which may be called the power of the scold, or the shrewish sanction – has the fatal defect, that it avails most against the least tyrannical superiors' (SW, 289). This kind of retaliatory and unauthorized power, he says, 'generally only establishes a counter-tyranny' that, like the power of tyrants, tends to encourage the worst and most irresponsible uses of power. 'It is the weapon of irritable and self-willed women; of those who would make the worst use of power if they themselves had it, and who generally turn this power to a bad use.' It is not a form of power available to 'amiable' or 'highminded' women (SW, 289).

Furthermore, although some women are able to get what they want *from the limited choices and possibilities open to them*, most women have little power and no authority to share in governing their marriages. Therefore, they have little power to determine the choices and actions available to them within their marriages. The limited power that married women possess, Mill says, is no substitute for their lack of freedom:

> Neither in the affairs of families nor in those of states is power a compensation for the loss of freedom. [A wife's] power often gives her what she has no right to, but does not enable her to assert her own rights ... By sinking her own existence in her husband; by having no will (or persuading him that she has no will) but his, in anything which regards their joint relation, and by making it the business of her life to work upon his sentiments, a wife may gratify herself by influencing, and very probably perverting his conduct, in those of his external relations which she has never qualified herself to judge of, or in which she is herself wholly influenced by some personal or other partiality or prejudice. (SW, 290)

In short, insofar as married women possess only the limited power of subordinates within their marriages, their freedom of self-government is likewise restricted.

Mill's primary response to this problem is his ideal of marital partnership within which men and women share power as equal partners. This ideal, despite some limitations, extends his principle of democratic self-government to both women and men in governing their marriages and families. He regards marital and family relations as an important site for governing conduct since they play an important role in determining the field of possibilities faced by each family member, individually and in matters of mutual concern. Accordingly, he says, 'Not a word can be said for despotism in the family which cannot be said for despotism in the state' (SW, 286). In other words, the criticisms that apply to political despotism also apply to despotic rule within families. There may be some benign or even 'benevolent' despots who exhibit paternalistic concern for those subject to their power, even to the degree that they grant their subjects certain freedoms. They are still despots, though, with unchecked power to reign over others as they see fit. Consequently, the freedom of others is protected, as Mill says in *Representative Government*, only 'on sufferance, and by a concession' from the despot (CRG, 402; cf. PPE, 759–63). Moreover, despots by definition deny those subject to their rule the freedom of self-government.

Mill recognizes that the family, like the state, needs to be governed. He insists, though, that this does not mean 'that some one person must be the ultimate ruler,' and that his democratic notion of marital partnership is the best form of government in two-parent families (SW, 290–1).[30] He explains this ideal in *The Subjection of Women* through an analogy with business partnerships. He says that the law does not 'ordain that one partner should administer the common business as if it was his private concern,' leaving others with only delegated powers (SW, 291). Furthermore, he says that experience does not

> show it to be necessary that any theoretical inequality of power should exist between the partners, or that the partnership should exist between the partners, or that the partnership should have any other conditions than what they may themselves appoint by their articles of agreement. Yet it might seem that the exclusive power might be conceded with less danger to the rights and interests of the inferior, in the case of [business] partnership than marriage, since he is free to cancel the power by withdrawing from the connexion. The wife has no such power [under existing laws], and even if she had, it is almost always desirable that she should try all measures before resorting to it. (SW, 291)

Mill's analogy between marriages and business partnerships is somewhat misleading, since marriages are not reducible to a contractual relationship, as he himself points out in *On Liberty*. Marriages typically give rise to moral obligations between parties that have no direct analogue in the ties that typically bind business partners, especially when children are involved (OL, 300; Mendus, 1989b). Still, his analogy is instructive: marriages, like business partnerships, can be established on an egalitarian basis whereby each partner has roughly equal power in deciding matters of mutual concern.

Ultimately, Mill balances his commitment to equality with his acceptance of different roles for husbands and wives. He contends that while married persons cannot consult their partners on all decisions, so that one person must frequently exercise 'sole control' over certain decisions, the decision maker need not 'always be the same person'

(SW, 291). 'The natural arrangement,' he says,

> is a division of powers between the two; each being absolute in the execu-
> tive branch of their own department, and any change of system and
> principle requiring the consent of both ... There would seldom be any
> difficulty in deciding such things by mutual consent, unless the marriage
> was one of those unhappy ones in which all other things as well as this,
> become subjects of bickering and dispute. The division of rights would
> naturally follow the division of duties and functions; and that is already
> made by consent, or at all events not by law, but by general custom,
> modified and modifiable at the pleasure of those concerned. (SW, 291)

In effect, he seeks to reconcile his views of equality and sexual difference
by democratizing the patriarchal bourgeois family norm.

This leaves some fundamental tensions in Mill's notion of sex equality.
He rightly contends that such a clear division of duties and decision-
making responsibilities in a marriage would be consistent with equality *if
it was itself determined and revisable by free and mutual agreement.* At the same
time, he says that inequality in 'the real practical decision of affairs' is
justified when it rests upon 'comparative qualifications,' such as the
greater wisdom of the older partner until both partners 'attain a time of
life at which' their age difference loses importance (SW, 291). Mill notes
that this basis for unequal decision-making authority tends to favour
men since they are 'usually the eldest.' Nonetheless, he maintains that it
is compatible with basic equality since it merely gives due recognition to
special knowledge or experience. He also says, 'There will naturally also
be a more potential voice on the side, whichever it is, that brings the
means of support' (SW, 291). Then he quickly adds, 'Inequality from this
source does not depend on the law of marriage, but on the general
conditions of human society, as now constituted. The influence of mental superiority, either general or special, will necessarily tell for much. It
always does at present' (SW, 291). His claim here that 'mental superiority' merits special authority builds upon his general view that superior
knowledge is the only legitimate basis for unequal political power (see
chs. 3 and 8).

Mill's defence of this kind of inequality has some shortcomings, especially when he extends it to marital relations. Notably, he fails to explain
just why we should expect the older partner in a marriage to have
'mental superiority' that justifies an *a priori* claim to extra authority. He
recognizes that questions of policy, whether for a family or for a state,

involve both instrumental knowledge and moral knowledge – that is, knowledge about the best way to achieve desired ends and knowledge about appropriate ends (L, Bk. VI, ch. 12; Thompson, 1976, 55–62). Yet he fails to consider that with respect to families, many (if not most) significant decisions also concern what he calls prudential and aesthetic judgments – that is, judgments about what is wise and about what constitutes a good or desirable way of life. For instance, Mill himself notes that decisions about having and educating children raise not only instrumental and moral considerations, but also aesthetic, religious, or spiritual considerations that involve different views of the good (PPE, 220–1, 765–6; OL, 301–3; 'ORG'; see ch. 4, above). Furthermore, while he maintains that moral, prudential, and aesthetic judgment require a 'cultivated mind,' he insists that this kind of mental cultivation is potentially attainable by virtually all adults (U, 215–16; and ch. 4, above). These considerations call into question general claims about the 'comparative qualification' of older partners. While age offers some benefits of knowledge and wisdom, these advantages are difficult to gauge for decisions that concern partners jointly.

At the same time, Mill's suggestion that the duties and responsibilities of partners should be determined by their mutual consent provides a democratic and egalitarian criterion for allocating greater decision-making authority to one partner or the other. One partner or the other is bound to have more expertise in certain matters, particularly with regard to instrumental knowledge. Yet it is always an open question just how such instrumental knowledge should be weighed against moral and aesthetic considerations; and such judgments are best made jointly. Such mutual consent also sustains mutual self-government.

There is a deeper flaw than this in Mill's view of marital partnership. His acceptance of the prevailing middle-class sexual division of labour in England undermines his claim that his marital ideal represents a free and equal contract between a man and a woman. In Mill's scenario, men and women consent to what Carole Pateman aptly calls the 'patriarchally ascribed status of superior husband and subordinate wife' (Pateman, 1984, 78). Although Mill seeks to transform marital relations, his democratic and feminist impulses are constrained by his view that when a woman chooses to marry a man she 'naturally' assumes primary responsibility for child rearing and housework. His 'partnership' remains patriarchal insofar as he gives married men's social and political ambitions outside of the family precedence over those of married women.[31] This is evident in how Mill addresses the issue of women's economic independence (see above). While he insists that the prospect of making an independent livelihood is necessary for women to be free to choose whether to marry, he fails to consider the importance of continuing economic independence and equality for married women. Thus, he criticizes marriage laws that undermine women's independence by denying them any rights to the property they bring into or acquire during marriage; but he fails to address adequately how the division of labour that makes the husband the primary wage earner while 'the wife superintends the domestic expenditure' perpetuates unequal decision-making authority within households (SW, 296–7, 297).[32]

b. Economic and Political Freedom

Mill further illuminates the relationship between freedom, power, and sex equality by illuminating how the power of gender unequally structures men's and women's opportunities to share in governing economic enterprises and in exercising political freedom. Notwithstanding his use of masculine pronouns, he applies his principle of democratic self-government – 'the liberty of each to govern his own conduct ... by such laws and social restraints as his own conscience can subscribe to' (SW, 336) – to both women and men with respect to industry and politics as well as marital relations. He succinctly addresses the links between these different domains when he defends the 'co-operative principle' in industrial organization in *Principles of Political Economy*. As I explain in Chapter 7, he promotes cooperative enterprises in which labourers govern their own work lives 'on terms of equality ... and ... under managers elected and removable by themselves' to advance the 'freedom and independence of the individual' in the 'industrial department' of modern societies (PPE, 775, 793). He adds that an economy based on co-operatives 'would be the nearest approach to social justice, and the most beneficial ordering of industrial affairs for the universal good ... *assuming of course that both sexes participate equally in the rights and in the government of the association*' (PPE, 794, emphasis added).

Mill promotes equal political freedom for women and men – that is, an equal voice in shaping the laws that govern them – on similar grounds.[33] He insists that the 'modern' principle that things go best for individual men and women when they are able to decide for themselves 'what they are and are not fit for, and what they shall and shall not be allowed to attempt' is applicable to politics as well as to personal life (CRG, 479). He declares in *The Subjection of Women*,

> To have a voice in choosing those by whom one is to be governed, is a
> means of self-protection due to every one, though he were to remain
> excluded from the function of governing: and that women are considered
> fit to have such a choice, may be presumed from the fact, that the law
> already gives it to women in the most important of all cases to themselves:
> for the choice of the man who is supposed to govern a women to the end of
> life is always supposed to be voluntarily made by herself. (SW, 301)

This formulation is a bit misleading given his ideal of marriage as a
partnership in which 'leading and following can be alternate and reciprocal' (SW, 294). His basic point, though, is simply that women and men
have the same capacity and rightful claim to determine how they are
governed by the state (CRG, 479–81). While he stops short of espousing
simple political equality among citizens – at least in the short run (see
ch. 8, below) – he maintains that sex differences are not a legitimate
basis for political inequalities. In addition, he says that giving women the
vote would encourage men to acknowledge them as equals, since politics
would be 'a joint concern' (CRG, 480). Meanwhile, leaving women
disenfranchised relegates them to exercising merely indirect political
influence through their capacity to influence the political activities of
their husbands or of other men (480–1). Mill contends, moreover, that
'it is a personal injustice to withhold from any one, unless for the
prevention of greater evils, the ordinary privilege of having his [or her]
voice reckoned in the disposal of affairs in which he [or she] has the
same interest as other people' (CRG, 469). He regards such 'control of
those who do make their business politics, by those who do not,' as a
fundamental aspect of political freedom ('AWEF,' 154; and SW, 336).

Along with equal voting rights, Mill also defends the equal right of
capable women to seek and hold office, even though he insists that to
actually 'exercise a public trust' is not essential to political freedom (SW,
301; see ch. 8, below). His reasoning here follows his more general
argument for opening occupations to whichever women or men are
qualified to fill them:

> With regard to the fitness of women ... to hold offices or practice profes-
> sions involving important public responsibilities; I have already observed
> that this condition is not essential to the practical question in dispute: since
> any woman, who succeeds in an open profession, proves by that very fact
> that she is qualified for it ... As long therefore as it is acknowledged that
> even a few may be fit for these duties, the laws which shut the door on those

exceptions cannot be justified by any opinion which can be held respecting
the capacities of women in general. (SW, 301)

That is, just as men must demonstrate their fitness through their success
in electoral competition, the same criterion should hold for women. The
law, therefore, should not bar all women from holding office just because some women may not be up to the task, any more than it should
bar all men from holding office because some of them are unfit for it.

Overall, Mill makes a ringing call for enabling women to share equally
in economic and political self-government; he sees this as a key aspect of
sex equality. Once again, though, his acceptance of the existing bourgeois sexual division of labour undermines his commitment to equal
freedom. In his view, the domestic responsibilities of women who are
wives and mothers preclude their equal participation in occupations
outside the home (see above). Yet insofar as equal participation in
public vocations is a necessary condition for equal participation in practices of economic and political self-government, the latter goal requires
an equal sharing of household labour and care giving among married
men and women.

III Conclusion

Owing largely to subsequent feminist struggles, key aspects of Mill's
feminist agenda have been achieved – though often partially and un-
evenly – in many parts of the world. These achievements range from
women's suffrage and the increasing presence of women as political
leaders to more equal marital relations and economic opportunities. Yet
these later achievements do not detract from Mill's earlier ones. He
persuasively highlighted several ways in which the subjection of women
undermined the goal of equal freedom for all, and he pointed the way to
a more democratic gendering of social and political power.

The powers of education and opinion must be used to foster mental
freedom and autonomy in both women and men; women as well as men
must be economically empowered to make their own livelihood; women
and men must have equal political rights; the law should be used to end
the subjection and abuse of women by men; and marital relations should
be democratically transformed into balanced (if not strictly equal) partnerships. This ambitious agenda illuminates the complementarity of
freedom and equality as well as freedom and power. 'The true virtue of
human beings,' Mill says, 'is fitness to live together as equals; claiming

nothing for themselves but what they freely concede to every one else; regarding command of any kind as an exceptional necessity, and in all cases a temporary one; and preferring, whenever possible, the society of those with whom leading and following can be alternate and reciprocal' (SW, 294).

As we have seen, though, his vision of equal freedom is limited by his incomplete account of the interplay between power and culture in constituting received norms of gender and sexuality. He illuminates how prevailing ideas about women's 'natures' are cultural constructs. Yet he misses four subtle ways in which power is exercised to propagate received knowledge of 'natural' gender roles and 'normal' sexuality. *First*, he fails to pursue his critique of the ideological character of existing gender norms to its logical conclusions. He accepted as natural a sexual division of labour that reflected the then prevailing English middle-class norm which provided greater freedom for men than for women. Meanwhile, his goal of equal freedom requires a more thoroughly equalized sexual division of labour between women and men. For instance, women and men who are married to each other can be equally free to pursue their own individual life plans to the extent that they either share domestic labour equally (e.g, cooking, cleaning, shopping, child rearing, caring for elderly parents) or freely and equally choose to assume different responsibilities (Phillips, 1997). Moreover, as Mill suggests, the latter division of labour can be an equally free choice for women and men only when both sexes face comparable social, political, and economic constraints and opportunities with regard to choosing their life plans. In this regard, public policies can do more than he proposes to promote equal freedom – for example, by fostering equal educational opportunities, equality with respect to marriage and divorce, equal pay for equal work, and affordable, high-quality child care.

Second, Mill's critique of received gender norms is also limited by his tendency to regard men as the 'human' norm in interpreting commonalities and differences between women and men. He takes such a male-centred position insofar as he implicitly construes the standard criteria for full labour market and political participation so that conditions distinctive to women, such as pregnancy and childbirth, count as 'disabilities' (Mendus, 1993, 213). Consequently, he actually supports equal freedom only for those women can fit the mold of the 'typical' (that is, male) wage earner – that is, those women who forgo marriage, child bearing, and motherhood. Yet even these women do not have fully equal freedom, since Mill expects them to sacrifice any desires they might have concerning marriage and children – something he does not ask of men.[34] Equal freedom for women and men requires an approach that does not highlight differences – where they actually exist – only as a basis for *unequal* treatment of women.[35] In this light, if we start with a commitment to equal freedom for women and men to pursue paid employment and to participate in politics, we can then adopt policies that take account of differences while supporting equal freedom.[36] This may require treating women *differently* than men in certain situations to achieve equality. For instance, for certain occupations to be equally open to both women and men, women and men may need different supporting conditions – for example, maternity leave for women; special protection for pregnant women against toxic chemicals – rather than the *same* treatment based on a standard of what is required by the 'normal' (male) worker (MacKinnon, 1989; Minow, 1990a; Cohen, 1991; Cornell, 1991).

Third, Mill was unable to see how the powers of education and opinion in Victorian England, which expressed dominant religious and cultural traditions (Anglican, English), constituted Victorian manhood and womanhood in terms of a naturalized or 'compulsory' heterosexuality (cf. Rich, 1980; Warner, 1993). That is, he uncritically adopted the received view that manhood and womanhood are always partly defined by sexual attraction to the other sex. For this reason, he was unable to see how the powers of education and public opinion are deployed against those who exhibit unconventional forms of manhood or womanhood – for example, 'masculine' or androgynous women and 'feminine' or androgynous men. Nonetheless, his principle of liberty supports wider sexual freedom and 'experiments in living' with regard to gender norms than that which he officially endorses.

Fourth, Mill fails to grasp how gender norms are socially constructed within power relations that are culturally variegated (Ong, 1988, 88). This limitation in Mill's feminism is integrally related to the non-interpretive character of his political theory (see chs. 2 and 3, above), which leads him to a one-sided account of how traditions perpetuate women's oppression. The relevant laws and customs arose, he says, not because they proved to be those 'most conducive to the happiness and well being' of all; rather, they merely ratified 'the fact that from the very earliest twilight of human society, every woman ... was found in a state of bondage to some man' (SW, 263–4). This system perpetuates 'the law of the strongest' in relations between the sexes even as 'modern civilization' increasingly repudiates this 'law' (SW, 265). 'The subjection of women to men being the universal custom, any departure from it appears quite naturally as unnatural,' even though 'the feeling is dependent on custom' (SW, 270).[37] In addition, he begins his analysis of the subjection of women with his assertion that respect for the free development of *all persons* – women and men – constitutes 'the peculiar character of the modern world' (SW, 272). What 'chiefly distinguishes modern institutions, ... modern life itself,' he says, 'is, that human beings are no longer born to their place in life, ... but are free to employ their faculties, and such favourable chances as offer, to achieve the lot which may appear to them most desirable' (SW, 272–3). In light of this progressive view of history, Mill implicitly posits one universal form of the subjection of women and one uniform trajectory of women's emancipation. Likewise, he construes religious and cultural traditions and customs that conflict with his modernist view of freedom strictly as barriers to the advance of freedom and well-being.[38]

My point is not that his analysis of how power operates through religious and cultural traditions is simply wrong. In fact, he sheds light on some general aspects of patriarchal power that operate in many contexts, including the powers of education with which men exert 'influence over the minds of women' (SW, 263, 271–2). Nevertheless, because he disregards the meaning that people's religious and cultural identities have for them, he fails to discern how the exercise of power is shaped by cultural differences (see chs. 1 and 4, above). Religious and cultural traditions are always *intertwined with* relations of power, but are seldom *reducible to* effects of power. As Ruth Bloch says, gendered meanings and practices in different cultures are expressive of efforts to give meaning to such things as spiritual fulfilment, aesthetic pleasure, anxieties of existence, and mysteries of procreation as much as they are manifestations of the power of men over women (1993, 95, 98). Mill overlooks the expressive–transcendent dimension of religious and cultural traditions, and as a result he insufficiently grasps what is at stake for women and men when the integrity of their religious or cultural identities is undermined.

Therefore, if we are to carry forward Mill's emancipatory feminist goals while respecting differences among women and among men, we need a more interpretive and pluralistic approach to feminist criticism than he provides – one that grasps the historical and cultural specificity of multiple forms of patriarchy (Grewal and Kaplan, 1994, 17–18).[39] People, as Charles Taylor says, are 'agents of self-definition' whose practices are partly constituted by their self-understandings (1985d, 118–19, and 117). This holds true even for people caught up in relations of domination (Spelman, 1988; Mohanty, 1991; Spivak, 1994). Accordingly, women with different class, caste, religious, cultural, ethnic, 'racial,' sexual, and national identities generally understand their struggles for freedom and other valued goals not simply *as women*, in a generic sense, but as Chinese women, Jewish women, Catholic women, Moslem women, white middle-class North American women, and so on. Confronting this diversity does not preclude highlighting general aspects of patriarchal oppression of the sort that Mill identifies; but criticizing women's oppression must be in part a local, contextual endeavour that addresses how particular women and men conceive of their gender identities in relation to their other social identities. This task must be localized *only in part*, however, because of the partial character of people's self-understandings – our own included. People rarely, if ever, have a thorough grasp of the power dynamics that shape their field of possibilities. Therefore, interpretative feminist criticism typically entails offering alternative interpretations of social relationships and practices that challenge agents' self-understandings.

Such an interpretive and pluralistic feminism enables us to confront the pervasiveness of women's oppression across cultures, as well as the diversity of its forms; at the same time, it calls upon us to acknowledge a plurality of forms of 'authentic' womanhood in relation to diverse ways of life or fundamental commitments. Moreover, in contrast to universalistic feminist criticism, such as Mill's, that focuses on oppression that all women presumably experience *as women*, this approach helps us account for resistance to feminist ideas among women who give normative priority to other aspects of their social identities – for example, fundamental religious or cultural commitments – over their identities as women.

In sum, Mill sheds considerable light on the necessary social conditions of equal freedom, but he fails to address sufficiently how promoting freedom sometimes conflicts with other valued goals, such as respect for diverse ways of life (Galston, 1995, 521; cf. Berlin, 1969c, 171–2; Parekh, 1994).[40] Still, respecting social diversity and cultural pluralism does not mean that feminists cannot appeal to freedom, in Mill's sense, to criticize different patriarchal traditions, practices, and ways of life. We can follow his lead in illuminating how different forms of patriarchy limit the freedom of women to direct the course of their own lives; we can offer new interpretations of various religious and cultural traditions; and we can support women who are actively contesting practices and traditions from within. Moreover, the constraints that patriarchal power imposes on women's agency make it imperative to watch for unarticulated or barely articulated forms of resistance by women. Under conditions marked by subordination, force, intimidation, violence, and educational pressures to fit into prescribed gender roles, women sometimes enact prevailing norms and practices without freely affirming them (Mathieu, 1990, 81–2; Spivak, 1994). In the end, if we are committed to supporting the freedom of individuals to, in Mill's words, 'use and interpret experience in [their] own way' to find fulfilment, then we also need to respect their fundamental beliefs (OL, 262; cf. Jones, 1994, 36).

7

Economic Freedom*

We are too ignorant either of what individual agency in its best form, or
Socialism in its best form, can accomplish, to be qualified to decide which of the
two will be the ultimate form of human society.
   ... The decision will probably depend mainly on one consideration, viz. which
of the two systems is consistent with the greatest human liberty and spontaneity.

John Stuart Mill, *Principles of Political Economy*

Mill's attention to the interplay between freedom and power in the
economic sphere is one of the most distinctive features of his liberalism.
Most importantly, he regards property – especially ownership and control of the means and instruments of production – as a key source of
social power; and he construes economic freedom in terms of the power
of individuals, individually and collectively, to direct the course of their
economic activities. Mill explains in his *Autobiography* that the 'criticisms
of the common doctrines of Liberalism' by St. Simonian socialists helped
convince him of 'the very limited and temporary value of the old political economy, which assumes private property and inheritance as indefea-
sible facts, and freedom of production and exchange as the *dernier mot* of
social progress' (A, 173, 175).

   In contrast to many other 'classical liberals,' Mill rejects the view that
the freedom of individuals in the economic sphere is maximized to the
extent that state power is restricted to protecting property and maintaining security. Moreover, despite his qualified support of *laissez-faire*, his

*Portions of this chapter originally appeared in 'J.S. Mill's Conception of Economic
Freedom,' *History of Political Thought* 20, no. 3 (Autumn 1999): 494–530.

conception of economic freedom strongly challenges the now common understanding of economic freedom in terms of capitalism, 'free markets,' 'free trade,' private property, and 'freedom of production and exchange.'[1] In Mill's view, these economic ideas and institutions have a tenuous relationship to the economic freedom of individuals, although they serve other ends, such as allocative efficiency. It is therefore misleading to say, as Pedro Schwartz does, that Mill regards capitalism as 'the system of economic freedom' (Schwartz, 1968, 12).[2]

As I will explain, Mill's view of economic freedom is a direct extension of his broader conception of freedom (see ch. 1). Rather than starting with the view that capitalism or any other system is a 'system of economic freedom,' Mill employs his broader conception of freedom to evaluate the merits of different economic systems. Furthermore, he is critical of existing capitalism for the 'restraints' it imposes on the economic freedom of individuals, and he favours significant reforms of the 'present system' – toward something akin to worker self-managed market socialism – as necessary for achieving maximal economic freedom.

Some previous interpreters of Mill's view of economic freedom, such as Schwartz, have tended either to misconstrue his broader conception of freedom or to misunderstand how it relates to his view of economic freedom. Other interpreters have begun to redress these errors, but without offering a sustained account of Mill's conception of economic freedom (for example, Ryan, 1983b; Smith, 1984; Hollander, 1985; Claeys, 1987; Riley, 1994, 1996). As Jonathan Riley emphasizes, 'A proper distinction between [the] respective doctrines of laissez-faire and of [individual] liberty is crucial for understanding Mill's art of political economy' (1998, 317; 1994, xlii). As I will explain, though, Mill's distinction between *laissez-faire* and individual liberty is just one part of his conception of *economic freedom*. The latter, like his broader conception of freedom, features both 'positive' and 'negative' aspects. It involves not only the absence of burdensome constraints on economic activities, but also the power of individuals to direct the course of their lives with respect to their economic activities and relationships. In such works as *Principles of Political Economy, On Liberty,* and his posthumously published *Chapters on Socialism,* Mill emphasizes three 'positive' aspects or enabling conditions of economic freedom: the 'mental freedom' or autonomy necessary for individuals to develop their own characters, preferences, and tastes; opportunities and resources for individuals to pursue effectively their own life plans and ideas of the good life; and opportunities for self-government within economic enterprises. In short, economic freedom, according to Mill, encompasses both practices of individual independence and practices of collective self-government – both the power of individuals, acting independently of others, to pursue their own life plans, and participation by associated individuals in governing economic enterprises.

This understanding of Mill's conception of economic freedom sheds new light on his view of the relative merits of capitalism and socialism and, in turn, the kind of economic system that would maximize individual economic freedom. It also illuminates his affinities to later 'revisionist' liberals like T.H. Green and John Dewey; sheds new light on important connections between the liberal and socialist traditions; and clarifies some unresolved issues in Mill's view of the political economy of freedom.

I Mill on Economic Freedom

a. Economic Freedom

Debate about 'economic freedom' is partly due to confusion regarding what we are referring to when we speak of economic freedom. Mill's view of economic freedom is a direct extension of his broader conception of freedom, which I examined earlier. Accordingly, he challenges the now prevailing conception of 'economic freedom' in Western capitalist countries. Economic freedom is now frequently construed as *equivalent to* 'free markets,' 'free trade,' 'free enterprise,' 'freedom of contract,' and even 'competitive capitalism.' For instance, Milton Friedman declares 'competitive capitalism ... a system of economic freedom' (1962, 4). Similarly, Michael Oakeshott conceives of economic freedom in terms of the unrestricted opportunities of individuals to accumulate and use private property: 'The institution of property most favourable to liberty is, unquestionably, a right to private property least qualified by arbitrary limits and exclusions ... The freedom which separates a man from slavery is nothing but a freedom to choose and to move among autonomous, independent organizations, firms, purchasers of labour, and this implies private property in resources other than personal capacity' (1991, 393–4). Friedman's and Oakeshott's conceptions of economic freedom resemble Mill's in their emphasis on the freedom of individuals to make choices and to move among autonomous organizations. In contrast to Mill, though, the former regard laws restricting individual property rights as unequivocally *freedom limiting*, and they fail to address the repressive power dynamics embedded in the notion of private property.[3]

Mill's conception of economic freedom shifted somewhat over time.

He made his largest shift, however, between the 1820s and 1848, when he published the first edition of his *Principles of Political Economy*. In the 1820s, Mill *did* regard capitalism as a system of economic freedom. In debates in 1825 with the Co-operative Society – consisting of followers of utopian socialist Robert Owen – Mill argued that state interference in the private ownership and control of property for egalitarian ends always restricts freedom. He added, however, that such restrictions are some-times justified, since freedom must be balanced against other values.[4] In the 1840s and thereafter he developed a significantly different position. First, he placed individual freedom firmly at the heart of his conception of a good society. Second, he contended that inequalities of property, opportunities, and economic power in capitalist societies were under-mining the effective freedom and individuality of the 'generality of labourers in [England] and most other countries' (PPE, 209).[5] Further-more, his view of a maximally freedom-supporting economic system drew considerably on socialist ideas.

Mill never systematically articulates his view of economic freedom, so we have to reconstruct it from his comments about the freedom of individuals within different economic arrangements. He highlights one key aspect of his view of economic freedom when he distinguishes the 'principle of individual liberty' from the 'doctrine of Free Trade' in *On Liberty* (OL, 293). There are good utilitarian grounds for both, he says, but the two principles are distinct:

> Both the cheapness and the good quality of commodities are most effec-tively provided for by leaving buyers and sellers perfectly free, under the sole check of equal freedom to the buyers for supplying themselves else-where. This is the so-called doctrine of Free Trade, which rests on grounds different from, though equally solid with, the principle of individual liberty ... As the principle of individual liberty is not involved in the doctrine of free trade, so neither is it in most questions which arise respecting the limits of that doctrine, as, for example, what amount of public control is admissible for the prevention of fraud by adulteration; how far sanitary precautions, or arrangements to protect workpeople employed in danger-ous occupations, should be enforced on employers. (OL, 293)[6]

Mill adds, 'Restrictions on trade, or on production for purposes of trade, are indeed restraints; and all restraint, *quâ* restraint, is an evil: but the restraints in question affect only that part of conduct which society is competent to restrain, and are wrong solely because they do not really produce the results which is desired to produce by them' (OL, 293). At the same time, he says that interference with trade *is* a question of liberty in 'all cases ... where the object of interference is to make it impossible or difficult to obtain a particular commodity.' The infringement of liberty at issue, though, is not that 'of the producer or seller, but on that of the buyer' (OL, 293). For *buyers*, the availability of desired goods may have a direct bearing on their freedom to pursue their preferred way of life. Regulations on trade, however, sometimes *enhance* the freedom of buyers by protecting them against deception, fraud, and harmful goods and services.[7] The freedom of producers or sellers is not affected in a comparable way unless either the restricted good is for some reason the only one they are able to produce and sell, or producing or selling *that particular good* is a component of their plans of life. This would be the case, for instance, if certain people were prohibited from pursuing their chosen craft or profession, such as practising 'alternative' medicine. Such restrictions might be justified, but they would still be restrictions of economic freedom.

Mill's principle of liberty is distinct from but also related to his conception of economic freedom. The domain of individual liberty that Mill seeks to protect encompasses both the economic and noneconomic interests and activities of individuals. When Mill outlines 'the appropriate region of human liberty,' he includes interests and activities that are integrally (though not exclusively) connected to economic institutions and relationships: 'liberty of tastes and pursuits; of framing the plan of our life to suit our own character; of doing as we like, subject to such consequences as may follow ... so long as what we do does not harm [others]' (OL, 226). Mill adds that 'from this liberty of each individual, follows the liberty, within the same limits, of combination among individuals; freedom to unite, for any purpose not involving harm to others' (OL, 226). Again, this set of liberty interests includes some activities that are not primarily economic – such as political organizing, participation in other voluntary associations, gathering with friends, and gathering with co-religionists – but it also encompasses some economic activities. Moreover, Mill notes that even liberty interests that are primarily noneconomic have economic aspects. For example, freedom of thought has economic dimensions linked to the 'the liberty of expressing and publishing opinions' (OL, 225–6).

Thus, the economic activities of individuals constitute a significant part of the 'domain of individual liberty' that I discussed in Chapter 5. Economic practices of individual liberty include the freedom of individuals to choose their occupations; to start businesses and enter into business partnerships; to join unions and participate in strikes; and to pursue their own good with their share of the produce of their labours. As I will explain later, though, Mill gives the freedom of individuals to set up capitalist firms a distinctly qualified status.

Mill addresses material and institutional conditions for economic freedom most strikingly when he discusses the 'restraints' to freedom imposed by existing capitalism and *likely* to be imposed by the 'communist' alternative to capitalism. Concerning existing capitalism, Mill says, 'The restraints of Communism would be freedom in comparison with the present condition of the majority of the human race. The generality of labourers in this and most other countries, have as little choice of occupation or freedom of locomotion, are practically dependent on fixed rules and on the will of others, as they could be on any system short of actual slavery' (PPE, 209). He amplifies this point in his *Chapters on Socialism*. Writing in the wake of the Reform Bill of 1867, Mill echoes the socialist critique of the limitations of the achievement by the working class of 'purely political rights,' such as the franchise. Despite all that has been done and will be done concerning the extension of franchises, he says,

> a few are born to great riches, and the many to a penury, made only more grating by contrast. No longer enslaved or made dependent by force of law, the great majority are so by force of poverty; they are still chained to a place, to an occupation, and to conformity with the will of an employer, and debarred by the accident of birth both from the enjoyments, and from the mental and moral advantages, which others inherit without exertion and independently of desert. (COS, 710)

In short, while working people are gradually achieving equal status as free citizens with regard to political rights, the great majority of them remain *economically unfree* within existing capitalism. That is, they are still restrained to a significant extent by poverty and powerlessness from choosing their occupations and manners of living and from having a voice in determining the rules that govern their work lives.

The latter aspect of unfreedom concerns the governance of firms. In Mill's view, establishing economic freedom in modern societies is not strictly a matter of enabling individuals to pursue independently their own desires and life plans. Since members of such societies are typically involved in relationships and institutions that make them interdependent, achieving economic freedom for all also requires practices of collective self-government within economic enterprises. In this regard, Mill contends that co-operatively managed economic enterprises would extend 'the freedom and independence of the individual ... [to] the industrial department' in modern societies (PPE, 793).

Finally, in contrast to how Mill analyzes the 'restraints' to freedom within the 'present system,' the unfreedom he associates with 'communism' largely concerns the prospects for supporting mental freedom and individuality (PPE, 209; COS, 745–6). What is crucial, he says, is 'which of the two systems is consistent with the greatest amount of human liberty and spontaneity' (PPE, 208). Any alternative system, he contends, must meet a difficult test: 'whether there would be any asylum left for individuality of character; whether public opinion would not be a tyrannical yoke; whether the absolute dependence of each on all, and surveillance of each by all, would not grind all down into a tame uniformity of thoughts, feelings, and actions' (PPE, 209). In Mill's view this kind of 'compression' of freedom is already a problem within the present capitalist system, but would be exacerbated under communism. As I noted in Chapter 1, he says in response to a misunderstanding of his criticism of communist ideas in the *Principles* that 'the drudgery to which hunger, and the fear of hunger, condemn the great mass of mankind, is the chief source which makes their lives inane and monotonous' ('CC,' 1179). 'If communism ... would make life a dull routine,' he explains, 'it is not because it would make everyone comfortable.' The chief danger posed by communism is that it would make the 'yoke of conformity' that afflicts the present society 'heavier instead of lighter.' He adds that even many rich people are unfree in the present society, not due to 'fear of want,' but due to their fear 'of other people's opinions': 'They do not cultivate and follow opinions, preferences, or tastes of their own, nor live otherwise than in the manner appointed for persons of their class. Their lives are inane and monotonous because (in short) *they are not free, because though able to live as pleases themselves, their minds are bent to an external yoke*' ('CC,' 1180, 1179, emphasis added). The unfreedom at issue lies in the inability of people overwhelmed by conformist pressures to conceive of and pursue *their own* desires and life plans, *even when* they are 'able to live as pleases them.'

As is the case with Mill's broader conception of freedom, then, considerations of economic freedom encompass each of the two distinct kinds of questions that Isaiah Berlin associates with 'negative' and 'positive' senses of freedom, respectively: 'What am I free to do or be?' and 'Who governs me?' (1969c, 130).[8] Mill recognizes potential tensions between these two forms of economic freedom – individual liberty and democratic self-government – but he regards both as indispensable and neither one as more essential than the other. Moreover, he regards a degree of autonomy sufficient to pursue our own desires and life plans as a condition of individual economic freedom.

b. Maximal Economic Freedom

For Mill, the goal of securing economic freedom for all is integrally related to his notion of 'social and distributive justice' (see ch. 2). Mill's goal is not the greatest *sum* of freedom, which might entail great freedom for some and little for others, but rather substantial freedom for all. He implicitly develops a notion of what I will call 'maximal economic freedom,' which he summarizes in the *Principles* as follows:

> The perfection both of social arrangements and of practical morality would be, to secure to all persons complete independence and freedom of action, subject to no restriction but that of not doing injury to others: and the education which taught or the social institutions which required them to exchange the control of their own actions for any amount of comfort or affluence, or to renounce liberty for the sake of equality, would deprive them of one of the most elevated characteristics of human nature. (PPE, 208–9)

According to Mill, *some* means of achieving greater equality limit freedom in significant ways – for instance, a command economy that administers equal wages to all indiscriminately. Yet maximizing economic freedom, in his view, requires considerable equality with respect to educational and occupational opportunities, income and property holdings, and opportunities to share in governing economic enterprises. In turn, Mill maintains that securing maximal independence and freedom of action entails that no one can have *complete* independence and freedom of action. Rather, restrictions on certain economic activities – such as the unlimited accumulation of private property, and activities harmful to others – are required to secure individual liberty and opportunities for democratic self-government for all.

Given Mill's fundamental commitment to the aggregative principle of 'utility as the ultimate appeal on all ethical questions' (OL, 224), it is important to be clear about just how he defends his commitment to equal economic freedom in terms of distributive rules of justice. Mill, as we have seen, insists that the appeal must be to 'utility in the largest sense, grounded on the permanent interests of man as a progressive being' (OL, 224). In turn, he offers a utilitarian case for maximal freedom based on his view that freedom and individuality are among the 'permanent interests' that are key components of human happiness and well-being (see ch. 2, above). He derives from his indirect utilitarianism and his understanding of basic human faculties the proposition that 'the perfection of both social arrangements and practical morality would be, to secure to all persons complete independence and freedom of action, subject to no restriction but that of not doing injury to others' (PPE, 208–9). At the same time, Mill does not support absolutely equal economic freedom, or regard maximal economic freedom as suitable or attainable within all stages of societal development. Accordingly, maximal economic freedom involves considerations of social justice and expedience, and it presumes an advanced degree of individual and societal development.

II The Political Economy of Freedom

a. Individual Liberty

As I have explained, Mill's conception of economic freedom encompasses both the freedom of individual independence, or individual liberty – of individuals acting independently of others to pursue their own good in their own way – and that of democratic self-government. Regarding individual liberty, Mill emphasizes three different aspects: first, the 'mental freedom' to develop individual character and preferences; second, equal opportunities for individuals to pursue occupations of their own choosing; and third, the exclusive right of each individual to his or her just share of the produce. The following six topics are central to Mill's view of the political economy of maximal individual liberty: the role of government; education; freedom of contract; distributive justice; taxation; and property rights.

THE ROLE OF GOVERNMENT

Although Mill is wary of excessive state action in economic matters, he supports state action to prevent harmful economic activities, establish universal education, provide poor relief, regulate labour contracts, pro-

mote equal opportunity, and regulate rights of property and inheritance. Mill summarizes his view of the proper role of the state in the
Principles when he discusses the 'grounds and limits of laissez-faire,' or
government noninterference. He distinguishes what he calls 'the authoritative form of government intervention' from intervention that is
'not authoritative.' This distinction is related to the one he makes in *On
Liberty* between issues of individual liberty and those of free trade. *Authoritative* intervention, he says, is that which 'may extend to controlling
the free agency of individuals. Government may interdict all persons
from doing certain things; or from doing them without its authorization.' In contrast, *nonauthoritative* intervention refers to 'when a government, instead of issuing a command and enforcing it by penalties, adopts
the course ... of giving advice, and promulgating information; or when,
leaving individuals free to use their own means of pursuing any object of
general interest, the government, not meddling with them, but not
trusting the object solely to their care, establishes, side by side with their
arrangements, an agency of its own for a like purpose' (PPE, 937).

Mill argues that authoritative 'intervention has a much more limited
sphere of legitimate action ... [and] requires a much stronger necessity
to justify it' than the nonauthoritative form (PPE, 937). Then, highlighting the liberty interests at stake, he says:

> There is a circle around every individual human being, which no govern-
> ment ... ought to be permitted to overstep ... That there is, or ought to be,
> some space in human existence thus entrenched around, and sacred from
> authoritative intrusion, no one who professes the smallest regard for hu-
> man freedom and dignity will call in question: the point to be determined
> is, where the limit should be placed ... I apprehend that it ought to include
> all that part which concerns only the life, whether inward or outward, of
> the individual, and does not affect the interests of others. (PPE, 938)

Two aspects of this formulation merit special attention. First, as in *On
Liberty*, Mill maintains that government should abstain from *authoritatively* interfering (that is, through legal penalties) with economic activities of individuals, or associated individuals, that fall within the self-
regarding domain of individual liberty. That is, government should not
use the force of law to interfere with economic activities that do not
impinge upon certain vital 'interests [of others], which ... ought to be
considered as rights' (OL, 276). Conversely, government has an obligation to use legal penalties to prevent conduct that would violate vital
interests of others (OL, 223, 276). Second, Mill identifies several govern-

ment economic activities, including restrictions on trade and production, that are nonauthoritative forms of intervention – that is, that do not restrict legitimate liberty interests. In other words, Mill conceives of the range of state actions that count as 'interference of the law with individual freedom' as a distinct subset of a broader range of possible state actions in economic matters (PPE, 938). Generally speaking, some state actions *do* interfere with individual liberty – for example, policies that restrict the capacity of some individuals to pursue occupations of their own choosing or their preferred way of life. Yet there are a number of economic activities that the state can and should undertake, according to Mill, to secure maximal economic freedom for all, including taxation, education, regulation of property rights and inheritance, regulation of labour contracts, and poor relief.

To summarize, Mill maintains that as a general rule the state should abstain from carrying out too much of the 'business of life' since it is best that 'a large portion of the affairs of the society should be left in the hands of the persons immediately interested in them' (PPE, 943). At the same time, to secure the economic freedom of all, state action is often justified to help bring about conditions and relationships that support such freedom. As he explains in an 1866 letter, 'The aid of Gov^t is often useful, and sometimes necessary, to start improved systems which once started are able to keep themselves going without further help' (letter to John Campbell, 4 April 1866, CW 16, 1155).[9]

EDUCATION

Mill's interest in education follows from his concern for mental freedom. People need to be educated, in his view, to develop the 'individual character and individual preferences' necessary to pursue their own manner of life (COS, 746). Moreover, he relates education for mental freedom to both forms of economic freedom – individual liberty and democratic self-government – since each requires that people develop their capacities for reasoning, deliberation, and judgment (OL, 262). As I explained in Chapter 4, Mill regards schooling, or formal education, as a crucial means of cultivating people's capacities for individuality and autonomy – at least when it engages 'active faculties.' At the same time, education 'in its larger acceptation' encompasses 'even the indirect effects produced on the character and on the human faculties, by things of which the direct purposes are quite different; by laws, by the forms of government, by the industrial arts, by modes of social life' ('IA,' 217).

Based on these considerations, Mill offers a two-pronged education policy. First, government has a responsibility to ensure that all members of society have access to educational opportunities necessary for them to develop mental freedom and pursue their own distinct life plans. Second, the state's role in regulating economic activities should be determined *in part* by the effects of particular policies on people's educations in the larger sense of their self-development. The second point is part of Mill's argument for *laissez-faire* as the general rule with respect to government intervention in the economy. 'The business of life,' he says, 'is an essential part of the practical education of a people ... Instruction is only one of the desiderata of mental improvement; another, almost as indispensable, is a vigorous exercise of the active energies; labour, contrivance, judgment, self-control' (PPE, 943). He adds that such intellectual cultivation through 'discussion and management of collective interests' should extend not just to a 'select few,' but to all members of society:

> It is therefore of supreme importance that all classes of the community, down to the lowest, should have much to do for themselves; that as great a demand should be made upon their intelligence and virtue as it is in any respect equal to; that government should not only leave as far as possible to their own faculties the conduct of whatever concerns themselves alone, but should suffer them, or rather encourage them, to manage as many as possible of their joint concerns by voluntary co-operation. (PPE, 944)[10]

Mill insists, though, that the 'present wretched education, and wretched social arrangements' are the greatest hindrance to the attainment of 'mental cultivation' and, in turn, mental freedom by all classes of society (U, 215; COS, 729, 745–6). In Mill's view, existing class divisions limit the educational opportunities of the working classes in two significant ways: first, access to formal education is largely determined by income; and second, the relationship between capitalists and wage labourers within capitalist firms gives workers little voice in management and, in turn, little opportunity to develop reasoning, judgment, and deliberation ('E,' 628; PPE, 763–4, 948–50). Consequently, Mill calls for government not simply to leave people alone to pursue their interests, but also to 'encourage them, to manage as many as possible of their joint concerns by voluntary co-operation.' To facilitate 'practical education' of all members with respect to the 'business of life,' the state must judiciously support 'voluntary' activities within civil society that exercise the 'active energies' of 'all classes of the community, down to the lowest' (PPE, 944).

Mill proposes a more clearly defined role for the state with respect to formal education. He identifies it as one of several important cases in which the usual objections to government interference either 'are altogether absent' or 'are overruled by counter-considerations of still greater importance' (PPE, 946). He says that the preferences of each individual are generally the best measure of what will satisfy her interests, but insists that there are goods, such as education, regarding which 'the demand of the market is by no means a test' of their worth. Thus, the claim that the consumer is always the best judge 'can be admitted only with numerous ... exceptions' (PPE, 947). Concerning education, Mill contends that people who lack education are frequently not competent judges of its worth: 'The uncultivated cannot be competent judges of cultivation. Those who most need to be made wiser and better, usually desire it least' (PPE, 947). He says it is undesirable to use 'funds derived from compulsory taxation' to do things that are 'already sufficiently done well by individual liberality,' but insists that the provision of formal education is not such a matter: 'Even in quantity it is, and it is likely to remain altogether insufficient, while in quality ... it is ... generally so bad as to be little more than nominal' (PPE, 948–50). 'Free trade' in education is inadequate, then, because poorer members of society are unable to afford sufficient education and uneducated consumers tend to seek too little (PPE, 950; 'E,' 622). Mill concludes, therefore, that it is 'the duty of government to supply the defect, by giving pecuniary support to elementary schools, such as to render them accessible to all the children of the poor' (PPE, 950; cf. OL, 301–2).

Mill says relatively little about the state's responsibility to ensure that everyone has access to the education she or he needs beyond elementary education to freely choose her or his occupation or career path.[11] He does address this issue in passing, however. He contends that everyone – the poor as well as the rich, women as well as men – should have sufficient educational opportunities not only to develop her or his capacities for mental freedom, but also to pursue 'the higher positions in life, including all which confer power or dignity, ... if [she or] he passed with real distinction through the course of instruction open to all' ('E,' 628).[12]

Finally, Mill argues that while government should ensure that adequate educational opportunities are available, it must not be permitted to claim a monopoly over formal education. Such broad control would give the government potentially despotic power to 'mould the opinions and sentiments of the people from their youth upwards,' which would undermine their mental freedom (PPE, 950; OL, 302). This is Mill's chief reason for doubting that 'Communism' would secure greater freedom than would capitalism. He explains that in a communist system, with decisions about education 'made for every citizen by the collective body,' any adults who have a dissenting view of how to educate their own children 'would have to rely for their chance of obtaining it upon the influence they could exercise in the joint decision of the community' (COS, 745). Consequently, the 'compression' of freedom and individuality that is already a great problem 'would probably be much greater under communism' (COS, 745–6). Note, however, that Mill criticizes communism in the *Principles* only after he points out that the 'restraints of Communism would be freedom in comparison with the present condition of the majority of the human race' (PPE, 209). In this regard, contemporary welfare-state capitalist societies mark a notable advance over the capitalism of Mill's time, largely to the degree that they have moved away from 'free trade' in education to provide universal access to formal education through compulsory taxation. In addition, he suggests that the danger of despotic state control over schooling would be avoided in certain 'socialist' reform plans.

FREEDOM OF CONTRACT

Mill's view of the relationship between freedom of contract and individual liberty is similar to his view of state responsibilities with regard to education. He says the presumption that each individual knows better than anyone else what is in her or his best interests 'breaks down entirely' for any person 'incapable of judging or acting for himself' – for example, people who are mentally incompetent or at an immature age (PPE, 951). For these persons, government action may be necessary to protect their interests. Regarding the principle of 'freedom of contract,' Mill says the question is not whether government should interfere 'with individuals, in the direction of their own conduct and interests, but whether it should leave absolutely in their power the conduct and interests of somebody else' (PPE, 951). The basic idea behind freedom of contract – that individuals should be free to voluntarily enter into contractual agreements and partnerships with each other to exchange labour, goods, and services – seems to follow logically from Mill's principle of liberty. Mill offers two qualifications, however, in light of how capitalist relations of production and exchange give some people undue power over 'the conduct and interests' of others at the expense of equal freedom for all.

First, Mill says that when it is extended to children, 'freedom of contract ... is but another word for freedom of coercion' (PPE, 952). That is, in the absence of laws restricting labour contracts with children, adults are left free to achieve *their* interests by coercing children. Not only are such contracts harmful to children, but part of this harm consists of restricting children's freedom by undermining their ability to develop their own characters and abilities and pursue their own life plans.

Mill's second qualification is rather different insofar as it concerns the freedom of adult wage earners, who presumably have the maturity to take care of themselves, and he makes it implicitly rather than explicitly. Mill agrees with socialist critics that the wage labour relationship in capitalist firms is harmful to workers because it forces them to accept working conditions that make them *dependent* on others rather than *self-dependent* or self-governing. Mill's critique of this dependence is similar to his argument that people should not be free to sell themselves into slavery. 'It is not freedom,' he says, for a person 'to be allowed to alienate his freedom' (OL, 299; cf. PPE, 953–4). The capitalist wage labour relationship is a problem because it confronts wage labourers with systemic relationships of unfreedom *despite* the fact that they enter into these relationships voluntarily. Moreover, Mill basically agrees with socialist arguments that workers do not really enter into these relationships freely, since without significant capital of their own most workers do not have the option of working for themselves or in relationships that do not involve dependence (PPE, 759–69).

DISTRIBUTIVE JUSTICE

On the broader issue of distributive justice, Mill also agrees with the socialist view that the presence of economic resources, such as income and wealth, is a necessary condition of freedom. As he says in 'Newman's Political Economy,' the distribution of the produce of society comprises the distribution of 'the means of life and enjoyment' ('NPE,' 444). In turn, when Mill declares that social reform should aim at 'combining the greatest personal freedom with ... just distribution,' he sees these goals as mutually supporting (PPE, xciii). Moreover, he links the issue of just distribution of *produce* to that of just distribution of *power* in the management of economic enterprises. Mill focuses on four interrelated aspects of distributive justice: the unjust distribution of produce in the present system; the difficulty of finding an uncontroversial principle of a 'just' distribution; inherited inequalities of wealth and opportunity; and gender inequality.

Regarding the present system of private property, Mill maintains that the present distribution of society's produce between the rich and the poor is 'obviously unjust ... so slightly connected as it is with merit and demerit, or even with exertion' ('NPE,' 444).[13] He explains that the usual justification for *private property* is that it 'assure[s] to all persons what they have produced by their labour and accumulated by their abstinence' through fair competition (PPE, 227, 218). Ideally, then, a system of private property

> would be accompanied by none of the initial inequalities and injustices which obstruct the beneficial operation of the principle in old societies. Every full-grown man or woman ... would be secured in the unfettered use and disposal of his or her bodily and mental faculties; and the instruments of production, the land and tools, would be divided fairly among them, so that all might start, in respect to outward appliances, on equal terms ... But the division, once made, would not again be interfered with; individuals would be left to their own exertions and to ordinary chances, for making an advantageous use of what was assigned to them. (PPE, 201–2)

Mill says, though, that these initial conditions have been absent wherever private property has been established, and that existing capitalist systems are far from the ideal: 'The laws of property have never yet conformed to the principles on which the justification of private property rests ... They have not held the balance fairly between human beings, but have heaped impediments upon some, to give advantage to others; they have purposely fostered inequalities, and prevented all from starting fair in the race' (PPE, 207). Given the initial inequities, Mill regards the equilibrium wage for working people that emerges from market competition under the present system as unjust. The primary problem, from Mill's perspective, is that the unequal initial distribution of property, which undermines equal starts, was itself established unjustly (see Hollander, 1985, 782).

Mill sometimes implies that a just system based on private property is possible, but he is ambivalent on this point. Consider his suggestion that in an ideal private property system, resources would initially be divided 'so that all might start ... on equal terms,' but the resulting distribution 'would not again be interfered with.' Mill's claim that if all started on equal terms the resulting distribution of goods should not be altered thereafter conflicts with his view that the law should offer some protection for individuals with respect to engagements that bind them 'in perpetuity.' The former principle would leave individuals to bear the full burden or reap the full benefits of early successes or failures forever after; yet Mill is generally reluctant to leave individuals with no security against early mistakes or misfortunes.[14] Moreover, his idealized scenario fails to address the restraints to freedom entailed when accumulated inequalities of wealth and resources are passed across generations, and when some members of society become dependent, as wage labourers, on the capital of others for their livelihood.

Mill addresses the issue of inherited wealth elsewhere, however. He says that 'inequalities of property which arise from unequal industry, frugality, perseverance, talents, and to a certain extent even opportunities, are inseparable from the principle of private property, and if we accept the principle, we must bear with the consequences' (PPE, 225).[15] Yet he also contends that the state can legitimately fix limits 'to what any one may acquire by the mere favour of others [through gifts or inheritance], without any exertion of his [own] faculties' (PPE, 225). Accordingly, as I will explain shortly, Mill calls for a heavy tax on inherited wealth to equalize opportunities across generations.

Mill alludes to his deeper doubts about the merits of a system based on private property when he qualifies his support for private property with the phrase 'if we accept the principle.' He looks to the socialist tradition for what he calls the highest standards of distributive justice – particularly the communist principle of equal division of produce and Louis Blanc's still 'higher standard' of 'apportionment according to need' (COS, 739). Mill expresses his greatest sympathy, however, for Fourierist socialism, which 'allow[s] differences of remuneration for different kinds or degrees of service to the community,' and he does not dwell on an ideal standard of just distribution (COS, 739, 747; PPE, 212).[16] This is partly due to his belief that realizing an ideal distribution would require considerable improvement in 'the intelligence and morality of the individual citizens' (COS 745; cf. Hollander, 1985, chs. 10–11; Riley, 1996). But it is also due to how Mill links the goal of a just distribution of produce to that of a just distribution of power within economic enterprises.

Mill emphasizes this connection in *Principles of Political Economy* when he speculates about 'the nearest approach to social justice ... possible ... to foresee' (PPE, 794). The central feature of his ideal is democratically reorganized industrial relations, which would give workers a voice in determining the distribution of wages within their firms, *rather than* any specific principle for the just distribution of produce. He points out that establishing worker self-managed firms will often conflict with the 'highest' standards of just distribution of produce.[17] Ultimately, then, Mill seems to place the goal of expanding freedom of workers through industrial democracy before that of achieving an ideal standard of just distribution of produce (see below).

Finally, as I explained in the previous Chapter, Mill's feminism also informs his view of distributive justice. At least as a broad principle, he defends the equal freedom of both women and men in the economic domain. Thus, when he suggests that establishing industrial co-operation would yield the 'nearest approach to social justice' presently foreseeable, he adds that this *assumes* 'that both sexes participate equally in the rights and in the government of the association' (PPE, 140). Mill insists that equal opportunity for both sexes with respect to industrial occupations is a direct extension of the principle that 'freedom of individual choice is ... the only thing [that] ... throws each operation into the hands of those who are best qualified for it' (SW, 273).[18]

TAXATION

Concerning the impact of taxation on individual liberty, Mill starts with the premise that there are no limits *in principle* to the positive activities that a government may undertake insofar as it leaves individuals 'free to use their own means of pursuing any object of general interest' (PPE, 937). He explains, 'When a government provides means for fulfilling a certain end, leaving individuals free to avail themselves of different means if in their opinion preferable, there is no infringement of liberty, no irksome or degrading restraint' (PPE, 938–9). Mill acknowledges, 'There is, however, in almost all forms of government agency, one thing which is compulsory; the provision of the pecuniary means' – that is, taxation (PPE, 939). Still, as Fred Berger explains, 'What is important about taxation [for Mill] is that, so long as its extent is limited, it leaves the people free to chart out the course of their own lives as they see fit; it imposes a way of life on no one' (1984, 180; cf. Brink, 1992).[19]

Mill develops this point in *On Liberty* by explaining how taxing certain goods can make their cost prohibitive. He contends that a policy of taxing 'stimulants' for the purpose of making them more difficult for people to obtain differs 'only in degree' from laws that simply prohibit their sale 'and would be justifiable only if [prohibition] were justifiable.' Mill adds, 'Every increase of cost is a prohibition, to those whose means do not come up to the augmented price; and to those who do, it is a penalty laid on them for gratifying a particular taste' (OL, 298). In short,

Mill regards taxation for legitimate public purposes as 'absolutely inevitable,' but holds that taxes that make certain commodities unaffordable to people with limited means effectively limit their freedom to choose their manner of life (OL, 298). He recognizes, moreover, that such taxes rarely impose this kind of burden on wealthy people; and in turn, he treats taxes on luxury goods differently.[20]

Given Mill's concern for how taxes on articles of consumption unequally burden the rich and poor, we might expect him to support graduated (or progressive) taxation – taxing a progressively larger percentage from larger incomes – as a general rule for just taxation and maximal individual liberty. Yet he contends that a proportional tax on incomes that is adjusted to exempt the income necessary to meet basic needs – which would make it *mildly* progressive – is the best standard for ensuring that each person bears 'his fair share of the burden' (PPE, 806–8). Each person, he says, would 'pay a fixed proportion, not of his whole means, but of his superfluities'; and such a tax would establish equality of sacrifice in the sense that everyone would 'be made to bear [the sacrifices] as nearly as possible with the same pressure upon all' (PPE, 809, 807).

Mill acknowledges, however, that there are some strong arguments in favour of graduated taxation as the standard for equal sacrifice. He notes that a 10 per cent tax on an income of 1,000 pounds may be a heavier burden than the same percentage tax on an income of 10,000 pounds, even if 5 pounds were given back to each for an exemption on the first 50 pounds of income to secure basic necessities (PPE, 808–10). In this view, proportional taxation imposes a gradually *diminishing* burden on people as their incomes increase because people tend to spend a progressively diminishing portion of their incomes on necessities as their incomes increase. He insists, though, that this appeal to what is now called the 'diminishing marginal utility' of each additional increment of income is 'too disputable ... to be made the foundation of any rule of taxation' (PPE, 810).[21] Therefore, he appeals to considerations of desert, or reward proportionate to 'industry and economy,' as the basis for choosing an adjusted proportional tax as the standard for equality of sacrifice. 'To tax the larger incomes at a higher percentage than the smaller,' he says, 'is to lay a tax on industry and economy; to impose a penalty on people for having worked harder and saved more than their neighbours' (PPE, 810–11).

Ironically, Mill's appeal to the principle of desert as a basis for favouring proportionate taxation is incongruous with his insistence that desert was far from being realized in the existing system of private property and capitalist management of firms. Insofar as the existing economic system is far from yielding reward in proportion to industry and effort, Mill's claim that a graduated income tax would entail 'a tax on industry and economy' is inapplicable to it. Consequently, his appeal to desert seems to *presuppose* the kind of transformation of the present capitalist system – *including* modified property rights, substantive equality of opportunity, and democratically managed enterprises – that constitutes his broader vision of distributive justice.[22]

Mill proposes a heavy tax on inherited wealth to help facilitate this transformation, along with a tax on the unearned portion of land rent (see PPE, 819–22). Due to inherited inequalities, he says, 'Many, indeed, fail with greater efforts than those with which others succeed, not from difference of merits, but difference of opportunities' (PPE, 811). He regards the freedom of persons to dispose of their personal property as they please – to enjoy, to give, or to exchange – as a component of their economic freedom (PPE, 215). He maintains, though, that while the principle of private property encompasses the right of individuals 'to what has been produced by others, if obtained by their free consent,' it *does not* entitle anyone without qualification to 'the fruits of the labour of others, transmitted to them without any merit or exertion of their own' (PPE 217, 208; cf. COS 750). He adds that while private property inevitably produces some inequality of opportunities, judicious legislation can go a considerable way to ameliorate this effect: 'If the tendency of legislation had been to favour the diffusion, instead of concentration of wealth ... the principle of individual property would have been found to have no necessary connexion with the physical and social evils which almost all Socialist writers assume to be inseparable from it' (PPE, 208). In turn, based on a distinction between the freedom to bequeath wealth to others and the right to inherit wealth, Mill recommends a heavy, *graduated* inheritance tax as 'both just and expedient' (PPE, 812). The right of bequest, he says, is part of the idea of private property since it involves the right of each person to exercise control over the fruits of his or her exertions (PPE, 218). The right to *inherit* wealth is quite different, however, since it involves what has been produced by others. Mill concludes, therefore, that heirs can rightfully claim the resources necessary to 'enable them to start with a fair chance of achieving by their own exertions a successful life,' but says there are great benefits to limiting what an individual may inherit to no more than 'the means of comfortable independence' (PPE, 221, 225).

Ironically, Mill's argument for progressive taxation of inherited wealth appeals to the logic of diminishing marginal utility that he rejects with respect to income taxes. He says that after a certain point the benefits of each additional increment of wealth, in terms of attainable 'pleasures and advantages,' diminish relative to the potential public benefits from redistributing it.[23] Yet if Mill's appeal to diminishing marginal benefits is valid with respect to wealth, then the same concept should also be applicable to incomes – *especially* in a system that fails to yield reward proportionate to exertion. Consequently, there is a stronger case than Mill allows, based on his own reasoning, for a progressive income tax to achieve both 'equality of taxation' and a more equal distribution of the resources for individual freedom (Berger, 1984, 179ff).

PROPERTY RIGHTS

Concerning property rights, Mill goes well beyond the issue of inherited wealth. He brings together classical liberal notions of ownership and desert with a socialist-influenced critique of property as a source of social power. He implicitly extends to the regulation of property rights the principle of policy that while the state must respect 'the liberty of each individual in what specifically regards himself, [it] is bound to maintain a vigilant control over his exercise of any power which it allows him to possess over others' – a corollary of his principle of liberty (OL, 301). He follows socialists in treating private ownership of *articles of consumption*, or personal property, differently from private ownership of the means of production. He regards the former as a necessary condition of the freedom of individuals to pursue their own manner of life; but he maintains that private ownership of the means of production has no necessary connection to individual economic freedom (COS, 738, 749ff). Moreover, since the means and instruments of production are intrinsically involved in trade, Mill places ownership of these things not in the domain of individual liberty, but in that of 'social morality.' He is particularly concerned about how private ownership of the instruments and means of production gives some people power over others.

Mill summarizes his view of private property as a source of social power most explicitly in 'Coleridge' with special reference to property in land. When the state permits any person to own more land than is necessary for subsistence, he says,

it confers on him power over other human beings – power affecting them in their most vital interests; and that no notion of private property can bar the right which the State inherently possesses, to require that the power which it has so given shall not be abused ... By giving this direct power over so large a portion of the community, indirect power is necessarily conferred over all the remaining portion ... And the State fails in one of its highest obligations, unless it takes these points under its ... superintendence; unless, to the full extent of its power, it takes means of ... securing the happiest existence to those employed on [the land], and for setting the greatest number of hands free to employ their labour for the benefit of the community in other ways. ('C,' 157–8)

Mill focuses his sharpest criticisms on private ownership of land, but he also criticizes the existing laws concerning ownership and control of 'moveable property' or capital. The latter, in Mill's view, is more readily justified than the former in terms of the usual rationale for private property. Private property in land lacks justification, Mill says, because 'land is a monopoly, not by acts of man, but of nature; it exists in limited quantity, not susceptible of increase' ('LLQ,' 672). In contrast, movable property or capital is expanded by human labour and, thus, is more likely than landed property to be accumulated by people through their own labour and abstinence.

Nevertheless, Mill emphasizes that accumulations of *movable* property also give some people undue power over others. Private ownership of the means of production gives property owners not only 'exclusive use or control over things,' but also power over the working people who depend on them for their livelihoods (COS, 750). This is the basis for his argument that freedom and justice would be better served if the existing division of power 'between the capitalist as chief, and work-people without a voice in management,' was replaced by co-operative associations in which all parties would share in managing economic enterprises (PPE, 775).

Overall, Mill insists that it would be wrong to conclude 'that all the rights now regarded as pertaining to property belong to it inherently' (COS, 750). Property rights can rightfully be modified, in Mill's view, when the change would be 'beneficial to the public and conducive to the general improvement,' as long as the existing proprietors are justly compensated by the state for the property they are 'dispossessed of' (COS, 753).[24] Elsewhere Mill argues – based on considerations of expedience *rather than* on considerations of justice – that 'the interests of society would in general be better consulted by laws restrictive of the acquisition of too great masses of property, than by attempting to regulate its use.' Yet he adds that society has the 'same right' to interfere with 'capital, and moveable property generally,' as it does with property in land (letter to Charles Eliot Norton, 26 June 1870, CW 17, 1740).[25] Mill remains ambivalent, however, with respect to both socialist alternatives and the role of the state in bringing about a new system of property rights and work relationships. Consequently, he refrains from offering a clear program of reform to secure economic freedom for all, apart from a set of reforms concerning landed property.[26]

b. Democratic Self-government

When Mill turns to the governance of economic enterprises, he promotes worker self-management to maximize freedom (Claeys, 1987). He contrasts the repressive power dynamics in standard capitalist enterprises with the liberatory power relationships found in worker self-governed co-operatives in his chapter 'On the Probable Future of the Labouring Classes' in the *Principles*. Mill begins by describing two opposing theories concerning the proper status for manual labourers – one of 'dependence and protection' and the other of 'self-dependence.' According to the first theory, 'the lot of the poor, in all things which affect them collectively, should be regulated *for* them, not *by* them. They should not be required or encouraged to think for themselves, or give to their own reflection or forecast an influential voice in the determination of their duty ... The relation between rich and poor, according to this theory (a theory also applied to the relation between men and women) should be only partly authoritative ... The rich should be *in loco parentis* to the poor, guiding and restraining them like children' (PPE, 759, Mill's emphasis).[27] This theory of dependence, in Mill's view, is manifest within capitalist firms in the power the 'employing' or capitalist class exercises over the labouring class, with 'the many who do the work being mere servants under the command of the one who supplies the funds' (PPE, 767–9). This relationship precludes the freedom of working people – that is, their self-government – within economic enterprises.

Mill contends that this 'patriarchal or paternal system of government' is becoming obsolete (PPE, 762–3). 'The civilizing and improving influences of association, and the efficiency and economy of production on a large scale,' he says, 'may be attained without dividing the producers into two parties with hostile interests and feelings' (PPE, 769). He explains:

The poor have come out of leading strings, and cannot any longer be governed or treated like children ... Modern nations will have to learn the lesson, that the well-being of a people must exist by means of the justice and self-government ... of individual citizens ...

... If the improvement [of human affairs] ... shall continue its course, there can be little doubt that the *status* of hired labourers will gradually tend to confine itself to the description of workpeople whose low moral qualities render them unfit for anything more independent: and the relation of masters and workpeople will be gradually superseded by partnership ...: in some cases, association of the labourers with the capitalist; in others, and perhaps finally in all, association of labourers among themselves. (PPE, 763, 769, Mill's emphasis)

In short, working people can now be governed according to the theory of self-dependence, which treats adult members of modern societies as self-governing beings.

Mill develops this democratic ideal in terms of what he calls the 'co-operative principle,' in reference to the co-operative societies of the time. His ultimate goal is to extend democratic self-government, on equal terms, to virtually all working people with respect to their economic enterprises, within a competitive market economy. The ideal form of industrial association, he says, 'is not that which can exist between a capitalist as chief, and workpeople without a voice in the management, but the association of the labourers themselves on terms of equality, collectively owning the capital with which they carry on their operations, and working under managers elected and removable by themselves' (PPE, 775). This form of association, he says,

would combine the freedom and independence of the individual, with the moral, intellectual, and economical advantages of aggregate production; and ... would realize, at least in the industrial department, the best aspirations of the democratic spirit, by putting an end to the division of society into the industrious and the idle, and effacing all social distinctions but those fairly earned by personal services and exertions ... In this or some such mode, the existing accumulations of capital might honestly ... become in the end the joint property of all who participate in their productive employment. (PPE, 793)

Mill refers to this form of association as 'the nearest approach to social justice, and the most beneficial ordering of industrial affairs ... which it is possible at present to foresee ... (... assuming of course that both sexes participate equally in the government of the association)' (PPE, 794).

One of Mill's guiding assumptions is that relationships of power and interdependence are unavoidable in modern economies. He says that 'large industrial enterprises' will dominate both agriculture and manufacturing due to economies of scale.[28] Therefore, most people *cannot* be freed from relationships of dependence in the economic domain by placing them 'in a condition in which they will be able to do without one another'; instead, extending economic freedom generally requires establishing practices of democratic self-government whereby people are enabled 'to work with or for one another in relations not involving dependence' (PPE, 768).

The co-operative principle represents the fullest expression of this idea, according to Mill, since it extends the 'democratic spirit' to 'all who participate in ... productive employment' in the 'industrial department.' No member of a co-operative is absolutely free to do as she or he pleases; yet all members share the freedom of self-government by sharing in management. Co-operatives, like any other enterprises, must establish certain general rules of discipline. Yet they offer a substantial gain in freedom by giving working people a voice in determining these rules, in comparison to standard capitalist firms, which subject working people to rules imposed by others. Mill explains, for instance, that managers of co-operatives are paid for the time they work like other members, although usually at the highest rate of pay; at the same time, 'the rule is adhered to, that the exercise of power shall never be an occasion of profit' (PPE, 784). Moreover, in the exercise of their power, managers are democratically accountable to the whole body of associated workers. Decisions made the distribution of wages for different jobs, the distribution of profits between new investments and expansion, and the extent of provisions made for the sick and disabled are collective concerns (PPE, 783–4).[29]

As Jonathan Riley points out, Mill does not abandon his usual concerns about intolerant majorities when he considers worker self-governed enterprises – particularly given his concerns about the existing education of working people (1994, xliii).[30] However, Mill addresses this issue with respect to communistic associations, not decentralized co-operative enterprises.[31] Majority tyranny is possible in democratic co-operatives, but there is little reason to believe that it poses a greater danger in an economy of decentralized co-operatives than in an economy dominated by traditional capitalist firms. Moreover, given the powers of surveillance and control now wielded in capitalist firms by owners and managers who are largely unaccountable to workers, there are good reasons to expect co-operative associations to be less burdensome.[32] As Mill notes, a decentralized system of co-operatives would be quite different in this regard from a unitary communistic society.

III Conclusion

Mill's view of the political economic order that will promote maximal economic freedom and social justice is full of hopes and anticipations. Some matters Mill wisely leaves open, but others require more resolution than he offers. Most importantly, as my reading brings to light, he is vague about what should be done to bring about the changes necessary to maximize economic freedom; and he offers no final judgment – and claims that none can yet be made – about whether some form of socialism or a radically reformed form of capitalism is compatible with the greatest amount of personal freedom. He is also vague about the freedom of those persons who, for the foreseeable future, would remain either unemployed or employed but – due to their 'low moral qualities' – in a status no 'more independent' than that of 'hired labourers' (PPE, 769). These questions test the limits of Mill's political economy of freedom.

My reading resolves some of these ambiguities by clarifying Mill's view of economic freedom. His conception of economic freedom applies his broader view of freedom – as the power of persons for self-determination – to economic activities. Accordingly, his account of economic freedom is central to his assessment of the choice between capitalism and socialism. To achieve Mill's goal of 'maximal' economic freedom would require *at the very least* a radically reformed kind of capitalism. For Mill, economic freedom encompasses two different forms of self-determination: the individual liberty for people to pursue occupations and leisure activities of their own choosing, *and* opportunities for them to share in democratic self-government within economic enterprises. Maximal economic freedom can be achieved, therefore, only by reforms that do away with most – if not all – inherited inequalities; and that establish roughly equal educational opportunities, a division of produce proportionate to productive contributions, and democratic self-government in economic enterprises. Moreover, his analysis strongly implies that such a decentralized system of worker-managed associations, *if and when it becomes possible*, would combine 'the greatest personal freedom with that just distribution of the fruits of labour, which the present laws of property do not profess to aim at' (PPE, xciii).

Thus, Mill's reluctance to declare which system is compatible 'with the greatest ... liberty and spontaneity' is largely due to how his preferred system differed from models of capitalism and socialism as they existed in his own time.[33] Nonetheless, his ideal of a decentralized system of co-operatives within a competitive market has important implications for understanding his relationship to the socialist tradition. Mill explicitly rejects communistic socialism, which entails centralized state management of all economic activities; yet he admires Fourierism, which emphasizes a decentralized economy and worker self-management while permitting differences of remuneration (COS, 739–46; PPE, 212–14).[34] Moreover, after making his case for co-operative associations, Mill comments: 'I agree, then, with the Socialist writers in their conception of the form which industrial operations tend to assume in the advance of improvement; and I entirely share their opinion that the time is ripe for commencing this transformation, and that it should by all just and effectual means be aided and encouraged' (PPE, 794). He explains that he disagrees with socialists concerning 'their declamations against [market] competition' and insists that market competition among enterprises will remain 'indispensable to progress' (PPE, 794).[35] Thus, aside from his defence of market competition – which is no longer rejected by all socialists – Mill's view of the political economy of freedom has important socialist aspects.[36]

Mill remains unclear about the details of his preferred system, though not without reason. He suggests that at least for the near term, individual capitalists with profit-sharing policies should continue to compete with co-operatives – partly to keep 'the managers of co-operative societies up to the due pitch of activity and vigilance' with regard to adopting improvements (PPE, 793). Yet he also envisions a gradual multiplication of co-operatives so that they will gradually absorb 'all work-people, except those who have too little understanding, or too little virtue' to be self-governed (PPE, 793). His ideal, then, is a far-reaching 'change in society' that would democratically reconfigure the 'industrial department.' He rather wistfully suggests that as this process unfolds, owners of capital will gradually shift from being old-style capitalists to lending their capital to co-operatives at diminishing rates of interest, 'and at last, perhaps, even to exchange their capital for terminable annuities.' This transition, he implies, would ultimately result in something close to socialism, since existing accumulations of capital would become, 'by a kind of spontaneous process, ... the joint property of all who participate in their productive employment' (PPE, 793).[37]

Five other issues require a clearer resolution than we can find within the parameters of Mill's analysis. *First*, Mill's assumption that modern economies will be dominated by large enterprises is largely valid, but fails to address the persistence of smaller firms alongside large firms. Consequently, Mill leaves open the questions of whether there will be, or should continue to be, a place for small-scale capitalistic entrepreneurs; and how such entrepreneurs should be integrated into a co-operative economy. *Second*, given Mill's wariness of state power and his hope for a 'spontaneous' transformation, he offers little guidance with respect to the actions the state might take to establish a decentralized co-operative economy. He sees no legitimate objection *in principle* to the state making policies to achieve this end, but he advises caution concerning the readiness of working people to assume the demands of 'conscience and intellect' that a decentralized co-operative economy would require of them.[38] He is cautiously optimistic, however, about the prospect of educating almost 'every person in the nation' for such freedom (COS, 746). *Third*, Mill never addresses two related macroeconomic issues: how to regulate relations between co-operative firms, and how to allocate resources in a co-operative-based national economy (Robbins, 1952, 159). *Fourth*, Mill assumes that the problem of democratic accountability is basically a national problem (cf. Held, 1993, 25). Thus, despite his attention to international trade, he fails to foresee how global labour markets and capital flows complicate the political task of maximizing economic freedom. Concerning each of these issues, Mill's contribution is limited by how he embraces socialist ideas at the level of the firm but not at the level of broader economic forces (Kuttner, 1992, 11–12).

Finally, Mill identifies two interrelated obstacles to including nearly all working people in a system that supports maximal economic freedom. First, there is the problem of providing productive employment at decent wages for everyone who wants a job.[39] Mill maintains that population control is essential in order to secure wages above subsistence level for all members of society (PPE, 762). He expects reproductive restraint to result from increasing education and the opening of industrial occupations to both sexes (PPE, 765). At the same time, Mill says that the state should provide the means of subsistence to destitute persons through compulsory taxation (PPE, 962). Thus, he supports a minimum 'safety net' of freedom from want. Second, Mill is not at all certain about whether everyone can be educated for a system of maximal economic freedom, or whether there will always be some persons who will have 'too little understanding, or too little virtue, to be capable' of being fully included (COS, 746–8; PPE, 793). As he notes, however, these are two challenges that – along with ecological limits to growth – any modern economic system must face (COS, 728–9; PPE, 755–6).

8

Political Freedom

There is no true democracy where large classes of the community are denied equality of political rights.

J.S. Mill, letter to Lucy Stone, 14 April 1868

Mill's fame as a proponent of individuality has led some commentators to regard him as a theorist of strictly individual as opposed to political freedom. R.H. Hutton, an early reviewer of *On Liberty*, articulates this charge against Mill as follows:

> The only liberty he would deny to the nation is the liberty to be a nation. He distrusts social and political freedom. There is a depressed and melancholy air about his essay in treating social and political organisms. He thinks strongly that individuals should be let alone, but virtually on the condition that they shall not coalesce into a society and have a social and political life that may react strongly on the principles of individual action. (Hutton 1975 [1859], 133)

This interpretation misses the mark, however, since it wrongly takes Mill's account of the appropriate bounds of individual liberty and of the collective authority of society in *On Liberty* as his complete view of modern social and political freedom. In fact, culminating with his *Considerations on Representative Government*, in 1861, and his political speeches and writings between 1866 and 1870, Mill develops an insightful account of the meaning and conditions of political freedom. Moreover, his account of political freedom in a representative democracy complements his defence of individual liberty and individuality.

As we have seen, Mill conceives of individual freedom in terms of both practices of individual liberty – that is, our freedom as independent individuals to pursue our own good in our own way – and practices of democratic self-government – that is, 'the liberty of each [individual] to govern his conduct by his own feelings of duty, and by such laws and social restraints as his own conscience can subscribe to' (SW, 336). His conception of political freedom is thus a direct extension of his principle of democratic self-government to politics. He conceives political freedom in terms of the capacity of citizens to share in shaping the laws that govern them. Therefore, he maintains that achieving political freedom for all members of a society requires a democratic form of government. At the same time, he champions representative rather than direct democracy. Political freedom does not require that citizens have a direct hand in making the laws and policies that govern them; it is achieved by establishing and perfecting institutions of representative government that will secure effective popular control over those persons who do the business of governing.

He outlines his view most starkly in an 1867 parliamentary speech in favour of women's suffrage:

> What is the meaning of political freedom? Is it anything but the control of those who do make their business politics, by those who do not? Is it not the very essence of constitutional liberty, that men come from their looms and forges to decide, and decide well, whether they are properly governed, and whom they will be governed by? And nations which prize this privilege the most, and exercise it most fully, are invariably those who excel the most in the common concerns of life. ('AWEF,' 154)

Similarly, in *Representative Government* he characterizes the political freedom established by representative democracy as that of each person being 'under no other external restraint than the necessities of nature, or mandates of society which he has his share in imposing, and which it is open to him, if he thinks wrong, publicly to dissent from, and exert himself actively to get altered' (CRG, 411).

According to Mill, in a representative democracy citizens exercise political freedom in two distinct but interrelated ways. First, they exercise final control over their local and national representatives through periodic competitive elections. Second, they participate in a surrounding public sphere of political discussion, surrounding the democratic state, that makes 'the whole public ..., to a certain extent, participants in the government' (CRG, 436). Occasionally, citizens also participate more directly in government, but this is the exception rather than the rule. Political freedom, in his view, is not a matter of each citizen getting just what he or she wants *before* participating in collective deliberations. Rather, it involves citizens sharing in processes of democratic deliberation and will formation. Furthermore, Mill's conception of political freedom goes hand in hand with his baseline conception of equality (see ch. 2, above). This is so despite his insistence on representative democracy and his support for unequal voting rights in *Representative Government*. Political freedom does not require that all citizens have equal power or influence in collective decision-making. Rather, it demands practices of representation and deliberation that yield a roughly equal consideration of the interests and perspectives of all members of the community.

As with his theory of freedom more generally, Mill develops his view of democratic political freedom in light of his theories of social power and individual and societal development. Concerning power, he insists that the control of *political power* is largely dependent on the distribution of *social power* in society.[1] Therefore, a political philosophy that seeks to comprehend the conditions of political freedom must build upon what he calls a broader 'social philosophy – a study of agencies lying deeper than forms of government, which, working through forms of government, produce in the long run most of what these seem to produce' ('AC,' 234; CRG, 380; 'Civ,' 173). For present purposes, what is especially important is how he answers this question: 'When it is said that the strongest power in society will make itself the strongest power in the government, what is meant by power?' (CRG, 380–1):

> To mere muscular strength add two other elements, property and intelligence, and we are nearer the truth, but far from having reached it. Not only is the greater number often kept down by a less, but the greater number may have a preponderance in property, and individually in intelligence, and may yet be held in subjection forcibly or otherwise ... To make these various elements of [social] power politically influential, they must be organized; and the advantage in organization is necessarily with those who are in possession of the government ... The power in society which has any tendency to convert itself into political power, is not power quiescent, power merely passive, but active power; in other words, power actually exerted; that is to say, a very small portion of all the power in existence. Politically speaking, a great portion of all power consists in will. How is it

possible, then, to compute the elements of political power, while we omit ... anything that acts on the will? (CRG, 381)

Two points here are especially important for understanding Mill's view of political freedom in a representative democracy. First, not only do different groups and classes in society possess different forms and sources of social power, but the group or class in society with the greatest social power will tend to control political power. Second, while different groups and classes in society have different sources of social power – for example, wealth, intelligence, strength in numbers – these various 'powers in society' differ with regard to the ease with which they can be 'convert[ed] ... into political power.'

Regarding modern democratizing capitalist societies, Mill places special emphasis on the class divide that opposes the numerical strength of the working classes against the wealth of the 'middle' or capitalist class. He also highlights two other forms of social power: the powers of education and public opinion, and the knowledge-based authority of the 'instructed minority' (see ch. 3, above). For example, he regards the distribution of voting rights as an important aspect of the distribution of power in society, since universal suffrage would give the labouring classes, as the numerical majority, the greatest voting power. Yet he points out that raw strength in numbers is not necessarily the most important 'power in society' since 'the greater number [is] often kept down by a less.' We need to pay special attention to the distribution in society of those 'active' forms of power that are more readily converted into political power, including anything that acts on people's wills. In this regard, he suggests that the wealthy and the 'instructed minority' have unique power to 'act on the wills' of 'average men' by shaping their 'persuasions and convictions' (CRG, 382).

While playing close attention to how the distribution of social power shapes control of political power, Mill also highlights the sovereign status of state power in relation to other forms of power in society. He says, 'the stake which an individual has in good government [by the state] is ... nothing less than his entire earthly welfare, in soul, body, and mind. The government to which he is subject has power over all his sources of happiness, and can inflict on him a thousand forms of intolerable misery' ('RWR,' 354–5; 'Ce,' 589). The state, in short, has potential power in modern societies to regulate, alter, and police all other social relationships and activities. With this in mind, he declares that political freedom is 'the most important liberty of the nation' (CRG, 432).

In light of his theories of social power and individual and societal development, Mill's view of democratic political freedom is dynamic and developmental in two key respects. First, he contends that democratic government requires an 'advanced state of civilization' in which the members of a society 'have become capable of being improved by free and equal discussion' (CRG, 413, 567; OL, 224). For Mill, this means chiefly European societies, including Australia, Canada, New Zealand, and the United States (CRG, chs. 4 and 18; 'FWNI'). I will leave aside this aspect of his theory for now, since my aim is to clarify his view of political freedom in democratizing societies. Second, with respect to those societies which he deems prepared for democratic government, his democratic theory has 'static' and 'dynamic' aspects. That is, he is concerned both with the kind of democratic institutions and practices appropriate to the existing state of these societies – the static aspect – and the kind of reformed democratic institutions appropriate for 'improved' circumstances – the dynamic aspect (Duncan, 1969, 68). Mill says in *Representative Government* that 'the goodness of a government conveniently divides itself [into two aspects], namely, how far it promotes the good management of the affairs of society by means of the existing faculties, moral, intellectual, and active, of its various members, and what is its effect in improving or deteriorating those faculties' (CRG, 404, 390–1).[2]

Mill supports equality of political rights as an ultimate goal. Nonetheless, his utilitarianism, combined with his theories of social power and individual and societal development, leads him to reject the idea that all citizens simply *as citizens* are entitled to an 'equal voice' in their government ('TPR,' 323; CRG, ch. 8). He contends that within the context of 'the state of society' as is it *currently composed*, particularly with existing class divisions and corresponding inequalities of education, strict political equality would undermine democratic deliberation and good government (CRG, 446–7). Conversely, he maintains that there are certain necessary social and economic conditions for achieving a *maximally free and egalitarian* form of representative democratic government – that is, one that enables all members of society to exercise effectively 'the full privileges of citizenship' (CRG, 411). Two conditions are chief among these. The first is a system of national education that fosters 'the virtues of self-help and self-government' (CRG, 410). This is basically his goal of educating everyone for freedom (see ch. 4, above). The second condition is the realization of his broader program of egalitarian-democratic social reform. This includes achieving equality between the sexes and the gradual replacement of existing capitalist work relations by a democratic, co-operative market economy (see chs. 6 and 7, above).

Mill's ambivalence about political equality and his emphasis on representative government give his democratic theory a rather élitist cast that has been rightly criticized (Burns, 1968; Mayer, 1968; Duncan, 1969; Pateman, 1970; Macpherson, 1977; Gutmann, 1980; Farr, 1993). It is important to recall, though, that he published his major political writings well before the enactment of universal suffrage in England (see below). Moreover, his ultimate democratic horizon of what I call *maximal political freedom* would go a long way toward securing equal political freedom for each citizen in a broadly democratic society.

I Representative Democracy

Mill begins his defence of representative democracy in *Representative Government* by challenging what he says is the common assumption 'that if a good despot could be ensured, despotic monarchy would be the best form of government.' The idea, he explains, is that if such a government could be an all-seeing one, this 'would ensure a virtuous and intelligent performance of all the duties of government' by establishing the best laws and the most effective administration (CRG, 399). He contends, however, that even if such a government was possible it would have a serious shortcoming with respect to the kinds of persons that would be 'formed' under it, particularly in terms of developing their 'active faculties' (CRG, 400). Mill explains, 'What should we then have? One man of superhuman mental activity managing the entire affairs of a mentally passive people ... The nation as a whole, and every individual composing it, are without any potential voice in their own destiny. They exercise no will in respect to their collective interests. All is decided for them by a will not their own' (CRG, 400). Even a modified despotism that observes 'many of the rules and restraints of constitutional government' would have serious limitations (CRG, 401–2). For instance, a limited monarchy might allow substantial public debate and thus some of the advantages of 'a free government'; but it would realize them 'in a very imperfect degree ... since however great an amount of liberty the citizens might enjoy, they could not forget that they held it on sufferance' (CRG, 402).

Mill therefore says that the ideally best form of government would be a 'completely popular government' that would make each citizen the 'only safeguard of his own rights and interests.' He explains,

> The ideally best form of government is that in which the sovereignty, or the supreme power in the last resort, is vested in the entire aggregate of the community; every citizen not only having a voice in the exercise of that

ultimate sovereignty, but being, at least occasionally, called on to take an
actual part in the government, by the personal discharge of some public
function, local or general ...

... [It is the form of government] in which the whole people participate;
that any participation, even in the smallest public function, is useful; that
the participation should everywhere be as great as the general degree of
improvement of the community will allow. (CRG, 403–4, 412)

Such a government would exercise citizens' active faculties by giving
everyone a voice in the government and, on occasion, more substantial
political experience – for example, jury duty, holding public office,
participation in public meetings (CRG, 404). It would thereby promote
what Mill calls *self-protection* and *self-dependence* – that is, the capacity of
citizens to defend their interests and take care of themselves (CRG, 404;
PPE, 759–69).

With respect to democratic politics, he is concerned with fostering
these qualities among citizens primarily to enable them to pursue their
legitimate interests in concert with others. Participation in democratic
politics fosters this civic virtue, he says, because it calls upon the private
citizen, 'while so engaged, to weigh interests not his own; to be guided,
in the case of conflicting claims, by another rule than his private partiali-
ties; to apply, at every turn, principles and maxims which have for their
reason of existence the common good ... He is made to feel himself one
of the public, and whatever is for their benefit to be for his benefit'
(CRG, 412). Democratic government is desirable, then, not only because
it promotes freedom and self-protection, but also because it calls forth
citizens' 'active' faculties of reasoning, judgment, and deliberation (CRG,
410–12; and see ch. 4, above).[3]

In the same breath, Mill maintains that the best attainable form of
democratic government in complex modern societies is *representative*
government. Direct democracy is unworkable 'since all cannot, in a
community exceeding a single small town, participate personally in any
but some very minor portions of the public business' (CRG, 412). Representative democracy abandons the goal of having all citizens share directly in making and administering the laws that govern them – the kind
of citizen participation found in the ancient Athenian polis (CRG, 411–
12).[4] Nonetheless, it leaves the citizens as a whole with 'the sovereignty,
or supreme controlling power in the last resort,' by giving them electoral
control over the public officials who carry out day-to-day governance
(CRG, 403–4). Political freedom, then, consists largely of the presence of

institutions of representative democracy that establish popular *control* of the government; it does not involve direct popular participation in the legislative or executive power.

To take the full measure of Mill's conception of political freedom in a representative democracy, we need to examine its details. He elaborates the interplay between political freedom and social power in relation to five key political institutions and supporting (or 'secondary') principles: democratic deliberation; equal representation; the public sphere of 'publicity' and political discussion; balance between local and national branches of government; and balance between popular participation and expert authority.

a. Equal Representation and Democratic Deliberation

Mill's principles of democratic deliberation and equal representation are central to his conception of political freedom in a representative government. He explains these principles in two pivotal chapters of *Representative Government*: 'Of the Proper Function of Representative Bodies' and 'Of True and False Democracy.' At first glance, he appears to quickly jettison the participatory aims of his democratic theory as soon as he considers the role representative assemblies. In tandem with his claim that the people should control the government through elected representatives, he says that there are distinct limits to what the representative assembly 'should itself do' (CRG, 422–4). While control over the government by elected representatives is crucial for popular sovereignty, the assembly should not itself exercise state power. Mill proposes to divide the legislative process between the assembly and a special Commission of Legislation. Commission members would be selected by and accountable to the representative assembly and specially trained in 'the business of making laws' (CRG, 430). The assembly would *initiate* and direct the legislative process by instructing the commission to draw up bills for particular purposes; the commission would then *draft* the legislation. In this way, Mill's proposal would significantly distance 'the whole people' from exercising actual political power, especially with regard to national governments, by curtailing the law-making powers of their elected representatives.

Still, although Mill seeks to limit the assembly's role in drafting laws, it is crucial to appreciate the role he intends it to have in democratic deliberation and law making. He sees the representative assembly as the chief forum within government for the people to express and refine their political opinions, interests, and wills. Thus, it is indispensable for establishing 'the most important liberty of the nation, that of being governed only by laws assented to by ... elected representatives' (CRG, 432). While the legislative commission would 'embody the element of intelligence' in law making, the representative assembly 'would represent that of will.' Although the assembly is not fit in Mill's view for 'doing the work' of legislation and administration, it *is* suited to the task 'of causing it to be done; of determining to whom or to what sort of people it shall be confided, and giving or withholding the national sanction to it' (CRG, 430). He explains,

> No measure would become a law until expressly sanctioned by Parliament; and Parliament, or either House, would have the power not only of rejecting but of sending back a Bill to the Commission for reconsideration or improvement. Either House might also exercise its initiative, by referring any subject to the Commission, with directions to prepare a law. The Commission, of course, would have no power of refusing its instrumentality to any legislation which the country desired. (CRG, 430)

While legislation would not be a direct expression of popular will, popular will, mediated through elected representatives, would set the general contours of public policy.

In this regard, the key feature of Mill's conception of political freedom is his view of the legislative assembly as literally the 'parliament' of the nation: the place of talk, debate, deliberation, unrestricted exchange of opinions, and expression of grievances. The function of the representative assembly is to

> watch and control the government: to throw the light of publicity on its acts: to compel a full exposition and justification of all of them which any one considers questionable; to censure them if found condemnable ... In addition to this, ... to be at once the nation's Committee of Grievances, and its Congress of Opinions; an arena in which not only the general opinion of the nation, but of every eminent individual whom it contains, can produce itself in full light and challenge discussion; where every person in the country may count upon finding somebody who speaks his mind, as well as or better than he could speak it himself ... where those whose opinion is overruled, feel satisfied that it is heard, and set aside not by a mere act of will, but for what are thought superior reasons, and commend themselves as such to the representatives of the majority of the nation, where every

party or opinion in the country can muster its strength, and be cured of any illusion concerning the number or power of its adherents. (CRG, 432)

Mill goes on to note that critics often misguidedly deride representative assemblies as 'places of mere talk and *bavardage*' (CRG, 432–3). They fail to appreciate the importance of such *talking* in a democratic state. At its best, such 'talking' fosters thoroughgoing deliberation regarding 'every interest and shade of opinion' so that collective decisions will involve all parts of the political community (CRG, 433). Critics of 'mere talk' would have a point if parliamentary debate and deliberation were completely severed from effective political power, but this is not what Mill proposes. While the Parliament's 'talking and discussion' would stop short of assuming legislative or administrative power, it would control and direct the government. The work of governing would thereby be 'the result of discussion' and would remain accountable to the 'unlimited latitude of suggestion and criticism' from elected representatives of the people (CRG, 433). This process would go a considerable way toward giving everyone a meaningful voice in his or her own self-government.

Mill further elaborates this notion of deliberative democracy in terms of his ideal of equal representation. He develops this ideal in the course of recommending Thomas Hare's model of 'personal representation,' which is a form of proportional representation. Mill explains the merits of Hare's electoral plan by contrasting it with the kind of 'winner-take-all' electoral system that is used in the United States to elect members of the Congress. In the latter system, representatives are determined by separate elections in single-member districts. Whoever wins a majority (or sometimes just a plurality) of the votes is elected to represent the district. Mill says that this system is a 'false democracy' because it fails to establish 'a really equal democracy ... [in which] every single individual [would] count for as much as any other single individual' (CRG, 449):

> The pure idea of democracy, according to its definition, is the government of the whole people, equally represented. Democracy as commonly conceived and hitherto practiced, is the government of the whole people by a mere majority of the people, exclusively represented. The former is synonymous with the equality of citizens; the latter, strangely confounded with it, is government of privilege, in favour of the numerical majority, who alone possess practically any voice in the State. (CRG, 448)[5]

In single-member district systems, in each given district the voters who constitute the majority gain exclusive representation. The majority's choice becomes the elected representative for everyone in the district, including those voters who favoured candidates with different views as well as nonvoters.[6] As a result, many people in each electoral district have no effective representation. Consequently, minority points of view tend to be excluded from representative assemblies.

Mill maintains that Hare's plan, in contrast, would achieve 'really equal democracy' by enabling virtually every elector to vote for a winning candidate and thereby have a voice in Parliament. Minority as well as majority perspectives would have a share of seats in Parliament roughly proportionate to their percentage of the popular support. Mill explains,

> In a representative body actually deliberating, the minority must of course be overruled; and in an equal democracy (since the opinions of the constituents, when they insist on them, determine the representative body) the majority of the people, through their representatives, will outvote and prevail over the minority and their representatives. But ... in a really equal democracy, every or any section would be represented, not disproportionately, but proportionately. A majority of the electors would always have a majority of the representatives; but a minority of the electors would always have a minority of the representatives. Man for man, they would be as fully represented as the majority. Unless they are, there is not equal government, but a government of inequality and privilege ... there is a part whose fair and equal share of influence in the representation is withheld from them; contrary to all just government, but above all, contrary to the principle of democracy, which professes equality as its very root and foundation. (CRG, 449)

In short, true democratic equality would give the majority the largest share of representation and the final say in collective decisions: 'the minority must yield to the majority, the smaller number to the greater.' Yet minorities would not be left without any representation (CRG, 449). They would have less representation than the majority, but they would be equally represented in processes of collective deliberation and decision making. To achieve this end, Mill proposes that representatives be elected on an at-large basis, with the number of voters being divided by the number of seats in the assembly, so that a certain quota of votes is necessary for a candidate to win a seat (CRG, 453–5; Thompson, 1976, 102–5).

Regarding political freedom, then, Mill gives two reasons for regarding Hare's plan as 'among the very greatest improvements yet made in the theory and practice of government' (CRG, 454). First, it would secure representation for 'every minority in the whole nation, consisting of a sufficiently large number to be, on principles of equal justice, entitled to a representative,' rather than for just 'two great parties alone' (CRG, 455). This would help realize Mill's goal of ensuring that every member of society can expect someone in Parliament to express his or her point of view so that 'those whose opinion is overruled, feel satisfied that it is heard, and set aside ... for what are thought superior reasons' (CRG, 432).[7] Second, voters would no longer face the prospect of being nominally represented by someone whose views they do not share or for whom they did not vote. Each individual voter would elect someone who basically shares her or his political views, and this would greatly enhance the identification of electors with their representatives. 'Under this relation,' Mill says,

> the tie between the elector and the representative would be of a strength, and a value, of which at present we have no experience. Every one of the electors would be personally identified with his representative, and the representative with his constituents. Every elector who voted for him, would have done so either because, among all the candidates for Parliament who are favourably known to a certain number of electors, he is the one who best expresses the voter's opinions, or because he is one of those whose abilities and character the voter most respects, and whom he most willingly trusts to think for him. (CRG, 455)

The last point distinguishes Hare's plan somewhat from other systems of proportional representation. Hare's plan places greater emphasis than other such plans on electing distinguished individuals to Parliament. Proportional representation (PR) electoral systems typically involve voters choosing among multiple parties, each with a slate of candidates that supports a common platform or philosophy. Each party gains a number of seats in the assembly roughly proportional to its share of the popular vote. Consequently, such systems encourage voters to choose among the different philosophical or ideological perspectives of different parties rather than focus on distinguished individual leaders. Hare's system, by contrast, provides for the representation of minority points of view in a way that coincides with Mill's aim of reserving a special place in democratic deliberations for the 'instructed minority' (CRG, 457). It does so by enabling distinguished individuals to win election independently of party organizations.

b. Political Equality and Class Division

There is a deep tension in Mill's view of political equality owing to his assessment of the class division in the existing condition of democratizing capitalist societies. While he emphasizes equal representation of all political perspectives in public deliberations, he is reluctant to support strictly equal political rights for all members of society. He maintains that people can fully share in political freedom and the educative effects of political participation only if they have a voice in how they are governed. Yet he also says that everyone is not entitled without qualification to an *equal voice*. He contrasts his view with that of more radical 'democratic reformers' as follows:

> A person who is excluded from all participation in political business is not a citizen ... To take an active interest in politics is, in modern times, the first thing which elevates the mind to large interests and contemplations; the first step out of the narrow bounds of individual and family selfishness ... The possession and exercise of political, and among others of electoral, rights, is one of the chief instruments both of moral and of intellectual training for the popular mind; and all governments must be regarded as extremely imperfect, until every one who is required to obey the laws, has a voice, or the prospect of a voice, in their enactment and administration.
>
> But ought every one to have an *equal* voice? This is a totally different proposition ... [Democratic reformers] say, that every one has an equal interest in being well governed, and that every one, therefore, has an equal claim to control over his own government. I might agree to this, if control over his own government were really the thing in question; but what I am asked to assent to is, that every individual has an equal claim to control over the government of other people. The power which suffrage gives is not over himself alone; it is over others also ... Now, it can in no sort be admitted that all persons have an equal claim to power over others. The claims of different people to such power differ as much, as their qualifications for exercising it beneficially. ('TPR,' 323, Mill's emphasis)[8]

In short, Mill insists that full citizenship requires a voice in government. Yet he also says that people with superior 'knowledge and intelligence' deserve a greater voice in the management of common concerns 'on the ground of greater capacity for the management of the joint interests' (CRG, 473–5, 478). This is why he proposed in the late 1850s and early 1860s, *given the existing state of society*, to enfranchise virtually everyone but to give plural (or extra) votes to citizens with higher educational or occupational attainments. His aim was to endow more educated citizens with 'a more potential voice' in government. In addition, he supported certain exclusions from fully universal suffrage, while keeping it 'accessible to all who are in the normal condition of a human being' (CRG, 472).[9]

To understand how Mill reconciles his case for plural voting with his commitment to equal representation, we need to consider his historical context, the static and dynamic aspects of his democratic theory, and how his theory of social power informs his class analysis of the existing state of society. Concerning his historical context, he defended plural voting in writings that he published before the English Reform Act of 1867 and before the establishment of universal primary education – principally in 'Thoughts on Parliamentary Reform' and *Representative Government*. Universal suffrage was not even seriously considered in the parliamentary debates that preceded the Reform Act of 1867.[10] In this light, Mill's support for nearly universal suffrage (not just manhood suffrage) combined with plural voting was a relatively democratic position, even if it was less so than that of some 'democratic reformers' of the time (Dilke, 1897; Zimmer, 1976; Ten, 1998). Furthermore, he gave plural voting a distinctly transitional place in his democratic theory in relation to the existing class structure. In this regard, his concern with the limited educational attainments of the labouring classes was the more straightforward and conventional part of his argument. Like many commentators in the 1860s, he contended that expanding suffrage would require a corresponding expansion of educational opportunities. This movement bore its first fruit in the Elementary Education Act of 1870 (Briggs, 1965, ch. 10; Lawson and Silver, 1973, 314ff).

Mill's argument, however, also has a more radically democratic dimension that is an extension of his theory of social power. This concerns his assessment of the implications for democratic politics of the class divisions in democratizing capitalist societies and his hopes for overcoming these divisions.[11] His class analysis shifts over time with the changing class structure, but he consistently warns that strictly equal political rights within the existing society would actually *undermine* equal representation. In his political writings of the 1830s he locates the primary class division in England in the division between the old aristocracy and the rising 'mass' of society. Here he includes in 'the mass' both the middle class, which was politically as well as economically ascendant, and the labouring classes, which were excluded from the suffrage reforms of 1832 and 1867 ('Civ,' 169; 'RR,' 23; 'TDA[II],' 166–7; Sarvacy, 1984). By the time of *Representative Government*, in 1861, he contends that in societies not divided by race, language, and nationality, the primary class division is between the class of employers (i.e., the 'middle' or capitalist class) and the labouring classes (CRG, 446–7). He includes among the class of employers 'not only retired capitalists, and the possessors of inherited wealth, but all that highly paid description of labourers (such as the professions) whose education and way of life assimilate them with the rich.' He includes among the class of labourers 'those smaller employers of labour, who by interests, habits, and educational impressions, are assimilated in wishes, tastes, and objects to the labouring classes.' These two classes not only have conflicting 'apparent interests' with respect to the existing economic order, but also possess different and conflicting forms of social (and potentially political) power (CRG, 447). The employing or middle class has unmatched wealth and property (in the form of movable property or capital) as well as considerable intellectual attainments; the labouring classes have unmatched strength in numbers.[12]

Against this backdrop, Mill concludes that the good of the whole community will be achieved in 'a state of society thus composed' only to the degree that representative democracy is organized to guard against the dangers posed by class-based politics. Each class must be prevented from using its power to promote its immediate 'class interests' (i.e., its 'sinister interests') at the expense of 'justice and the general interest' (CRG, 447). 'Looking at democracy,' he says, 'in the way it is most commonly conceived, as the rule of the numerical majority, it is surely possible that the ruling power may be under the dominion of sectional or class interest, pointing to conduct different from that which would be dictated by impartial regard for the interest of all' (CRG, 442). For present purposes, his most salient example of this danger is the class division common to all countries between 'a majority of poor, [and] a minority who, in contradistinction, may be called rich. Between the two classes, on many questions, there is a complete opposition of apparent interest' (CRG, 442). Mill suggests that even if we suppose that the majority will generally be 'sufficiently intelligent' to maintain the security of property, there is 'considerable danger' that the labouring classes will use their numerical superiority to enact policies that favour their narrow class interests. He warns, for instance, of legislative attempts to impose unfair tax burdens on the wealthy, artificially raise wages, and stifle 'improvements ... tending to dispense with any of the existing labour' (CRG, 442). He adds, 'It will be said that none of these things are for the *real* interest of the most numerous class' (Mill's emphasis), but he insists that this claim misses the crux of the problem:

> It is not what their interest is, but what they suppose it to be, that is the important consideration with respect to their conduct: and it is quite conclusive against any theory of government that it assumes the numerical majority to do habitually what is never done, nor expected to be done ... by any other depositories of power – namely, to direct their conduct by their real ultimate interest, in opposition to their immediate and apparent interest. (CRG, 442–3)

These considerations are the basis for Mill's support of plural voting in combination with universal suffrage between 1859 and 1861. During this time period he shares the widespread concern among the English élite about the rise of the labouring classes. He assumes that the labouring classes will tend to act in a unitary way to pursue their 'apparent' class interests.[13] Therefore, he concludes that fully equal political rights (that is, one person, one vote) would enable them to dominate government without an effective 'rival power' due to their collective strength in numbers (CRG, 459; cf. Briggs, 1965, ch. 10). With this scenario in mind, he supports plural voting as a temporary measure to maintain a balance of power between the two main classes (Sarvacy, 1984). He explains in *Representative Government*, 'The plurality of votes must on no account be carried so far, that those who are privileged by it, or the class (if any) to which it mainly belong, shall outweigh by means of it all the rest of the community' (CRG, 476). He adds that unless a mode of plural voting is established that gives superior influence to education 'and [is] sufficient as a counterpoise to the numerical weight of the least educated class; for so long, the benefits of completely universal suffrage cannot be obtained without bringing ... a chance of more than equivalent evils' (CRG, 477).

Mill clarified the transitional character of his support for plural voting in a parliamentary speech on the unsuccessful Reform Bill of 1866. In response to previous speakers who noted an inconsistency between the position he defended in his writings and the more egalitarian position he was now defending, he said, 'It may be that I have suggested plurality of votes ... The proposals I made had reference to universal suffrage, of which I am a strenuous advocate. It appeared to me that certain things were necessary in order to prevent universal suffrage from degenerating into the mere ascendancy of a particular class' ('RP,' 84–5). He went on to say that only one of the checks he had earlier proposed was 'equally desirable in any representative constitution – the representation of minorities' ('RP,' 85). Thus, while at different times he supports both Hare's system of personal representation and plural voting to prevent majority tyranny by the working classes within the existing circumstances, he gives the two proposals different roles in his democratic theory, especially after 1865. He supports plural voting as a conditional and temporary expedient, but he regards personal representation as a 'strictly democratic' mechanism for both present and future circumstances.[14]

To summarize, while Mill's temporary support for plural voting to prevent 'the mere ascendancy' of the labouring classes arguably favoured the middle class over the labouring classes, this was not his intention. He is by no means merely an apologist for the interests of the middle or capitalist class (cf. Macpherson, 1977). He maintains that even under existing conditions the working class requires the vote as a means of political freedom, self-protection, and self-development. Moreover, he also insists that some of the more important class interests of the labouring classes with respect to reform of the existing economic order actually correspond to 'their real ultimate interests' and, thus, to the general interest (see ch. 7, above). He explains, 'The reason why, in any tolerably constituted society, justice and the general interest mostly in the end carry their point, is that the separate and selfish interests of mankind are almost always divided; some are interested in what is wrong, but some, also, have their private interest on the side of what is right' (CRG, 447). What is necessary, then, is a democratic process that will enable the labouring classes to achieve their 'real' interests but prevent them from carelessly attaining their merely 'apparent' interests. I will return to this point later. More generally, he maintains that no class should have the power to unilaterally pursue its immediate class interests and policy preferences. Such supreme class power would undermine the effective freedom of other members of society, just as the exclusion of working men and women of all classes from political rights undermines their political freedom. In each case, the lack of political freedom is marked by the inability of individuals or groups to have a meaningful voice in public deliberations and collective political decisions.[15] Thus, even though he offers qualified support for strict equality of political rights, he nonetheless maintains his commitment to a baseline notion of political equality. Moreover, his ultimate goal, as I will explain later, is a form of representative democracy that enables all individual members of the political community to participate in processes of collective deliberation and decision making as equal citizens.

c. The Principle of Publicity and the Public Sphere

Political freedom, in Mill's view, relates not merely to the formal institutions of representative democracy. It also encompasses the broader channels of public discussion and political will formation outside the representative assemblies. He says that 'the utmost possible publicity and liberty of discussion' is essential to make the 'whole public ... to a certain extent, participants in the government' (CRG, 436). Concerning this aspect of political freedom, previous commentators have focused largely on Mill's strictures against any censorship that undermines 'the fullest liberty of professing and discussing ... any doctrine' (OL, 228n).[16] They have paid little attention to his understanding of how freedom of thought and discussion in the public sphere is mediated by the structure of ownership and control of the means of communication and by the distribution of social power in society. He addresses this topic only in passing, in the context of the formation of public opinion and the control of daily newspapers. Nonetheless, he illuminates the possibility of a kind of minority rule by the capitalist class. This danger to democratic politics runs directly counter to his more immediate worry: the impending political dominance of the labouring classes.

As we have seen, Mill says that to account for those forms of power in society that tend to make themselves 'politically influential' we need to pay special attention to the distribution of those 'active' forms of power that 'act on the will' (CRG, 381). He maintains, moreover, that the various forms of social power become politically influential only to the extent that they are organized to that effect (CRG, 381). Therefore, *any form of social power that acts on people's wills comprises a great part of political power* because it affects how different members of society are or are not organized politically (see above). Consequently, while different groups or classes in society possess different sources of social power (e.g., numerical strength, wealth, intelligence), those groups that have power to 'act on the wills' of others have a considerable advantage in gaining control of political power. Such power includes the 'power over human character' that is exercised by 'education and opinion' (U, 218; OL, 282).

With respect to democratic politics, Mill develops this point primarily in terms of the formation of public opinion and people's political wills in the public sphere. He construes the public sphere in terms of the network of newspapers, political tracts, journals of opinion, political clubs, and political parties that involves citizens in political debate and discussion. He says in *Representative Government* that some individuals and groups exercise power over other people's wills and actions by shaping their thoughts and opinions:

> To think that because those who wield the power in society wield in the end that of government, therefore it is of no use to attempt to influence the constitution of government by acting on opinion, is to forget that opinion is itself one of the greatest active social forces. One person with a belief, is a social power equal to ninety-nine who have only interests. They who can succeed in creating a general persuasion that a certain form of government, or a social fact of any kind, deserves to be preferred, have made the most important step which can possibly be taken toward ranging the powers of society on its side. (CRG, 381)

In other words, those persons who are able to influence or persuade others to support their views regarding the best form of government or best set of policies not only exercise direct power over others, but also are on the way to controlling state power. That is, they have gone a considerable way toward organizing the merely 'passive' power present in society into *active* political power that serves their interests. 'It is what men think that determines how they act,' Mill explains, 'and though the persuasions and convictions of average men are in a much greater degree determined by their personal position than by reason, no little power is exercised over them by the persuasions and convictions of those whose personal position is different, and by the united authority of the instructed' (CRG, 381).

Mill's hope is that 'the united authority of the instructed' will have the greatest influence over public opinion in political debates (Ten, 1998, 381). He contends that 'speculative thought is one of the chief elements of social power' and that the instructed, the chief agents of speculative thought, will tend to promote general rather than 'sinister' interests (CRG, 382).[17] Indeed, he has in mind 'the instructed minority' when he says that 'one person with a belief, is a social power equal to ninety-nine who have only interests.' His thought is that the person with a belief – that is, the instructed person – has *active* power to persuade others, while the ninety-nine persons with 'only interests' have 'merely passive power.' Thus, the working classes have unmatched *potential* power to control government due to their numerical strength. Yet they will realize this power only when they 'learn the habit' of expressing and forming their own opinions along with the 'habit of acting in concert' ('TDA[II],' 165).[18]

Mill emphasizes the power of the instructed minority to shape the opinions of others, but also recognizes that this is not the only group with power to 'act on the wills' of others. Recall that he says 'no little power is exercised over [average men] *by the persuasions and convictions of those whose personal position is different, and by the united authority of the instructed*' (CRG, 381, emphasis added). He develops this point most strikingly in his second article on Tocqueville's *Democracy in America* with reference to the role of newspapers in shaping public opinion. Describing the increasing power of public opinion in modern democratizing commercial societies, he writes,

> While individuals thus continually rose from the mass, the mass itself multiplied and strengthened; the towns obtained a voice in public affairs; the many, in the aggregate, became even in property more and more a match for the few ... The Reformation was the dawn of the government of public opinion. Even at that early period, opinion was not formed by the higher classes exclusively; and while the publicity of all State transactions, the liberty of petition and public discussion, the press – and of late, above all, the periodical press – have rendered public opinion more and more the supreme power, the same causes have rendered the formation of it less and less dependent upon the initiative of the higher ranks. ('TDA[II],' 162)

He points out, though, that while 'public opinion' is increasingly the 'supreme power' in modern politics, it is not a self-generated expression of the opinions and sentiments of the whole public. Instead, he regards newspapers and the periodical press as key agencies in the *formation* of public opinion. He names political unions, antislavery societies, and organizations of the working classes in England as important examples of the power of combined action of the masses. But then he insists,

> The real Political Unions of England are the Newspapers. It is these which tell every person what all other persons are feeling, and in what manner they are ready to act: it is by these that the people learn, it may be truly said, their own wishes, and through these that they declare them. The newspa-

pers and the railroads are solving the problem of bringing the democracy of England to vote, like that of Athens, simultaneously in one *agora*; and the same agencies are rapidly effacing those local distinctions which rendered one part of our population strangers to another; and are making us more than ever (what is the first condition of a powerful public opinion) a homogeneous people. ('TDA[II],' 165)[19]

Newspapers are the heart of the modern democratic *agora*. They establish the kinds of communicative links of discussion and debate among citizens that are the essential basis for democracy: access to information; exchange of ideas and perspectives; publicity and debate concerning political issues and acts of government. They spread 'knowledge and intelligence' to all the 'ranks' of society. Therefore, they are crucial to 'the habit of forming an opinion, and the capacity of expressing that opinion, [that] constitutes a political power' ('TDA[II],' 165). Mill adds,

> It is easy to scoff at the kind of intelligence which is thus diffusing itself; but it is intelligence still. The knowledge which is power, is not the highest description of knowledge only: any knowledge which gives the habit of forming an opinion, and the capacity of expressing that opinion, constitutes a political power; and if combined with the capacity and habit of acting in concert, a formidable one.
>
> It is in this last element, the power of combined action, that the progress of the Democracy has been the most gigantic. ('TDA[II],' 165)

In democratizing capitalist societies, then, the formation of public opinion becomes increasingly independent of the direction of the 'higher ranks' – that is, the aristocracy, the clergy, political élites. But it is now shaped in large part by newspapers and the periodical press.

Mill never systematically examines how the newspapers or other means of political communication can become means through which some individuals or groups in society exercise power over others by 'acting on their wills.' As I noted in Chapter 3, though, he highlights several 'tendencies of modern commercial society' that favour the 'middle class' in this regard – particularly the capitalist class that gathers wealth by 'the accumulation of capitals' ('TDA[II],' 164–6, 191–5). For instance, not only does he call the newspapers 'the real Political Unions of England,' but he also says elsewhere that the daily press in England represents the 'opinions and sentiments' of the middle class.[20] Moreover, with reference to England in 1840, he says that 'inequalities of property are apparently greater than in any former period in history' ('TDA[II],' 163). Accordingly, he 'partially' agrees with the view that the middle class will tend to dominate political power by using its 'property, intelligence, and power of combination,' in league with the aristocratic class, 'against any possible growth of those elements of importance in the inferior classes' ('TDA[II],' 166). 'Hardly anything now depends upon individuals,' he says, 'but all on classes, and among classes mainly upon the middle class. That class is now the arbiter of fortune and success' ('TDA[II],' 194).[21] He suggests that while democratizing trends usher in the political supremacy of public opinion, the middle class has unique power to *shape* public opinion – that is, to make what he calls 'bourgeois opinion' accepted as *public* opinion ('TDA[II],' 162, 189, 194–200).

Mill adds one further element to his analysis of the public sphere. He claims in an early letter that the existing political economy of newspaper publishing in England weakens and distorts public discussion. He says that the 'low state of the newspaper press' prevents the 'best thinkers' in England from 'direct[ing] public opinion' as they do in France. Therefore, he asserts the need for a new newspaper that would be 'a vehicle of intelligence ... conducted by men really in earnest about public objects, and really forming their opinions from some previous knowledge & not from the mere appearances of the moment, or the convenience of party advocacy.'[22] Furthermore, he suggests that some improvements of 'the social organisation' are needed before the 'instructed classes' can be expected to fulfil their ideal role of elevating political discussion in the public sphere. Principally, he says,

the great social sinister interests should be removed, since while these exist, those, who would otherwise be the instructed classes, have no motive to obtain real instruction in politics & morals, & are subjected to biases from which the students of the physical sciences are exempt. They can drive a trade in the ignorance and prejudices of others; they either write for the classes who have sinister interests, and minister to their selfishness or malevolence, or else, addressing themselves to the common people, they find in the well grounded discontent of the people against their institutions sufficient materials for acquiring popularity without either instructing their intellects, or cultivating right habits of feeling or judging in their minds.[23]

In short, insofar as newspapers and the periodical press are dominated by 'sinister interests,' they will fail to foster the greatest possible publicity and liberty of thought and discussion. Consequently, they will also fall short as means of popular political freedom.

Despite these concerns about the structural development of the public sphere, Mill remains hopeful. He sees some countervailing factors that he expects to facilitate open, democratic debate and discussion. For example, he celebrates what he regards as the educative and liberating effects on the working class of new institutions of public discussion, including 'the fiscal emancipation which gave existence to the penny press':

> The institutions for lectures and discussion, the deliberations on questions of common interest, the trade unions, the political agitation, all serve to awaken public spirit, to diffuse variety of ideas among the mass, and excite thought and reflection in the more intelligent ... The working classes are now part of the public; in all discussions on matters of general interest they, or a portion of them, are now partakers; all who use the press as an instrument may, if it so happens, have them for an audience; the avenues of instruction through which the middle classes acquire such ideas as they have, are accessible to, at least, the operatives in the towns. (PPE, 763–4)[24]

He expects that through these activities, and through improvements in 'school education,' the working classes will continue to increase their intelligence (PPE, 764). Therefore, he suggests that in 'the same proportion' as the working class becomes 'well paid, well taught, and well conducted ... will the opinions of that class tell, according to its numbers, upon the affairs of the county' ('TDA[II],' 166).[25]

Mill is obviously right that the working classes 'are now part of the public.' Unfortunately, though, he fails to reconcile this point with his observations about the greater powers of other groups, particularly the class of capitalists, to control the means of communication and thereby to *shape* public opinion in capitalist democracies. Working people are clearly 'an audience' for 'all who use the press as an instrument.' Yet Mill's observations about the political economy of the circulation of ideas and opinions in newspapers and journals of opinion suggest that working people lack equal power and equal freedom to shape public opinion and to make their own opinions politically influential. Moreover, when we extend his analysis of the public sphere to contemporary conditions, the prospects for free and democratic debate and discussion are even more troubling. The increasing degree of concentrated ownership and control over major media outlets by large private corporations – or what Mill calls the 'accumulation of capitals' – gives the capitalist class unmatched power to shape public opinion, including the political opinions of the labouring classes. Those individuals or groups that control major media outlets exercise enormous control over what becomes 'news,' how much time and space is devoted to serious political issues, how news is circulated, and what political perspectives are privileged or marginalized (Miller, 1996; Page, 1996; McChesney, 1997).[26]

Taken together, these considerations shed new light on Mill's view of the danger of 'majority tyranny' in modern democratic politics. In addition to his explicit concern about the threat of majority tyranny by the labouring classes, his analysis illuminates the danger of *minority tyranny* by the capitalist class. He says in *On Liberty* that at least in principle, democratic governments place political power in the hands of 'the people.' He adds, though, that 'such phrases as "self-government," and "the power of the people over themselves," do not express the true state of the case':

> The 'people' who exercise the power are not always the same people with those over whom it is exercised; and the 'self-government' spoken of is not the government of each by himself, but of each by all the rest. The will of the people, moreover, practically means the will of the most numerous or the most active *part* of the people; the majority, or those who succeed in making themselves accepted as the majority. (OL, 219, Mill's emphasis)[27]

Mill's more immediate worry in *On Liberty* and *Representative Government* is with the potential for tyranny by the working class majority once they learn 'to feel the power of government their power' (OL, 223). Nonetheless, his discussion of newspapers and periodicals also indicates how the capitalist class, although a numerical minority, might be able to make its opinions 'accepted as the majority' through its control over the major media outlets. This would enable it to promote its own immediate class interests *under the guise of popular democracy*.

Mill himself has two reasons to gloss over the threat to political freedom posed by concentrated corporate ownership of newspapers and other means of political communication. First, in his time newspapers and other means of mass communication in capitalist societies had not yet developed their present, highly oligopolistic character. Second, he implicitly offers a novel, liberal-democratic solution to the problem of capitalist class domination of the public sphere: along with legal protection for freedom of the press and freedom of thought and government regulation of monopolies, he also favours (and anticipates) *a gradual transition to a post-capitalist economy based on co-operative enterprises.* Insofar as the economic enterprises that constitute the primary means of communication in democratic societies are independent democratic co-operatives, we could expect greater pluralism and democratic accountability in the media. In turn, the dangers posed by media concentration and class domination would be largely averted.

d. Local and National Democracy

Turning back to the governmental framework needed to secure political freedom in modern societies, Mill contends that it is essential to divide government powers and responsibilities between 'central and local authorities' (CRG, 534). He says in the *Principles*,

> A democratic constitution, not supported by democratic institutions in detail, but confined to the central government, not only is not political freedom, but often creates a spirit precisely the reverse, carrying down to the lowest grade of society the desire and ambition of political domination ... In proportion as the people are accustomed to manage their own affairs by their own active intervention, instead of leaving them to the government, their desires will turn to repelling tyranny rather than to tyrannizing: while in proportion as all real initiative and direction resides in the government, and individuals habitually feel and act as under its perpetual tutelage, popular institutions develop in them not the desire for freedom, but an unmeasured appetite for place and power. (PPE, 944)

The national Parliament should serve as 'the great council of the nation' (CRG, 534). Meanwhile, 'all business purely local – all which concerns only a single locality – should devolve upon the local authorities' (CRG, 541). Mill reiterates his broader argument that the 'various liberties' that nourish representative democracy in national governments, including jury duty, reading newspapers, and participating in parliamentary elections, are vitally important 'both as securities for freedom and as means of general cultivation' (CRG, 535). He says, however, that local governments offer average citizens much greater opportunities than national governments to share directly in the affairs of government and to experience the political education that this entails:

> In the case of local bodies, besides the function of electing, many citizens in

turn have the chance of being elected, and many, either by selection or by rotation, fill one or other of the numerous local executive offices. In these positions they have to act, for public interests, as well as to think and to speak, and the thinking cannot all be done by proxy. It may be added, that these local functions, not being in general sought by the higher ranks, carry down the important political education which are the means of conferring, to a much lower grade in society. The mental discipline being thus a more important feature of local concerns than in the general concerns of the State. (CRG, 535–6; 'TDA[II],' 168)

On the matter of establishing political freedom in localities, Mill notes that in the New England states of the United States local functions of government 'are still exercised directly by the assembled people' themselves. He maintains, however, that this arrangement only works well in small communities that permit direct self-government by all citizens. Consequently, 'recourse must generally be had to the plan of representative sub-Parliaments for local affairs' (CRG, 535). Regarding the composition of local assemblies, he reiterates several points that he makes about national assemblies. Local assemblies should have 'a widely democratic basis,' especially given their role in 'popular education' (CRG, 536). The same provisions should be adopted for the representation of minorities as in the case of the national Parliament; and the same reasons exist for plural voting. At the same time, since the 'imposition and expenditure of local taxation' is the primary duty of local representatives, the electoral franchise should be reserved for those persons 'who contribute to the local [tax] rates, to the exclusion of all those who do not.' Furthermore, 'there is not so decisive an objection' as there is in the case of elections for the national assembly for 'making the plural voting depend ... on a mere money qualification.' This would give 'a greater proportional influence to those who have a larger money interest at stake' (CRG, 536). These provisions would restrict the 'widely democratic basis' that Mill seeks. Still, aside from the truly *democratic* principle of representation of minorities, he clearly intends for the other measures to have the same conditional role that he gives them in national politics.[28]

Finally, to determine the discretionary power appropriate for local authorities, Mill says that we need to balance certain disadvantages of localities with the advantages of central authorities (CRG, 542–5). He contends, for example, that the 'political instruction' of citizens in the virtues of self-government requires something other than simply maximizing their participation in public affairs: 'a school supposes teachers as well as scholars: the utility of instruction greatly depends on its bringing inferior minds into contact with superior [minds], a contact which in the ordinary course of life is altogether exceptional' (CRG, 539). In this regard, he warns that local governments are more likely than national governments to feature participants of 'low calibre' (538). Therefore, while local governments provide average citizens with more opportunities for direct involvement in government, central governments generally offer them greater exposure to 'the most instructed minds' (541–5).

Mill gives two further reasons for favouring considerable intervention by central governments in local affairs. First, the criteria that 'constitute good management of these things, are the same everywhere' (CRG, 541). 'Power may be localized,' he says, 'but knowledge, to be most useful, must be centralized' (CRG, 544). In other words, beneficial new knowledge regarding issues such as education and public health will have its greatest impact only insofar as it is made available throughout society. Such knowledge may originate in a particular locality, but only a central government can ensure that it becomes available throughout the nation. Second, while such things as paving, lighting, and cleaning the streets of a locality 'are of little consequence to any but its inhabitants,' other local matters are not of strictly 'local, as distinguished from national, importance' (CRG, 541). Examples include jails, police, and the local administration of justice. Local authorities will often have a distinct advantage in administering the details of such matters because of their greater knowledge of local circumstances (CRG, 543–4). Still, insofar as local issues touch upon such vitally important issues as 'security of person and property, and equal justice between individuals,' the central government should ensure that 'whatever are the best arrangements for securing these primary objects should be made universally obligatory' (CRG, 541–2). Localities, he says, 'may be allowed to mismanage their own interests, but not to prejudice those of others, nor violate those principles of justice between one person and another ... If the local majority attempts to oppress the minority, or one class another, the State is bound to interpose' (CRG, 544).[29]

By designating this special role for central governments, Mill opens the door for central authorities to limit considerably the discretionary power of local governments. Mill's resulting constitutional framework is best construed, as Oskar Kurer suggests, as a model of *deconcentration* rather than *decentralization* since it transfers 'authority from central to local government with little or no local discretion' (Kurer, 1989b, 294n35). Some power is localized, but the limits of local discretion are ultimately determined by the central government. Mill offers persuasive reasons for this intergovernmental division of freedom and power. Insofar as the central government limits the discretion of local governments to protect the 'security of person and property, and equal justice between individuals,' it serves as a crucial agent of freedom rather than simply a constraint to freedom. Just as the state must exercise vigilance regarding the social power that some people exercise over others (OL, 301), central governments have a crucial role in securing equal justice against unjust or oppressive local governments.

e. Popular Participation and the 'Authority of the Instructed'

One further component of Mill's view of the relationship between social power and political freedom concerns 'the authority of the instructed.' In light of his theory of authority, he gives this form of social power a special role in establishing political freedom within a 'rational democracy.' He consistently maintains that some trade-offs must be made (especially under then existing conditions) between maximizing opportunities for popular participation in government and ensuring competent governance 'by the deliberately-formed opinions of a comparatively few, specially trained for the task' ('RR,' 23).[30] As I explained in Chapter 3, however, he argues that reasoned deference to authority by ordinary citizens is fully compatible with democratic self-government.

Mill bases his argument here partly on his view as to the existing capacities of most citizens and partly on his view of the difficulty of attaining authoritative knowledge about the 'extensive subjects' that concern governments. He believes that there are no clear limits to the intellectual '*powers* of the mass of mankind'; yet most people's circumstances, especially regarding the burdens of making a living, greatly limit 'their possible *acquirements*' ('SOA,' 242, Mill's emphasis). In the same breath, he says that the division of labour in modern societies enables *some* people to 'dedicate themselves to the investigation and study of physical, moral, and social truths, as their peculiar calling' so that they 'can alone be expected to make themselves thorough masters of the philosophical grounds of those opinions which it is desirable that all should be firmly *persuaded*, but which they alone can entirely and philosophically *know*' ('SOA,' 242, Mill's emphasis). On the one hand, then, he supports the democratic view that 'the most important moral and political truths are simple and obvious, intelligible to persons of the most limited faculties, with moderate study and attention' ('SOA,' 242). On the other hand, he emphasizes the practical limitations of most people's commonsense understandings. He insists that a substantial number of truths in political matters require extensive study before they can be fully understood. 'When all is done,' he says, 'there still remains something which [most people] must always and inevitably take on trust' ('SOA,' 243).

Thus, while Mill supports democratic government, he warns against the danger of 'collective mediocrity' in democracies (CRG, 457). The general public demands 'that all things shall be made clear to each man's understanding – an indifference to the subtler proofs which address themselves to more cultivated and systematically exercised intellects' ('TDA[II],' 196, 179). Therefore, there must be a special role in politics for persons with 'more cultivated ... intellects' because attention to 'subtler proofs' is often crucial for choosing good public opinion policies. What is necessary 'is not that public opinion should not be, what it is and must be, the ruling power; but that, in order to [foster] the formation of the best opinion, there should exist somewhere a great social support for opinions and sentiments different from those of the mass' ('TDA[II],' 198). A 'rational' democracy, then, requires a combination of popular sovereignty and legislative and administrative processes that reserve a special role for the authority of the instructed. Ideally, this 'governing class' would not only evaluate subtle arguments that are beyond the comprehension of ordinary citizens, but would also be somewhat insulated from such 'sinister interests' as 'the unbalanced influence of the commercial spirit' (CRG, chs. 5–14; 'TDA[II],' 198, 196, 200–4). 'The interest of the people,' Mill explains, 'is, to choose for their rulers the most instructed and ablest persons who can be found, and having done so, to allow them to exercise freely, or with the least possible control – as long as it *is* in the good of the people, and not some private end, that they are aiming at' ('TDA[I],' 72, Mill's emphasis). He believes that the instructed minority will generally aim at the general good because it tends to be 'governed by higher considerations' rather than selfish class interests (CRG, 447, 457–8; 'TDA[II],' 198–204). Meanwhile, the power of the people to choose governing authorities constitutes 'that intervention of popular suffrage which is essential to freedom' (CRG, 527). The people must have the power 'to dismiss their rulers as soon as the devotion of those rulers to the interests of the people becomes questionable'; yet this 'freedom cannot produce its best effects' unless it is combined 'with trained and skilled administration' ('TDA[I],' 71–2; CRG, 440).

In developing these arguments, Mill implicitly highlights two distinct kinds of political competence: moral competence – the capacity to discern ends that promote justice and the general interest – and instrumental or technical competence – the capacity to grasp the best or most effective means to achieved the desired ends (Thompson, 1976, 55ff). These two kinds of competence are closely related to his distinction between 'art' and 'science.' 'Art' refers to the capacity to evaluate the appropriate *ends* of human conduct, or to determine what *ought* to be done. 'Science' concerns matters of fact; it is concerned with revealing the links between causes and effects in the world (L, 949; see ch. 2, above). In politics, Mill regards these two kinds of knowledge as largely distinct. He regards the drafting and administering of laws as essentially a technical exercise. In contrast, he sees both moral and technical knowledge at issue in the 'art' of politics – that is, determining what kinds of laws and policies there ought to be. In addition, he contends that ordinary citizens tend to have greater moral competence than instrumental competence. In Mill's view, the 'scientific' or technical aspects of politics, particularly in the area of political economy, are more like the demonstrable truths of mathematics: when all evidence is before us 'all the argument is on one side' (OL, 244). He maintains, though, that these are typically truths that can be grasped fully only by those who have gone through specialized studies: 'The multitude will never believe these truths until tendered to them from an authority in which they have as unlimited confidence as they have in the unanimous voice of astronomers on a question of astronomy' ('TDA[I],' 73n).[31] He recognizes that this comparison between politics and astronomy is problematic insofar as attaining really authoritative knowledge is much more difficult in politics due to personal and class biases (ACP, 267–79). Nonetheless, he maintains that those who have studied these matters extensively are generally more capable than average citizens to judge the 'philosophical grounds' of competing propositions.

Mill regards moral knowledge as more intrinsically contestable and more readily attainable by ordinary citizens because it concerns judgments about people's vital interests (see ch. 5, above). He includes political matters, along with morals, religion, and the business of life, among the 'infinitely more complicated' subjects regarding which typically 'the truth depends on a balance to be struck between two sets of conflicting reasons' (OL, 244–5). He summarizes his case for the moral competence of average citizens in *On Liberty* when he distinguishes matters of 'social morality' from matters that fall within province of individual liberty: 'On questions of social morality, of duty to others, the opinion of the public, that is, of the overruling majority, though often wrong, is likely to be still oftener right; because on such questions they are only required to judge of their own interests' (OL, 283).

Still, Mill maintains that in such matters the instructed minority can help foster 'a virtuous and enlightened public opinion' (CRG, 390). He expects that the opinion of 'the public' or the overruling majority will often be wrong, especially as long as class divisions cloud people's judgments (CRG, 441–7). Many people will mistake their immediate interests for their 'real' interests or pursue worthy but unattainable goals. Moreover, people need to develop their capacities for reasoning and judgment in order to distinguish their 'real' from their 'immediate' interests (CRG, 442–3; U, 214–16; ch. 4, above). Mill therefore looks toward the instructed minority to play an educative role in democratic deliberation. He says that 'though the superior intellects and characters will necessarily be outnumbered [in a democracy], it makes a great difference whether or not they are heard' (CRG, 457). His hope is that 'the majority of the people, through their representatives,' will prevail in an 'equal democracy,' but that the instructed minority will elevate public debate and deliberation (449, 460). He says, 'if the presence in the representative assembly can be insured, of even a few of the first minds in the country, ... the influence of these leading spirits is sure to make itself sensibly felt in the general deliberations' (CRG, 458). To the degree that they have a meaningful place in public deliberations they will be able to help 'keep popular opinion within reason and justice, and ... guide it from deteriorating influences which assail the weak side of democracy' (CRG, 460). For example, he says that in the existing class-divided society the instructed minority can sometimes tip the balance in favour of those whose class interests most closely correspond to justice and the general interest of society. Most members of the two dominant classes are motivated largely by their immediate class interests; but the instructed minority can often persuade a minority from each class to subordinate their immediate interests 'to reason, justice, and the good of the whole' (CRG, 446–7).[32]

Overall, Mill tempers the élitist tendency of his argument with its developmental aspect. He envisions increasing democratization of social and political relationships as a consequence of ongoing 'progress in the mass of the people in mental cultivation, and in the virtues dependent on it' (PPE, 764). This democratization would include a distinctly democratic kind of deference by average citizens to the authority of experts. The latter would be reasoned and freely given and, thus, fully compatible with self-government and an unwillingness to be governed by 'mere authority.' Furthermore, given the difficulties of gaining authoritative knowledge in matters of public policy, including serious obstacles to impartial judgment, deference to authority would never be unconditional or uncritical (see ch. 3, above). Mill says, 'Even supposing the most tried ability and acknowledged eminence of character in the representative, the private opinions of the electors are not to be placed entirely in abeyance. Deference to mental superiority is not to go the length of ... abnegation of any personal opinion' (CRG, 510). Such democratic authority requires that knowledge and understanding be sufficiently diffused among a population so that it 'would not be the blind submission of dunces to men of knowledge, but the intelligent deference of those who know much to those who know more' (ACP, 314). 'What is wanted,' he says in *Representative Government*, is not the complete absence of authority, 'but the means of making ignorance aware of itself, and able to profit by knowledge; accustoming minds which know only routine, to act upon, and feel the value of principles: teaching them to compare different modes of action, and learn, by use of their reason, to distinguish the best' (CRG, 545). Achieving this kind of democratic authority ultimately requires a liberal and democratic political culture that includes 'the check of the freest discussion and the most unreserved censure,' along with citizens who have developed their own capacities to think for themselves.[33]

II Maximal Political Freedom

Mill never elucidates his view of maximal political freedom, but it is the logical extension of his view of political freedom in the existing state of society to 'improved' circumstances. It is integrally linked to the dynamic, developmental side of his political theory. He says at the start of *Representative Government* that popular participation in a representative democracy 'should everywhere be as great as the general degree of improvement of the community will allow' (CRG, 411–12). In this regard, his ideal of maximal political freedom looks ahead to the development of a more democratic and egalitarian civil society to support a more equal and deliberative democratic politics. Based on his assessment that the class divide has overriding significance in democratizing capitalist societies, he pays special attention to the necessary political–economic conditions of his ideal. It follows that his conception of maximal political freedom needs to be understood in light of his claim in his

Autobiography that his 'ideal of ultimate improvement [goes] far beyond Democracy' toward 'the general designation' of socialism (A, 239). At the same time, he cautions that fully democratic politics and a democratic, co-operative-based economy will be viable only when 'the whole mass of the people' become prepared for the rights and duties that they would acquire under egalitarian democracy or socialism.[34] For this reason, he prefaces his allegiance to socialism and democracy in his *Autobiography* by explaining that by the 1840s he and Harriet Taylor Mill became 'much less democrats than I had been, *because so long as education continues to be so wretchedly imperfect*, we dreaded the ignorance and especially the selfishness and brutality of the mass' (A, 239, emphasis added). Still, despite his concerns about the existing virtues and capacities of the working class, his ultimate democratic horizon is clear.[35]

Extrapolating from his account of political freedom within the existing state of society, we can reconstruct Mill's conception of maximal political freedom as follows. *First*, he retains his view that political freedom in modern societies requires *representative* rather than direct democracy. Like Benjamin Constant, Mill maintains that modern societies are quite different from 'the ancient commonwealths' in which the freedom of citizens was conceived strictly in terms of 'a certain form of political organization' ('GELH,' 244; cf. Constant, 1989 [1819]). For Mill, politics, while important, is now only one of the domains of human freedom and self-development. As he says in *The Subjection of Women*, 'citizenship fills only a small place in modern life, and does not come near the daily habits or inmost sentiments' (SW, 295). Political freedom may be the 'most important liberty of the nation' (CRG, 432), but most people are usually preoccupied in their daily lives with other concerns and other freedoms. Therefore, Mill regards a division of labour between ordinary citizens (who periodically participate in politics) and elected representatives, law makers, and civil servants (who do most of the business of governing) as both necessary and desirable.

Second, Mill conceives of maximal political freedom in terms of *a democratically reformed model of representative government within a democratically reformed civil society*. Maximal political freedom, in his view, requires not only 'equality of political rights' (or the 'full privileges of citizenship') for virtually all adult men and women, but also modes of election, representation, and political discussion that give all citizens a roughly equal voice in political deliberations and decision making (CRG, 411).[36] He applies these principles to both local and national governments, and he maintains that their full realization requires five social conditions in addition to equal political rights: quality schooling to raise up the capacities of the labouring classes to the level of the higher classes (PPE, 759–69; OL, 299; CRG, ch. 10); equality between the sexes, as well as 'justly constituted' families that are 'schools' of freedom and equality (SW, 295); a co-operative economy that overcomes the existing class division between 'capitalist[s] as chief[s], and working people without a voice in the management' (PPE, 775); a free and open, liberal and democratic public sphere of political communication; and Hare's system of personal representation to ensure equal representation. Mill regards these various principles and institutional reforms of state and society as mutually reinforcing. For instance, quality education and a co-operative economic order are necessary, in his view, to establish the economic basis for a fully equal democracy. He maintains that it will become possible to establish a roughly equal voice for all individual members of society *as individuals* only insofar as the existing class divide is overcome (see sec. I: B). In addition, he insists that full and equal political freedom for all cannot be secured unless equality is achieved between the sexes. This must include not just equal political rights, but also marital partnerships and equal educational and economic opportunities that enable women to participate equally with men in paid employment and politics (SW, ch. 4; CRG, ch. 8).

Finally, Mill's goal of enabling the 'whole public' to participate freely and equally in political discussions in the public sphere outside of government is closely linked to his view of the political economy of freedom (see ch. 7). As I noted earlier, his ideal of 'the utmost publicity and liberty of discussion' has two components. First, he defends the liberal principle that there must be no active state or societal censorship of political ideas and opinions. Second, he begins to examine the political economy of the circulation of political ideas and the formation of public opinion. He suggests that public discussion tends to be constrained and corrupted to the degree that the means of communication are dominated by 'sinister interests.' In particular, his account of social power illuminates the danger to the democratic public sphere that is posed by oligopolistic, capitalist ownership and control of the mass media. Thus, a decentralized, democratic co-operative economy is a necessary condition for realizing his vision of 'the utmost publicity and liberty of discussion, whereby not merely a few individuals in succession, but the whole public, are made, to a certain extent, participants in the government, and sharers in the instruction and mental exercise derivable from it' (CRG, 436). Maximal political freedom, then, requires not only provisions for equal representation within representative assemblies – such as Hare's plan – but also social and economic reforms that foster equal participation in a free and democratic public sphere outside of government.

III Conclusion

To summarize, Mill's theory of representative democracy remains an indispensable starting point for understanding the meaning and conditions of political freedom in modern societies. It foreshadows in many respects how political freedom has since been established in many countries through representative government, universal suffrage, regular elections, and such basic political liberties as freedom of the press, freedom of expression, and freedom of association. Moreover, many contemporary democracies utilize some form of proportional representation to secure equal and pluralistic representation. Yet much of the continuing vitality of Mill's view of political freedom lies in the fact that his democratic horizon, including his view of maximal political freedom, presents a continuing challenge to every existing 'democracy.' Democratic politics, for Mill, is a more-or-less thing rather than an all-or-nothing thing; it is not secured once and for all merely by adopting a set of basic democratic rights and practices. His standard of a 'really equal democracy' requires modes of representation and deliberation in popular assemblies such that 'those whose opinion is overruled, feel satisfied that it is heard, and set aside ... for what are thought superior reasons'; and it calls for a surrounding public sphere of political discussion that enables 'the whole public' to share equally in political deliberations (CRG, 432, 436).[37]

Mill's challenge to existing democracies is even more far-reaching when we take into account his broader vision of democratic self-government. He deems continuing democratization of educational, economic, gender, and familial relations both possible and desirable in every existing 'democracy,' as well as in all those societies that have not yet achieved minimal democratic politics. For Mill, moreover, achieving maximal political freedom is integrally connected to the goal of achieving a free and democratic civil society. Such a society would secure the greatest possible freedom of thought and discussion, along with the individual liberty for people to pursue their own good in their own way so long as they do not impede the efforts of others to pursue theirs (OL, 225–6). But this is not all. It would also address the interrelationships between people, including the pervasive relationships of power that govern their lives. It would empower people to share freedom more fully and equally by educating them for freedom, fostering equality and mutuality between the sexes, and establishing practices of mutual self-government within families and work relations as well as in politics.

This last point highlights the dynamic, developmental character of Mill's democratic theory. One of the great strengths of his theory is his attention to the educative effects of social and political institutions. In this regard, Mill poses a powerful challenge to recent 'democratic revisionists' such as Joseph Schumpeter and Bernard Berelson (Schumpeter, 1950; Berelson et al., 1954). These theorists claim that most people are incapable of active democratic citizenship. Accordingly, they urge us to abandon the idea that democratic government can be government *by the people* in any tangible sense. We should reconceptualize democratic government, they say, in terms of periodic and competitive elections that empower the people to choose among competing governing élites (Schumpeter, 1950, ch. 22). Mill foreshadows these revisionists in his emphasis on representative government, his doubts about the existing capacities of most citizens, and his call for a special role for the 'instructed minority.' Yet he differs considerably from them when he emphasizes the developmental character of people's capacities for self-government and maintains that the 'mental cultivation' necessary for democratic self-government can 'be made the inheritance of [virtually] every person in the nation' (U, 215–16; COS, 746). Moreover, he contends that opportunities to share in democratic self-government are among the more important 'schools' for the virtues of self-government. Thus, while he favours a form of *representative* democracy that reserves a special role for the instructed minority, he looks forward to 'improved' circumstances in which all citizens will be capable of a substantial and (roughly) equal role in democratic politics.

Despite Mill's considerable achievement, his view of democratic political freedom is open to criticism on three main fronts: his understanding of the role of expert authority; his tentative analysis of a democratic public sphere and the dangers of minority rule; and his exclusive focus on the nation-state as the central site of modern politics. Concerning the first point, there are two important tensions in his view of the relationship between political freedom and the authority of the instructed. *First,* as I noted earlier, he contends that the prospect of attaining authoritative political knowledge is undermined by the complexity of political phenomena and by the impact of personal and class biases on social scientific inquiry (see ch. 2, above). His scepticism here is well-founded, even though he expects authoritative knowledge of political matters to become increasingly available. There is little 'united authority of the instructed' with regard to key political issues partly because people who study them intensively are generally as far as ever from reaching any consensus. This is true, moreover, even in the discipline of economics, which Mill regards as the area of sociological inquiry most readily amenable to scientific analysis.

Second, his distinction between the 'art' and 'science' of politics is problematic. We can generally delineate technical and moral *aspects* of different policy alternatives, whether in economics, education, or environmental protection. Still, political issues always involve both instrumental knowledge and moral judgment, and those persons who have technical proficiency in particular areas have no unique claim to moral competence (Dahl, 1989, ch. 5). For instance, economists can claim special expertise regarding, say, how raising the minimum wage will affect the level of unemployment in an economy, but they have no special *moral* competence concerning if, when, and how a society should adjust its minimum wage laws. Such policy decisions involve judgments about risks and ends that go beyond the technical expertise of economists.[38] Moreover, Mill's own emphasis on the educative dimension of political institutions and laws highlights how the *means* to a given *end* usually favour some values (or ends) over others. As V.W. Bladen says, 'means may become partially ends in themselves' (1965, xxxv). In this regard, Mill's proposals to reserve a special role for the 'instructed minority' as the best means of making and administering the laws *entails* certain ends. In the name of expert governance, he sacrifices some popular power and responsibility for self-government.

This last point figures prominently in the criticisms of Mill's democratic theory made by such theorists as Carole Pateman and C.B. Macpherson. These critics contend that Mill ultimately offers too little room for popular participation in politics to achieve either thoroughgoing democracy or the educative benefits that he seeks (Pateman, 1970; Macpherson, 1977). In Mill's model of representative democracy, most citizens most of the time would have little direct experience – even at the local level – with the business of government. In addition, he is perhaps overly sanguine in his belief that even limited participation by citizens tends to foster not just growth 'in range of ideas and development of faculties' of ordinary citizens, but also 'moral' instruction insofar as it enlarges their perspectives (CRG, 412).

With some minor revisions, the core of Mill's developmental conception of political freedom in a representative democracy largely withstands this participatory critique. He rightly points out that participation in politics is not the only domain of human freedom and self-development. Many members of modern societies are unavoidably too preoccupied with other activities and responsibilities to devote more than a fraction of their energies to politics. Therefore, *some* division of labour in politics between most citizens, on the one hand, and activists, politicians, and civil servants, on the other hand, seems to be required in complex modern societies (Dunn, 1993a; 1993b, ch. 1). Given this division of labour, Mill's ideas of equal representation, democratic deliberation, and a liberal and democratic public sphere offer significant resources for grasping how to make the 'whole public ... participants in government,' despite his ambivalence about political equality (CRG, 436). His broad vision of a maximally free and democratic society would considerably expand opportunities for all adult women and men to share in practices of democratic self-government and, thus, to be sharers in the intellectual and moral education that it provides. Furthermore, while Mill does not go as far as he might to consider new ways to expand citizen participation in the business of government, he certainly does not foreclose this approach to democratic reform.

To improve on this aspect of Mill's theory, we need to go beyond his account of the connections between social and political democratization to determine just what kind of equality among citizens is necessary if we are to secure tangible political freedom for all citizens (cf. Dahl, 1989, ch. 8; Dworkin, 1996; Bohman, 1997; Knight and Johnson, 1997). For instance, Mill's analysis of the necessary conditions for a free and democratic public sphere raises crucial issues that he only begins to address. What remains to be done is to extend his insights regarding the shaping of public opinion in light of the subsequent 'structural transformation of the public sphere' (Habermas, 1991). This analysis must address the multiplication of new means of communication – from radio and television to the Internet – as well as the global reach of these media and the increasingly concentrated ownership and control of major media outlets by major corporations (Garnham, 1992; McChesney, 1997). To achieve something close to 'really equal democracy' and maximal political freedom in our time, then, we need to go beyond Mill's suggestive remarks about newspapers to confront more directly than he does how inequalities of ownership, control, access, and accountability among citizens with respect to the mass media undermine democratic equality and political freedom.

Closely related to the limitations of Mill's account of the public sphere is the ambivalence of his broader class analysis. As we have seen, his class balance model of democratic politics in *Representative Government* is premised largely on his assessment of the impending rise of the labouring classes. Furthermore, his notion of maximal political freedom presupposes a post-capitalist transformation of existing class divisions. Arguably, though, the greatest threat to political freedom in a 'really equal democracy' in existing capitalist democracies is the unmatched social power of larger private corporations. These firms can often use their social power to set public agendas and limit possibilities for democratic deliberation and decision making for the entire polity (Lindblom, 1977; Bachrach and Botwinick, 1992, 148; Bohman, 1997, 339).[39]

Finally, Mill's conception of political freedom suffers from one further limitation – one that is common to many nineteenth and twentieth century democratic theorists. He assumes that political freedom is a national problem and that the nation-state is the ultimate locus of political power and democratic accountability (Held, 1993). The nation-state is likely to remain a focal point of political power and freedom for quite some time, so Mill's theory is not likely to become obsolete soon. Nonetheless, to adequately address increasingly dense global political, economic, and ecological interconnections, we need partially to reconceptualize the domains of democratic politics and political freedom in terms of major forms of power and governance that transcend the boundaries of nation-states. These new political domains include international institutions such as the United Nations, the World Bank, the World Trade Organization, and the International Monetary Fund; regional supranational institutions such as the European Union; and such 'private' enterprises as transnational corporations.

9

Mill and the Politics of Freedom

> We have had the morality of submission, and the morality of chivalry and generosity; the time is now come for the morality of justice.
>
> J.S. Mill, *The Subjection of Women*

Mill said in a letter to Pasquale Villari near the end of his life that his work 'lies rather among anticipations of the future than explorations of the past.'[1] Thus, there is considerable irony in the task of recovering his insights into the interplay between freedom and power in the context of contemporary struggles for freedom. In a profound way, his work still anticipates the future, even if he was overly optimistic about trends toward societal 'improvement.' His hopes and ideals regarding equality between the sexes, economic freedom, and a vibrant and deliberative form of democratic politics have nowhere been fully realized.

I set out in this study with two primary aims. My broader aim has been to contribute to a critical sociology of freedom by clarifying the complementary relationship between freedom and power. My second aim has been to offer a new interpretation of John Stuart Mill's political philosophy that highlights his insights into the interplay between freedom and power. Yet if I have succeeded so far in realizing my first aim, I have done so largely by pursuing my second. Here I intend partially to redress this balance, but mainly by reassessing key aspects of Mill's theory of freedom: his general account of the interplay between freedom and power; and his four 'secondary' principles for achieving maximal freedom for all members of society. Regarding Mill's theory as a whole, A.D. Lindsay nicely summarizes his achievement when he says, 'if we recognize that, just, because of his historical position, we cannot look for a complete systematic exposition, we may take his writings rather as pointing the way to a new philosophy than as constituting a new one in themselves' (1950, x).

I Rethinking Freedom and Power

Concerning what is at stake when members of modern societies debate and struggle for freedom, Steven Lukes suggests that what most people value is 'being in control of one's own life, or as much of one's life as possible' (1991, 63). Mill elaborates this point in relation to the interplay of freedom and power. Freedom, Mill shows, requires not just the absence of burdensome constraints, but effective powers of self-determination. He clarifies how practices of freedom are situated within the relationships of power that govern people's lives by shaping their capacities for free agency and structuring their fields of possible action. Since people are always situated within relations of power, their freedom cannot be construed as simply the absence of power or constraint, or even the number of options open to them within existing power relations. Instead, it must also be conceived in terms of their capacity to share in shaping the power relationships that govern their lives. As Mill says, the 'freedom of action of the individual' consists of 'the liberty of each to govern his [or her] own conduct by his [or her] own feelings of duty, and by such laws and social constraints as his [or her] conscience can subscribe to' (SW, 336, 337).

Mill reveals several ways in which the power of some persons *over* others limits the freedom of the latter. At the same time, he also highlights four ways in which the exercise of freedom is integrally related rather than opposed to the exercise of power. First, he maintains that having 'power over our own character[s]' to formulate and pursue our own desires and purposes – what we now call autonomy – is a necessary condition of our being fully free (L, 841). Second, Mill conceives of autonomy as a developmental power that people attain to the extent that the various power relationships situating them – that is, educational, political, economic, gender, and family relations – cultivate their capacities to think for themselves. Third, he maintains that freedom requires the presence of opportunities and material resources that enable people to pursue their aims and purposes. Fourth, he conceives of individual freedom in terms of the choices and actions of independent individuals, as well as practices of mutual self-government that enable individuals to share in determining what they are free to do and be.

My claim is that Mill is largely right on each of these points. His argument needs to be amended, though, insofar as he fails to recognize how different contexts of power and culture constitute different possibilities for free agency. To address this actuality, we need a view of freedom that is more pluralistic than his – one that acknowledges how people can freely pursue fundamental commitments and beliefs that they have not reflectively chosen. At the same time, as I said in Chapter 1, adopting such a pluralistic view of practices of freedom should not lead us to overlook Mill's insight into the significance of reflective choice, self-realization, and self-government to practices of freedom in modern societies. Moreover, due to his attention to the interplay between freedom and power, his understanding of the freedom of individuals to choose their own mode of life challenges the notion of 'freedom of choice' that is so widely celebrated in contemporary capitalist societies. Freedom is not advanced simply by offering people more choices, regardless of what the choices are. Rather, our freedom is expanded only insofar as we have tangible power to pursue 'our own good in our own way' and to share in practices of self-government.

II Four Principles of Freedom

To further elucidate the strengths and limitations of Mill's theory of freedom, I will turn once more to his four principles of freedom. As I explained in Chapter 2, he offers the following four principles as 'secondary principles' for realizing maximal freedom in modern democratizing societies: the principle of liberty; the principle of democratic self-government; social and distributive justice; and equality. Taken together, these principles address the individualistic and collective aspects of freedom with respect to the power relationships situating people.

a. The Principle of Liberty

Mill elaborates his principle of liberty most fully, and it is one of his great contributions to modern political theory and practice. The principle of liberty, again, is 'that the sole end for which mankind are warranted, individually or collectively, in interfering with the liberty of action of any of their number is ... to prevent harm to others' (OL, 223). This offers an invaluable framework for members of pluralistic modern societies to determine the respective limits of individual liberty and 'the power which can be legitimately exercised by society over the individual' (OL,

217). Due to the indeterminate character of the notion of 'harm to others,' the liberty principle is not quite the 'very simple' principle Mill says it is. I have argued, however, that this indeterminacy is largely a strength rather than a weakness. Mill regards the task of determining those individual interests that 'ought to be considered as rights' as a political task (OL, 276). Accordingly, he offers the liberty principle as a maxim of 'positive political morality' to guide democratic politics (CRG, 422). It highlights for citizens the dangers of imposing their ideas of the good life on others, including their notions of what is 'religiously wrong.' At the same time, it also allows for some variation of rights and duties across societies in relation to different cultural contexts.

Finally, my interpretation illuminates two corollaries that Mill derives from the principle of liberty to address more fully the interplay between freedom and power. First, he emphasizes that society has powers other than legal or moral punishment with which to foster morally responsible conduct; it also has 'all the powers of education' with which to make its members 'wise and good' (OL, 282). Second, he insists that while the state must respect 'the liberty of each individual in what specifically regards himself, [it] is bound to maintain a vigilant control over his exercise of any power which it allows him to possess over others' (OL, 301). In this regard, his distinction between the respective domains of individual liberty and social morality challenges the common distinctions between 'private' and 'public' spheres of life. Mill explains persuasively that many relationships and activities that are often regarded as 'personal' or 'private,' such as family relationships or control of 'private property,' are relations of power that involve moral obligations, including obligations of justice. Some private activities and relationships fall squarely within the province of individual liberty. Yet others fall outside the province of individual liberty and into that of law or morality. This is true, for example, of marital or parental relationships in which one or more persons exercise power over others in abusive ways. Similarly, 'private' property gives some property owners not only power over things, but also power over other persons. Accordingly, Mill supports efforts to reform existing property rights and work relationships in capitalist democracies, with the goal of fostering maximal economic freedom and social justice (see ch. 7). In sum, his principle of liberty provides a means for reconciling democratization of the state, industrial relations, education, and marital relations with protection for individuals against tyrannical majorities.

b. Democratic Self-government

Mill's principle of democratic self-government complements his principle of liberty. The liberty principle protects the freedom of independent individuals to pursue their own good in their own way within the province of individual liberty; the principle of democratic self-government aims to extend freedom to individuals with respect to the power relationships that govern their lives. Mill elaborates this principle in light of how people's lives are governed by economic, educational, familial, and political relations. Accordingly, in contrast to classical liberal and civic republican theorists, he demonstrates that the relevance of democratic self-government is not limited to the state.

Mill's aim of broadly extending the freedom of democratic self-government into key sites of power remains as controversial today as it was in his time. Consider, for instance, Samuel Huntington's important but ultimately deficient challenge to this participatory democratic ideal. Huntington notes that democratic procedures are 'only one way of constituting authority' and that in many cases 'claims of expertise, seniority, experience, and special talents may override the claims of democracy' (1997, 285). This point is well taken, but Mill's judgment is basically sound regarding the proper domains of the democratic principle. He makes a strong case for employing democratic self-government in politics, industrial relations, and marital relations to achieve maximal freedom for all members of society. At the same time, he refrains from extending democratic procedures to schools or to relations between parent and children. Children and students, in his view, do not merit the same status and authority as parents and teachers. This point, however, does not preclude such quasi-democratic institutions as student governments and relatively democratic parenting.

Mill's case for political and marital democracy is, in my view, indisputable – especially since his principle of liberty leaves room for couples to work out alternative domestic arrangements *by mutual consent.* His case for industrial or economic democracy is more controversial, although equally valid. It turns largely on considerations of freedom and justice. In addition, despite concerns about the existing capacities of working people for self-government, he points out that there are ultimately good economic grounds for discounting claims that capitalists, and managers accountable to capitalists have special talents and expertise that entitle them to exercise exclusive power in economic enterprises.[2] He adds, though, that 'the moral aspect of the question ... is still more important than the economical' (PPE, 768). Any program to promote and sustain economic democracy would necessarily limit the freedom of some members of society to accumulate and control unlimited amounts of property in the means and instruments of production. Yet it would do so to promote social justice and *greater overall freedom* among all members of society – what I have called maximal economic freedom. Finally, to achieve Mill's aims, proponents of economic democracy now need to give more attention than Mill does to the global reach of capitalist firms and the place of small-scale capitalist entrepreneurs in an economy composed largely of democratic firms (see ch. 7).[3]

c. Social and Distributive Justice

Mill's account of the situatedness of freedom within relations of power enables him to address insightfully the connections between freedom and justice. He shows that insofar as people always exercise freedom within some relations of power, including relations of mutual self-government, freedom has unavoidable distributive aspects. These latter are evident in terms of how a society distributes power and resources that are means of self-determination, as well as how it distributes basic rights and liberties. In this light, Mill's aim is not the greatest *sum* of freedom, which could mean great freedom for some and little for others. Rather, his aim is maximal freedom, which would yield considerable freedom for all adult members of society in all areas of life.

Mill theorizes the link between freedom and justice in two respects. First, individuals should be free to pursue their own good in their own way, in his view, as long as they act within the limits of respect for their moral obligations to others. Furthermore, he insists that the force of law – as opposed to the moral coercion of public opinion – should be used to restrict the conduct of individual members of society only when they violate those vital interests of others that ought to be considered as rights. Respect for *these interests* is an obligation of justice, and therefore it can and should be enforced by legal penalties. Second, he also applies considerations of social and distributive justice to the distribution of those powers and resources – including educational opportunities – that are essential to individuals if they are to develop autonomy and to exercise self-determination and self-government.

Mill's account of how the distribution of resources and power results in a particular distribution of freedom offers an important corrective to theorists Berlin and Rawls, who distinguish between freedom and the 'conditions of its exercise,' or liberty and the 'worth of liberty' (Rawls, 1971, 204).[4] Insofar as freedom means effective self-determination, it is misleading to separate freedom from the conditions of its exercise.[5] Thus, Mill helps us appreciate how freedom is at stake in struggles over social and distributive justice.

d. Equality

Mill's approach to the interplay between freedom and power leads him to provide a persuasive response to the claim that freedom and equality are competing values (cf. Berlin, 1969a, liii–liv; 1969c, 170). As he says in his second article on Tocqueville, 'Equality may be either equal freedom, or equal servitude' ('TDA[II],' 159). He sees freedom and equality as largely complementary or interdependent rather than as conflicting values. Some egalitarian policies or programs undermine freedom; even so, in many respects fostering equality is essential to fostering maximal freedom. Mill's developmental utilitarianism tempers his egalitarianism, at least in the short run. He distinguishes in many cases between the kind and degree of equality appropriate to people's existing capacities – particularly with respect to claims of democratic self-government – and the kind and degree of equality that would support maximal freedom in various domains. For present purposes, I will focus on how he conceptualizes the complementary relationship between equality and freedom.

Mill highlights how freedom and equality are mutually supportive of each other with respect to political, economic, and marital relations. Extending freedom to all members of society within these relationships requires relatively equal status and equal rights to self-government for each individual situated within these relationships: full and equal democratic citizenship; equality among worker-members (both women and men) in governing economic enterprises; and equality between spouses in marital partnerships. Furthermore, equal freedom for women and men requires broader equality between the sexes. Mill's conception of distributive justice allows for some inequality of income and wealth, which entails some inequalities of individual liberty, but only insofar as these inequalities correspond to differences in merit and exertion. At the same time, he explains that in order to achieve an economic system that bestows rewards proportionate to differences in merit, two egalitarian reforms of existing capitalism are required: first, a strong standard of equality of opportunity, including equal educational opportunities and sharp taxes on inherited wealth; and second, a transition to an economy based largely on democratic co-operatives, in which worker members collectively determine the distribution of wages and profits within firms (see ch. 7). All told, he shows that egalitarian policies that foster autonomy and equal opportunity and that empower people to share in self-government are necessary to achieve maximal social and political freedom.[6]

III Conclusion: The Politics of Freedom

Mill clarifies several aspects of the interplay between freedom and power. With respect to my goal of a critical sociology of freedom, however, his theory of freedom is limited by his flawed account of social change. He shows that extending freedom more fully and equally in modern societies demands an enormous *redistribution of power* in economic, political, educational, gender, and familial relationships. Yet he seriously underestimates the degree to which achieving such change requires social and political *struggle* to overcome vested interests. When he says that 'speculative thought is one of the chief elements in social power' and the chief agent of social transformation, he implies that when people collectively get their ideas right they generally shape their institutions accordingly (CRG, 382; L, 926; see ch. 2, above).[7] His faith in the power of speculative thought leads him to miss, first, the ideological dimension of freedom struggles – the latent struggle to conceptualize the meaning and conditions of freedom – and, second, the degree of manifest social and political struggle needed to bring about emancipatory change. These considerations relate to a shortcoming in Mill's theory of social power that I noted at the outset: his account of social power is richly sociological except insofar as it is insufficiently interpretive.[8]

First, concerning the ideological dimension of freedom struggles, it is important to recall that the controversy that Mill addresses in *On Liberty* is not the meaning and conditions of freedom, but rather the *rightful limits* of individual freedom. In his other major, sustained analyses of freedom, in *A System of Logic* and *An Examination of Sir William Hamilton's Philosophy*, he focuses on another controversy: the debate over free will and determinism. His own conception of freedom was soon challenged (see Hutton, 1975 [1859]; Ritchie, 1956 [1891]; Bosanquet, 1899; Hobhouse, 1956 [1911]), but he never considered the possibility that the very meaning and conditions of freedom would themselves become politically contested. However, debates over the meaning of freedom are by no means politically neutral, since conceptualizing 'freedom' involves contestable interpretations of the agents, obstacles, and goals constitutive of practices of freedom (MacCallum, 1973; Connolly, 1983, ch. 4; Taylor, 1985a). That being said, such controversy does not belie the fact that there are better and worse conceptions. Therefore, once we accept Mill's account of how freedom requires autonomy and power, we need to confront the paradox that freedom is now widely construed, at least in Anglophone countries, in terms of the absence of constraints or the nonrestriction of options (cf. Friedman, 1962; Berlin, 1969c; Taylor, 1979; Skinner, 1984; Flathman, 1987b).

For example, Milton Friedman's view of capitalism as a 'system of economic freedom' has become widely accepted, despite its limitations for those persons who are disempowered by the class structure of capitalist societies (see ch. 7). As Zygmunt Bauman notes, in the twentieth century there has been a shift in struggles for freedom 'away from the area of production and power and into that area of consumption. In our society, individual freedom is constituted as, first and foremost, freedom of the consumer; it hangs upon the presence of an effective market' (1988, 6–7; cf. Dunn, 1990). This 'consumer sovereignty' is an impoverished practice of freedom, though, insofar as it separates questions of freedom and unfreedom from realities of power and powerlessness. It leaves most people with little control over the power relationships that determine their working conditions and their livelihoods.[9]

Mill had envisioned a different future for modern societies. 'I am not charmed,' he says, 'with the ideal of life held out by those who think that the normal state of human beings is that of struggling to get on; that the trampling, crushing, and treading on each other's heels, which form the existing type of social life, are the most desirable lot of the human kind' (PPE, 754).[10] At the same time, he offers some insight into how this narrow view of freedom has become so prevalent, even among those whom it leaves significantly unfree, when he considers the ascendancy of the capitalist class and of '*bourgeois* opinion' ('TDA[II],' 194–5, Mill's emphasis). 'Wherever there is an ascendant class,' he says in *On Liberty*, 'a large portion of the morality of the country emanates from its class interests, and its feelings of class superiority' (OL, 221). Mill himself expects the working class to soon become ascendant; yet the eclipse of his view of economic freedom can be explained at least in part by the power of the capitalist class to promote a procapitalist view of freedom (Marx, 1978b [1848]; Bauman, 1988, chs. 3–4). In the United States, for instance, the *marketing* of the consumerist notion of freedom is pervasive. For example, several years ago I came across a fitting symbol of this phenomenon while walking on a beach. Someone had littered the beach with a disposable drinking cup from a 7 Eleven mini-market featuring the slogan 'Freedom of Choice,' along with trademarks for both Coca-Cola and Pepsi-Cola. The pitch, in short, was that 7 Eleven offered consumers 'freedom' to choose either Coke or Pepsi.

To develop an adequate critical sociology of freedom, then, we need to go beyond Mill's tentative insights into the connections between ascendant classes and prevailing moralities to develop a more explicit account of the ideological or discursive dimensions of freedom struggles. Such an account must go beyond Mill's political sociology of educational, class-based, and gender-based constraints upon freedom to address discursive practices of exclusion and marginalization, including those concerning 'race,' sexuality, and culture. In other words, we need to address the more subtle ways in which power operates to produce our knowledge about prevailing social practices and identities (Foucault, 1980a; Hoy, 1981; Bourdieu and Eagleton, 1992).

Second, Mill grossly underestimates the degree of *manifest* struggle needed to achieve emancipatory social change. He is better at outlining what a free society would look like than at offering us practical guidance on how to achieve it. This lacuna in his thinking is glaringly evident in his hopes for a relatively 'spontaneous' transition to a postcapitalist, co-operative based economy wherein the means of production would become 'the joint property of all who participate in their productive employment' (PPE, 793). As Alan Ryan comments, 'Mill contrived to get things as wrong as he ever did' on this score (1983b, 230). Mill's expectation here goes hand in hand with his optimistic view of education for freedom. He says in *Representative Government* that 'any education which aims at making human beings other than machines, in the long run makes them claim to have the control of their own actions' (CRG, 403). Accordingly, he maintains that as working people increasingly develop their capacities for self-dependence and self-government, there will be irresistible pressure to use the co-operative principle to extend the 'freedom and independence of the individual ... [into] the industrial department' in modern societies (PPE, 759, 769, 793).[11] Yet where industrial or workplace democracy has made significant (if partial) inroads in capitalist democracies – for example, in Germany and Sweden – this has been done only through strong labour movement activism, usually in association with working class–based socialist or social democratic parties (Bachrach and Botwinick, 1992, chs. 4–5). We can surmise, therefore, that maximal personal, economic, and political freedom for all men and women will only be achieved – if it ever is – through active struggle by disempowered classes and groups, and their allies, in the pursuit of freedom and justice.

Mill is right, then, when he says, 'The love of power and the love of liberty are in eternal antagonism' (SW, 338). This does not mean, however, that freedom and power *per se* are in 'eternal antagonism.' Maximizing freedom in a society cannot be achieved by *abolishing* power, but rather only by redistributing power to enable everyone to share more fully in practices of individual self-development and self-determination and collective self-government. This goal challenges those who have greater freedom and power within existing social and political institutions. The love of power in the sense of wielding 'power over' others is incompatible with the love of freedom because the latter demands a willingness among people to *share power with others*. Accordingly, the task of achieving greater freedom requires struggles to liberalize and democratize social and political power relationships against those who currently dominate them.[12]

To meet this challenge, a critical theory of freedom must address more fully than Mill's theory does the obstacles to struggles for greater freedom entailed in existing power dynamics. In this regard, Mill's account of the power men possess to sustain their power over women remains instructive. Women, he explains, must overcome not only the immediate power that men exercise over them in daily interactions, but also 'the whole force of education' with which men 'enslave their minds' (SW, 271). Today this point must be extended to encompass how gender is constructed through struggles over gendered meanings in the mass media, families, schools, and state institutions, and in the public economy.

Mill lacks a comparable theory of the state in democratic capitalist societies, although he offers important intimations of such a theory. He points out that state power must be analyzed in relation to the distribution of social power in a given society. Moreover, he aptly warns that the state is a dubious ally in freedom struggles insofar as state policies to ameliorate social problems often tend to increase state power at the expense of individual initiative ('Ce'; OL, ch. 5; PPE, 950). In the same breath, he correctly sees the state as a crucial instrument of justice (OL, 301). Still, we need a more sustained analysis than he provides of those elements of social power that are most readily converted into political power. This requires special attention to the unequal power generated by the class structure of capitalist democracies, and to the political role of major corporations.[13] In addition, we need a more complete account than Mill offers of the kinds of state action that foster freedom.

I suggested at the start of this chapter that Mill's theory of freedom still speaks to hopes of social progress. At the same time, his modernist vision of social 'improvement' and emancipation cannot be adopted for current conditions without amendment. In particular, his theory of societal development – which posits that all societies advance through similar stages of civilizational advancement – is the kind of historical 'grand narrative' that postmodernists rightly criticize (Lyotard, 1984). It has proved to be a poor guide for comprehending tendencies toward stability and change across different cultures and societies. Therefore, in league with his Eurocentric view of fully rational and free action, it calls into question the universalistic claims of his theory of freedom (see chs. 1–2). For instance, the tasks of educating people for freedom, applying the principle of liberty, and achieving equality between the sexes in all societies are far more complicated than Mill imagines. Moreover, we need to look beyond Mill's work if we are to address adequately the interplay of freedom and power with respect to freedom struggles concerning 'race,' ethnicity, nationality, sexuality, and cultural pluralism. Nonetheless, his thinking generally sheds light on these matters (Baum, 1997).

Mill's view of economic and political freedom faces still further obstacles when measured against existing political and economic realities. It has become commonplace to say that the prospect for achieving economic democracy and for deepening political democracy in existing capitalist representative democracies is minimal, especially in light of intensifying economic globalization. In Mark Lilla's words, 'The forces at work in shaping the economy and politics ... are simply too deep to permit such idle dreaming' (1998, 7; cf. Isaac, 1996). There *are* deep political, economic, and cultural forces working against Mill's goal of maximal economic and political freedom. Yet struggles for freedom continue, and possibilities for extending freedom have not been exhausted, even in existing capitalist democracies. It remains to be seen whether such emancipatory hopes are an idle dream, but it is not too late to seek a freer world.[14]

Notes

Introduction

1 Mill articulates his view of this modern project most explicitly in *The Subjection of Women*, ch. 1. For 'postmodern' challenges to this ideal, see Jean-François Lyotard (1984) and Anthony Giddens (1990).

2 Richard Ashcraft's way of contrasting Mill to contemporary liberals is basically sound – at least with respect to liberals who focus on narrower issues of individual liberty: 'If modern liberals have, to a significant degree, misunderstood the radical dimensions of Mill's political thought, it is because, unlike him, they have demonstrated little interest in exposing and criticizing the fundamental defects and injustices of the institutions that shape their daily lives' (1989, 126).

3 Thomas Hobbes provides a classic formulation of this conception in *Leviathan* (1651). He says, for example, 'By LIBERTY is understood, according to the proper signification of the word, the absence of externall Impediments: which Impediments, may oft take away part of a mans power to do what hee would; but cannot hinder him from using the power left him, according as his judgment, and reason shall dictate to him' (1968, 189). On the place of this view of freedom in modern liberalism, see Gray (1986).

4 On this point, see Foucault, 1983. Related criticisms of 'classical liberalism' are made by John Dewey (1946) and Hannah Arendt (1968). One contemporary liberal theorist who explicitly counterpoises freedom and power in this way is Giovanni Sartori (1987).

5 Representative thinkers in this tradition include Rousseau (1979 [1762]), Kant (1959 [1785]), Marx (1978b [1848]), T.H. Green (1962 [1880]), John Dewey (1980 [1935]), Hannah Arendt (1968), and, more recently, Carol Gould (1988) and Amartya Sen (1990a, 1990b).

6 The first definition of 'govern' listed in *The Oxford English Dictionary* is, 'To rule with authority, especially the authority of a sovereign: to direct and control the actions and affairs of (a people, a state or its members), whether despotically or constitutionally; to rule or relegate the affairs of (a body of men, corporation); to command the garrison of (a fort)' (*OED*, 2nd ed., v. 6: 708).

7 Even some sophisticated defenders of 'negative liberty' such as Isaiah Berlin sometimes write as if complete noninterference is the model of (negative) freedom. For instance, Berlin contrasts the 'negative' conception of freedom with the conception of freedom as 'liberation by reason' or 'self-direction or self-control' by pointing out that the latter 'is not the "negative" conception of a field (ideally) without obstacles, a vacuum in which nothing obstructs me' (1969c, 144).

8 I develop this point, however, in a way that diverges from Foucault's approach and converges with the emancipatory concerns of other recent 'radical' theorists of power. See Lukes (1974, 1986); Gaventa (1980); Hartsock (1985); Bowles and Gintis (1987); Isaac (1987); and Wartenburg (1988, 1990).

9 Mill conveys this basic difference between freedom and power when he says, in *The Subjection of Women*, 'The love of power and the love of liberty are in eternal antagonism' (SW, 338). Freedom and power are not in opposition *per se*, but people who love power, such as despots, tend to exercise power in ways that diminish the freedom of others.

10 Consider also the following passage, from Mill's *Principles of Political Economy*: 'There is a circle around every individual human being, which no government, be it that of one, of a few, or of the many, ought to be permitted to overstep ... That there is, or ought to be, some space in human existence thus entrenched around, and sacred from authoritative intrusion, no one who professes the smallest regard to human freedom and dignity will call in question' (PPE, 938).

11 The claim that Mill has a negative conception of freedom is defended by, among others, Holloway (1961); Berlin (1969b, 1969c); Spitz (1975); Ten (1980); Gray (1983); Berger (1984, 1985a); Rees (1985); McCloskey (1986); Riley (1988, 1991a); and Donner (1991). In R.H. Hutton stated this view as follows: 'Mill's essay regards "liberty" from first to last in its negative rather than its positive significance' (Hutton, 1975 [1859], 133). Similarly, John C. Rees, one of Mill's most influential contemporary interpreters, says, 'Mill is generally regarded ... as a leading exponent of the negative idea of liberty – "liberty is just the absence of restraint" – which prevailed in England until the Idealists' (1985, 175).

12 Berlin writes, '[Mill] is justly criticized for paying too much attention to purely spiritual obstacles to the fruitful use of freedom – lack of moral and intellectual light; and too little (although nothing like as little as his detractors have maintained) to poverty, disease, and their causes ... and for concentrating too narrowly on freedom of thought and expression. All this is true' (1969b, 198).

13 I owe this observation to Ed Fogelman.

14 This revisionist scholarship, pioneered by J.C. Rees (1961, 1966a, 1985) and Alan Ryan (1964, 1965, 1986, 1990), has been continued by such writers as Lyons (1976, 1979, 1982a, 1982b); G.L. Williams (1976a, 1976b); G.W. Smith (1980a, 1980b, 1984, 1989); Gray (1983, 1989a); Berger (1984); Semmel (1984); Skorupski (1989); and Donner (1991). Ryan, Lyons, Gray, Berger, and Skorupski in particular clarify what Gray calls the 'indirect' character of Mill's utilitarianism as it relates to his theory of justice and principle of liberty (Gray, 1989a). With the exception of Ryan, however, these interpreters pay relatively little attention to the significance of his understanding of social power apart from how it relates to his principle of liberty. See Ryan (1983a; 1983b; 1984).

15 Smith (1984) and Berger (1984) both refer to Mill's 'theory of freedom,' but they conceive of it too narrowly in terms of his principle of liberty and his developmental view of individuality. Berger goes a step farther by emphasizing the links that Mill makes between freedom and justice and freedom and equality (1984, chs. 4 and 5). Leslie Stephen, the early historian of utilitarianism, provides a better guide to the broad scope of Mill's theory by suggesting that together Mill's chief works comprise his 'theory of conduct' (1900, 245).

16 Two partial exceptions to this generalization are Kinzer (1988) and Ashcraft (1989).

17 This point has been addressed in part by Pateman (1970); Gutmann (1980); Shanley (1981); Ryan (1983b, 1984); Sarvasy (1984, 1985); Claeys (1987); and Ashcraft (1989).

18 Mill himself offers a cautionary note in *Principles of Political Economy* for those who would criticize his Eurocentrism without considering his historical context. In the course of discussing how many people once held firmly to erroneous mercantilist theories of wealth creation in economics, he says, 'It often happens that the universal belief of one age of mankind – a belief from which no one *was*, nor without an extraordinary effort of genius and courage, *could* at that time be free – becomes to a subsequent age so palpable an absurdity, that the only difficulty then is to imagine how such a thing can ever have appeared credible ... But let no one feel confident that he

would have escaped the delusion if he had lived at the time when it prevailed. All the associations engendered by common life, and by the ordinary course of business concurred in promoting it ... [so that] what we now think so gross an absurdity seemed a truism' (PPE, 4–5, Mill's emphasis).

19 I owe this distinction between 'sociological' and 'interpretive' views to Diana Saco. On the connections between power and knowledge, see Michel Foucault (1980a, 1980b) and Edward Said (1979).

20 This way of interpreting Mill's work is similar to the approach that he himself adopts in an 1833 article on the work of a political writer who went by the pseudonym of Junius Redivivus. He says, 'If the writer ... be wise and honest, the more we read of his writings, knowing them to be his, the more thoroughly we shall trust him, and the better we shall learn to comprehend him. Every one of his opinions or sentiments which comes to our knowledge helps us to a more perfect understanding of all the rest; and the light they reflect on each other is a protection to the author against having his meaning mistaken, worth all precautions taken together' ('WJR[I],' 370–1).

1: Mill's Conception of Freedom

1 The principle of liberty entails that a community can rightfully exercise power over the conduct of its members only to prevent 'harm to others' (OL, 223). Its purpose is to secure for individuals a large degree of freedom of thought and action by protecting them against social and political interference. See ch. 5, below.

2 Smith (1984), along with several other of Mill's interpreters, uses 'freedom' and 'liberty' interchangeably, and says that Mill does the same. Cf. Berlin (1969c); Gray (1983); and Berger (1984).

3 Paul Ziff (1960) and Hanna Fenichel Pitkin (1988) explain that in English *freedom* has a broader range of usage than *liberty*, which has more formal and legal connotations. The different roots of the concepts correspond to different contexts of usage and different shades of meaning. Pitkin explains, for instance, that 'the *frē-* family could characterize action as spontaneous, readily or gladly done, done of one's own accord, even zealously done. The 'liber-' family did not carry these meanings, despite its use for the capacity to choose between sin and goodness' (1988, 538).

4 Thus, Mill uses 'freedom' more frequently than 'liberty' in works such as *Representative Government* and *The Subjection of Women*, where he makes more far-ranging arguments about freedom; and he uses 'liberty' much more frequently in *On Liberty*: 'liberty' occurs 85 times in *On Liberty*, excluding the title and chapter titles, while 'freedom' occurs only 46 times. In *The*

Subjection of Women he uses 'freedom' 30 times and 'liberty' only 10 times; and in *Representative Government* he uses 'freedom' 38 times and 'liberty' 27 times.

5 Although Mill frequently uses masculine pronouns generically, referring to both women and men, he was an advocate of women's rights and even gave some attention to the problem of sexist language – particularly, to the misleading effects of 'using the masculine *pronoun* where both sexes are equally concerned.' See Mill in *The Examiner*, 1 June 1834 (CW 23, 729), quoted in Robson and Robson (1994, xvii).

6 Isaiah Berlin and Benjamin Gibbs have attributed to Mill a basically negative empiricist view of freedom. Berlin characterizes Mill as a defender of 'the definition of negative liberty as the ability to do what one wishes' (Berlin, 1969c, 139). Cf. Gibbs (1976, 81).

7 For Mill, though, freedom does not *mean* self-development or self-realization as it does for some theorists of freedom. This is important because, as John Gray explains, people may freely choose to sacrifice chances for self-development for other goals (1983, 58).

8 As Berlin points out, conceiving of freedom as simply 'the ability to do what one wishes' is problematic because it entails that freedom could be attained just as effectively by conditioning people to want less as by enabling them to satisfy their initial wants. See Berlin (1969a, xxxviii; 1969c, 139–40).

9 In 'Bentham' Mill refers to this power as the power of 'self-culture' or 'self-education' ('B,' 98). He understands this power as a *potential* power that we will generally realize, however, only under favourable circumstances. See ch. 3, below.

10 Johann Gottlieb Fichte provides a striking example of the potential for authoritarian governance entailed in such notions. He says, 'To compel men to adopt the right form of government, to impose Right upon them by force, is not only right, but the sacred duty of every man who has the insight and the power to do so' (quoted in Berlin, 1969c, 151, n1).

11 According to Mill, actions can only be counted as *virtuous* when they spring from decisions made after deliberation ('RBP'). Thus, in *Utilitarianism* he conceives of 'the person of confirmed virtue' not just as someone who has 'a confirmed will to do right,' but also as a person who has the strength of character necessary to make and pursue reflective and deliberate choices (U, 238, 237).

12 Mill uses the word autonomy only once in French, and in a way that connotes 'independence' or 'freedom from interference' rather than the current sense of the word in philosophy of action. In an 1871 letter to Émile Acollas, he says, 'Quant à la partie philosophique, vous savez

probablement par mon Essai sur la Liberté, dans quel sens et avec quelles limites j'entends notre principle common, celui de l'autonomie de l'individu.' ['As to the philosophical party, you probably know from my Essay on Liberty, in what sense and with what limits I understand our common principle, that of the autonomy of the individual.'] See letter to Émile Acollas, 20 September 1871, CW 17, 1831–32.

13 Accordingly, his view of free action is related to but distinct from his view of the capacity for higher pleasures. Cf. Donner (1991, chs. 6–8); and Smith (1991).

14 Jon Elster identifies a closely related but distinct phenomenon of 'sour grapes.' This is where persons who may have full *capacity* for autonomous agency restrictively adapt their preferences to 'second-best' options in light of the constraints they face. See Elster (1983, ch. 3).

15 Frankfurt (1971) explains that 'wantons' are motivated strictly by first-order desires – that is, desires that they do not reflect upon in light of more considered objectives. In contrast, persons with unimpaired capacities for rational action have the capacity to form second-order *volitions* – that is, the capacity to *will what they want to will.*

16 Gerald Dworkin explains that autonomy 'is not merely an evaluative or reflective notion, but includes as well some ability both to alter one's preferences and to make them effective in one's actions and, indeed, to make them effective because one has reflected upon them and adopted them as one's own' (1988, 17).

17 As Smith points out, though, Mill's view is more clearly paternalistic with regard to persons with 'infirmities of character' or 'inveterate' habits (U, 212; L, 840; and Smith, 1991, 247). Moreover, as I will explain later, Mill is strongly paternalistic with respect to non-Western cultures. He justifies this stance with the ethnocentric claim that just as children need others to take care of them, so too do 'states of society in which the race itself may be considered in its nonage' (OL, 224).

18 As Berlin says, the extent of a person's freedom depends not just on 'how many doors are open,' but also on 'how open they are, [and] upon their relative importance' to his or her life (1969a, xxxix–xl).

19 He says in *Representative Government* that the 'improvement' of human societies gradually leads people to abandon the 'inveterate spirit of locality' (CRG, 417). 'Experience proves,' he says, 'it is possible for one nationality to merge and be absorbed in another: and when it was originally an inferior or more backward portion of the human race the absorption is greatly to its advantage' (CRG, 549). On occasion, he exhibits a more subtle appreciation for the meaning and significance of religious and cultural values, and

for the need to take account of agents' self-understandings. For instance, in *Representative Government* he also emphasizes the need to take account of 'the religious feelings' of the people of India; and he makes similar points elsewhere (see esp. 'Carlyle's French Revolution'). Still, he never fully integrates these interpretive impulses into his approach to free action and social criticism. See Parekh (1994); and Baum (1997).

20 Letter to Charles Friend, 29 October 1869, CW 16, 1469, Mill's emphasis. Mill's standard of premises taken *from reason rather than from authority* refers to reasons that can be assessed on formal or logical grounds, independently of any appeal to received traditions or supernatural forces (OL, ch. 2; 'GH[I],' 290). His view is 'radical' in the Enlightenment sense of seeking to bring all beliefs and practices progressively under the scrutiny of critical reasoning.

21 Some contexts of choice, of course, are more heterogeneous in this regard than others.

22 Consider the case of my six-year-old friend Ben, who has been learning a Jewish identity from his parents and from his Jewish Sunday school. Recently he asked me, 'You're Jewish?' (His parents had recently told him that I am, but I am actually a nonbeliever with an equivocal Jewish identity.) His mom was nearby and she signalled me to refrain from giving him the atheistic and equivocal response that I would have given him had I answered more *freely.* I simply told him, 'Yes.' This raises the following questions: Would Ben be *more free* in a straightforward way if I had introduced him at his impressionable age to such alternative possibilities as atheism and a nonreligious Jewish identity? What does this mean for the intergenerational bonds that are partly constituted by parents passing on such religious and cultural identities? Cf. Kymlicka (1996); and Nickel (1994).

23 The same thing can be said of some aspects of our national, cultural, ethnic, and gender identities. These identities are arguably socially and politically constructed and, thus, learned; but this does not mean that we can simply put them on and take them off at will like a change of clothes.

24 This point might appear to be controverted by the frequency of religious conversions. This would be so, however, only if we misleadingly supposed that all religious conversions are something people consciously choose upon reflection. See Asad (1996); and Baum (1997).

25 Michael Sandel (1990) has called these two forms of religious freedom 'freedom of choice' – the freedom to choose our own way of life or our own set of beliefs – and 'freedom of conscience' – the freedom to practice our religion.

26 The questions are from Breyten Breytenbach (1986, 73). Cf. MacCallum (1973); and Patterson (1991).

27 Notably, however, these latter practices existed within distinctly patriarchal cultures. For the ancient Greek practice of self-mastery, see Foucault (1986, 78–93); for early Christian 'spiritual freedom,' see Patterson (1991, chs. 10–15); and for the Puritan view, see John Winthrop, 'A Little Speech on Liberty' (1645), in Levy (1988, 13–14).

28 Mill promotes respect for 'the religious feelings of the [Indian] people' (CRG, 570; and OL, 240–1n). Yet his view of fully free action, *in league* with his historical evolutionism, undergirds his support of British colonial rule in India until such time as the Indian people 'have become capable of improvement by free and equal discussion,' independent of appeals to inherited traditions (OL, 224; and CRG, ch. 18).

29 I develop this point more fully in Chap. 7. The broader historical intertwinement of freedom with slavery (and other forms of subordination) is Orlando Patterson's central theme in *Freedom* (1991).

30 Mill also contends that the kind of free action he promotes is uniquely conducive to full human flourishing (OL, ch. 3). This claim, however, is harder to substantiate as a universal truth about human beings than he suggests. Cf. Parekh (1994); Skorupski (1994); and Gray (1996).

31 Fish adds, 'Rather than a continuum, what we have is ... an array of structures of constraint, no one of which is more constraining than any other' (1989, 459).

32 Regarding self-immolation in India, A.L. Basham explains that in medieval times the lot of widows was so hard that 'it is not surprising that women often immolated themselves on their husbands' funeral pyres.' Through self-immolation a widow was able to escape the hardships of widowhood and be recognized as 'a virtuous woman' (*sati*). Despite legal prohibitions enacted in the nineteenth century, there have been some recent acts of self-immolation in India. See Basham (1959, 187); Hawley (1994); and Spivak (1994).

33 One further objection to this line of thought is that while conceptions of freedom such as Mill's originate in specific cultural contexts, they also 'travel' *across* cultures. Indeed, Mill's notion of freedom has travelled far (see, for example, Mackie [1998] on the translation of Mill's *On Liberty* into Japanese in 1871). Yet two further points need to be appreciated to grasp how Mill's conception of freedom is culture-bound. First, the diffusion of concepts and practices across cultures takes place in part through asymmetrical relations of power – through colonialism, capitalist globalization, migrations, and so on. This is not to say that transplanted conceptions and practices are necessarily 'inauthentic' in new contexts. Nor is it to deny that they are often transformed en route. My point, rather, is that we need to

take into account how the part that *power* plays in this process complicates the question of when concepts and practices are *freely* adopted (cf. Asad, 1993, chs. 5, 7; Clifford, 1992). Second, we need to address the losses as well as the gains involved in such cultural travelling. Mill implies that when nonliberal cultures adopt (or are taught or forced to adopt) his conception of freedom, the changes will be unequivocally progressive and emancipatory. He fails to consider what people with fundamental commitments to nonliberal ways of life might lose by adopting his view of conceptions of the good life as freely chosen and revisable. For instance, cultural assimilation of the Navaho people into the modern United States has undoubtedly brought them new practices of freedom, but it has also undermined their older practices of freedom, which, if Dorothy Lee is right, had great value in their own right.

2: Mill's Theory of Modern Freedom

1 I refer to 'democratizing societies' because none of the countries on which Mill bases his political analyses – principally England, France, and the United States – had established fully democratic states in Mill's time. Moreover, Mill says that 'a democratic state of society' *may or may not* coincide with a democratic form of government ('TDA[II],' 200); and his own implicit notion of democratization encompasses both states and civil societies.

2 Mill fails to adequately consider, however, that the social sciences differ from the natural sciences in that human beings, which are their subject matter, are self-interpreting beings whose reality is partly constituted by concepts with which and through which they understand and act within their social world (Taylor, 1985a). For further discussion of the limitations of Mill's philosophy in this regard, see Skorupski (1989, 275–82); and Baum (1997).

3 Mill says, 'We do not feel ourselves less free because those to whom we are intimately known are well assured how we will to act in a particular case. We often, on the contrary, regard the doubt what our conduct will be as a mark of ignorance of our character, and sometimes even resent it as an imputation' (L, 837).

4 He explains in *August Comte and Positivism*, 'The human beings themselves, on the laws of whose nature the facts of history depend, are not abstract or universal but historical human beings, already shaped, and made what they are, by human society' (ACP, 307).

5 At one point in *A System of Logic*, Mill expressly includes freedom among the

social phenomena amenable to social scientific investigation, even as he emphasizes the imprecise character of such research: 'The causes of every social phenomenon which we are particularly interested about, security, wealth, freedom, good government, public virtue, general intelligence, or their opposites, are infinitely numerous, especially the external or remote causes, which alone are, for the most part, accessible to direct observation. No one cause suffices of itself to produce any of these phenomena' (L, 884).

6 This point is central for understanding Mill's *indirect* version of utilitarianism. It closely resembles what is called *rule-utilitarianism*, according to which general utility is maximized when people follow a set of moral rules; and it differs from what is called *act-utilitarianism*, according to which promoting happiness should be the direct aim of all conduct. Mill outlines his view in a letter to Thomas Carlyle as follows: 'Though I hold the good of the species (or rather of its separate units) to be the ultimate end (which is the alpha and omega of my utilitarianism), I believe with the fullest belief that the end can in no other way be forwarded but by the means you speak of, namely, by each taking for his exclusive aim the development of what is best in *himself*' (12 January 1834, CW 12, 207). For further discussion, see Lyons (1976, 1979); Gray (1983); Berger (1984); Skorupski (1989); and Ryan (1990).

7 Mill explains in *Utilitarianism*, 'The ingredients of happiness are very various, and each of them is desirable in itself, and not merely when considered as swelling an aggregate ... They are desired and desirable in and for themselves; besides being means, they are part of the end' (U, 235; see Hoag, 1987, 422–3).

8 Mill says that it is 'better to be a human being dissatisfied than a pig satisfied; better to do Socrates dissatisfied than a fool satisfied' (U, 212).

9 Similarly, he says in *Principles of Political Economy*, 'After the means of subsistence are assured, the next in strength of the personal wants of human beings is liberty; and (unlike the physical wants, which as civilization advances become more moderate and more amenable to control) it increases instead of diminishing in intensity, as the intelligence and moral faculties are more developed' (PPE, 208).

10 In addition, as I explain in subsequent chapters, Mill maintains that freedom tends to foster autonomy: by exercising freedom, people also exercise their faculties of observation, reasoning, judgment, discrimination, firmness, and self-control, all of which are constitutive of free agency, or autonomy. In turn, freedom also contributes indirectly to utility by enhancing the well-being of individuals and by fostering social improvement.

11 In this regard, Mill understands political economy as being rather different from the notion of a science of government. He insists that the study of how people acquire and consume wealth (which is the subject of political economy) cannot be fully separated from the study of the broader societal contexts in which these activities take place; yet he says that political economy *can* be fruitfully pursued as a distinct branch of social science (L, 900–4). In contrast, he says that 'there can be no separate Science of Government ... [since] questions respecting the tendencies of forms of government' are thoroughly intertwined with 'all the circumstances [of particular societies] by which the qualities of a people are influenced' (L, 906).

12 For Mill, state power is by no means the only consequential locus of power relationships in modern societies. Yet in contrast to broader contemporary uses of the term 'political' to refer to (in Robert Dahl's words) 'any persistent pattern of human relationships that involves, to a significant extent, control, influence, power, or authority' (Dahl, 1991, 4; Phillips, 1991, ch. 4), Mill reserves the terms 'politics' and 'political' for institutions of the state.

13 Mill never describes these principles in this way. In *A System of Logic*, however, he outlines this general relationship concerning how the 'art' of attaining a certain objective involves deriving practical rules or precepts from the relevant science (see L, Bk. VI, ch. 12).

14 Mill refers to 'the principle of liberty' and 'the principle of individual liberty' (OL, 301, 293).

15 However, in his first review of Alexis de Tocqueville's *Democracy in America*, he speaks of the 'democratic principle' with reference to the development of democratic politics in the United States ('TDA[I],' 66). He calls democracy a form of government that 'works not only *for* the people, but, much more extensively than any other government, *by means* of the people' ('TDA[I],' 71, Mill's emphasis). In addition, in *Principles of Political Economy* Mill refers more broadly to the 'democratic spirit' in arguing in favour of economic co-operatives (see ch. 7, below).

16 As David Lyons and Fred Berger explain, Mill develops a theory of justice as well as a theory of freedom (Lyons, 1979, 1982a; Berger, 1984). Since my primary concern is with Mill's theory of freedom, however, I address his view of justice as a secondary principle for achieving freedom.

17 In this regard, Mill argues in *The Subjection of Women* that it is incompatible with justice to deny 'the equal moral right of all human beings to choose their occupations (short of injury to others) according to their own preferences' (SW, 300). Similarly, he asserts in an article on slavery and the Civil War in the United States that the North is on the side of 'justice and moral

principle' because of its opposition to slavery ('The Slave Power,' CW 21, 157). Cf. D. Goldberg (1993, 215–19).

18 As I will explain later, though, Mill's argument is not completely successful in this regard.

19 Mill says, 'The claims of different people to such power differ as much as their qualifications for exercising it beneficially' ('TPR,' 323).

20 Berger articulates Mill's 'baseline' conception of equality in terms of the following four points: '1. Substantive inequalities of wealth, education, and power are *prima facie* wrong, and require justification. 2. Substantive inequalities must not permit any to "go to the wall"; redistribution to provide subsistence must be guaranteed. 3. Inequalities must not undermine the status of persons *as equals* ... 4. Only *certain* kinds of grounds serve to justify inequality – that the inequality will make no one worse off, or that is the result of rewarding according to desert' (1984, 159–60).

21 Mill explains in a letter to Arthur Helps, 'As I look upon inequality as *in itself* always an evil, I do not agree with anyone who would use the machinery of society for the purpose of promoting it. As much inequality as necessarily arises from protecting all persons in the free use of their faculties of mind and body and in enjoyment of what these can obtain for them, must be submitted to for the sake of the greater good' (CW 15, 421, quoted in Berger, 1984, 164).

22 Recall his claim in his *Autobiography* that he offers 'no system' of political philosophy (A, 169). He goes on to say that he holds the 'conviction that the true system was something much more complex and many sided than I previously had any idea of' (A, 169). His point seems to be that his political philosophy is not limited to any one prevailing school of thought.

23 Mill does not conceive of all power relationships as equally suited for democratic self-government. For instance, he does not consider the possibility of extending democratic self-government to students in schools or to inmates in prisons. Moreover, while he argues that spouses should share in governing their families, he does not consider extending such power to their children.

24 There may be cases, for instance, when intervention or regulation by public authority may be justified but inexpedient. This is the case with some economic transactions, according to Mill.

25 Hart explains further, 'Individual persons and the *level* of an individual's happiness are for the utilitarian only of instrumental, not of intrinsic importance. Persons are merely the "receptacles" for the experiences which will increase or diminish aggregate welfare' (1982, 99, Hart's emphasis).

Mill's distinction between 'higher' and 'lower' pleasures further complicates this aggregative tendency in his thought (see Gray, 1989a, 221).

3: The Theory of Social Power

1 Richard Ashcraft (1989) provides a useful overview of Mill's understanding of social power. See also Feuer (1976); and Kinzer (1988, lviii–lxi). Richard Friedman (1968) offers a valuable discussion of Mill's view of the related concept of authority.

2 Similarly, in *The Subjection of Women* he contends that more equal rights and opportunities for women will 'increase ... the general fund of thinking and acting power' in society (SW, 336).

3 Within the 'three-dimensional' view of power developed by Steven Lukes (1974) and John Gaventa (1980), the first 'face' of power concerns the observable capacity of an agent (or agents) to achieve her (or their) goals by getting others to do what they would not otherwise do. The second 'face' is less readily observable in terms of who wins or loses in political struggles; it involves such things as control over agendas for action and the suppression of challenges to the status quo by less powerful agents. The latter, due to their relative powerlessness, may become resigned to situations and *opt out* of potential struggles to pursue their interests. The *third* face of power concerns not merely whether people act upon their perceived interests, but also how they learn to think about themselves and perceive their desires and interests.

4 Mill says in *On Liberty* that it is 'living belief which regulates conduct,' and that doctrines that 'have no hold on ordinary believers ... are not a power in their minds' (OL, 249).

5 Lukes characterizes his own view of power as 'radical' because it focuses on the role of broader 'social forces and institutional practices' that shape people's conduct and thereby create 'the possibility of false or manipulated consensus' (1974, 10, 24). Other radical theorists, such as Foucault, emphasize the construction of social identities. Mill begins to address this topic with respect to the social construction of traditional masculine and feminine identities. See ch. 6, below; and Berger (1984, 183).

6 Pitkin says that when we focus on 'power over' we are focusing on a relational form of power, but 'power to' is not necessarily relational in this sense: 'One may have power over another or others, and that sort of power is relational ... But he may have power to do or accomplish something all by himself, and that power is not relational at all; it may involve other people

if what he has power to do is a social or political action, but it need not'
(1972, 277). I have qualified this point by saying that power does not always
refer to a *direct* relationship between persons because even 'nonrelational'
exercises of power are generally rooted in the webs of social relations
through which people derive their 'power to X' (Isaac, 1987; Wartenberg,
1988).

7 Mill does not identify himself as a realist in matters of philosophy of science
and he is sometimes associated with empiricism. Nonetheless, he criticizes
empiricism in a manner similar to realists. He calls empiricism 'bad generalization *à posteriori*,' and he defines 'empiricism properly so called' as
'causation inferred from causal conjunction, without either due elimination, or any presumption arising from known properties of the supposed
agent' (L, 792). Cf. Isaac (1987, 22).

8 Mill adds, however, that 'under due limitations [this ascendancy] ... ought
not to be regarded as an evil. That class is the most powerful; but it needs
not therefore be all-powerful' ('TDA[II],' 200).

9 I return to this point in Chapter 8, where I also discuss more fully Mill's
class analysis of modern democratic politics, including his view of the composition of the different classes.

10 For instance, in *Utilitarianism* he says that 'the principles which lie under
justice are the source of its authority' (U, 252).

11 Similarly, Mill argues in his first article on Tocqueville that the character of
'political truths' is *not* such that the evidence of them 'could be made apparent at once to any person of common sense': 'Many of the truths of
politics (in political economy, for instance) are the result of a concatena-
tion of propositions, the very first steps of which no one who has not gone
through a course of study is prepared to concede ... The multitude will
never believe these truths, until tendered to them from an authority in
which they have as unlimited confidence as they have in the unanimous
voice of astronomers on a question of astronomy ... When there shall exist
as near an approach to unanimity among the instructed, on all the great
points of moral and political knowledge, we have no fear but that the many
will not only defer, but cheerfully acknowledge them as their superiors in
wisdom, and the fittest to rule' ('TDA[I],' 73–4n).

12 Insofar as social and political practices and relationships are partly constituted by local languages and by concepts of the agents who enact and reproduce them – the *interpretive* aspect of social reality – the problem of
'objectivity' is even more intractable than Mill recognizes. The 'truths'
attainable through social science are always bounded by linguistic and
cultural differences in ways that Mill fails to appreciate adequately.

13 This 'natural state' is comparable to what he refers to elsewhere as 'organic' periods in history. See ch. 2, above.

14 Mill views ancient Athens and Rome quite differently in this regard than he does non-Western societies such as India and China. Along with his claim that the 'authority of ancestors' in Athens and Rome 'did not supersede reason, but guided it,' he cites the Athenian statesman Demonsthenes' view that such authority was 'not merely an argument, but as one of the strongest arguments' ('SOA,' 293, 292).

15 Mill says that much of the world, including the entire East, 'has, properly speaking, no history, because the despotism of Custom is complete ... Custom is there, in all things, the final appeal; justice and right mean conformity to custom; the argument of custom no one, unless some tyrant intoxicated with power, think of resisting' (OL, 272). Mill sometimes speaks of 'the yoke of authority' to denote the kind of constraint imposed by traditional authority (see for example, 'B,' 78).

16 S.V. Pradhan remarks that with regard to India, Mill's theory of government 'supplies an eloquent apology for imperial occupation, and may be said to be the first respectable, philosophical expression of what was later to be called "the white man's burden"' (1976, 19–20). For further analysis of Mill's views on India, see Burns (1976); Zastoupil (1988); Mehta (1990); Moir (1990); Said (1993); and Parekh (1994, 1995).

17 Given his position in the British East India Company, this is not always true of his writings of India. Still, as Bhikhu Parekh says, Mill makes no 'careful study of the history, cultures, and social structures' of the non-European societies about which he generalizes (1994, 89).

18 In this regard, Mill's view of democracy differs substantially from that of more radical egalitarians as Marx, nineteenth-century anarchists, contemporary radical democratic anarchists (like Noam Chomsky and Murray Bookchin), and contemporary participatory democrats (like Carol Gould). Cf. Chomsky (1973); Marx (1974 [1871]); Gould (1988); Bookchin (1990); and ch. 8, below.

19 Elsewhere he says that understanding political truths is not something that 'could be apparent at once to any person of common sense, as well educated as every individual in the community might and ought to be ... The multitude will never believe these truths, until tendered to them from an authority in which they have as unlimited confidence as they have in the unanimous voice of astronomers on a question of astronomy' ('TDA[I],' 73n).

20 Mill's friend John Morley aptly summarizes his view of democratic authority: 'You must have authority, and yet must have obedience. The noblest

and deepest and most beneficent kind of authority is that which rests on an obedience that is rational, deliberate, and spontaneous' (1873, 241).

21 Mill coveys the gist of his view of the kind of 'mental cultivation' that is necessary to reconcile freedom with deference to authority in a passage in *Representative Government* on 'the function of popular institutions as a means of political instruction': 'It is but a poor education that associates ignorance with ignorance, and leaves [citizens], if they care for knowledge, to grope their way to it without help, and to do without it if they do not. What is wanted is, the means of making ignorance aware of itself, and able to profit by knowledge; accustoming minds which know only routine, to act upon, and feel the value of principles: teaching them to compare different modes of action, and learn, by use of their reason, to distinguish the best' (CRG, 545).

22 He says, for instance, that the limited power that women have to influence their families and politics is not 'a compensation for [their] loss of freedom.' A woman's power, he adds, 'often gives her what she has no right to, but does not enable her to assert her own rights' (SW, 290).

23 'Man is conceived by Bentham,' Mill writes, 'as a being susceptible of pleasures and pains, and governed in all his conduct partly by different modifications of self-interest, and the passions commonly classed as selfish, partly by sympathies, or occasionally antipathies, toward other beings' ('B,' 94; cf. L, 890).

24 Although he also pays considerable attention to the role of schools and other forms of education in governing people's lives, he does not call for extending self-government to schools and universities.

4: Education for Freedom

1 During the Reform debates of 1867, conservative commentators like Robert Lowe argued that further extensions of the franchise would degrade the franchise 'to the level of those persons who have no sense of decency or morality' (Lowe, *Speeches and Letters on Reform* [1867], pp. 61–2, quoted in Briggs, 1965, 499). On the general state of British formal education in this period, see Gillian Sutherland (1990).

2 Mill explains that our more complex ideas and states of consciousness are built up out of associations among more elementary impressions in relation to our awareness of similarities, differences, conjunctions, and successions among our sensations. This is sometimes a matter of 'Composition of Causes,' whereby the resulting phenomena are merely the sum of the effects of the separate causes (L, 852–3). Other complex mental phenomena,

such as autonomy, result from associations that combine like processes of 'chemical' rather than 'mechanical,' or merely additive, composition. In such cases, 'many impressions or ideas operating in the mind together' give rise to new ideas or impressions that are not 'simply the sum of the effects of those causes when separate,' and may even differ from them in kind (L, 853).

3 Mill acknowledges that his argument appears to be circular insofar as the desire for pleasure is still the motive, but he insists that this objection does not get to the crux of the matter: 'As we proceed in the formation of habits, and become accustomed to will a particular act or a particular course of conduct because it is pleasurable, we at last continue to will it without any reference to its being pleasurable' (L, 842).

4 At the same time, as I explain in Chapter 5, Mill makes a utilitarian case for fostering 'a large variety in types of character.'

5 Mill says in the *Logic* that differences of 'mental susceptibility' may be 'innate and ultimate facts,' the result of different life experiences, or the product of 'varieties of physical organisation' (L, 856). Moreover, physiological differences often have a psychological impact so that in 'even different *qualities* of mind, different types of mental characters, will naturally be produced by mere differences of intensity of the sensations' (L, 857; and 'NTA,' 223). When he turns to the relationship between sex and gender, this line of argument leads him to give some weight to the notion that sex differences might influence character development, even as he challenges the then prevailing gender dichotomies (SW, 276). His critique of the prevailing view builds upon his general tendency to attribute most differences in people's characters and capacities to differences in education and experiences (L, 859).

6 It is important to be clear about how far Mill's view is from racist views that attribute differences of conduct and intellectual ability between groups of people to 'inherent natural differences' between them. As Mill says in the *Principles*, 'Of all the vulgar modes of escaping from the consideration of the effects of social and moral influences on the human mind, the most vulgar is that of attributing the diversities of conduct and character to inherent natural differences' (PPE 319). See also Mill's 1850 article, 'The Negro Question.'

7 In his *Autobiography* Mill explains the role of the empowering mode of instruction in his own early education, which his father directed: 'Most boys or youths who have had much knowledge drilled into them, have their mental capacities not strengthened, but overlaid by it. They are crammed with mere facts, and with the opinions or phrases of other people, and

these are accepted as a substitute for the power to form opinions of their own ... Mine, however, was not an education of cram.' His father, he says, 'strove to make the understanding not only go along with every step of the teaching, but, if possible, precede it' (A, 33–4).

8 Mill reprints this very passage in *A System of Logic*, where he adds that 'social existence is only possible by a disciplining of those more powerful propensities, which consists in subordinating them to a common system of opinions' (L, 926). Unfortunately, Mill associates moral restraint and autonomy in 'Coleridge' with 'manliness of character.' This should be considered, however, in light of his view of prevailing 'feminine' character (see above).

9 Foucault says that the individual 'assumes responsibility for the constraints of power; he makes them play spontaneously upon himself; he inscribes in himself the power relation in which he spontaneously plays both roles,' the one who disciplines and the one who is disciplined (1979, 202–3).

10 He warns in *On Liberty*, 'Wherever there is an ascendant class, a large portion of the morality of the country emanates from its class interests, and its feelings of class superiority' (OL, 221).

11 Mill says in 'Coleridge' that one of the things that can build a feeling of allegiance between a people and their government is the feeling that 'may attach itself to the principles of individual liberty and political equality' ('C,' 134).

12 Richard Rorty explains, 'Socialization has to come before individuation, and education for freedom cannot begin before some constraints have been imposed' (1989, 200). Individuation and socialization are so deeply intertwined, however, that it is somewhat misleading to say that one precedes the other.

13 Consider, for instance, the élitist political subtext of Mill's discussion of self-control in 'Nature.' He says that the 'unnatural' character of self-discipline is apparent not only in the long tutelage of children, but also in 'the very imperfect manner in which it is acquired by persons born to power, whose will is seldom resisted, and by all who have been early and much indulged; and in the marked absence of the quality in savages, in soldiers and sailors, and in a somewhat less degree in nearly the whole of the poorer classes in this and many other countries' ('N,' 395).

14 Letter to Charles Friend, 29 October 1868, CW 16, 1469, Mill's emphasis. In the same letter he says, 'I do not think it right either oneself to teach, or to allow any one else to teach one's children, authoritatively, what ever that one does not from the bottom of one's heart & by the clearest light of reason, believe to be true ... One assuredly has no right to incumber the reason & entangle the conscience of one's children' (pp. 1468–9). Reli-

giously committed parents, of course, would insist that their beliefs are
consistent with the 'light of reason,' but Mill holds that such beliefs are
based on authority but *not* on reason.

15 He develops this point further in 'Dr. Whewell on Moral Philosophy.' There
he criticizes education within ecclesiastical institutions, in which instructors
must 'vow adherence to a set of opinions made up and prescribed' as
authoritative truths. He asks, 'How can intellectual vigour be fostered by
the teaching of those who, even as a matter of duty, would rather that their
pupils were weak and orthodox, than strong with freedom of thought?'
('WMP,' 168).

16 Mill is not strictly opposed to the teaching of those parts of the Old and
New Testaments 'which are either poetical or properly historical, ... *as
history* in places of education'; but he opposes using schools to 'inculcate all
that is contained in those books ... as matter ... of positive religious belief'
(letter to Rev. Thomas W. Fowle, 9 February 1867, CW 16, 1235–6, Mill's
emphasis). He maintains that *secular* rather than merely 'unsectarian' (but
basically Christian) education is the only kind of education 'provided by
the public' that is really 'education for all' ('Secular Education' [1850], CW
28, 4). Cf. Ryan (1998, 528).

17 In another 1868 letter, Mill says that in supporting 'compulsory education'
he intends 'that all parents should be required to have their children
taught certain things, *being left free to select the teachers*, but [with] the sufficiency of the teaching being ensured by a government inspection of
schools & by a real & searching examination of pupils' (letter to Rev.
Leopold John Bernays, 8 January 1868, CW 16, 1347, emphasis added).

18 As we have seen, however, he makes a related argument in combination
with his view of societal development to justify colonial rule by a 'more
civilized people' over an 'uncivilized' people, as long as the former aim at
preparing the latter to govern themselves (CRG, 567–8; OL, 224; 'FWNI,'
120, 118).

19 Isaiah Berlin is basically right when he remarks that 'Mill's psychology has
become antiquated and grows more so with every discovery that is made'
(1969b, 198).

20 He makes a highly suggestive comment in this regard in 'Bentham.' He says
that while Bentham's approach to morality addresses the need to regulate
people's 'outward actions,' it fails to address the educative aspect of morality – that is, its influence on people's 'affections and desires.' Therefore,
Bentham has little to offer with respect to determining moral standards for
'those facts in human life which tend to influence the depths of the character quite independently of any influence on worldly circumstances – such,

for instance, as the sexual relations, or those of the family in general, or any other social and sympathetic connexions of an intimate kind' ('B,' 98). Mill never really develops this insight, however.

21 Once again, Mill is aware of this difficulty. In an 1846 newspaper article on Ireland, in which he talks of the need to 'correct' the habits and characters of the Irish peasants, he says, 'You will never change people but by changing the external motives which act on them, and shape their way of life from the cradle to the grave ... The real effective education of a people is given them by the circumstances by which they are surrounded ... What shapes the character is not what is purposely taught so much as the unintentional teaching of institutions and relations ('The Condition of Ireland' [20], 19 November 1846, CW 24, 955).

22 Robert Heilbroner cautions, 'Empathetic parenting and supportive institutions can undoubtedly instill many social routines, but they cannot produce "liberated" behavior – that is, behavior free of sublimated rage, denials of many kinds, and acting-out of fantasies of oppression, both in an active as well as a passive mode' (1993, 314).

5: The Principle of Liberty

1 Mill explains in a letter to Theodore Gomperz that his objective in *On Liberty* is to protect 'moral, social, and intellectual liberty ... against the despotism of society whether exercised by governments or public opinion" (4 December 1858, CW 15, 581).

2 Mill says in a letter to Peter Alfred Taylor that 'the distinction between a government by general laws & one of arbitrary edicts is ... absolutely essential to good government under any constitution.' This distinction, he adds, is especially important under 'popular government, for most other governments are under some check from fear of the majority; but when the majority is itself the government, the check is only in its own breast, & depends on a strong conviction in the popular mind of its necessity' (28 May 1869, CW 17, 1608).

3 He explains in *An Examination of Sir William Hamilton's Philosophy* that in considering issues of moral responsibility and punishment, he starts from 'the reality of moral distinctions' with respect to what is right and wrong, just and unjust (EHP, 461, 456–7). I will return to this point later.

4 Previous commentators have aptly called this the domain of 'other-regarding' conduct, although Mill does not use this phrase, to complement what Mill calls the domain of 'self-regarding conduct.'

5 Mill elaborates on this point in 'Centralization' in 1862. Agreeing in part

with the French writer Charles Brook Dupont-White on the need for some centralized state power, he says, 'Has not the State necessarily a wider range of action, when it is expected to protect the slave, the wife, the child, the debtor, instead of leaving them to the will and pleasure of masters, husbands, fathers, and creditors? These primitive superiors once had power of life and death over those who were subject to them. It was the State which freed the weaker party from this despotism. The State alone could have done it, and on the state rests the duty of doing it, wherever it remains to be done ... As long as any wrongful authority is exercised by human beings over one another, the State has still the duty of abolishing it' ('Ce,' 589).

6 John Rawls says that a religious, philosophical, or moral doctrine 'is fully comprehensive when it covers all recognized values and virtues within one rather precisely articulated scheme of thought' (1989, 240).

7 Mill implicitly *does* promote a 'thin' conception of the good insofar as he maintains that freedom, autonomy, and individuality are basic ingredients of human well-being (Larmore, 1990). In this regard, it is important to appreciate both Mill's pluralistic view of the means to happiness and the limits that his substantive commitments impose upon certain kinds of diversity. I will return to these points later.

8 When Mill says that one person forcefully stopping another person from crossing an unsafe bridge when there is 'no time to warn him of the danger' entails no 'real infringement of his liberty,' he adds, 'when there is not a certainty, but only a danger of mischief, no one but the person himself can judge the sufficiency of the motive which may prompt him to incur the risk: in this case, therefore, (unless he is a child, or delirious, or in some state of excitement or absorption incompatible with the full use of the reflecting faculty) he ought, I conceive, to be only warned of the danger; not forcibly prevented from exposing himself to it' (OL, 294).

9 He says in *Principles of Political Economy* that the '*laisser-faire* principle' that each individual is 'the best judge of his own interests' breaks down in cases where a given individual 'may be incapable of judging or acting for himself; may be a lunatic, an idiot, an infant: or though not wholly incapable, may be of immature years and judgment' (PPE, 951). In such cases, he says, 'The most interested is not the best judge of the matter, nor a competent judge at all' (Ibid.).

10 As Patrick Devlin explains, 'When a state recognizes freedom of worship and of conscience, it sets up a problem for jurists which they have not yet succeeded in solving. Now, when the law divides right from wrong, it cannot appeal to any absolute authority outside itself as justifying the division' (1965, 86).

11   Letter to George Grote, 10 January 1862, CW 15, 762.
12   Letter to George Grote, 762.
13   Letter to George Grote, 762.
14   Mill's formulation is a bit misleading here. He generally uses the notion of 'imperfect obligations' in a way which suggests that individuals have what David Lyons calls 'good samaritan' obligations *to particular persons* that are obligations of benevolence (1982a; see also Berger, 1984; Riley, 1988). A classic example is a case where we come across a drowning person whom we are in a position to save. This constitutes an obligation of benevolence insofar as it is something that we would generally say a person deserves moral censure for not doing with regard to this person and at this time.
15   As Mill notes parenthetically, these considerations are basic to arguments for civil disobedience to challenge unjust laws (U, 242).
16   Mill seems to argue otherwise in 'Use and Abuse of Political Terms' when he considers the right of a person to publish his opinions. He says, 'a man has no *right* to do that which is *wrong*, though it may often happen that nobody has a right to *prevent* him from doing it' ('UAPT,' 10, Mill's emphasis). The first part of this assertion is a bit at odds with Mill's usual position, however. At the same time, he subsequently remains true to his basic point here: when a person claims a right to publish his or her opinions, he or she takes on certain moral obligations, such as that of being *truthful*. In this sense, we might say that he or she has no moral right to consciously publish falsehoods, but may have a legal right to do so. Furthermore, Mill supports libel laws to address this problem (see 'OLP').
17   Some commentators have called such effects on others 'morality-dependent harms.' See Honderich (1982); and Ten (1991).
18   Mill explains in his early essay, 'Use and Abuse of Political Terms,' that 'no man in his sound senses considers himself to be *wronged* every time he does not get what he desires; every man distinguishes between what he thinks another man *morally bound* to do, and what he merely *would like* to see him do; between what is morally criminal, a fit subject for complaint or reproach, and what excites only regrets, and a wish that the act had been abstained from' ('UAPT,' 9, Mill's emphasis).
19   Mill's strong case for 'the fullest liberty of professing and discussing, as a matter of ethical conviction, any doctrine, however immoral it may be considered' (OL, 228n) might seem to complicate matters further. Arguably, though, he would distinguish between the 'liberty of professing ... any doctrine' and the freedom of people to do so any way they please, whether through hateful utterances or through modes of expression that maintain respect for others (Vernon, 1996). I cannot discuss this point further here,

however. Later I discuss more fully the relevance of Mill's argument to contemporary debates about sexuality.

20 I suspect that Mill would support something on the order of the U.S. Fair Housing Act, which does not apply to rentals of single-family homes by their owners, rooms in such homes, or owner-occupied buildings with fewer than five units (Carter, 1993, 15). My guess is that he would accept that people have a special interest at stake when it comes to renting out space in their home, but have no comparable interest if, say, they own and rent rooms in a large apartment building or are owner-employers of something larger than a small family business. In the latter cases there are overriding public interests at stake that call for nondiscrimination laws. For relevant discussions of contemporary U.S. antidiscrimination law, see Carter (1993); and Sunstein (1998).

21 Consider the pressures that gay and lesbian couples commonly face against public displays of affection, such as holding hands in public.

22 Mill contends in 'Utility of Religion' that 'the deterring force of the unfavourable sentiments of mankind does not consist solely in the painfulness of knowing oneself to be the object of those sentiments; it also includes all the penalties which they can inflict: exclusion from social intercourse and from the innumerable good offices which human beings require from one another; the forfeiture of all that is called success in life; often a great diminution or total loss of means of subsistence; positive ill offices of various kinds, sufficient to render life miserable, and reaching in some states of society as far as actual persecution to death' ('UR,' 411).

23 In this regard, there is a superficial resemblance between Mill's position and Patrick Devlin's, which I quoted at the outset, that society ultimately 'must be the judge of what is necessary to its own integrity if only because there is no other tribunal to which the question can be submitted' (1965, 118).

24 He says in *Utilitarianism*, for instance, that unusual circumstances sometimes require different judgments than ordinary circumstances as to what is morally obligatory: 'particular cases may occur in which some other social duty is so important, as to overrule any one of the general maxims of justice. Thus to save a life, it may not only be allowable, but a duty, to steal, or take by force, the necessary food or medicine' (U, 259).

25 In the U.S. Supreme Court case *Bowers v. Hardwick* (1986), for instance, Justice Byron White, writing for the Court's majority, said, 'Proscription against [consensual sodomy by homosexuals] has ancient roots' (in Goldberg, 1994, 119). Chief Justice Warren Burger added in his concurring opinion, 'Condemnation of that conduct of those practices is firmly rooted

in Judeo-Christian moral and ethical standards' (Goldberg, 1994, 121). Based on this reasoning, the Court upheld the constitutionality of a Georgia sodomy law as it related to the prohibition of 'homosexual sodomy.'

26 Mill never considers homosexuality, and as I noted in Chapter 4, he takes a dim view of sexual passions generally. Nonetheless, he extends his view that consenting adults ought to have perfect freedom to do as they please, to sexual relations, as long as those relations do not cause harm to others. He maintains that the situation changes when sexual relations produce children, and he supports birth control. He summarized his view in a letter: 'What any persons may freely do with respect to sexual relations should be deemed to be an unimportant and purely private matter, which concerns no one but themselves. If children are the result, then indeed commences a set of important duties towards the children, which society should force upon the parents much more strictly than it does now. But to have held any human being responsible to other people and to the world for the fact itself, without the consequence, will one day be thought one of the superstitions and barbarisms of the infancy of the human race' (*The Letters of John Stuart Mill*, vol. 2, ed. Hugh S.R. Elliot [London, 1910], p. 382, quoted in Packe, 1954, 319).

27 Thus, the prohibition against murder is recognized by people with divergent moral and religious beliefs as an obligation of justice, but not *simply* because of the biblical commandment 'Thou shall not kill.' That is, the *wrongness* of murder does not rest solely on its being regarded as a 'sin.'

28 Gerald Bradley, for example, calls homosexuality 'victimless immorality,' and he maintains that 'immoral actions, even if not harmful to innocent bystanders, may be prohibited.' He rests his case on what he calls a 'shared moral substance of solidaristic spirit' that relates to 'God's plan for mankind' (1991, 28–9, 33–4). See also Devlin (1965, 118).

29 As Justice Harry Blackmun says in his dissenting opinion in *Bowers v. Hardwick*, 'the mere knowledge that others do not adhere to one's value system cannot be a legally cognizable interest, ... let alone an interest that can justify invading the houses, hearts, and minds of citizens who choose to live their lives differently' (in Goldberg, 1994, 131).

30 Devlin attempts to offer such an argument. He claims that homosexuality poses 'intangible harm' to the 'integrity' of society (1965, 116–18). His argument, however, is either circular – that is, he construes 'integrity of society' *in terms of* the special status accorded to heterosexual relationships, especially heterosexual marriages – or is little more than what Mill once referred to as 'vague and indefinite' fears of a minority group ('OEC,' 152). For Mill, claims about the 'integrity of society' might be relevant for

determining rightful limits of individual freedom (OL, 276); but they must
be more substantial than Devlin's. For a more sympathetic account of
Devlin's concerns, see Mitchell (1970).

31 Mill's argument supports Foucault's position that there should be unrestricted 'freedom of sexual choice [but] not of freedom of sexual *acts* because there are some sexual acts like rape which should not be permitted
whether they involve a man and a women or two men' (1988, 288,
Foucault's emphasis).

32 Our conduct, of course, often has unintended effects on others, so it is
sometimes difficult to specify the domain of morality in such cases. For
instance, the ways in which health care costs are spread across modern
societies raises the issue of whether or not individuals have any duties to
others to avoid conduct that might impose such costs upon them. In this
regard, Mill cautions that we may need to accept some 'inconvenience ...
for the sake of the greater good of human freedom' (OL, 282).

33 Recall Mill's comment that 'public opinion for the most part enjoins the
same things which are enjoined by the received social morality; that morality being ... the summary of the conduct which each one of the multitude
... desires others should observe towards him' ('UR,' 410). See ch. 4, above.

34 Similarly, Mill's friend John Morley asks in an 1873 essay, 'Can anyone's
opinion or any serious part of conduct be looked upon as truly and exclusively self-regarding?' (1873, 238).

6: Freedom, Sex Equality, and the Power of Gender

1 Mill does not use the term 'patriarchy.' In *Principles of Political Economy*,
however, he refers to the authoritarian structure of the capitalist workplace
as an example of what he calls 'the patriarchal or paternal system of government.' He includes the power of men over women as another example
of this (PPE, 762). He also insists that the force of law should be brought to
bear against 'the domestic life of domestic tyrants' (PPE, 952).

2 Mill highlights the connection between oppressive and repressive when he
contrasts past justifications for gender inequality based on 'the interest of
society, by which was meant the interests of men,' with current justifications
of such inequality: 'In the present day, power holds a smoother language,
and whosoever it oppresses, always pretends to do so for their own good:
accordingly, when anything is forbidden to women, it is thought necessary
to say ... that they are incapable of doing it, and that they depart from their
real path of success and happiness when they aspire to it' (SW, 299).

3 He does not consider the gender socialization of men as a constraint upon

their freedom. The prevailing 'masculine' socialization of men fosters self-will, a desire for self-government, and an unwillingness to submit to the will of others (SW, 271, 292–5). Yet Mill also says that men's dominance fosters self-centred and despotic characters among them.

4 He says, moreover, 'that the possessors of the power have facilities in this case, greater than in any other, to prevent any uprising against it' (SW, 318).

5 Mill notes that an upper-class woman can often get relief from household 'superintendence,' but she still faces considerable limitations to self-development *as a woman*: 'She has still devolving on her the management for the whole family of its intercourse with others – of what is called society, and the less the call made on her by the former duty, the greater is always the development of the latter ... All this is over and above the engrossing duty which society imposes exclusively on women, of making themselves charming' (SW, 318).

6 At the same time, Mill responds in *The Subjection of Women* to the claim that women accept their position 'voluntarily' partly by noting that 'a great number of women do not accept it' (SW, 270).

7 Eliza Southgate, a young woman in the United States at the start of the nineteenth century, conveys the weight of this kind of constraint strikingly in a letter to a cousin in 1802: 'In the choice of life one ought to consult their own dispositions and inclinations, their powers and talents ... I have often thought what profession I should choose were I a man. I have always thought if I felt conscious of possessing brilliant talents, the law would be my choice ... [But] I thank Heaven I was *born* a women. I have now only patiently to wait till some clever fellow shall take a fancy to me and place me in a situation, I am determined to make the best of it' (letter to Moses Porter, May 1802, in Cott, 1972, 108–9, emphasis in the original).

8 This tendency has led some commentators to claim that his feminism departs from utilitarianism by appealing to claims of rights and justice independent of utility (cf. Ten, 1991; OL, 224). Yet Mill's argument follows logically from his indirect utilitarianism and his view of the politics of rights (see ch. 5, above). Women have a moral right to share equally with men in the regulation of their affairs, individually and collectively, because this claim corresponds to interests that are so vital to their well-being that it ought to be considered as a right ('WS[I],' 373–4; SW, 300, 293–4).

9 His views of sexuality and sexual freedom are an exception. He accepts Victorian taboos about sexual pleasure, along with the view that women tend to be more passive sexually than men.

10 Mill reiterates this point in *A System of Logic*: 'A long list of mental and

moral differences are observed, or supposed to exist, between men and women; but at some future, and, it may be hoped, not distant, period, equal freedom and an equally independent social position come to be possessed by both, and their differences of character are either removed or totally altered' (L, 868). For further discussion, see Howes (1986); Tulloch (1989); Urbinati (1991).

11 Mill officially relies on 'empiricism properly so called,' according to which 'causation [is] inferred from causal conjunction, without either due elimination, or any presumption arising from known properties of the supposed agent' (L, 792). He distinguishes this view from a crude form of empiricism that he calls 'bad generalization *à posteriori*' (L, 792). As I explained in Chapter 4, though, in theorizing the self he makes some assumptions about 'known properties of the supposed agent.'

12 He explains further, 'What women by nature cannot do, it is quite superfluous to forbid them from doing. What they do, but not so well as men who are their competitors, competition will suffice to exclude them from ... Whatever women's services are most wanted for, the free play of competition will hold out the strongest inducements to them to undertake' (SW, 280).

13 He makes this point more emphatically in his early essay on marriage and divorce. He says that equal freedom for women and men requires that both 'have the power of gaining their own livelihood' ('MD[I],' 77). He adds, however, 'It does not follow that a woman should *actually* support herself because she is *capable* of doing so: in the natural course of events she will *not* ... In a healthy state of things, the husband would be able by his single exertions to earn all that is necessary for both' ('MD[I],' 74–5, Mill's emphasis). At other times he is more ambivalent. For example, in an 1869 speech on women's suffrage he calls for equal opportunities for women in political and economic activities outside the household, but he also contends that 'capable women' tend to develop special skills in managing their households that can be used to manage establishments to help the poor and to manage public finances. Then he says, 'If the home is a women's natural sphere (and I am not at all called upon to contradict the assertion) these depths of politics which need the faculties that can only be acquired at home, are a women's natural sphere too' (WS[I],' 377).

14 He does not consider the possibility that this outcome, when it occurs, may itself be the legacy of the sexist ideology that he challenges.

15 In the United States, for instance, a 1993 study by the Family and Work Institute estimated that working women still do 87 per cent of the shopping, 81 per cent of the cooking, 78 per cent of the cleaning, and 63 per

cent of the bill paying among married couples. See Steven A. Holmes, 'Is This What Women Want?' *New York Times*, 15 December 1996, sec. 4, p. 5.

16 My point is not that we have no grounds for judging what is good or bad for children. Rather, it is that at some point, beyond a few widely acknowledged basic needs and moral wrongs, such judgments are inevitably complicated by people's different conceptions of the good.

17 He says, for example, that it does not 'avail anything to say that the nature of the sexes adopt them to their present functions and position, and renders these appropriate to them' (SW, 276).

18 He says, 'women will never be what they should be, until women, as universally as men, have the power of gaining their own livelihood: until therefore, every girl's parents have either provided her with independent means of subsistence, or given her an education qualifying her to provide those means for herself' ('MD[I],' 77). See also SW, 298.

19 He says further in *On Liberty* that when marriages bring 'third parties into existence, obligations arise on the part of both parties towards those third persons, the fulfillment of which ... must be greatly affected by the continuance or disruption of the relation.' He adds, though, 'It does not follow, nor can I admit, that these obligations extend to requiring the fulfillment of the contract at all costs to the reluctant parties to the contract' (OL, 300).

20 Letter to Henry Keylock Rudsen, 22 July 1870, CW 17, 1751. He adds that he accepts the 'proposition that human freedom should not be interfered with, except by such precautions as are necessary to prevent injury to society); but what those precautions are, in this particular case, is precisely the question to be discussed, and it can only be determined justly or expediently by the joint experience, and with the full force and well-considered concurrence, of both sexes' (p. 1751). See also Mill's letter to John Nichol, 18 August 1869, CW 17, 1634.

21 As I noted in Chapter 4, he insists on 'the superiority of the mental over bodily pleasures' (U, 211). He holds the concern for sexual pleasure will count for less and less in people's pursuit of happiness as they develop their appreciation for 'higher' moral and intellectual pleasures. He also contrasts enslavement to sexual passions with the liberating use of reason that distances us from our 'animal' natures (Mendus, 1989a; Robson, 1976). In this regard, Mill's utilitarianism is more conservative than Jeremy Bentham's hedonistic utilitarianism. Bentham's view led him to a more favourable view of sexual pleasure, sexual freedom, and homosexuality (Crimmins, 1990).

22 Early draft of the *Autobiography* (CW 1, 236). Accordingly, his marital ideal is basically a kind of desexualized friendship in which partners with 'culti-

vated faculties' jointly seek the 'higher pleasures' of intellectual communion rather than the 'lower pleasures' found in sexual relations (SW, 335–6; 'MD[I]'). See Mendus (1989a, 182).

23 He says in an 1870 letter to Lord Amberly, 'I think it is most probable that this particular passion will become with men, as it already is with a large number of women, completely under the control of reason' (2 February 1870, CW 17, 1693). James Walvine explains, 'Middle-class Victorians, and their medical and social spokesmen, regularly denied that sexual activity could be in the least bit pleasurable for women' (1978, 44).

24 Mill's view of birth control was highly controversial. He was arrested at age seventeen for distributing pamphlets about birth control (Packe, 1954, 56–7). Later, in an 1868 letter, he responded sympathetically to efforts to promote birth control, to someone who sent him a pamphlet on birth control: 'Nothing can be more important than the question to which it relates ... About the expediency of putting it into circulation in however quiet a manner you are the best judge. My opinion is that the morality of the matter lies wholly between married people themselves, and that such facts as those which the pamphlet communicates ought to be made known to them by their medical advisers. But we are very far from that point at present, and in the meantime everyone must act according to his own judgment of what is prudent and right' (Mill, quoted in Packe, 58–9).

25 In his article on the French Revolution of 1848, he calls the belief 'that one of the most important and responsible of moral acts, that of giving existence to human beings, is a thing respecting which there scarcely exists any moral obligation, and in which no person's discretion ought on any pretense to be interfered with,' is an outmoded 'superstition' ('VFR,' 387).

26 Mill was prescient regarding how continuing human economic and population growth would increasingly squeeze out spaces for solitude and for habitats for other animal species. He says that even when population does not grow beyond the capacity of human beings to supply all people with 'food and raiment,' it can ravage nonhuman nature: 'A world from which solitude is extirpated, is a very poor ideal ... Nor is there much satisfaction in contemplating the world with nothing left to the spontaneous activity of nature; and every rood of land brought into cultivation, which is capable of growing food for human beings; every flowery waste or natural pasture ploughed up, all quadrupeds or birds which are not domesticated for man's use exterminated as his rival for food, every hedgerow or superfluous tree rooted out, and scarcely a place left where a wild shrub or flower could grow without being eradicated as a weed in the name of improved agriculture' (PPE, 756).

308 Notes to pages 184–91

27 Similarly, working couples could better combine these two kinds of work if the standard work week was reduced from forty hours to, say, thirty-two or thirty-five.

28 In this regard, Mill is on the right track when he defends 'comparative qualifications' of older partners in marriages in relation to 'the general conditions of human society, *as now constituted*' (SW, 291, emphasis added).

29 In the 'Statement on Marriage' that he wrote for his marriage to Harriet Taylor, he says that they both disapprove of 'the whole character of the marriage relation as constituted by law ... for this among other reasons, that it confers upon one of the parties to the contract, legal power and control over the person, property, and freedom of action of the other party, independent of her wishes and will' ('Statement on Marriage,' CW 21, 99). Concerning their marriage, he says, 'I declare it to be my will and intention, and the condition of the engagement between us, that she retains in all respects whatever the same absolute freedom of action, and freedom of disposal of herself and of all that does or may belong to her, as if no marriage had taken place' (99).

30 Mill's ideal of marital partnership is based at least in part on his friendship and intellectual partnership with Harriet Taylor. See Rossi (1970); Shanley (1981); Rose (1983); and Mendus (1989a).

31 Mill expresses this view most strikingly in his early essay on marriage and divorce. In addition to emphasizing that women must be able to gain their own livelihood, he says, 'In a healthy state of things, the husband would be able by his single exertions to earn all that is necessary for both: and there would be no need that the wife should take part in the providing of what is required to *support* life: it will be for the happiness of both that her occupation should rather be to adorn and beautify it ... If she loves, her natural impulse will be to associate her existence with him she loves, and to share *his* occupations' ('MD[I],' 77, 75–6, Mill's emphasis). He refers to equality here in terms of 'that affection of *equality* which alone deserves to be called love' ('MD[I],' 77, Mill's emphasis). While he emphasizes equal freedom for women more forcefully in *The Subjection of Women*, he does not abandon these underlying premises.

32 This is so, as I noted earlier, even though he acknowledges that whichever partner 'brings the means of support' into a marriage will tend to have a greater voice in mutual decisions (SW, 291; cf. Shanley, 1998, 415). Here Mill would have benefited by following Harriet Taylor's lead in 'The Enfranchisement of Women.' In response to the claim that giving women 'freedom of occupation' would diminish wages by crowding the labour market, she emphasizes the significance of economic independence for

married women as a necessary condition of marital equality ('EW,' 427, 426). Even if it turned out that husbands and wives would earn no more together than husbands earn alone, there would be a gain in equality as 'the women would be raised from the position of a servant to that of a partner' ('EW,' 428). Such economic partnership would brace women against tyrannical men who might otherwise claim 'to be sole earners, and the sole dispensers of what is earned' ('EW,' 428).

33 Along with arguing for equality in his writings, he worked with women's suffrage associations and introduced legislation to enfranchise women in 1866 and 1867 during his term in Parliament.

34 His view is thus an example of what Susan Moller Okin (1991) calls calls 'false gender neutrality' insofar as he claims to identify 'neutral' conditions for equal participation in public life. It is not gender neutral, though, since it is based on a 'masculine' conception of the standard worker as someone who does not get pregnant.

35 Martha Minow calls this the 'dilemma of difference.' She explains that when we identify particular characteristics with which to differentiate people from each other we are not only 'classifying the world; we are [also] investing particular classifications with consequences and positioning ourselves in relation to those meanings' (1990a, 3). That is, our classifications *make* particular differences salient in relation to particular social and political practices – for example, child rearing, housework, education, employment, political rights, laws.

36 Katha Pollitt warns, however, that such 'difference' feminism also poses some dangers for the goal of equality: '[It] says, in effect: this is what women are like, this is the kind of life they lead, so let's shape social policy and law to acknowledge and reflect it' (1994, 194). This takes us back to the 'dilemma of difference' insofar as assertions of difference may be used for discriminatory purposes. Still, claims of difference do not inevitably produce discriminatory effects, and acknowledging that women and men may sometimes need different treatment does not by itself preclude radical changes in family arrangements or gender roles (p. 195).

37 This noninterpretive tendency is also evident in his writings on religion. For instance, in 'The Utility of Religion' he analyzes religion's 'utility' as a form of power that instils in people a 'system of moral duties,' but he fails to consider what people's religious identities mean to them: 'We propose to inquire whether the belief in religion, considered as mere persuasion, apart from its truth, is really indispensable to the temporal welfare of mankind' ('UR,' 407, 405; and 'T,' 429–31, 442, 488).

38 He says in *Representative Government*, for instance, that the 'improvement' of

human societies gradually leads people to abandon the 'inveterate spirit of locality' (CRG, 417). 'Experience proves,' he says, 'it is possible for one nationality to merge and be absorbed in another: and when it was originally an inferior or more backward portion of the human race the absorption is greatly to its advantage' (CRG, 549). See also ch. 1, sec. V, above; and Kymlicka (1995, 5).

39 I develop this point more fully in Baum (1997), from which these last few paragraphs are drawn.

40 Consider Debra Kaufman's recent study of 150 newly orthodox Jewish women in major urban areas across the United States in the mid-1980s. Twenty-five of the women identified with or participated in the women's movement in the late 1960s and early 1970s, but they 'eventually were disappointed by what they perceived to be the concerns of the early women's movement. For many, the focus on individual rights and personal independence left the larger issues of "how to live one's life" in a meaningful manner unformulated' (1994, 352).

7: Economic Freedom

1 Mill does refer to capitalism, however, as the 'voluntary' system and as 'the system of individual agency' (PPE, 947, 961, 970). In *Principles*, he also uses such phrases as 'setting free' capital, 'freedom of commercial intercourse,' and 'free' competition; yet he consistently distinguishes these concepts from the economic freedom of individuals (see PPE, 82–3, 130, and 140).

2 Like Schwartz, Lionel Robbins focuses on Mill's support for *laissez-faire* as the general rule for the role of government in the economy, and says that Mill supports the basic notion of the classical economists (Smith, Ricardo, etc.) regarding 'the system of economic freedom': 'For them, an organization of production, based, in the main, on private property, was an essential complement to a system of freedom of choice as regards consumption and provision for the future' (Robbins, 1952, 187). Similarly, Abram Harris misconstrues Mill's conception of economic freedom in light of Mill's support for *laissez-faire* and his principle of liberty: '[Mill] considered freedom in economic relations, that is to say, freedom of exchange in markets, to be an essential condition and, hence, an ingredient of freedom in general.' Harris goes on to construe Mill's conception of 'economic freedom' in terms of 'his opposition to government interference with exchange relations' (1958, 40). See also Gray (1986, 74–5).

3 Likewise, in a recent survey of 'economic freedom' in different countries, scholars associated with Freedom House and *Freedom Review* assess relative

economic freedom in terms of how well governments secure for their citizens the right to own property, earn a living, operate a business, invest their earnings, trade internationally, and 'participate in all aspects of a market economy' (Messick, 1996, 6–7).

4 Calling for an economic system that leaves individuals with 'the greatest possible freedom of action,' he adds, 'I am not one of those, who set up liberty as an idol to be worshipped, and I am even willing to go farther than most people in regulating and controlling when there is a special advantage to be obtained ... I presume, however, ... that there is a pleasure in enjoying perfect freedom of action; that to be controlled, even if it be for our own good, is in itself far from pleasant, and that other things being alike, it is infinitely better to attain a given end by leaving people to themselves than to attain the same end by controlling them' ('Cooperation: Closing Speech,' CW 26, 320–1).

5 See also 'VFR,' 389. Around 1845, Mill developed considerable sympathy for various socialist ideas as an extension of his commitment to liberal individualism (Sarvasy, 1985; Hollander, 1985; Claeys, 1987). Moreover, he emphasizes the historical variability of economic institutions and ideas and, thus, criticizes those *disciples* of the 'founders of political economy' who 'believe themselves to be provided with a set of catch-words, which they mistake for principles – free-trade, freedom of contract, competition, demand and supply, the wages fund, individual interest, desire of wealth, &c. – which supersede analysis, and are applicable to every variety of cases without the trouble of thought' ('LLQ,' 671). See also 'MVC,' 215.

6 'Such questions involve considerations of liberty,' Mill says, 'only insofar as leaving people to themselves is always better, *caeteris paribus*, than controlling them; but that they may be legitimately controlled for these ends is in principle undeniable' (OL, 293).

7 Thus, a law requiring warning labels on poisonous drugs 'may be enforced without violation of liberty: the buyer cannot wish not to know that the thing he possesses has poisonous qualities' (OL, 294). Turning to the practices of gambling and prostitution, Mill says that the principle that people should be free to consult others about what they should do must be qualified with respect to 'classes of persons ... [whose very] mode of living [is] ... opposed to ... the public weal. Fornication ... must be tolerated, and so must gambling; but should a person be free to be a pimp, or to keep a gambling-house?' (OL, 296). He says that the latter activities, as matters of trade, can rightfully be restricted, but that to safeguard the freedom of buyers we should proceed cautiously before punishing the seller or 'accessory, when the principal is (and must be) allowed to go free' (OL, 293, 297).

8 Mill's understanding of two distinct but interrelated forms of economic freedom parallels his broader effort to balance *political freedom* – the freedom of citizens to share in determining the laws and public policies governing them – with *individual liberty*. See chs. 5 and 8.

9 Mill makes this point while expressing his support for the Labouring Classes' Dwelling Bill of 1866, which sought to help local authorities, public companies, and private individuals finance new housing stock (CW 17, 1155n2). He makes a similar argument in the *Principles* with respect to poor relief (PPE, 961).

10 Mill also argues that 'the business of life is better performed when those who have an immediate interest in it are left to take their own course, uncontrolled either by the mandate of the law or by the meddling of any public functionary' (PPE, 946). Similarly, in *On Liberty* he opposes government intervention to do things for people 'instead of leaving it to be done by themselves, individually, or in voluntary combination' (OL, 305).

11 He provides an explanation for this omission, though, in *Chapters on Socialism* when he says 'we are still only in the first stage of that movement for the education of the whole people' (COS, 729). Primary education was established on a national basis by the Education Act of 1870; secondary education only began to gain adequate financial support following the Balfour government's Education Act of 1902. Still, we now need a more systematic account than Mill provides of how unequal social and economic conditions undermine the goal of equality of opportunity.

12 Discussing the idea of educational endowments to broaden access to formal education, Mill insists that justice requires not only provisions for the poor, but also 'equal provision ... for the education of both sexes' ('E,' 629).

13 Mill also says 'the capricious distribution of the means of life and enjoyment [between rich and poor], could only be defended as an admitted imperfection.' He adds that 'nothing valid can be said against socialism in principle; and ... attempts to assail it, or defend private property, on the ground of justice, must inevitably fail' ('NPE,' 444).

14 He says 'the maxim of leaving contracts free, is not applicable without great limitations in case of engagement in perpetuity' (PPE, 954). In addition, he supports public assistance for the poor on the condition that it does not 'dispense with self-help'; and he says 'the true idea of distributive justice ... consists not in limiting but in redressing the inequalities and wrongs of nature' (PPE, 961, 808).

15 Elsewhere he says, 'That all should indeed start on perfectly equal terms, is inconsistent with any law of private property' (PPE, 207).

16 In an 1861 letter, Mill discusses the difficulty of laying down a 'general rule'

of just distribution in present circumstances: 'The insuperable difficulty is that there being no principle of equality to rest the settlement upon, any decision must be arbitrary, dependent upon the direction of the judge's sympathies' (letter to Samuel Paull, 23 November 1861, CW 15, 749).

17 Mill notes that worker-managed co-operatives in France generally abandoned the principle of equal wages for the apportionment of remuneration, beyond a fixed minimum for all, 'according to the work done' (PPE, 782).

18 Mill does not claim that everyone is entitled to get the occupation or manner of life that she or he desires. Justice, in his view, requires that everyone have an equal opportunity to develop the skills that will qualify her for the occupation of her choice and receive fair consideration in the competition for occupations and offices (see OL, 104–5; 'WS[I],' 374).

19 Mill's view is therefore quite different from the libertarian view articulated by Robert Nozick, according to which taxing the product of someone's labour is comparable to a kind of involuntary servitude (see Nozick, 1974).

20 Concerning luxury taxes, he says in the *Principles*, 'I disclaim all asceticism, and by no means wish to see discouraged ... any indulgence ... which is sought from a genuine inclination for, and enjoyment of, the thing itself.' He adds, however, that a large portion of expenditures on luxuries by the wealthier classes is incurred for the sake of appearances rather than 'for the sake of the pleasure afforded by the things ... and I cannot but think that expenditure of this sort is a most desirable subject of taxation' (PPE, 869; cf. PPE, 809).

21 He says that while government *must* account for people's 'sacrifices of real comfort,' a graduated tax requires legislators to make questionable judgments regarding 'sacrifices of the imaginary dignity,' such as 'whether the person with 10,000 pounds a year cares less for 1000 pounds than the person with only 1000 pounds a year cares for 100 pounds, and if so how much' (PPE, 810).

22 Riley suggests that the desert principle may be realizable under a reformed capitalism where revenues would be distributed 'entirely between workers and savers in proportion to the (marginal and/or average) physical products of their own labour and capital' (1996, 60). Mill's inconsistency here appears to be an error of omission: he never brings together his critique of existing capitalism's failure to achieve the desert principle with his argument about proportionate versus progressive taxation.

23 Regarding the prospect of taxing all but one-fifth of a large inheritance, Mill says, 'it must be apparent to every one, that the difference to the happiness of the possessor between a moderate independence and five times as

much, is insignificant when weighed against the employment that might be given, and the permanent benefits diffused, by some other disposal of the four-fifths' (PPE, 225).

24 Mill further illuminates his view of private property in an 1850 letter to Frederick Furnivall. He says that the principle of property 'is a great advance, both in justice & utility, above the mere law of force, but far inferior to the law of community; & there is not & cannot be any reason against the immediate adoption of some form of this last, unless it be that mankind are not yet prepared for it' (letter to Frederick Furnivall, 22 November 1850, CW 14, 51). See also Mill's letter to Furnivall of 27 November 1850 (CW 14, 53–4).

25 Mill's concern in this letter is to defend his distinction between rights respecting land and rights respecting movable property (letter to Charles Eliot Norton, 26 June 1870, CW 17, 1739).

26 Mill's proposed reforms include not only taxes on inheritance and rents, but also the more radical proposal that the state buy up land that becomes available on the market from large land owners and then 'leasing it, either to small farmers with due security of tenure, or to co-operative associations of labour' ('LLQ,' 683; see also 'LTR').

27 Paternalistic power, he adds, is prone to all those abuses of power which are usually found in relationships that give one class of persons unchecked power over others: 'To be under the power of some one, instead of being as formerly the sole condition of safety, is now, speaking generally, the only situation which exposes to grievous wrong. The so-called protectors are now the only persons against whom, in ordinary circumstances, protection is needed. The brutality and tyranny with which every police report is filled, are those of husbands to wives, of parents to children' (PPE, 761).

28 'Labour is unquestionably more productive,' Mill says, 'on the system of large industrial enterprises; the produce, if not greater absolutely, is greater in proportion to the labour employed' (PPE, 768).

29 Mill adds that co-operatives also offer some advantages with respect to productivity. Most importantly, they would overcome 'the standing feud between capital and labour' whereby wage earners have little interest in the enterprise other than 'to earn their wage with as little labour as possible' and employers have little concern for the workers apart from their labour (PPE, 791–2, 769).

30 Riley says, 'Even under decentralized socialism, intolerant majorities within producer associations would be likely to suppress unconventional ideas and impose a uniform private lifestyle on all of the members' (1994, xlii).

31 Mill says, 'In Communist associations private life would be brought in a

most unexampled degree within the dominion of public authority, and there would be less scope for the development of individual character than has hitherto existed' (COS, 425–6; PPE, 203–5, 209). Mill develops this point most strikingly with respect to education (see above).

32 With reference to the experience of French industrial associations, Mill says that rather than instituting looser rules of discipline than those found in 'ordinary workshops,' workers established stricter rules. He adds, however, that 'being rules self-imposed, for the manifest good of the community, and not for the convenience of an employer regarded as having an opposite interest, they are far more scrupulously obeyed, and the voluntary obedience carries with it a sense of personal worth and dignity' (PPE, 780–1).

33 On the character of this system in relation to 'socialism' and 'capitalism,' cf. Robbins (1952, 159–60); Riley (1994, xxix–xxxviii); and Riley (1996). Mill's model is more clearly socialist if we accept Alec Nove's recent definition of a socialist society as one in which 'the major part of the means of production of goods and services are not in private hands, but are in some sense socially owned and operated, by state, socialized or cooperative enterprises' (1987, 398).

34 Mill says of a Fourierist system, 'The free choice of individuals as to their manner of life would be no more interfered with than would be necessary for gaining the advantages of co-operation in the industrial operations' (COS, 748).

35 In his 1852 preface to the *Principles*, he adds that the success of recent co-operative associations in France shows 'that the time is ripe for a larger and more rapid extension of association among labourers, than could have been successfully attempted before the culminated democratic movements in Europe' (PPE, xciii). He also says that in his chapter 'On the Futurity of the Labouring Classes' he has 'endeavored to designate more clearly [than in the previous editions] the tendency of the social transformation, of which these associations are the initial step; and ... to disconnect the co-operative cause from the exaggerated ... declamations against competition, ... indulged in by its supporters.'

36 As is well known, Mill says in his *Autobiography* regarding his and Harriet Taylor's 'ideal of ultimate improvement' that they moved 'far beyond Democracy, ... [to] the general designation of Socialists' (A, 239). Mill reiterates this point in an 1868 letter to Peter Deml. 'It would not be a correct view of my opinions,' he says, 'to suppose that I think everything wrong in the doctrines of Socialism; on the contrary I think there are many elements of truth in them, & that much good may be done in that direction, especially by the progress of the Cooperative Movement.' Mill then refers Deml

to the chapter of the *Principles* that I have been discussing (letter to Peter Deml, 22 April 1868, CW 16, 1389).

37 Mill defines socialism as 'the joint ownership by all members of the community of the instruments and means of production' so that 'the division of the produce among the body of owners must be a public act' (COS, 738). Given Mill's emphasis on worker self-management as an aspect of freedom, a co-operative form of capitalism would approach his ideal of maximal economic freedom *if* it could combine private ownership of the means of production with *worker control* of enterprises. For an account of Mill's view of the 'spontaneous' transformation, see Riley (1996, 64–8).

38 Mill says in 1852 that he has never regarded his objections to the best socialist theories as conclusive, but warns that 'the low moral state of mankind generally and of the labouring classes in particular, renders them at present unfit for any order of things which would presuppose as its necessary condition a certain measure of conscience & intellect' (letter to Karl D. Heinrich Rau, 20 March 1852, CW 14, 87; see also PPE, 763; COS, 746–9).

39 Mill lacks the more recent feminist appreciation of domestic labour as productive labour for which there should be fair monetary compensation (see Folbre, 1994).

8: Political Freedom

1 Mill says in 'Civilization,' 'The distribution of constitutional power cannot long continue very different from that real power, without a convulsion' ('Civ,' 173).

2 This 'spirit of improvement' is basic to Mill's revised, indirect version of utilitarianism. The aim of good government, in his view, is not to satisfy the existing desires and 'immediate interests' of the population, but to realize as much as possible what he calls 'utility in the largest sense, grounded on the permanent interests of man as a progressive being' (OL, 224). See Ryan (1973); and Hampsher-Monk (1992, 387).

3 Graeme Duncan says that insofar as 'participation is supported simply for its supposed educative or moralizing effects, it would not need to amount to self-government or self-determination' (1969, 76). Yet it is clear, as Alan Ryan notes, that Mill also insists that 'persons at a certain level in human development are, essentially, sovereign agents, who have a right to govern themselves' (1983, 53).

4 Notably, though, the free citizens of Athens were an exclusive group (Hornblower, 1993).

5 Mill notes that it is *possible*, where a particular majority is the majority in

every electoral district, for a national majority to elect representatives in every district so that 'no other class could succeed in getting represented anywhere' (CRG, 450).

6 A significant number of voters in the United States vote for 'major party' candidates whom they regard as the 'lesser of two evils' in cases where neither of the two major parties adequately represents their views. This is true, for instance, of libertarians who vote for Republicans and of socialists and Greens who vote for Democrats. Voting for a Libertarian, Socialist, or Green Party candidate generally means voting for a sure loser, since such 'minor' party candidates are rarely able to get the electoral majority (or plurality) necessary to win a seat in Congress. Consequently, such minority perspectives are underrepresented. Cf. Richie and Hill (1998).

7 Elsewhere he says that representation of minorities is necessary to establish a 'deliberative assembly' that is based on 'the real, instead of nominal representation of every individual elector' ('RWR,' 358).

8 He reiterates this point in *Representative Government*: 'In all human affairs, every person directly interested ... has an admitted claim to a voice, and when his exercise of it is not inconsistent with the safety of the whole, cannot be justly excluded from it. But though every one ought to have a voice – that every one should have an equal voice is a totally different proposition' (CRG, 473).

9 He proposes to exclude from suffrage those persons who pay no taxes, receive parish relief, and cannot meet minimal standards of 'reading, writing, and calculating,' while hoping that in the long run the suffrage would become universal (CRG, 470–3). He says, though, 'These exclusions are not in their nature permanent. They exact such conditions only as all are able, or ought to be able, to fulfill if they choose' (p. 472). Still, Mill's concern with self-protection, self-dependence, and equal representation provides grounds for rejecting even these presumably temporary exclusions (Ten, 1998, 384).

10 Mill himself introduced legislation for women's suffrage in the House of Commons in 1866, and then again in 1867 ('Electoral Franchise for Women,' CW 28, 91–2; 'AWEF'). Women's suffrage was not achieved, however, until much later: women aged 30 or more were enfranchised in 1918; women between 21 and 30 not until 1928. The Reform Act of 1867 enfranchised male householders in the boroughs, nearly doubling the small electorate (from about 9 per cent of the population aged 20 and over to 16 per cent); the Reform Act of 1884 enfranchised householders in the rural counties (increasing the electorate to about 28.5 per cent of the population in 1886). The Reform Act of 1918 established nearly full *manhood* suffrage.

See 'Parliament,' in *The Encyclopaedia Britannica,* vol. 17 (Chicago: The Encyclopaedia Britannica, 1971), 383.

11 Wendy Sarvacy aptly states that Mill's democratic theory in *Representative Government* 'is best understood as appropriate for a period of transition between liberal-capitalism and democratic-socialism, because it both reflects the incompatibility of democracy and capitalism and seeks to facilitate the necessary social transformation' (1984, 568).

12 By the 1860s Mill saw the English aristocracy as increasingly marginal. Yet it still had significant political power despite its declining social power relative to the other two classes. This was presumably due to its historical control over the British government, since 'those who are in possession of the government,' according to Mill, have an advantage in making the 'elements of [social] power politically influential' (CRG, 381).

13 He says that manhood suffrage would give the numerical majority potentially 'absolute power, if they chose to exercise it,' and that this majority 'would be composed exclusively of a single class, alike in biases, prepossessions, and general modes of thinking' (CRG, 467). He adds, 'the great majority of voters, in most countries, and emphatically in [England], would be manual labourers; and the twofold danger, that of too low a standard of political intelligence, and that of class legislation, would still exist, in a very perilous degree' (CRG, 473).

14 He explains, 'On the principle of justice ... and on the principle of democracy above all, the representation of minorities appears to me an absolutely necessary part of any representative constitution which it is intended should permanently work well' ('RP,' 85). See also Mill, 'On Hare's Plan,' 29 April 1865, CW 25, 1210; CRG, 477. For further discussion, see Zimmer (1976); and Sarvacy (1984).

15 James Bohman makes a closely related point concerning the social power, or what he calls 'agency freedom,' of more powerful groups in modern democratic states: 'Such groups can substitute their more direct agency freedom (or their social power) for their social [that is, political] freedom mediated through institutions that disperse power. In this case, powerful groups do so by limiting the extent of the social freedom – for all those involved – by limiting the available options for deliberation for the whole polity' (1997, 331, 339).

16 See also Mill, 'On the Liberty of the Press' (1825), in Mill (1959); and 'The French Law Against the Press' (19 August 1848, CW 25, 1115–18). Commentators who focus on this aspect of Mill's argument about freedom of thought and discussion include Wishy (1959); Wollheim (1973, xix–xx); Levi (1975); Thompson (1976, 81); Habermas (1991, 132–8); and Kinder and Herzog (1993, 348–50).

17 In an 1829 letter to Gustave D'Eichthal, Mill refers to the 'instructed' as a potential 'pouvoir spirituel' (spiritual power) in society. His ideal is that 'the body of the people, that is, the uninstructed, shall entertain the same feelings of deference & submission to the authority of the instructed, in morals and politics, as they at present do in the physical sciences.' He sees this situation developing in tandem with 'the diffusion of knowledge among the labouring classes & the consequent improvement of their intellects.' He further elaborates this idea with regard to the prospect of 'regenerating' society by shaping people's opinions: 'It is not sufficiently considered by many zealots for even right opinions, that you have done little or nothing for a man when you have merely given him an opinion. An opinion suggests hardly anything to an uninformed mind; it may become a watchword, but it can never be a moving & influencing and living principle within him ... It is therefore of little use altering men's opinions ... until you have brought their minds to a higher state of cultivation, of which better opinions are the natural & and almost spontaneous growth (letter to Gustave D'Eichthal, 7 November 1829, CW 12, 40, 42).

18 He says in *On Liberty*, 'The majority have not yet learnt to feel the power of the government their power, or its opinions as their opinions' (OL, 223). He expects this situation to soon change, though.

19 Similarly, he says in *On Liberty* that in modern 'politics it is almost a triviality to say that public opinion now rules the world. The only power deserving the name is that of the masses, and of governments while they make themselves the organ of the tendencies and instincts of masses' (OL, 268). Then he adds, 'Those whose opinions go by the name of public opinion, are not always the same sort of public: in America they are the whole white population; in England, chiefly the middle class. But they are always a mass, that is to say, a collective mediocrity. And what is a still greater novelty, the mass do not take their opinions from dignitaries in Church or State, from ostensible leaders, or from books. Their thinking is done for them by men much like them selves, addressing them or speaking in their name ... through the newspapers' (OL, 268–9).

20 He speaks of 'the middle classes of this country, whose opinions and sentiments are represented by the daily press.' Then, concerning debates over trade unions, he adds, 'The middle classes of London, through their organs the London newspapers, are now manifesting ... [their] feelings [of fear and anger], on the subject of Trades' Unions' ('Notes on the Newspapers,' no. IV, June 1834, CW 6, 218, 220).

21 He expresses similar concern about the power of the wealthy in 'Rationale of Representation': 'In every country where there are rich and poor, the administration of public affairs would, even under the most democratic

constitution, be mainly in the hands of the rich ... Not only have the
wealthy and leisured classes ten times the means of acquiring personal
influence, ten times the means of acquiring intellectual cultivation, which
any person can bring into cultivation with them' ('RR,' 26).

22 Letter to Gustave D'Eichthal, 7 November 1829 (CW 12, 39). In this spirit,
Mill later worked on a plan to give an existing paper, *The Examiner*, 'a circulation among the working classes, as well as to give it a new character in
some other respects' (letter to Frederic Harrison, 13 April 1873, CW 17,
1949).

23 Letter to Gustave D'Eichthal, 7 November 1829 (CW 12, 40).

24 In an early article he says that the impending removal of taxes on newspapers and political tracts will invigorate public debate in England: 'There
will now ... be vastly greater facilities than ever were before known for the
diffusion of important truth among the people, and also of mischievous
error ... In the immensely increased number of readers which will be the
effect of the cheapness of newspapers and political tracts, any writers of
talent may hope, whatever be their sentiments, to find the quantity of support necessary for a moderate degree of success, without prostituting themselves to the hired advocacy of the opinions in vogue ('Notes on the
Newspapers,' nos. VI, August 1934, CW 6, 262).

25 Mill expects the public sphere to be a key arena through which the working
classes will increasingly realize their potential political power. Reflecting on
the Reform Act of 1867, he says, 'The instruments [of this movement] will
be the press, public meetings and associations, and the return to Parliament of the greatest possible number of persons pledged to the political
aims of the working classes' (COS, 707).

26 A related aspect of this corporate capitalist bias is the dependence of major
media outlets, such as newspapers and television networks, on the advertis-
ing revenues by other major corporations. See Bagdikian (1997).

27 He warns against the 'tyranny of the majority' immediately following this
passage. Since 'the people' are rarely *all* the people, he says, they 'may
desire to oppress a part of their number; and precautions are as much
needed against this as against any other abuse of power' (OL, 219).

28 His willingness to support a 'money qualification' for plural voting in local
elections is a bit anomalous, but it relates directly to his concern with maintaining a balance of power between the working and middle classes. He
apparently believes that there is greater danger that the working classes
would exercise a kind of class domination in local governments than in
national government.

29 With respect to public relief, for instance, he says that the well-being of the

labouring classes depends to a large degree 'upon the adherence to certain fixed principles ... Though it belongs essentially to the local functionaries to determine who, according to those principles, is entitled to be relieved, the national parliament is the proper authority to prescribe the principles themselves' (CRG, 544).

30 Maximizing popular accountability, he says, is not 'the sole requisite of good government.' Therefore, 'expediency may require that we should sacrifice some portion of it, or (to speak more precisely) content ourselves with a somewhat less approximation to it than might possibly be attainable, for the sake of some other end.' The other goal is the need for 'government by a select body' ('RR,' 23). See also CRG (ch. 15); and Thompson (1976, ch. 2).

31 He holds out hope that the class of established truths will gradually expand as a consequence of social and intellectual progress. 'As mankind improve,' he says, 'the number of doctrines which are no longer disputed or doubted will be constantly on the increase: the well-being of mankind may almost be measured by the number and gravity of the truths which have reached the point of being uncontested' (OL, 250).

32 He explains, 'When ... the instructed in general can be brought to recognize one social arrangement, or political or other institution, as good, and another as bad, one as desirable, another as condemnable, very much has been done towards giving to the one, or withdrawing from the other the social force that enables it to subsist' (CRG, 382).

33 'Appendix,' D&D 1, 472. See also ch. 4, above.

34 Mill discusses the 'unprepared state of the labouring classes' in a letter to Dr. Adolf Soetbeer on the prospects for socialism (18 March 1852, CW 14, 85). Similarly, in a later letter to Auberon Herbert, he says that workers need to learn how 'the higher virtues ... are needed to enable a democracy & above all any approach to socialism to work in any satisfactory manner' (letter to Auberon Herbert, 29 January 1872, CW 17, 1869–71). He elaborates the political economic side of his democratic theory in an 1864 speech on industrial co-operation, as follows: 'It is only when the entire working class shall be as much improved as the best portion of them now are that our hopes will be realized, and the whole mass of the people will practically adopt cooperation' ('Cooperation,' CW 28, 8). He goes on to say that the goal of economic co-operation 'cannot advance further than the minds and morals of the people engaged in it,' but then adds, 'This is the millennium towards which we strive' ('Cooperation,' 9).

35 Thus, he says in 'Civilization' that those who think 'the masses unprepared for complete control over their government ... will exert [their] utmost efforts in contributing to prepare them' ('Civ,' 174; cf. OL, 299).

36 He declares 'equality of political rights' his goal in a letter to Lucy Stone dated 14 April 1868 (CW 16, 1385). Elsewhere, he qualifies the inclusiveness of his democratic ideal by excluding the 'insane persons, [and] persons convicted of a crime' from voting rights; but he does not discuss this issue further ('TPR,' 322n).

37 Mill's ideal of 'really equal democracy' thus has some affinities to Robert Dahl's view (1989) that actually existing 'democracies' are more accurately construed as 'polyarchies' that establish 'rule of the many' but not equal self-government by all. His concern with democratic deliberation is carried forward by current proponents of 'deliberative democracy.' See also Bohman and Rehg (1997).

38 This point does not undermine Mill's observation that in many political matters most people must rely on the expertise of those who have studied them intensively. Those of us who cannot fully assess the grounds of different views of, say, the prospect of global warming often have no recourse but to rely at least in part on the views of often conflicting authorities in such matters.

39 Mill is not far off target when he says in 1840 that 'the ascendancy of the commercial class in modern society and politics is inevitable, ... [and that] it is chimerical to hope to overbear or outnumber the middle class' ('TDA[II],' 200). Yet the political *dominance* of this class as opposed to its *ascendancy* in the nineteenth century is not inevitable. I will return to this point in Chapter 9.

9: Mill and the Politics of Freedom

1 Letter to Pasquale Villari, 28 February 1872 (CW 17, 1873).

2 For recent arguments that support Mill's claims on this score (see Dahl, 1985); Bowles and Gintis (1987, ch. 3; 1993b); and Alcaly (1997). Mill and other theorists note some difficulties for democratic enterprises with regard to risk-taking and innovation (cf. Mill, PPE, 793; Bowles and Gintis, 1993b, 392–5). These difficulties do not appear to be insurmountable, however.

3 Regarding the latter issue, Michael Walzer offers a useful suggestion. He says that we can leave space for entrepreneurial activity, but insist that at some 'point in the development of an enterprise ... it must pass out of entrepreneurial control' and be reorganized according to democratic principles (1983, 303).

4 Berlin claims that the idea that a redistribution of power and resources can expand freedom confuses 'liberty and the conditions of its exercise' (1969a, liii–liv).

5 The issue is rather different if we speak of liberty rather than freedom, as I explained in Chapter 1, although Berlin and Rawls use the two terms interchangeably. We can indeed distinguish between having certain liberties and having the means with which to exercise one's liberties. Similarly, being *at liberty* to do something is not the same thing as *being free to do it.*

6 In this regard, Mill's theory of freedom foreshadows David Held's ideal of 'democratic autonomy,' according to which 'individuals should be free and equal in the determination of the rules by which they live' (1989, 165). Held explains, 'the concept of liberty presupposed by the model of democratic autonomy allows in some respects a smaller range of actions for certain groups of individuals ... some [would] no longer have the scope to, for instance, accumulate a vast amount of resources, or pursue their own careers at the expense of the careers of their lovers, wives or children. The liberty of persons within the framework of democratic autonomy will have to be one of progressive accommodation to the liberty of others. While, therefore, the scope of action may be limited for some in certain respects, it will be radically enhanced for others' (186). For related egalitarian arguments, see Norman (1987); and Lukes (1991, 59)

7 In *Representative Government,* for instance, he offers the case of the ending of slavery as 'a conclusive example how far mere physical and economic power is from being the whole of social power.' He says, 'It was not by any change in the distribution of material interests, but the spread of moral convictions, that negro slavery has been put an end to in the British Empire and elsewhere' (CRG, 382).

8 He errs by severing sociological analysis of power relationships from the web of meanings through which people interpret their experiences. The structural dimension of power relationships cannot be separated, however, from the cultural (that is, meaningful) dimension.

9 Undoubtedly, popular assent to this view of freedom has been fueled by the fact that much of the 'middle class' in contemporary capitalist societies (as opposed to the capitalist class that Mill refers to as the middle class) now own some stock shares or mutual funds. For example, with reference to the United States, the fact that about 51 per cent of adults now say they own stocks or mutual funds has led at least one commentator to speak of the '*democratization* of capitalism' (Weisburg, 1998, 29, emphasis in the original). This notion is highly misleading, however, given the concentration of income-producing wealth in capitalist countries (see note 13). Nonetheless, it figures into prevailing interpretations of freedom and democracy.

10 Regarding the pursuit of riches he adds, 'I know not why it should be a matter of congratulation that persons who are already richer than anyone needs to be, should have doubled their means of consuming things which

give little or no pleasure except as representative of wealth ... It is only in the backward countries of the world that increased production is still an important object: in the most advanced, what is economically needed is a better distribution' (PPE, 755).

11 Mill's naïve hope of a spontaneous economic transformation contrasts with his view of the difficulty of achieving the emancipation of women. Thus, he says in a late letter, 'The emancipation of women and co-operative production are, I fully believe, the two great changes that will regenerate society. But though the latter of these may grow without much help from the action of Parliaments and Congresses, the former cannot' (letter to Parke Godwin, 1 January 1869, CW 17, 1535).

12 Mill says, 'Where there is the least liberty, the passion for power is the most ardent and unscrupulous. *The desire for power over others* can only cease to be a depraving agency among mankind, when each of them individually is able to do without it' (SW, 338, emphasis added).

13 In the United States, for example, the richest 1 per cent of households control about 40 per cent of the country's wealth. The total wealth of the top 1 per cent is even greater when we focus on income-producing wealth, excluding equity in personal residences. See 'The Rich Get Richer,' *The New York Times*, 18 April 1995, A24; and Bachrach and Botwinick (1992, 173n7).

14 Apologies to Alfred (Lord) Tennyson and Robert F. Kennedy.

Bibliography

Works by Mill

I. Standard Editions of Mill's Works Cited

Dissertations and Discussions, vols. 1 & 2. New York: Haskell House. 1973. Reprint of the 1859 edition.
The Collected Works of John Stuart Mill. 1963–91. General ed., John M. Robson. 33 volumes. Toronto: University of Toronto Press.

II. Other Editions Used

Mill, John Stuart. 1910. *The Letters of John Stuart Mill,* 2 vols. Ed. Hugh S.R. Elliot. London: Longman's Green & Co.
– 1950. *John Stuart Mill's Philosophy of Scientific Method.* Ed. Ernest Nagel. New York: Hafner Publishing.
– 1957. *Autobiography* [1873]. Ed. Currin V. Shields. Indianapolis: Bobbs-Merrill.
– 1959. *Prefaces to Liberty: Selected Writings of John Stuart Mill.* Ed. Bernard Wishy. Boston: Beacon Press.
– 1965. *Mill's Ethical Writings.* Ed. J.B. Schneewind. New York: Collier Books.
– 1970. *The Subjection of Women.* In J.S. Mill and Harriet Taylor Mill. *Essays on Sex Equality.* Ed. by Alice Rossi. Chicago: University of Chicago Press.
– 1975. *On Liberty.* Ed. David Spitz, annotated sources and background criticism. New York: W.W. Norton.
– 1991. *On Liberty and Other Essays.* Ed. John Gray. Oxford: Oxford University Press.

III. Books, Articles, and Speeches Used

'The Admission of Women to the Electoral Franchise' (1867), *CW* 28.
'Aphorisms: A Fragment' (1837), *D&D* 1.
'Appendix' (1835), *D&D* 1.
'Armand Carrel' (1837), *D&D*, 1.
August Comte and Positivism (1865), *CW* 10.
'Austin on Jurisprudence' (1863), *CW* 21.
'Austin's Lectures on Jurisprudence' (1832), *CW* 21.
Autobiography, *CW* 1.
'Bain's Psychology,' CW 11.
'Bentham' (1838), *CW* 10.
'Carlyle's French Revolution' (1837), *CW* 20.
'Centralization' (1862), *CW* 19.
Chapters on Socialism (1879), *CW* 5.
'Civilization' (1836), *D&D* 1.
'The Claims of Labour' (1845), *D&D* 2.
'Coleridge,' CW 10.
'Comment on Plato's *Gorgias*' (1834/35), in Mill, 1965.
Considerations on Representative Government (1861), *CW* 19.
'Constraints of Communism' (3 August 1850), *CW* 25.
'Cooperation: Closing Speech' (1825), *CW* 26.
'Cooperation: First Speech' (1825), *CW* 26.
'Cooperation: Intended Speech' (1825), *CW* 26.
'Cooperation: Notes' (1825), *CW* 26.
'Dr. Whewell on Moral Philosophy' (1852), *D&D* 2.
'Editorial Notes to *James Mill's Analysis of the Phenomena of the Human Mind*' (1869), *CW* 31.
'The Education Bill [1]' (25 March 1870), *CW* 29.
'The Education Bill [2]' (4 April 1870), *CW* 29.
'Endowments,' CW 5.
'Essay on Marriage and Divorce' (circa 1831–32), in Mill and Mill, 1970.
An Examination of Sir William Hamilton's Philosophy, *CW* 9.
'A Few Observatons on Mr. Mill' (1833), Appendix D, *CW* 1.
'A Few Words on Non-Intervention' (1859), *CW* 21.
'Grant's Arithmetic for Young Children and Exercises for the Improvement of the Senses' (23 October 1835), *CW* 24.
'Grote's Aristotle' (1873), CW 11.
'Grote's History of Greece [I]' (1846), *CW* 11.
'Grote's History of Greece [II]' (1853), *CW* 11.

'Grote's Plato' (1866), *CW* 11.

'Guizot's Essays and Lectures on History' (1845), *D&D* 2.

'Inaugural Address Delivered to the University of St. Andrews' (1867), *CW* 21.

'Ireland' (1825), *CW* 6.

'Land Tenure Reform' (1871), *CW* 5.

'Leslie on the Land Question' (1870), *CW* 5.

'Maine on Village Communities' (1871), *CW* 30.

'Michelet's History of France' (1844), *D&D* 2.

'Miss Martineau's Summary of Political Economy' (1834), *CW* 4.

'Nature' *CW* 10.

'The Negro Question' (1850), *CW* 21.

'Newman's Political Economy' (1851), *CW* 5.

'On Genius' (1832), *CW* 1.

On Liberty (1859), *CW* 18.

'On Religion and Guardianship' (1846), in Mill, 1959.

'On the Definition of Political Economy and on the Method of Investigation Appropriate to it' (1836), in Mill, 1950.

'On the Liberty of the Press' (1825), in Mill, 1959.

'Perfectibility' (1828), *CW* 26.

'Periodical Literature: Edinburgh Review' (1824), *CW* 1.

Principles of Political Economy (1848–71), CW 2 & 3.

'Sedgwick's Discourse' (1835), *CW* 10.

'A Prophesy' (1838), *D&D* 1.

'Rationale of Representation' (1835), *CW* 18.

'Recent Writers on Reform' (1859), *CW* 19.

'Remark's on Bentham's Philosophy' (1834), *CW* 10.

'Representation of the People' (five speeches, 12 April 1866–31 May 1866), *CW* 28.

'Reorganization of the Reform Party' (1839), *CW* 6.

'The Right and Wrong of State Interference with Corporation and Church Property' (1833), *D&D* 1.

'The Savings of the Middle and Working Classes' (1850), *CW* 5.

The Subjection of Women, *CW*, 21; and Mill and Mill, 1970.

'Spirit of the Age' (1831), *CW* 22.

A System of Logic (1843), *CW* 7 & 8.

'Taine's De L'Intelligence,' *CW* 11.

'Theism' (1874), CW 10.

'Thornton on the Claims of Labour' (1869), *CW* 5.

'Thoughts on Parliamentary Reform' (1859), *CW* 19.

'Thoughts on Poetry and its Varieties' (1833), *D&D* 1.

'De Tocqueville on Democracy in America [I]' (1835), *CW* 18.
'De Tocqueville on Democracy in America [II]' (1840),' *CW* 18.
'The Right of Property in Land' (1873), *CW* 25.
'Use and Abuse of Political Terms' (1832), *CW* 18.
Utilitarianism, CW 10.
'Utility of Religion,' *CW* 10.
'Vindication of the French Revolution of February 1848, in Reply to Lord
    Brougham and Others' (1849), *D&D* 2.
'Women's Suffrage [1]' (18 July 1868),*CW* 29.
'Women's Suffrage [2]' (26 March 1870), *CW* 29.
'Women's Suffrage [3]' (12 January 1871), *CW* 29.
'Writings of Junius Redivivus [I]' (1833), *CW* 1.
'Writings of Junius Redivivus [II]' (1833), *CW* 1.

IV. Mill, with George Grote

'Taylor's Statesman' (1837), *CW* 19.

V. Harriet Taylor Mill, with John Stuart Mill

'Enfranchisement of Women' (1851), in Mill and Mill, 1970; and *D&D* 2.
'Papers on Women's Rights' (1847–1850?), *CW* 21.
'Remarks on Mr. Fitroy's Bill for the More Effectual Prevention of Assaults on
    Women and Children' (1853), *CW* 21.

VI. Harriet Taylor Mill

'Essay on Marriage and Divorce' (circa 1831–32), in Mill and Mill, 1970.

Secondary Sources

Aiken, Henry David. 1962. 'Utilitarianism and Liberty: John Stuart Mill's
    Defense of Utilitarianism.' In Aiken, *Reason and Conduct: New Bearings in
    Moral Philosophy*. New York: Alfred A. Knopf.
Alcaly, Roger. 1997. 'Reinventing the Corporation.' *New York Review of Books* 44
    (10 April).
Anschutz, R.P. 1953. *The Philosophy of John Stuart Mill*. Oxford: Clarendon Press.
Appiah, Kwame Anthony. 1993. *In My Father's House: Africa in the Philosophy of
    Culture*. New York: Oxford University Press.
Arendt, Hannah. 1968. 'What Is Freedom?' In Arendt, *Between Past and Future*,
    enlarged ed. New York: Penguin.

Arneson, Richard. 1979. 'Mill's Doubts about Freedom under Socialism.' In *New Essays on John Stuart Mill and Utilitarianism.* Ed. Wesley E. Cooper, Kai Nielsen, and Steven C. Patten. Guelph: Canadian Association for Publishing in Philosophy.

Asad, Talal. 1993. *Genealogies of Religion: Discipline and Reasons of Power in Christianity and Islam.* Baltimore: Johns Hopkins University Press.

– 1996. 'Comments on Conversion.' In *Conversions to Modernities: The Globalization of Christianity.* Ed. Peter van der Veer. New York: Routledge.

Ashcraft, Richard. 1989. 'Class Conflict and Constitutionalism in J.S. Mill's Thought.' In *Liberalism and the Moral Life.* Ed. Nancy Rosenblum. Cambridge: Cambridge University Press.

Bachrach, Peter, and Aryeh Botwinick. 1992. *Power and Empowerment: A Theory of Participatory Democracy.* Philadelphia: Temple University Press.

Bagdikian, Ben H. 1997. *The Media Monopoly.* 5th ed. Boston: Beacon Press.

Bain, Alexander. 1882. *John Stuart Mill: A Criticism with Personal Recollections.* London: Longmans, Green.

– 1886. *Emotions and the Will* [1859]. New York: D. Appleton.

Basham, A.L. 1959. *The Wonder That Was India.* New York: Grove Press.

Baum, Bruce. 1997. 'Feminism, Liberalism, and Cultural Pluralism: J.S. Mill on Mormon Polygyny.' *Journal of Political Philosophy* 5 (September).

Bauman, Zygmunt. 1988. *Freedom.* Minneapolis: University of Minnesota Press.

Benn, Stanley I. 1975–76. 'Freedom, Autonomy, and the Concept of a Person.' *Proceedings of the Aristotelian Society* 76.

Benson, Paul. 1991. 'Autonomy and Oppressive Socialization.' *Social Theory and Practice* 17 (Fall).

Berelson, Bernard, Paul Lazarsfeld, and William McPhee. 1954. *Voting.* Chicago: University of Chicago Press.

Berger, Fred R. 1984. *Happiness, Justice, and Freedom: The Moral and Political Philosophy of John Stuart Mill.* Berkeley: University of California Press.

– 1985a. 'Paternalism and Autonomy.' In *The Restraint of Liberty.* Vol. 7. *Bowling Green Studies in Applied Philosophy.* Bowling Green, OH.

– 1985b. 'Reply to Professor Skorupski.' *Philosophical Books* 26 (October).

Berlin, Isaiah. 1969a. 'Introduction.' In Berlin, *Four Essays on Liberty.* London: Oxford University Press.

– 1969b. 'John Stuart Mill and the Ends of Life.' In Berlin, *Four Essays on Liberty.*

– 1969c. 'Two Concepts of Liberty.' In Berlin, *Four Essays on Liberty.*

Berlin, Isaiah, and Ramin Jahanbegloo. 1992. 'Philosophy and Life: An Interview with Isaiah Berlin.' *New York Review of Books* 39 (28 May).

Bhabha, Homi K. 1985a. 'Signs Taken for Wonders: Questions of Ambivalence and Authority under a Tree Outside Delhi, May 1817.' *Critical Inquiry* 12 (Autumn).

– 1985b. 'Sly Civility.' *October,* no. 34 (Fall).

Bladen, V.W. 1965. 'Introduction.' in *The Collected Works of J.S. Mill*, vol. 2: *Principles of Political Economy*.

– 1968. 'John Stuart Mill: Economic Contributions.' *International Encyclopedia of the Social Sciences*, vol. 10. New York: Macmillan.

Bloch, Ruth. 1993. 'A Culturalist Critique of Trends in Feminist Theory.' *Contention* 2 (Spring).

Bogen, James, and Daniel M. Farrell. 1978. 'Freedom and Happiness in Mill's Defense of Liberty.' *The Philosophical Quarterly* 28 (October).

Bohman, James. 1997. 'Deliberative Democracy and Effective Social Freedom: Capabilities, Resources, and Opportunities.' In James Bohman and William Rehg (1997).

Bohman, James, and William Rehg, eds. 1997. *Deliberative Democracy: Essays on Reason and Politics*. Cambridge: MIT Press.

Bookchin, Murray. 1990. *Remaking Society: Pathways to a Green Future*. Boston: South End Press.

Bosanquet, Bernard. 1899. *The Philosophical Theory of the State*. London: Macmillan.

Bourdieu, Pierre, and Terry Eagleton. 1992. 'Doxa and Common Life.' *New Left Review* 191 (January/February).

Bowles, Samuel, and Herbert Gintis. 1987. *Democracy and Capitalism: Property, Community, and the Contradictions of Modern Social Thought*. New York: Basic Books.

– 1993a. 'Memo to Clinton: Economics.' *Tikkun* 8 (January/February).

– 1993b. 'A Political and Economic Case for the Democratic Enterprise.' In *The Idea of Democracy*. Ed. David Copp, Jean Hampton, and John E. Roemer. Cambridge: Cambridge University Press.

Bradley, Gerald V. 1991. 'The Constitution and the Erotic Self.' *First Things*, no. 16 (October).

Brady, Alexander. 1977. 'Introduction.' *Collected Works of John Stuart Mill*. Vol. 18. *Essays on Politics and Society*.

Breytenbach, Breyten. 1986. *End Papers: Essays, Letters, Articles of Faith, Workbook Notes*. New York: Farrar, Straus & Giroux.

Briggs, Asa. 1965. *The Making of Modern England, 1784–1867*. New York: Harper & Row.

Brink, David O. 1992. 'Mill's Deliberative Utilitarianism.' *Philosophy and Public Affairs* 21 (Winter).

Britton, Karl. 1989. 'Mill, John Stuart.' In *The Concise Encyclopedia of Western Philosophy and Philosophers*. New revised ed. Ed. J.O. Urmson and Jonathan Ree. London: Unwin Hyman.

Brown, D.G. 1978. 'Mill on Harm to Others' Interests.' *Political Studies* 26 (September).

Brown, Robert. 1984. 'J.S. Mill: The Structure of Social Science.' In Brown, *The Nature of Social Laws. Machiavelli to Mill.* Cambridge: Cambridge University Press.

Burke, Edmund. 1973 [1791]. *Reflections on the Revolution in France*, with Thomas Paine's *The Rights of Man.* New York: Anchor Books.

Burns, J.H. 1968. 'J.S. Mill and Democracy, 1829–61.' In *Mill: A Collection of Critical Essays.* Ed. J.B. Schneewind. Garden City: Anchor Books.

– 1976. 'The Light of Reason: Philosophical History in the Two Mills.' In *James and John Stuart Mill: Papers of the Centenary Conference.* Ed. John M. Robson and Michael Laine. Toronto: University of Toronto Press.

Burnstein, Daniel. 1992. '"The Very Culture of Feelings": Poetry and Poets in Mill's Moral Philosophy.' *Utilitas* 4 (May).

Caillé, Alain. 1992. 'Utilitarianism and Anti-Utilitarianism.' *Thesis Eleven*, no. 33.

Capaldi, Nicolas. 1973. 'Mill''s Forgotten Science of Ethology.' *Social Theory and Practice* 2 (Fall).

Carlisle, Janice. 1991. *John Stuart Mill and the Writing of Character.* Athens: University of Georgia Press.

Carter, Stephen L. 1993. 'Stuck with a Satanist? Religious Liberty in a Regulated Society.' *Commonweal* 120 (13 August).

Chomsky, Noam. 1973. *For Reasons of State.* New York: Vintage Books.

Chopra, Y.N. 1994. 'Mill's Principle of Liberty.' *Philosophy* 69 (October).

Christman, John. 1988. 'Constructing the Inner Citadel: Recent Work on Autonomy.' *Ethics* 99 (October).

– 1989. 'Introduction.' In *The Inner Citadel: Essays on Individual Autonomy.* Ed. Christman. New York: Oxford University Press.

Claeys, Gregory. 1987. 'Justice, Independence, and Industrial Democracy: The Development of John Stuart Mill's Views on Socialism.' *Journal of Politics* 49 (February).

Clifford, James. 1992. 'Travelling Cultures.' In *Cultural Studies.* Ed. Lawrence Grossberg, Cary Nelson, and Paula Treicher. New York: Routledge.

Cohen, Jean L. 1991. 'About Women and Rights.' *Dissent* 38 (Summer).

Collini, Stephan, Donald Winch, and John Burrow. 1983. 'The Tendency of Things: John Stuart Mill and Philosophic Method.' In Collini, Winch, and Burrow, *The Noble Science of Politics: A Study in Nineteenth Century Intellectual History.* Cambridge: Cambridge University Press.

Connolly, William E. 1983. *The Terms of Political Discourse.* 2nd ed. Princeton: Princeton University Press.

– 1987. 'Modern Authority and Ambiguity.' In *Nomos.* Vol. 29. *Authority Revisited.* Ed. J. Roland Pennock and John W. Chapman. New York: New York University Press.

Constant, Benjamin. 1989 [1819]. 'On the Liberty of the Ancients as Compared with the Liberty of the Moderns.' In Constant, *Political Writings*. Trans. and ed. Biancamaria Fontana. Cambridge: Cambridge University Press.

Coole, Diana H. 1988. 'J.S. Mill: Political Economist, Utilitarian and Feminist.' In Coole, *Women in Political Thought: From Ancient Misogyny to Contemporary Feminism*. Sussex: Wheatsheaf Books.

– 1993. 'Constructing and Deconstructing Liberty: A Feminist and Poststructuralist Analysis.' *Political Studies* 41 (March).

Cooper, Wesley E., Kai Nielsen, and Steven C. Patten, eds. 1979. *New Essays on John Stuart Mill and Utilitarianism*. Guelph: Canadian Association for Publishing in Philosophy.

Cornell, Drucilla. 1991. 'Sex-Discrimination Law and Equivalent Rights.' *Dissent* 38 (Summer).

Cott, Nancy F., ed. 1972. *Roots of Bitterness: Documents of the Social History of American Women*. New York: E.P. Dutton.

Cowling, Maurice. 1975. 'The Illiberalism of John Stuart Mill.' In Mill, 1975.

Cranston, Maurice. 1987. 'John Stuart Mill and Liberty.' *Wilson Quarterly* 11 (Winter).

Crimmins, James E. 1990. *Secular Utilitarianism: Social Science and the Critique of Religion in the Thought of Jeremy Bentham*. New York: Oxford University Press.

Dahl, Robert A. 1985. *A Preface to Economic Democracy*. Berkeley: University of California Press.

– 1989. *Democracy and Its Critics*. New Haven: Yale University Press.

– 1991. *Modern Political Analysis*. 5th ed. Englewood Cliffs, NJ: Prentice Hall.

Delmar, Rosalind. 1986. 'What Is Feminism?' In *What is Feminism? A Re-Examination*. Ed. Juliet Mitchell and Ann Oakley. New York: Pantheon Books.

Devlin, Patrick. 1965. *The Enforcement of Morals*. Oxford: Oxford University Press.

Dewey, John. 1946. 'Liberty and Social Control.' In Dewey, *Problems of Men*. New York: Philosophical Library.

– 1954 [1927]. *The Public and its Problems*. Chicago: The Swallow Press.

– 1966 [1916]. *Democracy and Education: An Introduction to the Philosophy of Education*. New York: Free Press.

– 1980 [1935]. *Liberalism and Social Action*. New York: Perigee Books.

Dilke, Charles W. 1897. 'John Stuart Mill, 1869–1873.' *Cosmopolis* 5 (March).

Dirks, Nicholas B., Geoff Eley, and Sherry Ortner. 1994. 'Introduction.' In *Culture/Power/History: A Reader in Contemporary Social Theory*. Ed. Dirks, Eley, and Ortner. Princeton: Princeton University Press.

Di Stefano, Christine. 1991. 'John Stuart Mill: The Heart of Liberalism.' In Di

Stephano, *Configurations of Masculinity: A Feminist Perspective on Modern Political Theory*. Ithaca: Cornell University Press.

Donald, James. 1992. 'Dewey-eyed Optimism: The Possibility of Democratic Education.' *New Left Review* 192 (March/April).

Donner, Wendy. 1987. 'Mill on Liberty of Self-Development.' *Dialogue* 26 (Summer).

– 1991. *The Liberal Self: John Stuart Mill's Moral Philosophy*. Ithaca: Cornell University Press.

Duncan, Graeme. 1969. 'John Stuart Mill and Democracy.' *Politics* 4 (May).

Dunn, John. 1989. '"Bright Enough for All Our Purposes": John Locke's Conception of a Civilized Society.' *Notes and Records of the Royal Society of London* 43.

– 1990. 'Liberty as a Substantive Value.' In Dunn, *Interpreting Political Responsibility*. Princeton: Princeton University Press.

– 1993a. 'Conclusion.' In *Democracy: The Unfinished Journey, 508 BC to AD 1993*. Ed. Dunn. Oxford: Oxford University Press.

– 1993b. *Western Political Thought in the Face of the Future*. Cambridge: Cambridge University Press.

Dworkin, Gerald. 1988. *The Theory and Practice of Autonomy*. Cambridge: Cambridge University Press.

Dworkin, Ronald. 1977. *Taking Rights Seriously*. Cambridge: Harvard University Press.

– 1996. 'The Curse of American Politics.' *New York Review of Books* 43 (17 October).

Eisenach, Eldon J. 1989. 'Self-Reform as Political Reform in the Writings of John Stuart Mill.' *Utilitas* 1 (November).

Elshtain, Jean Bethke. 1991. 'Feminism.' In *The Blackwell Encyclopedia of Political Thought*. Ed. David Miller, with Janet Coleman, William Connolly, and Alan Ryan. Oxford: Basil Blackwell.

Elster, Jon. 1983. *Sour Grapes*. Cambridge: Cambridge University Press.

Elster, Jon., and Karl Ove Moene, eds. 1989. *Alternatives to Capitalism*. Cambridge: Cambridge University Press.

Evans, Michael. 1989. 'John Stuart Mill and Karl Marx: Some Problems and Perspectives.' *History of Political Economy* 21 (Summer).

Farr, James. 1993. 'Framing Democratic Discussion.' In *Reconsidering the Democratic Public*. Ed. George E. Marcus and Russell L. Hanson. University Park: Pennsylvania State University Press.

Feuer, L.S. 1976. 'John Stuart Mill as a Sociologist: The Unwritten Ethology.' In *James and John Stuart Mill: Papers of the Centenary Conference*. Ed. John M. Robson and Michael Laine. Toronto: University of Toronto Press.

Fish, Stanley. 1989. 'Critical Self-Consciousness.' In Fish, *Doing What Comes Naturally: Change, Rhetoric, and the Practise of Theory in Literary and Legal Studies.* Durham: Duke University Press.

– 1996. 'Why We Can't All Get Along.' *First Things,* no. 60 (February).

Flathman, Richard E. , ed. 1973. *Concepts in Social and Political Philosophy.* New York: Macmillan.

– 1987a. 'Convention, Contractarianism, and Freedom.' *Ethics* 98 (October).

– 1987b. *The Philosophy and Politics of Freedom.* Chicago: University of Chicago Press.

Folbre, Nancy. 1994. *Who Cares for the Kids? Gender and the Structures of Constraint.* London. Routledge.

Foot, Phillippa. 1966. 'Free Will as Involving Determinism.' In *Free Will and Determinism.* Ed. Bernard Berofski. New York: Harper and Row.

Foucault, Michel. 1979. *Discipline and Punish: The Birth of the Prison.* Trans. Alan Sheridan. New York: Vintage Books.

– 1980a. *The History of Sexuality.* Vol. 1. Trans. Robert Hurley. New York: Vintage Books.

– 1980b. *Power/Knowledge: Selected Interviews and Other Writings.* Ed. Colin Gordon. New York: Pantheon Books.

– 1983. 'The Subject and Power.' In Herbert Dreyfus and Paul Rabinow, *Michel Foucault: Beyond Structuralism and Hermeneutics,* 2nd ed. Chicago: University of Chicago Press.

– 1986. *The Uses of Pleasure.* Trans. Robert Hurley. New York: Vintage Books.

– 1988. 'Sexual Choice, Sexual Act: An Interview.' In Michel Foucault, *Politics, Philosophy, and Culture: Interviews and Other Writings, 1977–1984.* Ed. Lawrence D. Kritzman. New York: Routledge.

Frankfurt, Harry G. 1971. 'Freedom of the Will and the Concept of a Person.' *Journal of Philosophy* 68 (14 January).

Fredman, L.E., and B.L.J. Gordon. 1967. 'John Stuart Mill and Socialism.' *The Mill News Letter* 3 (Fall).

Friedman, Milton. 1962. *Capitalism and Freedom.* Chicago: University of Chicago Press.

Friedman, Richard B. 1966. 'A New Exploration of Mill's Essay *On Liberty.' Political Studies* 14 (October).

– 1968. 'An Introduction to Mill's Theory of Authority.' In *Mill: A Collection of Critical Essays.* Ed. J.B. Schneewind. Garden City, NY: Anchor Books.

– 1973. 'On the Concept of Authority in Political Philosophy.' In Flathman, 1973.

– 1984. Review of John Gray, *Mill on Liberty: A Defense. The Mill News Letter* 19 (Winter).

– 1987. 'Authority.' In *The Blackwell Encyclopedia of Political Thought.* Ed. David

Miller, Janet Coleman, William Connolly, and Alan Ryan. Oxford: Basil Blackwell.

Friedrich, Carl Joachim. 1963. 'Independence and Participation: Dimensions of Political Freedom.' In Friedrich, *Man and His Government.* New York: McGraw-Hill.

Galeotti, Anna Elisabetta. 1993. 'Citizenship and Equality: The Place for Toleration.' *Political Theory* 21 (November).

Galston, William. 1995. 'Two Concepts of Liberalism.' *Ethics* 105 (April).

Garforth, F.W. 1979. *John Stuart Mill's Theory of Education.* New York: Barnes and Noble.

– 1980. *Educative Democracy: John Stuart Mill on Education and Society.* Oxford: Oxford University Press.

Garnham, Nicholas. 1992. 'The Media and the Public Sphere.' In *Habermas and the Public Sphere.* Ed. Craig Calhoun. Cambridge: MIT Press.

Gaventa, John. 1980. *Power and Powerless: Quiescence and Rebellion in an Appalachian Valley.* Urbana: University of Illinois Press.

Gert, Bernard. 1972. 'Coercion and Freedom.' In *Nomos.* Vol. 14: *Coercion.* Ed. J.R. Pennock and J.W. Chapman. Chicago: Aldine-Atherton.

Gibbons, John. 1990. 'J.S. Mill, Liberalism, and Progress.' In *Victorian Liberalism: Nineteenth Century Political Thought and Practice.* Ed. Richard Bellamy. London: Routledge.

Gibbs, Benjamin. 1976. *Freedom and Liberation.* London: Chatto and Windus, for Sussex University Press.

Giddens, Anthony. 1990. 'Modernity and Utopia.' *New Statesman and Society* (2 November).

Goldberg, David Theo. 1993. 'Modernity, Race, and Morality.' *Cultural Critique,* no. 24 (Spring).

Goldberg, Jonathan, ed. 1994. *Reclaiming Sodom.* New York: Routledge.

Goldinger, Milton. 1976. 'Mill's Attack on Moral Conservatism.' *Midwest Studies in Philosophy* 1.

Gould, Carol. 1988. *Rethinking Democracy: Freedom and Cooperation in Politics, Economy, and Society.* New York: Cambridge University Press.

Gray, John. 1980. 'On Negative and Positive Liberty.' *Political Studies* 28 (December), rpt. in Gray, 1989b.

– 1983. *Mill on Liberty: A Defense.* London: Routledge and Kegan Paul.

– 1986. *Liberalism.* Minneapolis: University of Minnesota Press.

– 1989a. 'Indirect Utility and Fundamental Rights.' In Gray, 1989b.

– 1989b. *Liberalisms: Essays in Political Philosophy.* London: Routledge.

– 1989c. 'Mill's and Other Liberalisms.' In Gray, 1989b.

– 1991. 'Introduction.' In John Stuart Mill, *On Liberty and Other Essays.* Ed. John Gray. Oxford: Oxford University Press.

– 1996. 'Postscript.' In Gray, *Mill on Liberty: A Defense*, 2nd ed. London: Routledge.

Gray, John, and G.W. Smith, eds. 1991. *J.S. Mill 'On Liberty' in Focus*. London: Routledge.

Green, Leslie. 1995. 'Internal Minorities and Their Rights.' In *The Rights of Minority Cultures*. Ed. Will Kymlicka. Oxford: Oxford University Press.

Green, Philip. 1992. 'A Few Kind Words for Liberalism.' *The Nation* 255 (28 September).

Green, Thomas Hill. 1962 [1880]. 'Liberal Legislation and Freedom of Contract'. In *Communism, Fascism, and Democracy*. Ed. Carl Cohen. New York: Random House.

Grewal, Indepral, and Caren Kaplan. 1994. 'Introduction: Transnational Feminist Practices and the Question of Postmodernity.' In *Scattered Hegemonies*. Ed. Grewal and Kaplan. Minneapolis: University of Minnesota Press.

Gutmann, Amy. 1980. *Liberal Equality*. Cambridge: Cambridge University Press.

– 1995. 'Civic Education and Social Diversity.' *Ethics* 105 (April).

Habermas, Jürgen. 1991. *The Structural Transformation of the Public Sphere*. Trans. Thomas Burger, with the assistance of Frederick Lawrence. Cambridge: MIT Press.

Hall, Catherine. 1992. 'Private Persons versus Public Someones: Class, Gender, and Politics in England, 1780–1850.' In Hall, *White, Male, and Middle Class: Essays in Feminism and History*. Cambridge: Cambridge University Press.

Halliday, R.J. 1968. 'Some Recent Interpretations of John Stuart Mill.' *Philosophy* 43 (January).

Hamburger, Joseph. 1982. 'Introduction.' In *Collected Works of John Stuart Mill*. Vol. 6: *Essays on England, Ireland, and the Empire*. Toronto: University of Toronto Press.

– 1991. 'Religion and *On Liberty*.' In *A Cultivated Mind: Essays on J.S. Mill Presented to John M. Robson*. Toronto: University of Toronto Press.

Hampsher-Monk, Ian. 1992. *A History of Modern Political Thought: Major Political Thinkers from Hobbes to Marx*. Oxford: Blackwell.

Harris, Abram L. 1958. *Economics and Social Reform*. New York: Harper and Brothers.

Hart, H.L.A. 1979. 'Between Utility and Rights.' In *The Idea of Freedom*. Ed. Alan Ryan. Oxford: Oxford University Press.

– 1982. 'Natural Rights: Bentham and John Stuart Mill.' In Hart, *Essays on Bentham: Studies in Jurisprudence and Political Theory*. Oxford: Clarendon Press.

Hartsock, Nancy C.M. 1985. *Money, Sex, and Power: Toward a Feminist Historical Materialism*, Boston: Northeastern University Press.

Hawley, John Stratton, ed. 1994. *Sati, the Blessing and the Curse: The Burning of Wives in India*. New York: Oxford University Press.

Hayek, Friedrich A. 1960. *The Constitution of Liberty.* Chicago: University of Chicago Press.

Heilbroner, Robert. 1993. 'Does Socialism Have a Future?' *The Nation* 257 (27 September).

Held, David. 1989. *Political Theory and the Modern State.* Stanford: Stanford University Press.

– 1991. 'Editor's Introduction.' In *Political Theory Today.* Ed. David Held. Stanford: Stanford University Press.

– 1993. 'Democracy: From City-States to Cosmopolitan Order?' In *Prospects for Democracy: North, South, East, West.* Ed. David Held. Stanford: Stanford University Press.

Herbert, Christopher. 1991. *Culture and Anomie: Ethnographic Imagination in the Nineteenth Century.* Chicago: University of Chicago Press.

Hexter, J.H. 1983. 'The Birth of Modern Freedom.' *Times Literary Supplement* (21 January).

Himmelfarb, Gertrude. 1963. 'Introduction.' In J.S. Mill, *Essays on Politics and Culture.* Ed. Himmelfarb. Garden City, NY: Anchor Books.

– 1974. 'Introduction.' In John Stuart Mill, *On Liberty.* Ed. Himmelfarb. Hammondsworth: Penguin Books.

– 1993. 'Liberty: "One Very Simple Principle"?' *American Scholar* 62 (Autumn).

Hirsch, Gordon D. 1975. 'Organic Imagery and the Psychology of Mill's "On Liberty".' *The Mill News Letter* 10, no. 2.

Hirschmann, Nancy J. 1996. 'Towards a Feminist Theory of Freedom.' *Political Theory* 24 (February).

Hoag, Robert W. 1986. 'Happiness and Freedom: Recent Work on John Stuart Mill.' *Philosophy and Public Affairs* 15 (Spring).

– 1987. 'Mill's Conception of Happiness as an Inclusive End.' *Journal of the History of Philosophy* 25 (July).

Hobhouse, Leonard. T. 1956 [1911]. 'Liberalism.' In *The Liberal Tradition: From Fox to Keynes.* Ed. Alan Bullock and Maurice Shock. Oxford: Oxford University Press.

Hobbes, Thomas. 1968. *Leviathan.* Ed. and intro. By C.B. Macpherson. Harmondsworth: Penguin Books.

Hollander, Samuel. 1985. *The Economics of John Stuart Mill.* Vol. 2. Toronto: University of Toronto Press.

Hollis, Martin. 1972. 'J.S. Mill's Political Philosophy of Mind.' *Philosophy* 47 (October).

Holloway, Harry. 1961. 'Mill's Liberty, 1859–1959.' *Ethics* 71 (January).

Honderich, Ted. 1982. '"On Liberty" and Morality-dependent Harms.' *Political Studies* (30).

Hornblower, Simon. 1993. 'Creation and Development of Democratic Institutions in Ancient Greece.' In *Democracy: The Unfinished Journey, 508 BC to AD 1993.* Ed. John Dunn. Oxford: Oxford University Press.

Howes, John. 1986. 'Mill on Women and Human Development.' *Australian Journal of Philosophy.* Supplement to vol. 64 (June).

Hoy, David Couzens. 1981. 'Power, Repression, Progress: Foucault, Lukes, and the Frankfurt School.' *TriQuarterly*, no. 52 (Fall).

Hughes, William H. 1972. 'More on Mill's Socialism.' *The Mill News Letter* 7 (Spring).

Huntington, Samuel. 1997. 'The Democratic Distemper.' In *Ideological Voices: An Anthology in Modern Political Ideas.* Ed. Paul Schumaker, Dwight C. Kiel, and Thomas W. Heilke. New York: McGraw-Hill.

Hutton, R.H. 1975 [1859]. 'Mill on Liberty.' In Mill, 1975.

Isaac, Jeffrey. 1987. 'Beyond the Three Faces of Power.' *Polity* 20 (Fall).

– 1996. 'The Poverty of Progressivism: Thoughts on American Democracy.' *Dissent* 43 (Fall).

Jones, Peter. 1994. 'Bearing the Consequences of Belief.' *Journal of Political Philosophy* 2 (March).

Kant, Immanuel. 1959 [1785]. *Foundations of the Metaphysics of Morals and What Is Enlightenment?* Trans. and intro. by Lewis White Beck. Indianapolis: Bobbs-Merrill.

Kaufman, Debra Renee. 1994. 'Paradoxical Politics: Gender Politics among Newly Orthodox Jewish Women in the United States.' In *Identity Politics: Cultural Reassertions and Feminisms in International Perspective.* Ed. Valentine M. Moghadam. Boulder, CO: Westview Press.

Kinder, Donald R., and Don Herzog. 1993. 'Democratic Discussion.' In *Reconsidering the Democratic Public.* Ed. George E. Marcus and Russell L. Hanson. University Park: Pennsylvania State University Press.

Kinzer, Bruce. 1988. 'Introduction.' In *Collected Works of John Stuart Mill.* Vol. 28: *Public and Parliamentary Speeches.* Toronto: University of Toronto Press.

Knight, Jack, and James Johnson. 1997. 'What Sort of Equality Does Deliberative Democracy Require?' In *Deliberative Democracy: Essays on Reason and Politics.* Eds. James Bohman and William Rehg. Cambridge: MIT Press.

Krouse, Richard W. 1982. 'Two Concepts of Representation: James and John Stuart Mill.' *Journal of Politics* 44 (May).

Krouse, Richard, and Michael S. McPherson. 1988. 'The Logic of Liberal Equality: John Stuart Mill and the Origins of the Political Theory of the Welfare State.' In *Responsibility, Rights, and Welfare: The Theory of the Welfare State.* Ed. J. Donald Moon. Boulder, CO: Westview Press.

Kukathus, Chandran. 1995. 'Are There Any Cultural Rights?' In *The Rights of Minority Cultures.* Ed. Will Kymlicka. Oxford: Oxford University Press.

Kurer, Oscar. 1989a. 'John Stuart Mill on Government Intervention.' *History of Political Thought* 10 (Autumn).

– 1989b. 'John Stuart Mill on Democratic Representation and Centralization.' *Utilitas* 1 (November).

Kuttner, Robert. 1992. 'Liberalism, Socialism, and Democracy.' *American Prospect*, no. 9 (Spring).

Kymlcka, Will. 1995. 'Introduction.' In Kymlicka, ed., *The Rights of Minority Cultures*. Oxford: Oxford University Press.

– 1996. *Multicultural Citizenship*. Oxford: Clarendon Press.

Larmore, Charles. 1990. 'Political Liberalism.' *Political Theory* 18 (August).

La Selva, Samuel. 1987. 'Selling Oneself into Slavery: Mill and Paternalism.' *Political Studies* 35 (June).

Lawless, Andrew. 1980. 'The Ontology of Discipline: From Bentham to Mill.' *Canadian Journal of Political and Social Theory* 4, no. 3.

Lawson, John, and Harold Silver. 1973. *A Social History of English Education*. London: Methuen.

Lee, Dorothy. 1959. *Freedom and Culture*. Prentice-Hall.

Levi, Albert William. 1975. 'The Value of Freedom: Mill's Liberty (1859–69).' In Mill, 1975.

Levy, David. 1980. 'Libertarian Communists, Malthusians and J.S. Mill Who Is Both.' *The Mill News Letter* 15 (Winter).

Levy, Michael B. Ed., 1988. *Political Thought in America: An Anthology*. 2nd ed. Chicago: Dorsey Press.

Lichtman, Richard. 1963. 'The Surface and Substance of Mill's Defense of Freedom.' *Social Research* 30 (Winter).

Lilla, Mark. 1998. 'A Tale of Two Reactions.' *New York Review of Books* 45 (14 May).

Lindblom, Charles. 1977. *Politics and Markets: The World's Political Economic Systems*. New York: Basic Books.

Lindsay, A.D. 1950. 'Introduction.' In J.S. Mill, *Utilitarianism, Liberty, and Representative Government*. New York: E.P. Dutton.

Loesberg, Jonathan. 1986. 'The Philosophic Context of Mill's Autobiography.' In Loesburg, *Fictions of Consciousness: Mill, Newman, and the Reading of Victorian Prose*. New Brunswick: Rutgers University Press.

Long, Douglas G. 1977. 'Appendix: Bentham and J.S. Mill on Liberty.' In *Bentham on Liberty: Jeremy Bentham's Idea of Liberty in Relation to His Utilitarianism*. Toronto: University of Toronto Press.

Lukes, Steven. 1973. *Individualism*. Oxford: Basil Blackwell.

– 1974. *Power: A Radical View*. London: Macmillan.

– 1986. 'Introduction.' In *Power*. Ed. Steven Lukes. New York: New York University Press.

– 1987. 'Perspectives on Authority.' In *Nomos*. Vol. 29. *Authority Revisited*. Ed. J. Roland Pennock and John W. Chapman. New York: New York University Press.

– 1991. 'Equality and Liberty: Must They Conflict?' In *Political Theory Today*. Ed. David Held. Stanford: Stanford University Press.

Lyons, David. 1976. 'Mill's Theory of Morality.' *Nous* 10 (May).

– 1979. 'Mill's Theory of Justice.' In *Values and Morals*. Ed. A.I. Goldman and J. Kim. Dordrecht: D. Reidel Publishing.

– 1982a. 'Benevolence and Justice in Mill.' In *The Limits of Utilitarianism*. Ed. Harlan B. Miller and William H. Williams. Minneapolis: University of Minnesota Press.

– 1982b. 'Utility and Rights.' In *Nomos*. Vol. 24. *Ethics, Economics, and the Law*. Ed. J. Roland Pennock and John W. Chapman. New York: New York University Press.

Lyotard, Jean-François. 1984. *The Postmodern Condition: A Report on Knowledge*. Trans. Geoff Bennington and Brian Massumi. Minneapolis: University of Minnesota Press.

MacCallum, Gerald C. 1973. 'Negative and Positive Freedom.' In Flathman, 1973.

Macedo, Stephen. 1995. 'Liberal Civic Education and Religious Fundamentalism: The Case of God v. John Rawls.' *Ethnics* 105 (April).

MacIntyre, Alasdair. 1987. 'Relativism, Power and Philosophy.' In *After Philosophy: End of Transformation?* Ed. Kenneth Baynes, James Bohman, and Thomas McCarthy. Cambridge: MIT Press.

Mackie, Vera. 1998. 'Freedom and the Family: Gendering Meiji Political Thought.' In *Asian Freedom: The Idea of Freedom in East and Southeast Asia*. Ed. David Kelly and Anthony Reid. Cambridge: Cambridge University Press.

MacKinnon, Catherine A. 1989. 'Sex Equality: On Difference and Domination.' In MacKinnon, *Toward a Feminist Theory of the State*. Cambridge: Harvard University Press.

Macpherson, C.B. 1973. *Democratic Theory: Essays in Retrieval*. Oxford: Oxford University Press.

– 1977. *The Life and Times of Liberal Democracy*. Oxford: Oxford University Press.

McChesney, Robert W. 1997. *Corporate Media and the Threat to Democracy*. New York: Seven Stories Press.

McCloskey, H.J. 1963. 'Mill's Liberalism.' *Philosophical Quarterly* 13 (April).

– 1986. 'Mill's Liberalism.' In *Political Thinkers*. Ed. David Muschamp. New York: St Martin's Press.

McPherson, Michael. 1982. 'Mill's Moral Theory and the Problem of Preference Change.' *Ethics* 92 (January).

Magid, Henry. 1965. 'Introduction.' In J.S. Mill, *On the Logic of the Moral Sciences.* Indianapolis: Bobbs-Merrill.

Majeed, J. 1990. 'James Mill's "The History of British India" and Utilitarianism as a Rhetoric of Reform.' *Modern Asian Studies* 24 (May).

Mandelbaum, Maurice. 1971. 'Man as a Progressive Being.' In Mandelbaum, *History, Man, and Reason: A Study in Nineteenth-Century Thought.* Baltimore: Johns Hopkins University Press.

Marx, Karl. 1974 [1871]. *The Civil War in France.* In Marx, *The First International and After: Political Writings.* Vol. 3. 1864–1883. Ed. and intro. by David Fernbach. New York: Vintage Books.

– 1978a [1844]. 'Contribution to the Critique of Hegel's *Philosophy of Right:* Introduction.' In *The Marx–Engels Reader.* 2nd ed. Ed. Robert C. Tucker. New York: W. W. Norton.

– 1978b [1848]. 'Manifesto of the Communist Party.' In *The Marx–Engels Reader.* 2nd ed. Ed. Robert C. Tucker. New York: W.W. Norton.

Mathieu, Nicole-Claude. 1990. 'When Yielding Is Not Consenting: Material and Psychic Determinants of Women's Consciousness and Some of Their Interpretations in Ethnology' (Part 2). *Feminist Issues* 10 (Spring).

Mayer, David Y. 1968. 'John Stuart Mill and Classical Democracy.' *Politics* 3 (May).

Mehta, Uday S. 1990. 'Liberal Strategies of Exclusion.' *Politics and Society* 18 (December).

Mendus, Susan. 1986/87. 'Liberty and Autonomy.' *Proceedings of the Aristotelian Society* 37.

– 1989a. 'The Marriage of True Minds: The Ideal of Marriage in the Philosophy of John Stuart Mill.' In *Sexuality and Subordination: Interdisciplinary Studies of Gender in the Nineteenth Century.* Ed. Susan Mendus and Jane Rendall. London: Routledge.

– 1989b. 'To Have and to Hold: Liberalism and the Marriage Contract.' In *Liberalism and Recent Legal and Social Philosophy.* Ed. Richard Bellamy. Stuttgart: Franz Breiner Verlag Wiesbaden GMBH.

– 1993. 'Losing the Faith: Feminism and Democracy.' In *Democracy: The Unfinished Journey, 508 BC to AD 1993.* Ed. John Dunn. Oxford: Oxford University Press.

– 1994. 'John Stuart Mill and Harriet Taylor on Women and Marriage.' *Utilitas* 6 (November).

Messick, Richard. 1996. 'The World Survey of Economic Freedom.' *Freedom Review* 27.

Meyers, Diana T. 1992. 'Personal Autonomy or the Deconstructed Subject? A Reply to Hekman.' *Hypatia* 7 (Winter).

Miller, David. 1989. '"Autonomous" v. "Autarchic" Persons.' *Government and Opposition* 24 (Spring).

Miller, Mark Crispin. 1996. 'Free the Media.' *The Nation* 262 (3 June).

Minow, Martha. 1990a. *Making All the Difference: Inclusion, Exclusion, and American Law.* Ithaca: Cornell University Press.

– 1990b. 'Putting Up and Putting Down: Tolerance Reconstructed.' In *Comparative Constitutional Federalism: Europe and America.* Ed. Mark Tushnet. New York: Greenwood Press.

Mitchell, Basil. 1970. *Law, Morality, and Religion in a Secular Society.* London: Oxford University Press.

Mohanty, Chandra Talpade. 1991. 'Under Western Eyes: Feminist Scholarship and Colonial Discourse.' In *Third World Women and the Politics of Feminism.* Ed. Mohanty, Ann Russo, and Lourdes Torres. Bloomington: Indiana University Press.

Moir, Martin. 1990. 'Introduction.' In J.S. Mill, *CW*, 30: *Writings on India.* Toronto: University of Toronto Press.

Morley, John. 1873. 'Mr. Mill's Doctrine of Liberty.' *Fortnightly Review* 20 (August).

Mouffe, Chantal. 1988. 'Radical Democracy: Modern or Postmodern?' In *Universal Abandon? The Politics of Postmodernism.* Ed. Andrew Ross. Minneapolis: University of Minnesota Press.

Nedelsky, Jennifer. 1989. 'Reconceiving Autonomy: Sources, Thoughts, and Possibilities.' *Yale Journal of Law and Feminism* 1 (Spring).

Nicholson, Peter. 1998. 'The Reception and Early Reputation of Mill's Political Thought.' In *Cambridge Companion to John Stuart Mill.* Ed. John Skorupski. Cambridge: Cambridge University Press.

Nickel, James. 1994. 'The Value of Cultural Belonging.' *Dialogue* 33 (Fall).

Norman, Richard. 1987. *Free and Equal: A Philosophical Examination of Political Values.* Oxford: Oxford University Press.

Nove, Alec. 1985. 'Feasible Socialism? Some Social-Political Assumptions.' *Dissent* 32 (Summer).

– 1987. 'Socialism.' In *The New Palgrave: A Dictionary of Economics*, Vol. 4. Ed. John Eatwell et al. London:

Nozick, Robert. 1974. *Anarchy, State, and Utopia.* New York: Basic Books.

Oakeshott, Michael, 1991. 'The Political Economy of Freedom.' In Michael Oakeshott, *Rationalism in Politics and Other Essays.* New and expanded edition. Foreward by Timothy Fuller. Indianapolis: Liberty Press.

Okin, Susan Moller. 1979. *Women in Western Political Thought.* Princeton: Princeton University Press.

– 1991. 'Gender, the Public and the Private.' In *Political Theory Today.* Ed. David Held. Stanford: Stanford University Press.

Ong, Aihwa. 1988. 'Colonialism and Modernity: Feminist Re-presentations of Women in Non-Western Societies.' *Inscriptions*, nos. 3/4.

Oswald, Donald J. 1990. 'J.S. Mill's *a priori* Deductive Methodology: A Case Study in Post-Modern Philosophy of Science.' *Review of Social Economy* 48 (Summer).

Packe, Michael St John. 1954. *The Life of John Stuart Mill.* New York: Macmillan.

Page, Benjamin I. 1996. 'The Mass Media as Political Actors.' *PS: Political Science and Politics* 29 (March).

Parekh, Bhikhu. 1994. 'Superior People: The Narrowness of Liberalism from Mill to Rawls.' *Times Literary Supplement* (25 February).

– 1995. 'Liberalism and Colonialism: A Critique of Locke and Mill.' In *The Colonization of Imagination: Culture, Knowledge and Power.* Ed. Jan Nederveen Pieterse and Bhikhu Parekh. London: Zed Books.

Parry, Geraint. 1994. 'Making Democrats: Democracy and Education.' In *Democracy and Democratization.* Ed. Geraint Parry and Michael Moran. London: Routledge.

Pateman, Carole. 1970. *Participation and Democratic Theory.* Cambridge: Cambridge University Press.

– 1983. 'Feminism and Democracy.' In *Democratic Theory and Practice.* Ed. Graeme Duncan. Cambridge: Cambridge University Press.

– 1984. 'The Shame of the Marriage Contract.' In *Women's Views of the Political World of Men.* Ed. Judith H. Stiehm. Dobbs Ferry, NY: Transnational Publishers.

Pateman, Trevor. 1982. 'Liberty, Authority and the Negative Dialectics of J.S. Mill.' *Radical Philosophy*, no. 32 (Autumn).

Patterson, Orlando. 1991. *Freedom.* Vol. 1: *Freedom in the Making of Western Culture.* New York: Basic Books.

Patton, Paul. 1989. 'Taylor and Foucault on Power and Freedom.' *Political Studies* 37 (June).

Pelczynski, Zbigniew, and John Gray, eds. 1984. *Conceptions of Liberty in Political Philosophy.* New York: St Martin's Press.

Phillips, Anne. 1991. *Engendering Democracy.* University Park: Pennsylvania State University Press.

– 1997. 'Sexual Equality and Socialism.' *Dissent* 44 (Summer).

Pitkin, Hanna Fenichel. 1972. *Wittgenstein and Justice.* Berkeley: University of California Press.

– 1988. 'Are Freedom and Liberty Twins?' *Political Theory* 16 (November).

Plamenatz, John. 1960. 'In What Sense Is Freedom a Western Idea?' *Current Law and Social Problems.* Vol. 1. Toronto: University of Toronto Press.

Pollitt, Katha. 1994. 'Feminism at the Crossroads.' *Dissent* 41 (Spring).

Popper, Karl. 1950. *The Open Society and Its Enemies.* Vol. 2. Princeton: Princeton University Press.

Pradhan, S.V. 1976. 'Mill on India: A Reappraisal.' *Dalhousie Review* 56 (Spring).

Quinton, Anthony. 1989. 'Phenomenalism.' In *The Concise Encyclopedia of Western Philosophy and Philosophers*. New rev. ed. Ed. J.O. Urmson and Jonathan Ree. London: Unwin Hyman.

Rawls, John. 1971. *A Theory of Justice*. Cambridge: Harvard University Press.

– 1988. 'The Priority of Right and Ideas of the Good.' *Philosophy and Public Affairs* 17 (Fall).

– 1989. 'The Domain of the Political and Overlapping Consensus.' *New York University Law Review* 64 (May).

– 1996. *Political Liberalism*. With a new introduction. New York: Columbia University Press.

Rees, John C. 1961. 'Individualism and Individual Liberty.' *Il Politico* 26.

– 1966a. 'A Re-Reading of Mill on Liberty,' with a 1965 Postscript. In *Limits of Liberty: Studies of Mill's On Liberty*. Ed. Peter Radcliff. Belmont, CA: Wadsworth Publishing.

– 1966b. 'Was Mill for Liberty?' *Political Studies* 14 (February).

– 1968. 'John Stuart Mill: Political Contributions.' *International Encyclopedia of the Social Sciences*. Vol. 10. New York: Macmillan.

– 1985. *John Stuart Mill's 'On Liberty.'* Ed. G.L. Williams. Oxford: Clarendon Press.

Rich, Adrienne. 1980. 'Compulsory Sexuality and Lesbian Existence.' *Signs* 4 (Summer).

Riley, Jonathan. 1988. *Liberal Utilitarianism: Social Choice Theory and J.S. Mill's Philosophy*. Cambridge: Cambridge University Press.

– 1991a. 'Individuality, Custom, and Community.' *Utilitas* 3 (November).

– 1991b. '"One Very Simple Principle."' *Utilitas* 3 (May).

– 1994. 'Introduction.' In John Stuart Mill, *Principles of Political Economy and Chapters on Socialism*. Ed. with an introduction by Jonathan Riley. Oxford: Oxford University Press.

– 1996. 'J.S. Mill's Liberal Utilitarian Assessment of Capitalism Versus Socialism.' *Utilitas* 8 (March).

– 1998. 'Mill's Political Economy: Ricardian Science and Liberal Utilitarian Art.' In *Cambridge Companion to John Stuart Mill*. Ed. John Skorupski. Cambridge: Cambridge University Press.

Ritchie, D.G. 1956 [1891]. 'The Principles of State Interference.' In *The Liberal Tradition: From Fox to Keynes*. Ed. Alan Bullock and Maurice Shock. Oxford: Oxford University Press.

Robbins, Lionel. 1952. *The Theory of Economic Policy in Classical Political Economy*. London: Macmillan.

– 1967. 'Introduction.' In *The Collected Works of J.S. Mill*. Vol. 5: *Essays on Economics and Society*. Toronto: University of Toronto Press.

Robson, John M. 1976. 'Rational Animals and Others.' In *James and John Stuart Mill: Papers of the Centenary Conference*. Ed. John M. Robson and Michael Laine. Toronto: University of Toronto Press.

Robson, Ann P., and John M. Robson. 1994. 'Introduction.' In *Sexual Equality: Writings by John Stuart Mill, Harriet Taylor Mill, and Helen Taylor*. Ed. Ann P. Robson and John M. Robson. Toronto: University of Toronto Press.

Roellinger Francis X., Jr, 1952. 'Mill on Education.' *Journal of General Education* 6 (July).

Rorty, Richard. 1989. 'Education without Dogma: Truth, Freedom, and Our Universities.' *Dissent* 36 (Spring).

Rose, Nicholas. 1995. 'Towards a Critical Theory of Freedom.' In *Classes*. Ed. Patrick Joyce. Oxford: Oxford University Press.

Rose, Phyllis. 1983. 'Mr and Mrs Mill.' *The Nation* (6–13 August).

Rossi, Alice S. 1970. 'Sentiment and Intellect: The Story of John Stuart Mill and Harriet Taylor.' In J.S. Mill and H.T. Mill, *Essays on Sex Equality*. Ed. A.S. Rossi. Chicago: University of Chicago Press.

Rousseau, Jean-Jacques. 1979 [1762]. *The Social Contract*. Trans. Maurice Cranston. Harmondsworth: Penguin.

Ruben, David-Hillel. 1989. 'Realism.' In *The Concise Encyclopedia of Western Philosophy and Philosophers*. New rev. ed. Eds. J.O. Urmson and Jonathan Ree. London: Unwin Hyman.

Ryan, Alan. 1964. 'Mr. McCloskey on Mill's Liberalism.' *Philosophical Quarterly* 14.
– 1965. 'John Stuart Mill's Art of Living.' *The Listener* (21 October).
– 1973. 'Two Concepts of Politics and Democracy: James and John Stuart Mill.' In *Machiavelli and the Nature of Political Thought*. Ed. M. Fleisher. London: Croom Helm.
– 1974. *J.S. Mill*. London: Routledge and Kegan Paul.
– 1983a. 'Mill and Rousseau: Utility and Rights.' In *Democratic Theory and Practice*. Ed. Graeme Duncan. Cambridge: Cambridge University Press.
– 1983b. 'Property, Liberty, and *On Liberty*.' In *Of Liberty*. Ed. A. Phillips Griffiths. Cambridge: Cambridge University Press
– 1984. 'Utility and Ownership.' In *Utility and Rights*. Ed. R.G. Frey. Minneapolis: University of Minnesota Press.
– 1986. 'Mill's Essay *On Liberty*.' In *Philosophers Ancient and Modern*. Ed. Godfrey Vesey. Cambridge: Cambridge University Press.
– 1987. 'Mill and Weber on History, Freedom and Reason.' In *Max Weber and His Contemporaries*. Ed. Wolgang J. Mommsen and Jurgen Osterhammel. London: Allen and Unwin.
– 1990 [1970]. *The Philosophy of John Stuart Mill*. 2nd ed. Atlantic Highlands, NJ: Humanities Press International.

– 1991. 'Sense and Sensibility in Mill's Political Thought.' In *A Cultivated Mind: Essays on J.S. Mill Presented to John M. Robson*. Toronto: University of Toronto Press.

– 1998. 'Mill in a Liberal Landscape.' In *Cambridge Companion to John Stuart Mill*. Ed. John Skorupski. Cambridge: Cambridge University Press.

Said, Edward W. 1979. *Orientalism*. New York: Vintage Books.

– 1993. 'Nationalism, Human Rights, and Interpretation.' In *Freedom and Interpretation: The Oxford Amnesty Lectures 1992*. Ed. Barbara Johnson. New York: Basic Books.

Sandel, Michael. 1982. *Liberalism and the Limits of Justice*. Cambridge: Cambridge University Press.

– 1984. 'Introduction.' In *Liberalism and Its Critics*. Ed. Michael Sandel. New York: New York University Press.

– 1990. 'Freedom of Conscience or Freedom of Choice?' In *Articles of Faith, Articles of Peace: The Religious Liberty Clauses and the American Public Philosophy*. Eds. James Davison Hunter and Os Guinness. Washington, D.C.: Brookings Institution.

Sartori, Giovanni. 1987. *The Theory of Democracy Revisited*, Part Two: The Classic Issues. Chatham, NJ: Chatham House Press.

Sarvasy, Wendy. 1984. 'J.S. Mill's Theory of Democracy for a Period of Transition Between Capitalism and Socialism.' *Polity* 16 (Summer).

– 1985. 'A Reconsideration of the Development and Structure of John Stuart Mill's Socialism.' *Western Political Quarterly* 38 (June).

Scanlon, James P. 1958. 'J.S. Mill and the Definition of Freedom.' *Ethics* 68 (April).

Schumpeter, Joseph. 1950. *Capitalism, Socialism, and Democracy*. New York: Harper and Row.

Schwartz, Pedro. 1968. 'John Stuart Mill and Socialism.' *The Mill News Letter* 4 (Fall).

– 1972. *The New Political Economy of John Stuart Mill*. English translation. Durham: Duke University Press.

Semmel, Bernard. 1984. *John Stuart Mill and the Pursuit of Virtue*. New Haven: Yale University Press.

Sen, Amartya. 1990a. 'Individual Freedom as a Social Commitment.' *New York Review of Books* 37 (14 June).

– 1990b. 'Justice: Means versus Freedoms.' *Philosophy and Public Affairs* 19 (Spring).

– 1993. 'India and the West: Our Distortions and Their Consequences.' *New Republic* 208 (7 June).

Shanley, Mary L. 1981. 'Marital Friendship and Slavery: John Stuart Mill's Subjection of Women.' *Political Theory* 9 (May).

– 1998. 'The Subjection of Women.' In *Cambridge Companion to John Stuart Mill.* Ed. John Skorupski. Cambridge: Cambridge University Press.

Skinner, Quentin. 1984. 'The Idea of Negative Liberty: Philosophical and Historical Perspectives.' In *Philosophy in History.* Ed. Richard Rorty, J.B. Schneewind, and Quentin Skinner. Cambridge: Cambridge University Press.

– 1986. 'The Paradoxes of Political Liberty.' In *The Tanner Lectures on Human Values.* Vol. 7. Salt Lake City: University of Utah Press.

Skorupski, John. 1985. 'The Parts of Happiness.' *Philosophical Books* 26 (October).

– 1989. *John Stuart Mill.* London: Routledge.

– 1994. 'John Stuart Mill and Liberalism' (letter to the editor). *Times Literary Supplement* (25 March).

Smith, G.W. 1980a. 'J.S. Mill on Edger and Reville: An Episode in the Development of Mill's Conception of Freedom.' *Journal of the History of Ideas* 41 (July/September).

– 1980b. 'The Logic of J.S. Mill on Freedom.' *Political Studies* 28 (June).

– 1984. 'J.S. Mill on Freedom.' In Pelczynski and Gray, 1984.

– 1989. 'Freedom and Virtue in Politics: Some Aspects of Character, Circumstances and Utility from Helvetius to J.S. Mill.' *Utilitas* 1 (May).

– 1990. 'Markets and Morals: Self, Character and Markets.' In *Philosophy and Politics.* Supplement of *Philosophy*: Royal Institute of Philosophy Supplement 26. Ed. G.M.K. Hunt. Cambridge: Cambridge University Press.

– 1991. 'Social Liberty and Free Agency: Some Ambiguities in Mill's Conception of Freedom.' In *J.S. Mill – 'On Liberty': In Focus.* Ed. John Gray and G.W. Smith. London: Routledge.

Smith, Paul. 1989. 'Liberalism as Authority and Discipline.' *Historical Journal* 32 (September).

Spelman, Elizabeth V. 1988. *Inessential Woman: Problems of Exclusion in Feminist Thought.* Boston: Beacon Press.

Spitz, David. 1975. 'Freedom and Individuality: Mill's *Liberty* in Retrospect.' In Mill, 1975.

Spivak, Gayatri Chakravorty. 1994. 'Can the Subaltern Speak?' In *Colonial Discourse and Postcolonial Theory: A Reader.* Ed. Patrick Williams and Laura Christman. New York: Columbia University Press.

Stephen, James Fitzjames. 1975 [1873]. 'Mill's Fallacies.' In Mill, 1975. Republished from Stephen, *Liberty, Equality, Fraternity* (London, 1873).

Stephen, Leslie. 1900. *The English Utilitarians.* Vol. 3. London: Duckworth.

Stokes, Mary. 1989. 'A Response to Susan Mendus' Paper, "To have and to Hold: Liberalism and the Marriage Contract."' In *Liberalism and Recent Legal and Social Philosophy.* Ed. Richard Bellamy. Stuttgart: Franz Breiner Verlag Wiesbaden GMBH.

Stolzenberg, Nomi Maya. 1993. '"He Drew a Circle That Shut Me Out": Assimilation, Indoctrination, and the Paradox of Liberal Education.' *Harvard Law Review* 106 (January).

Sumner, L.W. 1979. 'The Good and the Right.' In Cooper, Nielsen, and Patten, 1979.

Sunstein, Cass R. 1998. 'Sexual Equality vs. Religion: What Should the Law Do?' *Boston Review* 23 (October/November).

Sutherland, Gillian. 1990. 'Education.' In *Cambridge Social History of Britain, 1750–1950*. Vol. 3. Ed. F.M.L. Thompson. Cambridge: Cambridge University Press.

Taylor, Carole Anne. 1993. 'Positioning Subjects and Objects: Agency, Narration, Relationality.' *Hypatia* 8 (Winter).

Taylor, Charles. 1979. 'What's Wrong with Negative Liberty?' In *The Idea of Freedom*. Ed. Alan Ryan. London: Oxford University Press.

– 1985a. 'Interpretation and the Sciences of Man.' In Taylor, 1985c.

– 1985b. 'Rationality.' In Taylor, 1985c.

– 1985c. *Philosophy and the Human Sciences, Philosophical Papers* 2. Cambridge: Cambridge University Press.

– 1985d. 'Understanding and Ethnocentricity.' In Taylor, 1985c.

Ten, C.L. 1969. 'Mill and Liberty.' *Journal of the History of Ideas* 30 (January–March).

– 1980. *Mill on Liberty*. Oxford: Oxford University Press.

– 1991. 'Mill's Defense of Liberty.' In *J.S. Mill – "On Liberty": In Focus*. Ed. John Gray and G.W. Smith. London: Routledge.

– 1998. 'Democracy, Socialism, and the Working Classes.' In *Cambridge Companion to John Stuart Mill*. Ed. John Skorupski. Cambridge: Cambridge University Press.

Thalberg, Irving. 1978. 'Socialization and Autonomous Behavior.' *Tulane Studies in Philosophy* 28.

Thompson, Dennis F. 1976. *John Stuart Mill and Representative Government*. Princeton: Princeton University Press.

Thompson, John B. 1989. 'The Theory of Structuration.' In *Social Theory and Modern Societies: Anthony Giddens and His Critics*. Ed. David Held and John B. Thompson. Cambridge: Cambridge University Press.

Tulloch, Gail. 1989. *Mill and Sexual Equality*. Hemel Hempstead, UK: Wheatsheaf.

Tully, James. 1988. 'Governing Conduct.' In *Conscience and Casuistry in Early Modern Europe*. Ed. Edmund Leites. Cambridge: Cambridge University Press.

– 1989. 'Wittgenstein and Political Philosophy: Understanding Practices of Critical Reflection.' *Political Theory* 17 (May).

Urbinati, Nadia. 1991. 'John Stuart Mill on Androgyny and Ideal Marriage.'
Political Theory 19 (November).

Vernon, Richard. 1996. 'John Stuart Mill and Pornography: Beyond the Harm
Principle.' *Ethics* 102 (April).

Waite, Mary E. 1983. 'Why Mill Was for Paternalism.' *International Journal of
Law and Psychiatry* 6.

Walvine, James. 1978. 'Sinful Recreations.' In Walvine, *Leisure and Society, 1830–
1950*. London: Longman Group.

Walzer, Michael. 1983. *Spheres of Justice: A Defense of Pluralism and Equality*. New
York: Basic Books.

– 1994. 'Objectivity and Social Meaning.' In *The Quality of Life*. Ed. Martha
Nussbaum and Amartya Sen. Oxford: Clarendon Press.

Warner, Michael. 1993. 'Introduction.' *Fear of a Queer Planet: Queer Politics and
Social Theory*. Minneapolis: University of Minnesota Press.

Wartenberg, Thomas E. 1988. 'Situated Social Power.' *Social Theory and Practice*
14 (Fall).

– ed. 1990. *The Forms of Power: From Domination to Transformation*. Philadelphia:
Temple University Press.

Weber, Max. 1972 [1919]. 'Politics as a Vocation.' In *From Max Weber*. Ed. H.H.
Gerth and C.W. Mills. New York: Oxford University Press.

– 1973 [1922]. 'The Types of Authority and Imperative Co-ordination.' In
Flathman, 1973.

Weinstein, D. 1991. 'The Discourse of Freedom, Rights and Good in Nineteenth-century English Liberalism.' *Utilitas* 3 (November).

Weisburg, Jacob. 1998. 'United Shareholders of America.' *New York Times Maga-
zine* (25 January).

West, Henry R. 1976. 'Mill's Moral Conservatism.' *Midwest Studies in Philosophy*
1.

Williams, Geraint L. 1976a. 'Introduction.' In *John Stuart Mill on Politics and
Society*. Ed. Geraint L. Williams. Glasgow: Fontana/Collins.

– 1976b. 'Mill's Principle of Liberty.' *Political Studies* 24 (June).

– 1980. 'A Brief Reply to D.G. Brown on Mill.' *Political Studies* 28 (June).

Winch, Donald. 1970. 'Introduction.' In John Stuart Mill, *Principles of Political
Economy*. Books IV and V, along with Book II as an Appendix. Ed. Donald
Winch. Harmondsworth: Penguin.

Winthrop, John. 1988 [1645]. 'Little Speech on Liberty.' In *Political Thought
in America: An Anthology*. 2nd ed. Ed. Michael B. Levy. Chicago: Dorsey
Press.

Wishy, Bernard. 1959. 'Introduction.' In *Prefaces to Liberty: Selected Writings of
John Stuart Mill*. Boston: Beacon Press.

Wittgenstein, Ludwig. 1980. *Culture and Value.* Trans. Peter Winch. Chicago: University of Chicago Press.

– n.d. *Lectures and Conversations on Aesthetics, Psychology and Religious Belief.* Ed. Cyril Barrett. Berkeley: University of California Press.

Wolfe, Alan. 1993. 'The Politics of Privacy, Left and Right.' *Harper's* 228 (May).

Wolff, Robert Paul. 1968. *The Poverty of Liberalism.* Boston: Beacon Press.

Wollheim, Richard. 1973. 'Introduction.' In John Stuart Mill, *Three Essays.* Oxford: Oxford University Press.

Wrong, Dennis. 1988. *Power: Its Forms, Bases, and Uses.* With a new preface. Chicago: University of Chicago Press.

Young, Robert M. 1973. 'Association of Ideas.' *Dictionary of the History of Ideas.* Vol. 1. New York: Charles Scribner's Sons.

Zastoupil, Lynn. 1988. 'J.S. Mill and India.' *Victorian Studies* 32 (Autumn).

Ziff, Paul. 1960. *Semantic Analysis.* Ithaca: Cornell University Press.

Zimmer, Louis B. 1976. 'John Stuart Mill and Democracy, 1866–7.' *The Mill News Letter* 11 (Winter).

Index

Aiken, Henry David, 168
Aquinas, St Thomas, 170
Ashcraft, Richard, 279n
Austin, John, 85–6
authority, 37, 78, 83–100, 120, 126,
  217; democratic, 293 n. 20; and
  freedom, 84–5, 97–8, 125, 294
  n. 21; of the instructed minority,
  231, 246, 255, 263–4; modern,
  93–8; political, 135–6; and power,
  98–100; of received opinions, 125,
  143–4, 166; of society, 140; traditional, 87–93
autonomy, 8,14, 22–35, 43, 55,
  103–5, 112, 115, 120–1, 127–9,
  139, 148, 165, 167–9, 173–4, 176,
  193, 200, 206, 209, 268, 272, 275,
  283 n. 12, 284 n. 16, 288 n. 10;
  development of, 105–12, 125, 180,
  295 n. 2; and heteronomy, 30–3,
  132. *See also* individuality; self-
  formation

Bauman, Zygmunt, 6, 275
Bentham, Jeremy, 17, 67–9, 84, 94–5,
  128, 171, 294 n. 23, 297 n. 20, 306
  n. 21

Berelson, Bernard, 263
Berger, Fred R., 65, 216, 281 n. 14,
  289 n. 16
Berlin, Isaiah, 11, 15, 22, 40, 273, 280
  n. 7, 281 n. 12, 283 n. 6, 283 n. 8,
  284 n. 18, 297 n. 19, 322 n. 4
birth control, 302 n. 26, 307 n. 24
Bladen, V.W., 264
Blanc, Louis, 215
Bloch, Ruth, 196
Bohman, James, 318 n. 15
Bowers v. Hardwick, 301 n. 25, 302
  n. 29
British colonialism, 11, 16, 90, 286
  n. 28
British East India Company, 17, 59,
  293 n. 17
Britton, Karl, 108

capitalism. *See* political economy,
  capitalism
Carlyle, Thomas, 57, 288 n. 6
Carr, Rev. Henry William, 104, 111
character, 28, 29, 38, 105–6, 110–11,
  124, 131; confirmed, 106, 107;
  feminine, 120; formation of, 118,
  120. *See also* ethology, science of

China, 17, 58, 91, 293 n. 14
civil disobedience, 300 n. 15
civilization, 17, 79, 185, 278, 288 n. 9
civilized societies, 59, 126, 136, 162,
    232, 297 n. 18
classes, social, 79, 80; aristocracy,
    248–9, 318 n. 12; capitalists, 219,
    220, 225, 244, 245, 248, 250–1, 275;
    middle classes, 80, 81, 231, 242,
    244, 248–9, 319 n. 20, 320 n. 28;
    working classes, 80, 82, 114, 184,
    210, 215, 220, 221, 225, 231, 241–5,
    247, 250–1, 261, 275–6, 316 n. 38,
    320 n. 28, 321 n. 34. See also politi-
    cal economy; suffrage
Coleridge, Samuel Taylor, 57, 84
colonialism, 149
communism. See political economy,
    communism
communitarianism, 15
Comte, Auguste, 57, 58, 86
conformity, 26
Constant, Benjamin, 260
co-operative enterprises. See political
    economy, co-operative enterprises
Cowling, Maurice, 53
culture, 36–43, 132, 146, 149–50,
    161, 167, 168–70, 174, 185, 195–7,
    270, 276, 284 n. 19, 285 n. 23,
    286 n. 33, 292 n. 12; patriarchal,
    182–3, 185–6, 190, 196–7, 286
    n. 27. See also patriarchy
custom, 30, 37–38, 89–91, 93, 146,
    148, 161, 168–9, 174, 177

Dahl, Robert, 289 n. 12, 322 n. 37
democracy, 80, 84, 87, 92, 94–6, 131,
    136–7, 159–61, 169–71, 234, 248,
    250–1, 262, 289 n. 15; and capital-
    ism, 215, 240–5, 248–52, 261,

265, 277–8; deliberative, 235–40,
    258–63, 265, 267, 317 n. 7, 322
    n. 37; and democratization, 130,
    132, 258–9, 262, 270, 277, 287 n. 1;
    direct, 229, 234, 260; Mill's demo-
    cratic theory, 16, 233, 235, 262,
    321 n. 34; — developmental aspect
    of, 232, 258–66; rational, 87,
    255–6; representative, 16, 135,
    228, 231, 233–59; — Commission
    of Legislation, 160, 235–6; — and
    expert authority, 235; — and local
    self-government, 252–5; — and
    popular participation, 234–5, 259,
    265; — proportional representa-
    tion, 238–9. See also public sphere
democratic self-government, 9, 18,
    24, 122, 185, 193, 206, 207, 209,
    221–4, 229, 255, 258–9, 262, 265,
    268, 271, 273, 290 n. 23; Mill's
    principle of, 15, 46, 59, 60, 61–2,
    63–4, 84, 104, 122, 136, 173, 187,
    191, 229, 271–2
democratic societies, 135, 138, 179
despotism, 90, 93, 149, 187, 233, 293
    n. 15, 298 n. 1
Devlin, Patrick, 134, 299 n. 10, 301
    n. 23, 302 n. 30
Dewey, John, 201
discipline, 122–8; and moral respon-
    sibility, 123–5
discrimination, practices of, 158,
    162; and antidiscrimination laws,
    301 n. 20
divorce. See family, marriage, and
    divorce
Duncan, Graeme, 316 n. 3
Dworkin, Gerald, 284 n. 16

eccentricity, 168

ecology. *See* political economy, ecology
education, 16, 20, 51, 103–33, 154, 163, 232, 241, 272, 294 n. 24; authoritative, 126–7; broad sense of, 111–13, 118; constricting modes of, 119, 174; and economic enterprises, 120; educative relationships, 5, 104, 133; empowering, 114–15, 295–6 n. 7; formal, 112–18, 133, 209–12, 250, 261, 312 n. 11; for freedom, 103–33, 138, 139, 226, 232, 276, 278; and gender and family relations, 120; and mass media, 133; national, 232; parental responsibility for, 126–7; and pluralism, 127, 133; policy, 115–18, 127–8; political, 252–4, 265, 294 n. 21; postsecondary, 117; powers of, 11, 26, 34, 78, 82–3, 124, 131, 135–6, 166–8, 173, 193, 195–6, 231, 245, 270, 277; and rational conduct, 124; schooling. *See* formal education; and self-discipline, 122–8, 131; state-sponsored, 116, 127–8, 210–12. *See also* ethology
Education Act of 1870, 127, 241, 312 n. 11
Education Act of 1902, 312 n. 11
egalitarianism, 16, 33, 64–5, 86, 97, 104, 176, 180, 186, 190, 192–5, 232, 243, 259–66, 273–4; and élitism, 128–31, 258–9, 296 n. 13
élites, 248, 263
Elster, Jon, 284 n. 14
England, 18, 59, 76, 79, 91–2, 114, 128, 162, 185, 190, 247–9, 280 n. 11, 287 n. 1, 319 n. 19
Enlightenment, 285 n. 20

equality, 63, 97, 192, 206, 214, 232, 237; between the sexes, 18, 100, 188, 191, 193–5, 216, 226, 261, 267, 273, 305 n. 13, 308 n. 31, 309 n. 36; and freedom, 115, 120, 132, 176, 181, 183, 193, 212, 261; and inequality, 189, 191, 213–4, 218, 232, 290 n. 21; Mill's baseline conception of, 230, 244, 290 n. 20; Mill's principle of, 15, 46, 60, 63–5, 173; political, 64, 176, 233, 240–5, 260–4, 265–6, 296 n. 11, 322 n. 36, 322 n. 37. *See also* egalitarianism; justice
ethnicity, 278, 285 n. 23
ethology, science of, 49, 51, 55, 111–12, 132, 174; and education for freedom, 111–13; ethological laws, 111–12
Eurocentrism, 126, 162, 281 n. 18
European Union, 266

family, 98, 142, 173, 188, 190, 261, 262, 270, 294 n. 22, 309 n. 36; and authority, 189; children, 98, 142–3, 149, 179, 181, 183–4, 186, 188, 190, 194, 271, 290 n. 23, 296 n. 13, 296 n. 14; and domestic abuse, 143, 182, 314 n. 27; and traditional gender roles, 178–80, 184, 309 n. 36. *See also* marriage
female circumcision (female genital mutilation), 42
feminism, 16–17, 172, 173, 190, 193, 196–7, 216, 304 n. 8, 316 n. 39
Fish, Stanley, 41, 286 n. 31
Flathman, Richard, 7
Foucault, Michel, 7–8, 71, 280 n. 8, 291 n. 5, 296 n. 9, 303 n. 31; and disciplinary society, 125

France, 249, 287 n. 1
Frankfort, Henry, 32, 284 n. 15
freedom, 5–10, 13, 15, 18, 107, 145, 160, 165, 167, 282 n. 3, 282 n. 4, 283 n. 8; and choice, 147, 165, 185, 187, 310 n. 2; of conscience, 142, 144, 155, 163, 285 n. 25, 299 n. 10; constraints to, 7, 172–3, 175, 199, 204, 205, 215, 268, 276, 281 n. 12, 303–4 n. 3; critical sociology of, 3, 267, 274, 276–7; and culture, 36–43, 44; and determinism, 107. See also free will; economic, 20, 35, 40, 41, 115, 199–227, 275, 278; — maximal, 206–7, 272; — Mill's conception of, 201–6; and gendered inequalities, 172–98; ideological struggles over, 274–6; individual, 135, 138, 141, 143–51, 156–8, 163, 165, 168–70, 177–8, 180, 183, 191, 198, 200, 201, 207–21, 222, 229, 244, 268; manifest struggles over, 276–7; maximal, 63, 206–7, 221, 224, 227, 232, 269, 272–3, 276; mental, 24–5, 107, 112, 115–16, 131; Mill's conception of, 5, 10, 21–44, 45, 134, 139, 205; Mill's theory of, 5, 12–13, 20, 45–70, 115, 267, 323 n. 6; — static and dynamic aspects, 130; moralized conceptions of, 30; negative conceptions of, 5–6, 11, 18, 21, 23, 25, 27, 268, 280 n. 7, 280 n. 11; political, 20, 94–5, 136, 138–9, 173, 181, 191, 228–66, 278, 312 n. 8; — maximal, 233, 259–62; and power, 5–10, 34–6, 72, 142, 166, 172–3, 183–4, 191–4, 199, 253–5, 267–9, 272, 274–8, 280 n. 9; of the press, 251, 262; religious,

144, 155, 163, 285 n. 25, 299 n. 10; reproductive, 183, 226; of self-government, 119, 188; sexual, 182, 306 n. 21; situatedness of, 7, 20, 34–5; spheres of, 13; of thought, 203, 245, 250–1, 262, 297 n. 15. See also liberty
Freedom Review, 310 n. 3
free trade. See political economy
free will, 10–11, 27, 28, 274
French Revolution of 1848, 307 n. 25
Friedman, Milton, 201, 275
Friedman, Richard, 291 n. 1

Gaventa, John, 291 n. 3
gender, 5, 34, 67, 121, 172–98, 213, 262, 277, 285 n. 23, 295 n. 5; femininity and masculinity, 195, 291 n. 5, 296 n. 8; patriarchal gender relations, 120, 173, 182, 303 n. 1, 303 n. 3 (see also culture, patriarchal); power of, 172–6, 180–9, 193–8; and education, 174–6
genius, 110, 129
Germany, 276
Gert, Bernard, 9
Gibbs, Benjamin, 283 n. 6
globalization, 266, 278, 286 n. 33
govern/government, broad sense of, 7, 100–2, 280 n. 6
Gray, John, 32, 161, 169, 281 n. 14, 283 n. 7
Green, Thomas Hill, 201
Guizot, François, 78

happiness, 12–13, 115, 145, 151, 163, 165. See also pleasure; utilitarianism, greatest happiness principle
Hare, Thomas, 237–9, 261

harm principle, 139–41, 158, 161, 169, 270. *See also* liberty, principle of
Harris, Abram, 310
Hart, H.L.A., 67–8, 290 n. 25
Hartsock, Nancy, 6
Hegel, G.W.F., 17
Heilbroner, Robert, 298 n. 22
heterosexuality, 173, 184, 302 n. 30; compulsory, 195
history, periods of, 58
Hobbes, Thomas, 279 n. 3
homosexuality, 158–9, 162–5, 301 n. 26, 302 n. 28, 302 n. 30, 306 n. 21
human nature, 110, 206, 287 n. 4
Humboldt, Wilhelm von, 130
Huntington, Samuel, 271
Hutton, R.H., 228, 280 n. 11

improvement, societal, 130, 222, 232, 243, 267, 278, 284 n. 10, 288 n. 10, 316 n. 2. *See also* societal development
India, 17, 18, 42, 58, 59, 90, 126, 285 n. 19, 286 n. 28, 286 n. 32, 293 n. 14, 293 n. 16
individual development, 55, 56–7, 130, 134, 207, 230, 232; mental cultivation, 113, 116–8, 210, 263, 294 n. 21
individualism: methodological, 50; Mill's social view of, 50
individuality, 14, 21, 29, 43, 54, 107, 131, 143, 145, 146, 163, 168–9, 202, 205, 207, 209, 228, 230. *See also* autonomy
interests, 18, 145, 151, 246–50, 257–8, 270, 274; apparent, 243, 258; class, 242–4, 296 n. 10; gen-

eral, 244; real, 243, 258; sinister, 246, 249, 256, 261
International Monetary Fund, 266
Ireland, 298 n. 21

justice, 46, 55, 62–3, 115, 150, 156, 207, 244, 277, 289 n. 16, 289 n. 17, 292 n. 10; administration of, 254; and democratic politics, 159–60, 239, 242, 244, 254–5, 257–8, 318 n. 14; and equality, 177; social and distributive, 15, 55, 60, 62–3, 191, 206, 272–3, 312 n. 12, 312 n. 14, 313 n. 18; and utility, 281 n. 14, 304 n. 8. *See also* political economy, distributive justice; rights

Kinzer, Bruce L., 84
Kurer, Oskar, 254

Labouring Classes Dwelling Act of 1866, 312 n. 9
labour movement, 276
laissez-faire. See political economy, *laissez-faire*
Lee, Dorothy, 40, 287 n. 33
liberalism, 5, 15, 18, 133, 136, 199, 201, 279 n. 3, 311 n. 5; classical, 9, 271, 279 n. 4; and negative freedom, 5, 25
libertarianism, 313 n. 19
liberty, 23–5, 90, 132, 135–44, 147–8, 150, 156–61, 163, 165, 170, 174, 203, 206, 209, 212, 215, 224, 228–9, 269, 277, 282 n. 3, 282 n. 4, 296 n. 11, 311 n. 6, 311 n. 7, 312 n. 8; of conscience (*see* freedom of conscience); of discussion, 245, 247, 250; principle of, 13–4, 15, 23, 46, 59, 60–1, 63, 66, 104, 122,

134–5, 138–9, 143–50, 154, 161–2, 164, 166–71, 173, 183, 202–3, 212, 219, 269–71, 282 n. 1, 289 n. 14, 310 n. 2; province of individual, 139–43, 155, 183, 203, 208, 219, 257, 270–1; — and conceptions of the good, 146, 147, 150, 157, 165, 262, 269–70. *See also* self-regarding conduct

Lilla, Mark, 278
Lindsay, A.D., 267
Locke, John, 105, 170
Lukes, Steven, 7, 9, 71, 83, 268, 291 n. 3, 291 n. 5
Lyons, David, 281 n. 14, 289 n. 16, 300 n. 14

MacCallum, Gerald, Jr., 6–7
Macpherson, C.B., 16, 22, 264
Malthus, Thomas, 183
marriage, 142, 148, 178, 180–8, 194, 306 n. 19, 308 n. 32; and divorce, 180–1, 194; marital partnership, 185–91, 261, 308 n. 30; marital rape, 182; and normative heterosexuality, 179. *See also* heterosexuality; homosexuality
Marx, Karl, 17, 293 n. 18
mass media. *See* political economy of the means of communication
mental cultivation. *See* individual development, mental cultivation
Mill, Harriet Taylor. *See* Harriet Taylor
Mill, James, 17, 105, 128
Mill, John Stuart. Works: *Auguste Comte and Positivism*, 86, 156, 160, 287 n. 4; *Autobiography*, 12, 105, 128, 199, 260, 290 n. 22, 295 n. 7, 306 n. 22, 315 n. 36; 'Bain's Psy-

chology,' 108, 109; 'Bentham,' 19, 20, 34, 48, 53, 70, 84, 101, 283 n. 9, 297 n. 20; 'Carlyle's French Revolution,' 285 n. 19; 'Centralization,' 64, 72, 298 n. 5; *Chapters on Socialism*, 100, 200, 204, 312 n. 11; 'Civilization,' 79, 129, 316 n. 1, 321 n. 35; 'The Claims of Labour,' 113–4, 118; 'Coleridge,' 19, 20, 122, 219, 296 n. 8, 296 n. 11; *Considerations on Representative Government*, 20, 23, 73–4, 83, 112, 119, 120, 130, 136, 138, 143, 188, 228–30, 232, 235, 241–3, 246, 251, 259, 276, 282 n. 4, 285 n. 19, 294 n. 21, 309 n. 38, 317 n. 8, 323 n. 7; *An Examination of Sir William Hamilton's Philosophy*, 10–11, 23, 105, 274, 298 n. 3; 'On Genius,' 114, 119; 'Inaugural Address Delivered to the University of St Andrews,' 103, 112; 'Nature,' 109, 124, 296 n. 13; *On Liberty*, 10, 19, 20, 21, 23, 24, 26, 27, 29, 34, 37, 50, 56, 59, 60, 75, 83, 84, 88, 90, 107, 112, 124, 125, 129, 130, 131, 134, 136, 141, 188, 200, 202, 208, 216, 228, 251, 274, 275, 284 n. 12, 296 n. 10, 298 n. 1, 306 n. 19, 312 n. 10, 319 n. 18, 319 n. 19; *Principles of Political Economy*, 12, 21, 23, 26, 90, 101, 113, 120, 121, 122, 171, 191, 199, 200, 202, 205, 206, 208, 215, 280 n. 10, 281 n. 18, 288 n. 9, 289 n. 15, 299 n. 9, 310 n. 1, 315 n. 35; 'Spirit of the Age,' 85, 86; *A System of Logic*, 10, 12, 19, 21, 23, 27, 45, 46, 57, 65, 106, 274, 287 n. 5, 289 n. 13, 295 n. 5, 296 n. 8, 304 n. 10; 'Statement on Marriage,' 308 n. 29; *The*

Subjection of Women, 20, 21, 23, 24, 36, 42, 54, 61, 76, 91, 98, 100, 109, 122, 172, 174, 188, 191, 260, 267, 280 n. 9, 282 n. 4, 289 n. 16, 290 n. 2, 308 n. 31; 'Thoughts on Parliamentary Reform,' 64, 76, 99, 241; 'Use and Abuse of Political Terms,' 300 n. 18; *Utilitarianism*, 19, 53, 70, 82, 113, 140, 150, 283 n. 11, 288 n. 7, 292 n. 10, 301 n. 24; 'Utility of Religion,' 82, 125, 132, 309 n. 37; 'Dr Whewell on Moral Philosophy,' 297 n. 15

Minow, Martha: dilemma of difference, 309 n. 35

morality. *See* utilitarianism, domain of morality

Morley, John, 293 n. 20, 303 n. 34

nationality, 278, 284 n. 19, 285 n. 23
nation-states, 266
natural sciences, 287 n. 2
Nedelsky, Jennifer, 8
negative liberty. *See* freedom, negative conceptions of
newspapers, 81, 245, 247–9, 252, 319 n. 20, 320 n. 22, 320 n. 24. *See also* political economy of the means of communication
Nozick, Robert, 15, 313 n. 19

Oakeshott, Michael, 201
Okin, Susan Moller: false gender neutrality, 309 n. 34
oppression, 102. *See also* despotism; persecution, logic of; tyranny; women, subjection of
Owen, Robert, 28, 202

Parekh, Bhikhu, 169, 293 n. 17

Parliament, 237–9, 252, 253
Parry, Geraint, 104
Pateman, Carole, 16, 190, 264
paternalism, 119, 146, 148–9, 284 n. 17, 314 n. 27
patriarchy, 303 n. 1. *See* culture, patriarchal; gender, patriarchal gender relations
persecution, logic of, 156, 162, 170
Pitkin, Hanna Fenichel, 24, 75, 282 n. 3, 291 n. 6
pleasure, 12, 106, 295 n. 3; higher and lower, 111, 128, 284 n. 13, 291 n. 25, 306 n. 21, 307 n. 22. *See also* happiness; utilitarianism
pluralism, 155, 157, 162, 167, 169–71, 196, 269, 299 n. 7; cultural, 276
political economy, 257, 264, 289 n. 11, 292 n. 11; capitalism, 16, 41, 119, 119, 202, 204, 212–14, 221, 223–6, 232, 240–1, 248–9, 259, 270–1, 273, 313 n. 22, 315 n. 33, 316 n. 37, 323 n. 9; communism, 204, 205, 211–2, 223–4, 314 n. 31; co-operative economy, 232, 261, 276, 321 n. 34; co-operative enterprises, 11, 35, 82, 191, 222–4, 252, 260, 273–4, 314 n. 29, 315 n. 35; distribution of wealth, 213, 215, 218; and distributive justice, 213–16, 222; and ecology, 227, 266; economic enterprises, 200, 215, 221–4, 271; of education, 207, 224, 226, 312 n. 11; employment, 226, 264; and freedom, 199–227, 261, 265–6; freedom of contract, 201, 207, 212–13; free trade, 200, 201, 202, 211; industrial relations, 215–16, 222–3, 225, 276, 314 n. 27,

315 n. 32; *laissez-faire*, 122, 143,
200, 208, 210, 299 n. 9; market
competition, 222, 225, 315 n. 35;
of the means of communication,
245, 249–52, 261, 265, 320 n. 26;
poverty, 11, 204, 207, 312 n. 14;
property, 143–4, 154, 183, 186,
191, 199, 201, 202, 206, 213–15,
218–21, 230, 242, 254–5, 270, 310
n. 2, 312 n. 13, 312 n. 15, 314 n.
24; — and power, 219–20; role of
government, 207–21, 226–7; socialism, 16, 200, 204, 212, 215, 219,
221, 224–6, 260, 276, 311 n. 4, 312
n. 13, 314 n. 30, 315 n. 33, 315
n. 36, 316 n. 37, 321 n. 34; —
Fourierist, 215, 225, 315 n. 34;
taxation, 207, 211, 215, 216–19,
226, 243, 253; — of inheritance,
313 n. 23, 314 n. 26; — of luxuries,
313 n. 20; — progressive, on incomes, 217, 219, 313 n. 21; —
progressive, on wealth, 218; —
proportional, on incomes, 217;
wages, 215, 223, 226, 274, 308 n.
32; worker self-management, 200,
215, 223, 224, 273, 313 n. 17, 316
n. 37
Popper, Karl, 50
postmodernism, 4, 278, 279 n. 1
power, 5–10, 11, 15, 17–18, 19, 21–2,
25, 168, 212, 213, 223; active, 230,
231, 245, 246; corporate, 266, 277;
educative (*see* education, powers
of); and gender (*see* gender, power
of); and knowledge, 18; Mill's
conception of, 72–5; Mill's theory
of, 71–102, 134; oppressive, 172–3,
195–8; passive, 230, 247; political,
6–8, 15, 135, 199, 230–1, 246,

250–1, 253–5, 277, 289 n. 12, 319
n. 18, 319 n. 19; of public opinion,
135, 138, 159, 165, 173, 193, 195,
231, 245 (*see also* public opinion,
moral coercion of); radical view of,
291 n. 5; redistribution of, 274,
276–8; relationships of, 7. 9, 14,
22, 23, 35, 61, 66–7, 104, 132,
172–4, 262, 268, 271, 274, 290 n.
23, 323 n. 8; of self-formation,
28–9, 34; social, 56, 66, 199, 230–1,
235, 241
Pradhan, S.V., 293 n. 16
property. *See* political economy, property
psychology, 49–50, 55, 132; associationist, 105–11, 132, 294 n. 2; and
character, 106; and cognitive
capacities, 106–7, 110; — imagination, 107, 110, 128; — poetic natures, 110; and consciousness, 105;
and gender, 109; and improvement, 105; and mental phenomena, 105; and the mind: — laws of,
105, 109, 111; — phenomenalist
and realist accounts of, 108–9; —
presocialized, 109; and physiology,
109–10; and the self, 108–9; and
the will, 106
public opinion, 25, 80–2, 92, 96, 167,
246–51, 256; moral coercion of,
138, 167, 168, 173. *See also* power
or public opinion
public sphere, 229, 235, 245–52,
261–2, 265, 320 n. 25
punishment, 123–4, 140, 151, 158

race, 102, 173, 276, 278, 295 n. 6
Rawls, John, 15, 67, 273, 299 n. 6
Rees, John C., 27, 280 n. 11, 281 n. 14

religion, 88–9, 126–7, 132, 133, 144, 154–5, 158, 162, 170, 180, 185, 195–7, 203, 257, 270, 284 n. 19, 285 n. 22, 285 n. 24, 286 n. 26, 302 n. 27, 309 n. 37; Catholicism, 150; and choice, 39, 285 n. 22; Christianity, 88, 163, 185; Church of England, 127; and free action, 37–40, 42–3; Jews, 163, 310 n. 40; Mormons, 170; Moslems, 163; religious minorities, 159; religious toleration, 144, 170

representation, 229–30, 317 n. 5; equal, 232, 235–41, 261–2, 265, 317 n. 9; of minorities, 239–40, 244, 253, 317 n. 7, 318 n. 14

representative democracy. See democracy, representative

representative government, 59, 229. See also democracy, representative

rights, 54, 63, 68–70, 93, 122, 151–4, 157, 170, 178, 193, 204, 207, 289 n. 17, 300 n. 16; abstract or natural, 159, 170–1; and democratic politics, 159–65; group, 170; and justice, 63, 153; legal, 93, 153, 160, 186; moral, 68–9, 153; political, 244, 260–2; voting, 230 (see also suffrage); women's, 187. See also justice

Riley, Jonathan, 223

Robbins, Lionel, 310 n. 2

Robson, John, 109

Rorty, Richard, 296 n. 12

Rose, Nicholas, 3

Rousseau, Jean-Jacques, 54

Ryan, Alan, 12, 163, 276, 281 n. 14, 316 n. 3

St Simonians, 57, 199

Sandel, Michael, 15, 22, 23, 285 n. 25

Sarvasy, Wendy, 318 n. 11

satî (widow self-immolation), 42, 286 n. 32

secularism, 11, 21, 22, 24, 55, 62, 100, 106–8, 118, 121, 176, 224, 267–8, 272, 297 n. 16, 316 n. 3

self-development, 16, 25, 63, 146–7, 260, 304 n. 5

self-formation, 107, 173

self-realization, 41, 44

self-regarding conduct, 22, 60, 66, 121, 139–42, 146–8, 158–60, 167, 298 n. 4

sexism, 18, 283 n. 5, 305 n. 14

sexual harassment, 165

sexuality, 17, 163–5, 182–5, 193, 276, 304 n. 9, 306 n. 21. See also heterosexuality; homosexuality

Schumpeter, Joseph, 263

Schwartz, Pedro, 276

Skorupski, John, 281 n. 14

slavery, 147–8, 286 n. 29, 289–90 n. 17, 323 n. 7

Smith, G.W., 10, 23, 25, 139, 281 n. 15, 282 n. 2, 284 n. 17

social control, 138, 166

socialist tradition, 201, 202. See also political economy, socialism

social movements, 10, 276–7

social science, 133, 287 n. 2, 289 n. 11; realist and empiricist epistemologies of, 292 n. 7, 305 n. 11

social tyranny. See tyranny, social

societal development, 17, 207, 230, 232, 297 n. 18; Mill's theory of, 55, 56, 57–9, 134; social statics and social dynamics, 57. See also societal improvement

sociology, 49, 55, 86, 132
Spencer, Herbert, 68
Stephen, Leslie, 281 n. 15
suffrage, 79, 204, 256, 317 n. 9; manhood, 318 n. 13; plural voting, 16,
  241, 243, 253, 320 n. 28; Reform
  Acts, 104, 204, 241, 242, 294 n. 1,
  317–8 n. 10, 320 n. 25; universal,
  231, 240, 242; women's, 174, 176,
  191, 229, 305 n. 13, 309 n. 33, 317
  n. 10
Sweden, 276

Taylor, Charles, 7, 43, 146
Taylor, Harriet, 172, 182, 186, 260,
  308 n. 30, 308 n. 32, 315 n. 36
Ten, C.L., 53
theory, 13, 46, 55; moral, 13, 19,
  52–5; scientific, 13, 46–52, 55–9
Tocqueville, Alexis de, 17, 64, 76, 79,
  92, 247, 273, 289 n. 15, 292 n. 11
traditions, 145
transnational corporations, 266
tyranny: domestic, 182, 185–7, 301
  n. 1; majority, 156, 223, 244, 251,
  270, 320 n. 27; minority, 156, 251;
  political, 137–8, 159; social, 26, 64,
  124, 137–8, 159

United Nations, 266
United States, 92, 162, 275, 287 n. 1,
  304 n. 7, 305 n. 15, 317 n. 6
utilitarianism, 12, 55, 67–70, 143,

144, 146, 156, 159, 171, 202, 207,
  232, 281 n. 14, 288 n. 7, 290 n. 25,
  304 n. 8, 306 n. 21, 316 n. 2; and
  the Art of Life, 12, 48, 65, 69, 140;
  and domain of morality, 69, 139–
  41, 150–63, 165, 219, 257, 270, 303
  n. 32, 303 n. 33; — obligations of
  benevolence, 152, 154; — obligations of justice, 152–4, 160, 163,
  272; — relativity of moral obligations, 169–70 (see also punishment);
  greatest happiness principle, 12,
  54, 68, 143, 144, 150, 171; and
  practical reasoning, 69–70, 162;
  utility principle, 12, 54, 67, 143,
  144, 206; varieties of, 288 n. 6
virtue, 29, 156–7, 162, 193, 283 n. 11;
  and discipline, 123–4; and education, 111; and freedom, 29, 111,
  121; and representative democracy, 232, 233, 234, 253, 258, 260

Walzer, Michael, 8, 13, 322 n. 3
Weber, Max, 87, 93
women: emancipation of, 176–98,
  216, 324 n. 11; subjection of,
  172–98, 120–1. See also family;
  gender; marriage; suffrage, wom-
  en's
World Trade Organization, 266

Ziff, Paul, 282 n. 3